FLIGHT TRAINING:

TAKING THE SHORT APPROACH

FLIGHT TRAINING:

TAKING THE SHORT APPROACH

Written & Illustrated by David Diamond

Aviation Supplies & Academics, Inc.
Newcastle, Washington

Flight Training: Taking the Short Approach
Written and Illustrated by David Diamond
Email: ShortApproach@AirDiamond.com
Internet: AirDiamond.com

Aviation Supplies & Academics, Inc.
7005 132nd Place SE
Newcastle, Washington 98059-3153
Email: asa@asa2fly.com
Internet: www.asa2fly.com

Published 2004 by Aviation Supplies & Academics, Inc.
Printed in Canada.

07 06 05 04   9 8 7 6 5 4 3 2 1

ISBN 1-56027-556-1
ASA-SHORT-APP

Editors: Jackie Spanitz (Technical); Jennie Trerise (Production)
Cover design: Sandi Harner
Layout design: David Diamond

Library of Congress Cataloging-in-Publication Data

Diamond, David
  Flight training : taking the short approach / written and illustrated by David Diamond.
    p. cm.
  Includes index.
  ISBN 1-56027-556-1
1. Airplanes–Piloting. 2. Flight training. I. Title.

TL710.D53 2004
629.132'52'071–dc22

                        2004022597

Special thanks to:

THE INSTRUCTORS

It took not one, but two of the world's best flight instructors to teach me to fly: *Eliot Floersch*, who taught me that flying is something you must feel—something for which you needn't over-plan; and *April Gafford*, who taught me that flying is something you must consider—something for which you cannot over-plan. Their individual perspectives helped me better understand and appreciate the art and science of aviating. Every time I rock the cockpit, so to speak, I'm thankful for their guidance. And every time I do something stupid, I have them to blame.

Eliot and April: The two of you are with me on every flight I make, from *"lights, camera, action"* to *"airspeed, VASI, centerline."* (By the way, the tower wants you to call them.)

THE PARENTS

My father used to take me to airports to watch airplanes when I was an even younger kid. He'd enjoy a cigar while I gawked at the metal birds crawling onto the runways. One day, painted on the side of a big red, white and blue jet I saw taxiing for takeoff at LAX, I saw the words "LED ZEPPELIN." I couldn't believe the luck of seeing Led Zeppelin's airplane in person! At that moment I knew I had to become a rock star, even though moments earlier I wanted to become a pilot. I could be both, I explained to my father. "Careful you don't become a jack of all trades and master of none," my father warned. Well Dad, I never really mastered any of it, but I'm having one hell of a good time trying. I wish you could have been around long enough to see the outcome.

My mother, on the other hand, was always more than willing to encourage me as my interests wandered randomly from subject to subject. Her belief in me ensured I would never lack that last bit of insanity one requires to take on the highly unlikely over and over again. With no musical training, I have platinum records. With no art education, I have published illustrations. With no college degree, I have written a book. Maybe one day she'll see that all the fortune I've enjoyed in my life was not because of the date I was born, but because of the woman to whom I was born.

My stepfather was the first pilot I ever met. He flew F86 Sabres in the Korean War, which are apparently—as he reminds me—faster than Cessna 172s. After the war, his CFI—some guy named Gus Grissom—tried to recruit him into a new NASA program Grissom was involved with, which I think had something to do with thermometers. Anyway, lucky for me my stepfather didn't go. Had he gone, I might have missed out on all the inspiration he gave me to learn to fly. Not to discount his or Grissom's contributions to aviation and our country, but I'm confident history will remember *my* contributions as being at least as valid. Right? I mean, hell, they didn't even know how to use GPS.

THE FRIENDS & FAMILY

Throughout this book, and in many of the illustrations I do for others, the fictitious product names, airplane tail numbers and other obscure details seen in the images are actually secret codes of thanks to my friends and family. Nothing is random. From the friends I made while writing this book at coffee houses around San Francisco, to the ones I've had for decades—and even my bandmates from the 1980s—everyone of them has, at some point, been the reason I got through the day.

THE PUBLISHER

Once this book was finished, I asked aviation author Barry Schiff to recommend a publisher. He encouraged me to contact ASA. "They're a good outfit," he said. Barry, you were correct. Jackie, Jennie, Sandi, Mike, Fred and everyone else at ASA: Thanks for taking the chance and allowing me to be me. (As much as legally, morally, ethically and humorously possible.)

Foreword

I'm a student pilot. I've been one since October of 1999, and I plan to remain one for as long as airplanes continue to fly.

Don't get me wrong; it's not like flight training has been such a breeze for me that I just can't give up the easy victories. I've done a bunch of different things in my life and not one of them has impaled me upon the level of challenge and frustration that flight training has hurled my way.

The more I learn about aviation, the more I realize that a pilot just can't ever know enough. I'd rather learn my tough lessons from research than experience.

Some argue a different perspective, seeing aviation as a puzzle already solved: "A Boeing 777 flies by the very same principles as the Wright Brothers' flyer," an airline captain once told me. "Little changes in aviation."

The principles he spoke of are conceptual basics, much like those that liken a little kid's Matchbox to a big kid's Maserati: they both roll across the Earth's surface.

But I think this pilot does the advancement of aviation a disservice by thinking in these terms. The mystery of making an heavier-than-air craft fly has been solved, that's true. And a 777 really does fly by the same basic principles that launched the Wright Brothers' flyer into our history books.

But I'd sure rather entrust my life to a 777.

That's because aviation safety has evolved dramatically since those early days. We hear about air crashes on the evening news today only because they remain newsworthy. Events that are common are not newsworthy.

That's the aviation safety statistic I trust most. Every time I hear of a downed airplane in the news I'm reminded of how safe air travel has become.

But it's not yet perfect.

We build beautiful aircraft, and we do amazing things with them, but until we can land them in one piece every time, the puzzle has not been solved.

An airplane flies because of the talents of aircraft designers, builders, mechanics and pilots. Conversely, when one goes down, the finger can point no further than at one of those groups. The root cause of every airplane crash can be categorized into one or more of the following:

- Bad design

- Bad maintenance

- Bad judgement

The good news is that these are all human factors over which we have some control. Aircraft designers and mechanics can do more to improve *aircraft* safety, and pilots can do our part to improve *aviation* safety.

The entire aviation community must accept responsibility for every downed airplane. If we don't, we won't learn. Don't be lulled into a sense of invincibility because some government agency describes aviation in a positive light: "A new government study confirms that more people die in their sleep each day than in airplane crashes."

I can remember growing up and hearing aviation's beloved mantra: "Air travel is the safest mode of transportation." You've probably heard it too. Statistically, air travel is very safe. But let me tell you that you'd rather break an alternator belt in your car than in your airplane. And you'd be much more at ease as a lost bus driver than a lost pilot. And when your engine fails, you'll be much happier if all it means is that you have to raise the main sail.

Airplanes are amazingly safe, until something goes wrong. This is why the primary goal of aviation, from aircraft design to maintenance to piloting, is ensuring that *nothing* goes wrong. Aircraft mishaps still make the news because we collectively do such a good job of attaining that goal.

As pilots, there's little we can do about bad airplane design or negligent maintenance. We can verify an airplane's airworthiness only to an extent. What we can do to increase our chances of making each landing a safe one is to expand our aviation know-how so that we can better handle those rare instances when bad design or negligent maintenance bites us in our airborne asses.

You are handed your pilot's license the day the Federal Aviation Administration (FAA) determines you can safely and competently fly an airplane. We call this your *checkride*. But a year later you'll be thunderstruck at how insane the FAA was to think you were ever safe and competent back then.

Learning to fly really starts *after* you get your pilot's license. Once your certified flight instructor (CFI) has offered her last phrase of advice and the pressure of your checkride passes, you will take notice of the art and science of flying for the very first time. One by one the little things your CFI chirped in your ear all throughout your training will start to make sense. The fear and self-doubt you felt as a student pilot will subside as you realize that you actually learned more in your flight training than you thought you did.

This book won't teach you how to fly an airplane. My goal is help you work through the flight training process more effectively and efficiently by giving you a sense of what to expect. This book explores some of the stuff that makes a good pilot better and a bad pilot realize that aviation wasn't meant for everyone.

There's a lot to know. Better pilots know more—which is not to say that the more you know, the better a pilot you become. You become a better pilot by applying what you've learned in ways that make sense to you, and by being proactive in your continued flight education.

Ensure that you never, ever forget, and that you never stop learning.

Good pilots are more than masters of stomach-turning aerobatics and perfect landings. Good pilots can think faster than their airplanes can fly and good pilots know the difference between "legal" and "safe."

Good pilots are those for whom the cockpit presents no surprises.

In the end you will have taught yourself to fly: Do a good job!

ABOUT THIS BOOK

For years before I started my flight training I had many questions about the process. Where should I train? How much would it cost? How long would it take?

But what *I knew* that I didn't know was only the tip of my iceberg of ignorance. I had made many assumptions about flying itself that were simply not accurate: I expected that my pilot's license would offer me a freedom beyond any I had ever known. I could take a plane and go anywhere at any time. No more baggage check, no more flight delays.

Unfortunately, flying is not as freedom-filled as I had hoped. There are financial and other limitations that are very real. Most flight schools (and the FAA, which governs the aviation industry) won't tell you about this stuff up front because they want you hooked.

Had I known then what I know now, I would have still learned to fly. I just would have done it with fewer disappointments and more realistic expecta-tions. I hope this book will give you a good sense of what to expect from aviation during and after your flight training.

In this book I focus on issues involving flight training for a private pilot certificate to fly a single-engine airplane.

If you're already taking flying lessons, this book might offer some ideas and solutions that your flight instructor hasn't mentioned. If you read something here that you haven't already been taught—I'm confident that you will!—discuss it with your instructor. The conversation will be valuable.

This book is ideal for those who have not started flight lessons. I don't assume any aviation knowledge on the part of the reader, so you won't feel lost. Further, much of the early sections can help you glide into flight lessons with the confi-dence that you've made some good decisions.

Every pilot in the world started his or her training at square one.

Consider the following page square one.

Intro

WHY FLY?

Everyone has different reasons for learning to fly. Actually, that's probably not true. Most of us are drawn to flying because it seems fun. Our long-term aviation goals, however, might differ.

Are you in it for a wild weekend or a killer career?

AVIATION AS A CAREER

When I was a youngster I wanted to fly Concordes for Air France. I'm not sure why I chose Air France—maybe because I saw an Air France pilot one day and thought he looked cool in his uniform. As fate would have it, commercial aviation wasn't in the cards for me. But it might be for you.

"Professional pilot" can mean many things. Flying for the likes of United Airlines or KLM is only one part of the story. Regional or commuter airlines, police and fire departments, freight carriers and big companies (and big egos) with private jets, are also viable options for the professional pilot.

As you might imagine, flying commercially requires advanced ratings beyond your initial private pilot certificate. But more than advanced ratings, flying commercially takes a tremendous commitment. Piloting just isn't one of those careers that people use just to pay the bills:

"Ultimately I see myself working in Fast Food, but for now I just fly 747s transatlantic for Lufthansa while I fine-tune my burger-flipping skills."

It just doesn't work that way.

If you want to fly commercially, make that decision before you start your flight training or as soon thereafter as possible. It'll make all the difference in how you go about your training and what you need to expect of yourself.

THE AVIATION ECONOMY

Profitable careers in aviation are cyclical in nature, depending largely on the economy. Airlines seem to either have too many pilots or not nearly enough.

If the economy is down, it's not only hard to get airline jobs, it can be hard to keep them. I know of a few pilots that were laid off within their first year with their dream airlines.

It would do you good to spend some time at a local airport or flight school and talk to pilots about the current "aviation economy." Even if you don't find any airline pilots with whom you can shoot the breeze, you can pick the brains of flight instructors who are, in many cases, airline-bound themselves. (More on that later.) One phenomenon about aviation folk is that you will be hard-pressed to find someone unwilling to drone on about the subject for hours on end. There is just no such thing as a pilot without an opinion on aviation.

PILOT PAY AND PERKS

Pilots can earn respectable livings. This, of course, is dependent on many variables. Larger carriers pay better than smaller ones. Pilots with seniority take home more than rookies. And those at the controls of larger aircraft, carrying more passengers or cargo, tend to be paid accordingly.

New hires typically fly right-seat in smaller airplanes for the first few years, and they earn (salted) peanuts while doing so. Senior pilots flying larger aircraft can make more than $200,000 per year.

The chart below shows some real-world career examples. The figures used are rounded, taken from one of the top three U.S. companies in each of the categories listed. The fact is: by the time you're ready to apply for commercial jobs, the salary situation will have likely changed. So consider this chart more an example of the range of pay available to pilots.

The figures shown are monthly earnings based on an average number of flight hours flown. Regulations prevent career pilots from flying more than 100 hours per month, so these figures assume something less than that. All U.S. major airlines currently guarantee pilots a monthly minimum number of flight hours of between 65 and 85.

A pilot's actual pay is determined on several factors:

- Actual hours flown each month

- Crew position (first officer or captain)

Job Title (Year)	Regional Carrier		Major Airline		Major Cargo	
	Small	Large	Small	Large	Small	Large
First Officer (1st)	1,500	1,500	2,800	2,800	2,200	2,200
First Officer (5th)	2,200	2,500	8,000	12,500	6,600	7,900
First Officer (10th)	2,300	2,500	8,900	13,800	7,200	8,600
First Officer (15th)	2,300	2,500	9,200	14,800	7,400	8,900
First Officer (20th)	2,300	2,500	9,200	14,800	7,400	8,900
Captain (1st)	2,400	4,000	12,000	19,000	8,200	9,800
Captain (5th)	2,700	4,500	12,500	19,500	10,700	12,800
Captain (10th)	3,100	5,200	13,100	20,500	11,200	13,500
Captain (15th)	3,200	5,900	13,400	20,500	11,500	13,700
Captain (20th)	3,200	6,000	13,400	20,500	11,500	13,700
Cool Uniform?	Yes	Yes	Yes	Yes	Yes	Yes

- Aircraft type

- Type of route (international pays more than domestic)

- Seniority

- Time of day (night flights pay better than day flights)

- Special navigation requirements (over-water flights pay better than over-land)

Most airlines put new hires in the right seat (first officer) before they become captains of their own airplanes.

Some airlines employ flight engineers in addition to first officers and captains. A flight engineer is a position that some older aircraft, like the DC-10 and 727 require. Automated systems on newer aircraft have made this position increasingly rare. If an airline still flies one of those older airplanes, they will require flight engineers and might consider this their entry-level position. Flight engineer salaries are usually a bit less than those of first officers.

The greyed cells in the chart depict situations that are unlikely. For example, it's unlikely that anyone would still be the first officer of a small airplane flying for a regional past his 15th year. If by that time you haven't become captain or at least moved up to a larger aircraft, something's terribly wrong. Similarly, it's unlikely that one would still be flying as a first officer at a major airplane past her 15th year.

Promotions in the airlines are based on seniority. When you are hired, you are assigned a seniority number. This number determines when you are due for a promotion. The bad part of this is that good pilots might see morons promoted before them. The good part is that pilots can "see" their futures more clearly. This system makes it possible for a pilot to estimate when he will be moving to the left seat and start enjoying the associated salary bump.

If you're serious about flying for a particular airline, one trick is to get hired on with that airline as a flight attendant during your flight training. Your work schedule will likely be flexible enough to accommodate your flight training and the big bonus is that some airlines will honor your seniority as a flight attendant when you transition to pilot. Another benefit is a guaranteed interview for a pilot position when you're ready. There are usually many pilots vying for commercial positions and interviews can be tough to get. If those benefits aren't enough, you'll be immersed in the very environment you plan to be working in later. You'll learn the ropes, and make some connections which can only help you later on. Some airlines also have mentoring programs in which a more senior pilot will advise an aspiring pilot throughout her training.

It's interesting to note the difference in starting salaries between the airline and the cargo carrier. This is likely because most new pilots would rather fly in the glamour of the friendly skies than in an airplane that's part of the tightest ship in the shipping business. But it's also because most cargo flights take place at night, and pilots usually get paid more for night flights.

Benefits wise, career pilots have it made. Flying on your company airline or even another airline is typically free, as long as an open seat is available. Passes for friends and family members are also common and either cheap or free. But the best part of commercial aviation might be the work schedule. Many commercial pilots work less than 15 days per month!

Traditional "job" benefits are available to pilots:

- Family medical/dental insurance plans

- Sick leave

- Profit sharing and 401k plans

A few extras are also part of the package:

- Per diem for away time – Pilots are given spending cash for the time they spend away from home each month. The monthly average for time away is 300 hours. The per diem is about $1.90 per hour. That's a cool $570 extra dollars per month.

- Disability/loss of license – Disability insurance is no stranger to most employed folks. But most worker's jobs don't depend on successfully passing a medical exam every six months. Medical conditions that can be inconveniences for others, can be career killers for pilots.

The Federal Aviation Administration (FAA) forces airline pilots to retire at age 60. Airlines help compensate for this forced early retirement by offering generous retirement packages. Some airlines offer 60% of the pilot's salary. So if a lucky dog retires while earning $200,000 a year, she could still be raking in $120,000 annually just for sitting around local airport lounges and talking about the good ol' days.

EDUCATIONAL REQUIREMENTS

Most major airlines require their pilots to have four-year college degrees. This isn't always the case—there are pilots flying without them—but when competition for open spots gets fierce, you can bet that the college kid is going to get the gig.

Add the cost of college to your flight training and you're looking at $100,000 in education expenses before you ever put on your first shoulder-striped shirt.

If you know aviation is going to be your career, consider attending a college that offers an aviation degree. That way you're killing two birds with one student loan payment.

REQUIRED EXPERIENCE

Larger carriers typically require more flight experience of their new hires than do the regionals. This makes the regional carriers a popular career entry point. Let's not assume that less stringent experience requirements make regional airlines unsafe. There are (usually) two pilots driving the bus. The one in the left seat—the captain—is the one with all the experience. New hires are usually stuck in the right seat for a while.

That said, not all airlines are the same. Safety records vary and you should do your homework before you agree to sit in either seat for an airline.

The flight experience employers seek is gained from—you guessed it—flying airplanes. The gotcha here is that flying airplanes is expensive. Most commercial-bound cockpit jockeys would go broke from aircraft rental fees long before they amassed the experience required by the airlines. Many pilots opt to become *certified flight instructors* (CFI) to get those hours. Think about it: students pay for the airplane rental and the CFIs get to log the time too—what a deal for the CFI.

Once upon a time, military-trained pilots could be reasonably sure of getting on with the major airlines once their tours of duty were complete. But budget cuts have resulted in less flight time for military personnel, making the armed services a less attractive training route for those with long-term commercial aviation goals. Further, the military is requiring longer tours of duty than before. A pilot might be required to fly for Uncle Sam for many years before he'll be available to the airlines.

That said, airlines do love G.I. Joes and Janes. The discipline endured during military training is the exact type of atmosphere the airlines like to maintain. Maybe they feel that those military pilots are less like to break under pressure.

CAREER KEEP-IN-MINDS

Seniority is everything in commercial aviation. Choose your professional path wisely and monitor it closely. You might start out in the right seat of a smaller jet with designs on a 747 of your own one day. But you'll find that the more seniority you acquire in the smaller plane, the more money you make. And after being the captain of a 737 for a while, you might find a pay cut to sit in the right seat of a 747 to be hard to swallow.

Moving from a regional to a major airline can also drop you to the back of the seniority line. Even if the regional is owned by a major, there might not be a "follow through" program to allow pilots to retain seniority when moving up.

Don't consider your aviation training separate from your scholastic training if it's not too late. A Harvard Business degree might look good to Merrill Lynch—and it might get you from Economy to Business Class—but it's not likely to get you into the cockpit any sooner than a Marketing degree from Berkeley. However an aviation degree from a four-year college might move you to the front of many employment lines.

Keep yourself in shape. Eat well, work out, don't smoke, don't do drugs and keep your drinking to a minimum if you need to drink at all. Mother nature works against you when it comes to piloting. As you age, your body will start threatening your career with ailments that would mean little to most other professionals. But a pilot's career can be cancelled for some surprisingly benign reasons. (We'll talk about medical certifications later.) Your body needs all the help you can give it. Start living healthfully now and don't let up.

A Department of Transportation/FAA study showed that pilots live on average five years longer than the general population. Is this because we keep ourselves in better shape? Or is it because no one wants to die when there's an airplane to fly? Think about it: How many 55-year olds do you think could pass a physical exam that suggests they're as healthy as a 25 year old? Most middle-aged Americans are not physically fit to be commercial pilots.

This last keep-in-mind is my favorite: Do the right thing *all the time*. A DUI might be a drag when it comes to renewing your auto insurance, but rest assured that Delta, United, FedEx and UPS will slam the cockpit door in your face if you have a DUI on your record. A drug offense? Forget it. The FAA has access to DMV and criminal records.

Think about your commercial aviation aspirations carefully. In the meantime, take care of your health and stay out of trouble.

AVIATION FOR FUN

Most pilots in the United States, myself included, are private pilots, meaning we have no authority to fly commercially. The FAA is very specific about what we can and cannot do with our licenses. For example, if you take your friends flying, you are still required to pay your fair share of the airplane rental or other costs. The FAA simply will not permit a non-commercial pilot to be compensated in any way for piloting services. (Your CFI will go over this and other excruciating regulations affecting your pilot license.)

The freedoms far outweigh the limitations, however, so don't let that flying-for-free thing get you down.

Some pilots have their own airplanes and some rent. You'll probably rent at first, and might continue to do so forever. Airplanes are expensive to buy and maintain, so it often makes little economical sense to own one. If you're like me, you'll spend countless hours crunching numbers to try to come up with a scenario where ownership makes financial sense. I'm still trying.

One of the most fun things to do with your pilot's license is to pack up for the weekend and fly someplace great. This is possible regardless of whether you own your own airplane or not. Many flight schools and clubs will let members take planes overnight. There might be a minimum number of rental hours per day charged, but this depends on your school. I've found that it's easiest to get planes over holiday weekends since most people are busy with family and friends and don't fly during those times.

For my first over-nighter I took a Cessna 172 (and my pet Labrador "Clint") from San Carlos, California, (just south of San Francisco International) down to Santa Ana's John Wayne Airport, some 400 miles south. It was a Thanksgiving weekend and I felt as though I had the skies to myself. The radios were silent for most of the flight. A few times I asked air traffic control to verify my altitude or position just to hear another voice! Now, granted, the flight would have been faster and cheaper on Southwest or United than it was on Air David, but it would not have been nearly as fun. Clint seemed to tolerate the flight well enough, considering I didn't serve peanuts or even Scooby Snacks.

Setting that airplane down on John Wayne's massive 19R (pronounced, "one niner right") runway—which absolutely dwarfed the small Cessna!—was quite rewarding. I had grown up in Southern California and used to go to John Wayne Airport (then called Orange County Airport) with my father to watch the airplanes on weekends. I'd seen countless airplanes land on that runway as a kid and always dreamed that I'd do it myself one day.

On the day I left John Wayne, I was second in line to depart behind an American Airlines 757. Believe me when I tell you that you have never really *seen* a 757 until you're staring into the business end of its powerful twin jet engines from the cockpit of a dinky little airplane like the Cessna 172. (For reference, a quick blast from those engines could have easily sent my airplane flipping backward. We'll talk more about the dangers involving runway proximity to large jets later on.)

The flight home was amazing and uneventful at the same time. There's nothing quite like the feeling of being alone at 10,500 feet as the sun sets on the horizon and you wonder: "Is that an engine problem I hear, or just a snoring Labrador?"

What more can be said about flying for fun? Flying *is* fun and becomes more so as you gain experience.

THE PROCESS OF LEARNING TO FLY

The sometimes sad process of flight training works like this:

You take lessons from someone the FAA has certified to be competent to teach you what you need to know. As mentioned, this is your certified flight instructor. Your CFI might be young or old, male or female, sweet or stern, and good or bad at teaching abstract concepts like flight to wingless creatures like us.

Most of your lessons will be in an airplane, but some will be on the ground. Others might include time in a flight simulator.

Your first lesson will probably be in an airplane because this lesson is more an attempt to hook you on flight than it is to actually teach you anything about flying. Instructors that start students out by talking about flight theory are probably very lonely CFIs.

After your CFI determines you're ready, you'll fly solo for the first time and your CFI will endorse your logbook to say you have soloed. The number of hours required to reach this milestone varies from individual to individual. I soloed at about 20 hours, but remember, this process wasn't easy for me. You might solo far sooner than that, or not.

Where you train plays a role here too. I trained in San Carlos which is right in the middle of the San Francisco Bay Area—a very busy airspace. Students in this region typically take a bit longer to prepare for solo flight because there's much to know about airspace and radio communications. (Even still, I took longer than most!)

Once you've soloed, you're free to take an airplane up by yourself and fly to any legal place within a 25 nautical mile radius of your home airport. I say "legal" here because airspace or other restrictions might limit where you can go. For example, students from my flight school were not permitted to fly into San Francisco International Airport's airspace during solo flights.

Your CFI will note in your flight logbook which local airports you can use for landing practice. Absolutely everything you do as a student pilot is under the watchful eye of your CFI and the FAA. This is not to say that you can't take an airplane up without someone watching over you, but everything about your flight has to be within limits set by your CFI. For example, I was limited to landing only at nearby Half Moon Bay airport (or, obviously, San Carlos) and I could not take off with more than a 5 knot crosswind (wind hitting the airplane from the side) or a 10 knot headwind (wind hitting the airplane from the front). There were visibility and cloud ceiling limits placed on me too. (Knots are the unit of measure we use to rate velocities in aviation, such as wind speed and airspeed. More on that later.)

It was flight bondage. But it was for a good reason.

After your solo flight, the thrust of your training will turn to navigation and prepping you for your *real* first solo flight: the solo cross country.

For aviation purposes, "cross country" simply means flying and landing at an airport a certain distance from your home airport. For students, this is 50 nautical miles. Many agree this is the first major milestone for a student pilot. The solo is a big one too, but not as big as getting yourself from point A to point B based on your own flight plan, navigation and common sense.

Your solo cross country flights are restricted too. You and your CFI will choose your destination airport. A CFI will have to sign you off for the trip the day of the flight. This ensures that someone more knowledgeable than yourself (in theory) has verified that weather is good, your flight plan makes sense, and all the pieces are in place.

My first solo cross country was from San Carlos to Chico, California, some 160 miles away. This is much farther away than legally required, but I figured that if I was going to get lost, it wouldn't really matter how far away I was from home. It's easy enough to get lost within minutes of departure—distance means nothing.

I will never forget the day. It was a beautiful day in the San Francisco Bay Area, but the winds were forecast to be howling by the time I got back. My CFI asked what I would do if the winds were too strong when I returned. I told her that I would divert to another airport. This was the correct answer and she gave me the sign-off in my logbook.

While at least one other CFI looked on with disbelief that she was letting me go, I preflighted (prepared and checked out) the airplane and gave her a hug good-bye. The flight to Chico was uneventful until air traffic control (ATC) started vectoring me away from Sacramento International Airport as I neared the area.

Were they crazy? Didn't they know that I was on a preplanned, inflexible student solo flight? Didn't they know that as a moronic student pilot I was capable of any potential disaster? I figured that it would be their fault if I became the hood ornament on a Southwest Airlines 737. (Though I know now this was exactly what they were trying to prevent.)

This was lesson number one for this flight: Things don't always go as planned. I survived the unexpected vectors and got myself back on course without making the evening news.

I felt downright giddy when I saw Chico's vast runway in the distance. I'd made it! I called the tower to let them know I was inbound. They issued my landing clearance and told me what the winds were doing.

At that moment I turned white and my stomach got vectors all its own—straight to my throat.

The winds were blowing at 17 knots, but I didn't quite catch from which direction. The wind direction makes all the difference because if the winds were crossing the runway, I was in big trouble. I couldn't land in a crosswind like that! So I timidly asked the tower to repeat the winds, which they were happy to do. (Not much air-traffic up in Chico, so I'm sure they were just happy for the conversation.) The winds were coming right down the runway, which was good news. Strong surface winds aren't so bad when they hit you head on. (More on winds later.)

I realized these winds were a full 7 knots stronger than I was authorized to land in. My "legal" option was to skip the landing and head back to San Carlos. But I knew that I'd be approaching San Carlos low on fuel and having no idea if the winds there had become just as bad. A big part of pilot training is learning to make good decisions. Well good or not, I had made my decision.

I landed on Chico's enormous runway without incident. And then, in my post-touchdown bliss, I managed to roll right past the first off-ramp to the taxiway. (Taxiways are the surfaces used to get to and from the runway.) There was a commercial airplane waiting to land behind me and there I was strolling down the 10,000 foot runway searching for a way off. The tower politely asked me to get my "#@$" off the runway as soon as possible, which I did, but was I ever embarrassed.

Now if you're new to flight training, that situation won't seem so funny. But consider this: my airplane needed about 800 feet max to stop rolling after touchdown in those headwinds. And I landed

Figure 1: *A LONG WAY FROM HOME* Standing proud beside my airplane in Chico, I had just survived my first solo cross-country flight. I had no idea the ordeal that awaited me on my way back to San Carlos.

on a 10,000 foot runway and couldn't find a way off of it. I couldn't gun it to the end of the runway because the headwinds were so strong that if I had gone any faster I would have been airborne again.

You'll laugh about this one day if you do the same thing.

I refueled the airplane, had some lunch and got myself ready for the trip back home. I called everyone (and I mean *everyone*!) to let them know I had made it. I called for a weather update and, as expected, the winds were kicking up down south.

I couldn't very well stay in Chico for the rest of my life, and eventually it would be getting dark. So I got back in the airplane and figured that I'd stick to my original plan of finding a windless alternate airport if needed.

After taking some photos of myself standing by the airplane, I bid Chico a fond farewell and was airborne once again on my way home. It was this flight home where I started becoming a *real* pilot. I knew I was headed into unforgiving winds and I had to land somewhere. After all, takeoffs are optional but landings are mandatory.

Figure 2: *UNSCHEDULED LAYOVER* Roaring winds at San Carlos diverted me to Hayward where I couldn't resist snapping another photo while I awaited "rescue."

As soon as I was close enough to get a radio signal, I checked the San Carlos weather. San Carlos was reporting a crosswind of 18 knots, which is in excess of Cessna's suggested 15-knot maximum for the airplane, let alone my own limitations. So I started collecting weather reports from local airports. I checked San Jose, Palo Alto, Oakland and Hayward. Hayward won with only a 10-knot headwind.

So when the time was right, I aborted my plans for San Carlos and headed to Hayward. I landed, easily finding my way off the runway this time, and took some more pictures. I called my flight school to tell them where I was. They were thrilled that I had the wherewithal to not brave the San Carlos winds.

Me too. But now I was stuck in Hayward. Piloting was lonely work, I reckoned.

Another CFI was sent over to pick me up. As luck would have it, it was my old CFI, the one who couldn't believe that my new CFI had let me make the trip. I knew he'd be in "told you so" mode because that was his style. But I was so relieved that I wouldn't have to deal with those winds, I didn't care.

Boy was I wrong. He made me fly the plane back to San Carlos and complete my cross country flight with him by my side. Much to the surprise of both of us, I landed the airplane pretty well, even in those unforgiving winds.

And so was the end of my first solo cross country and the beginning of the last phase of my training.

Students are required to have at least 5 hours of solo cross country flight time before their check-rides. I made a few more flights after that one, but all paled in comparison to that Chico trip, my first solo cross country flight.

After you have logged at least 40 hours of flight time (it took me over 140 hours!) and your CFI has determined you are ready, your skills are tested by an FAA *designated pilot examiner.* As mentioned, this test is called your *checkride.* (Somewhere along the line you also take a multiple choice *knowledge test.*)

If you pass your checkride, you're immediately legal to take an airplane packed with flammable fuel and precious loved ones (or vice versa) just about anywhere: over open water, populated areas, mountainous terrain—you name it—and you can fly day or night.

Still feeling woefully inadequate as a pilot, after I passed my checkride I opted to immediately continue my pilot training by working on my instrument rating. (The instrument rating allows you to fly by reference to cockpit instruments in reduced visibility.) Personally, I don't think that the FAA should consider the instrument rating as an option. It's just too important. But the FAA can be suspiciously generous in what it allows us to do with our licenses. The United States of America, for example, is the only country on Earth that permits pilots without instrument ratings to fly at night.

More theories on FAA motivations later.

WHAT TO EXPECT

Knowing what to expect up front might help make or break your decision to dive into flight lessons. Many student pilots find themselves giving up on their training part-way through because they misjudged one or more of the significant commitments necessary to finish.

MONEY MATTERS

Every aspect of aviation is expensive. (Except airport overnight tie-down fees, which are oddly reasonable by comparison to everything else. Go figure.)

No one can honestly tell you how much learning to fly is going to cost because the final cost differs for everyone. Factors include the area in which you live, the type of airplane you choose for your training, and most significantly, the speed at which you are able to absorb it all.

Steer clear of flight schools that promise to get you through the program for "one low monthly payment" or an all-inclusive fee. Remember, it's the FAA-appointed examiner that ultimately determines you're ready to be a pilot, not the flight school.

Learning to fly is not something that should be budgeted too tightly. If a tight budget is a reality for you now, it might be best to save your pennies a while longer before you start your training. If you ever have to stop your lessons for financial reasons, you might never start it up again. At the very least, you'll have to do some serious backtracking to return to where you left off.

The area you call home matters too. Some parts of the country are simply more expensive than others. Airplane rental rates and CFI fees can vary considerably. Other regional factors matter too. Learning in a major metropolitan area with large nearby airports usually ends up costing more because there is more to learn. No worthwhile CFI is going to turn you loose in the skies above San Francisco, Los Angeles, Chicago or New York without being certain that you're aware of the airspace, know how to avoid it (or transition it legally and safely), and feel comfortable talking with local air traffic control facilities.

These Big City add-ons will cost you up front, but the long-term benefit is significant. It's like learning to drive in a city as opposed to a township with only one main road; you're better prepared for anything.

TIME

The entire discussion about money can be equally applied to time. After all, time is money. The longer you spend in your rented airplane with your rented CFI, the bigger the bill. And the longer it takes you to "get it," the longer you spend in your rented airplane with your rented CFI. The math is easy.

And what about your day job? Can you afford to take 3 to 4 hours off twice a week for lessons? If you can, then you're in great shape. Training once a week just isn't enough. You end up spending too much of each lesson reviewing what you learned the previous week. Consistency is key in flight training.

Conversely, training too much can be a nightmare. Let's say you have the time and money to train five days a week. Do you have the mental capacity to absorb that much information? There is a lot of reading and "thinking" involved in flight training. Give yourself time to grasp what you've learned between lessons.

When I first started my training I was flying as much as possible at the advice of my CFI. (Surprise.) But I found that it just wasn't helping. Remember, you teach yourself to fly. Your CFI is just there to make sure you don't kill yourself in the process. I needed the downtime to consider what I'd learned and where I needed work.

Many student pilots that don't have job flexibility rely on the weekends for flight training. But there are several disadvantages to weekend training. Other students aside, licensed pilots fly more on weekends too. This makes for booked-up airplanes, crowded airports and spoken-for CFIs.

Also consider weather. If a big storm system moves in on Saturday, there's probably less chance of adequate flying weather on Sunday. Lessons that are staggered throughout the week might better your odds of hitting good weather consistently.

So how long does it all take? Some flight schools will tell you that some students complete their training in "as little as three months." Yeah, well some don't too. It took me ten months, and that was going consistently the entire time. Now keep in mind that I took longer than many students for reasons I'll admit to throughout the book. But assume you'll need at least six months. If you finish sooner, then you'll impress your friends and have some time reserved in your schedule to go flying.

Again, regional areas can affect this considerably. Student pilots in Billings, Montana probably get their licenses sooner than do students in San Francisco. But then again, San Francisco-trained pilots will likely have little fear of the airspace surrounding Billings.

MEDICAL QUALIFICATIONS AND CONSIDERATIONS

The FAA wants to make sure you're healthy enough to fly. Healthy, of course, is a relative term. I went into my first FAA medical exam fearful that the doctor would discover some rare untreatable disease that no "ordinary" doctor could have possibly diagnosed. I was sure a permanent quarantine was imminent and that I'd never see the light of day again, let alone fly an airplane.

On the contrary, I left my medical exam scratching my balding head. Was that all there was? I was given a clean bill of health, but felt as though I had undergone more rigorous physical exams by suit tailors.

There are three classes of medical certificates: first-class, second-class and third-class. Airline transport pilots must hold a valid first-class certificate. Commercial pilots (corporate jets, crop dusters, sight-seeing pilots, etc.) must hold a valid second-class certificate. A third-class medical certification is all that's required for private pilots. [FAR 61.23]

Note: That little "FAR" notation at the end of the previous paragraph is the Federal Aviation Regulation number that applies to the topic discussed. I'll refer to regulations that way throughout the book so you can easily find them.

Each certificate class is good for a given period of time before it must be renewed. (For the record, a pilot certificate never expires, but is only valid with a current medical certificate.)

If I remember my first third-class exam correctly, the doctor took my blood pressure, checked my eyes and ears, checked my urine for something— I'm not sure what—discussed my general health history and asked if I could help fix his office computer. That was it.

For my most recent exam I opted for a first-class certificate. I was curious to see if I could pass it, but I was more curious to see what it entailed. If you're over 35 years of age when you apply for a first-class certificate you must either have the examiner give you an EKG, or you must provide one that's less than 60 days old, and preferably not something you purchased on eBay. My examiner did mine and I'm happy to say that "beautiful" was the word he used to describe it.

If a career with the airlines is your goal, you might as well go for a first-class medical certificate now. No sense in completing your training to learn you have some health issue that will prevent you from ever flying the friendly skies. If you have non-airline commercial aspirations—crop dusting, flying corporate planes, flight instructing, etc.—then go for the second-class medical certificate.

There's another reason that it's a good idea for you airline-bound pilots to go for the more stringent first-class each time you get a medical exam. It's going to be many years between the time you start your training and the time you'll actually need your first-class certificate. In that time your body will change. If at any point along the way you find that you can no longer qualify for a first-class certificate, you can make alternate career plans before you've wasted too much time and money.

This is not to say that you need to keep your first-class certificate valid as a first-class certificate. Over time, unless renewed, a first-class certificate effectively reverts to a second- and finally third-class certificate. So even if you go for the first-class certificate, you won't need to go for exams any more frequently than if you had applied for a third-class certificate.

EXAM REQUIREMENTS

The medical requirements for the three certificate classes are surprisingly similar. In fact, when reading through the section of the Federal Aviation Regulations (FARs) that covers the requirements [FAR Part 67, Subparts B, C, D] you have to look pretty hard to catch the differences.

First off, we'll cover the differences between each class.

- **Eyes** – First- and second-class certificates require that vision be correctable to 20/20 for distance and 20/40 for near vision. Third-class requires only 20/40 for both near and distance vision. First- and second-class certificates also require a few additional eye tests to check for conditions

that are far too medical for me to understand, let alone explain.

- **Cardiovascular** – A first-class certificate requires that applicants over 35 years of age pass an EKG test.

That's it for the differences. Now for the similarities.

- **Eyes** – So long as your vision is correctable to the levels mentioned above, and you have normal fields of vision or any other "hidden" problem that affects your eyes, you should be okay on the eye test. If you are color-blind to any degree you might receive a restriction on your certificate that says you cannot fly at night or when light signals are required. (Light signals are used by control towers to communicate with aircraft when radios aren't functioning.) There are a number of tests used to determine the degree to which a person can perceive color correctly. So don't give up now just because you know you're color-blind. Talk to an aviation medical examiner (AME) about your options.

- **Ears, nose, throat and equilibrium** – Can you hear and understand normal conversation? Can you decipher some test tones? Are you free of any other medical factors that might hinder your hearing? If all is well, you should do fine on this part of the exam too.

- **Mental** – Here the FAA is looking for a history of mental concerns, including severe personality disorders, psychosis, and substance abuse or dependency. If you've had one or more of these conditions, you might run into trouble. Those in rehab from drug or alcohol problems must remain sober for a period of 2 years before their certificate will be issued.

- **Neurologic** – The concerns here are epilepsy, black-outs for no apparent reason, and other similar conditions. The certificate application form asks if you've ever become unconscious. I said yes because I was knocked out in a skateboard accident as a kid. This was a black-out *with* a good reason, my doctor told me, so it didn't disqualify me.

- **Cardiovascular** – Do you have a history of heart disease? We're talking about *you*, not your family members. You won't be turned down because Uncle Charlie once had a heart attack. If your heart is okay, you should be okay too.

- **General medical condition** – This is catch-all category that the FAA uses to ensure that something doesn't sneak through the other categories.

Two of the more common problems pilots face at their medical exams are high blood pressure and diabetes. While these are genuine medical concerns, they might not automatically disqualify you from the rating you seek. If your condition is treatable via medication, you might be okay. Expect some extra paperwork and some delays, but don't give up because you *think* something might disqualify you.

My medical examiner has be doing FAA exams since 1962. He sums it up like this:

"The FAA wants pilots to pass their exams. This process isn't in place to limit the number of people flying airplanes. The FAA's main concern is that a pilot doesn't become incapacitated while flying. As such, their two biggest areas of concern are neurologic and cardiovascular."

The Federal Aviation Regulations list medical requirements in detail. You can find them in Part 67.

CHOOSING A MEDICAL EXAMINER
Your CFI can help you find a local FAA-designated aviation medical examiner (AME). The cost of the exam varies. My third-class exam was $80. My first-class exam was $85 plus another $60 for the EKG, and that was three years after the third-class exam. Health insurance won't likely cover the exams. (In retrospect, this was one of the more affordable aviation expenses!)

The FAA maintains an online database of AMEs. Find a link to it on my website. (See address below.) This webpage includes all the basic contact information you'll need along with the doctor's medical specialty and what, if any, pilot rating he or she holds.

(Note: Internet addresses change from time to time. To ensure you'll always be able to reach the online resources I mention in this book, I've set up a webpage of pointers to the various sites. Find it at **http://AirDiamond.com/sa**)

Should you care if an examiner flies or specializes in, say, internal medicine?

I've heard some horrible stories about medical examiners flunking pilots. Most of the time these examiners weren't pilots themselves. This is certainly not to say that examiners who are pilots are letting people slide through with subpar health. But an examiner who is also a pilot might be more apt to help a borderline applicant squeeze through by suggesting FAA-approved treatments or other options that a non-pilot examiner might not even think about. Pilots know what it's like to want to fly.

Taking that a step further, lets say that you do have diabetes. Without medication there's no way you'll get your certificate. And even with medication you'll have to provide proof from your doctor that your condition is well under control. Wouldn't it be most convenient if your AME was also your regular doctor? The FAA says this is just fine. In these cases, you have only one doctor to deal with and that one doctor sees to it you get the treatment you need while the FAA gets the paperwork it wants. Trying to coordinate two doctors can be difficult. A non-FAA doctor will have no interest in what treatments the FAA has blessed. He might prescribe a pill that simultaneously cures your ills and invalidates your medical certificate.

Get your medical certificate as soon as possible. If you have any doubts about passing your medical exam, it might be a good idea to get one even before you start your training, just to be sure. You are required to have your medical certificate before your first solo flight.

ENGLISH: IT'S ALL YOU'LL EVER NEED

English is the international language of aviation. If you're reading this book now, then you know all the English you'll need.

The ability to read, write and speak conversational English is required by the FAA. If English is not your forté, then bone up. Air traffic controllers worldwide are relying upon you to know the difference between words like "climb" and "descend," and "left" and "right."

So does this mean that everyone on the aviation airwaves has mastered English? Hardly. I'm often amazed that air traffic controllers are able to make sense of some of the mutterings I hear while flying. The seriousness of the issue can't be overstated. Many air accidents have been attributed to communication breakdowns.

If you fly into non-English speaking regions of the world, you might hear other languages spoken over the radio. Though not condoned by the International Civil Aviation Organization (ICAO)—the folks who make the *international* rules we fly by—when controllers and pilots speak the same language natively, they tend to use that language in aviation communications too. The jury is still out on the dangers, if any, of this. But consider this: if a pilot and controller have just a "passing" knowledge of English, we might all be better off if they speak in a tongue that ensures they understand one another.

PROFICIENCY TESTS

There are three proficiency tests you must pass to get your private pilot license:

- Written (Knowledge)
- Oral
- Practical

THE WRITTEN TEST

"The written," as you'll hear it referred to, is a 60-question multiple choice test with three possible answers per question. You are required to choose the "best" answer of the three. This test is also referred to as the *knowledge test* because it is no longer actually written, but taken on a computer.

Tests are given by authorized testing centers throughout the country. Mine cost $75. Your flight school can help you find the test center closest to your area.

The FAA considers a score of 70% or better passing. But many claim that the higher your score, the easier your oral test will be, as discussed shortly.

Groundschool is a great way to bone up for the written, but there are other options too. If you learn well on your own, you can use any number of do-it-yourself programs. Some are book-based while others use videos, DVDs or CD-ROMs. I've seen plenty of pilots do well on the written after using only self-help tools, but I'm a groundschool junkie myself. (Groundschool advantages are discussed in "Groundschool: yes or no?" on page 36.)

The FAA makes most of the test questions available to students for study purposes. Becoming familiar with the questions ahead of time is a good thing. Not that you have to memorize them to get a good score, but these questions can be tricky. It's not uncommon for a question to have two seemingly "good" answers. You need to carefully study the wording used to determine which of the answers is better.

Sometimes a question is asked "backward," meaning that you assume it's asking a certain thing, but in fact a discreet little "not" or other negating term lost in the complex sentence structure reverses the logic. Be careful.

Start studying the written test materials as soon as possible and take the test as soon as you're ready. You'll need to have successfully completed the written test before the day of your checkride. Take the written well in advance of your checkride. The last thing you'll want to be doing while prepping for your checkride is to also be prepping for the written.

THE ORAL TEST (CHECKRIDE PART 1)

Both the oral and practical tests are given as part of your checkride. The oral portion is a question and answer test given by your examiner. Technically, this test continues throughout your entire checkride, even the practical portion. So don't assume that once you get into the airplane you can start spouting erroneous information.

As mentioned, many feel that the better you do on your written test, the easier your oral test will be. This, of course, depends on your examiner. But it's safe to say that a student that barely squeaked by on his or her written might be drilled a bit harder.

The oral covers basically everything you learn during your flight training. Some questions are actual questions, while other times the test might just see like a conversation about aviation between you and your examiner. All the while, however, the examiner is paying attention to what fact or fiction comes from your mouth.

My oral test went pretty well. My CFI and I had prepped for almost two weeks beforehand to make sure I passed. (And that I didn't embarrass her!) I was asked questions about charts (maps), airspace, FAA regulations and some "what would you do if" situations, too. The FAA is big on scenario-based questions.

After about 10 minutes, my examiner stopped that oral-only portion of the test saying, "Well it's obvious you've got this stuff down." So the moral of the story might be to bore your examiner with correct, yet verbose answers.

Just make sure your desire to impress doesn't take you into areas where your knowledge thins. Some examiners love to let a student hang himself out to dry with overly detailed responses to simple questions and then fire back with even tougher questions:

"So, Jimmy, in your response to my question about your airplane's rudder system, you mentioned how it worked just like the rudder on a 747. Tell me more about the 747's rudder system."

Poor Jimmy.

Due to bad weather, I had to delay the practical portion of my checkride for another day. Interesting to note: it's up to the student to cancel a checkride for bad weather or airplane maintenance reasons. If I had decided that day to go ahead with the flight portion, I would have failed for bad decision-making with regard to weather.

THE PRACTICAL TEST (CHECKRIDE PART 2)

I've heard it said that many examiners know if a student will pass or fail his or her checkride before they even get into the airplane. This, I guess, comes from years of experience. An examiner once told me that based on the written test score, the sign-off of a reputable CFI, the student's level of confidence and a successful oral test, he knew exactly how the student would fly. But since the FAA requires the practical test, it's given regardless of any foresight on the examiner's part.

For the practical portion of your test you are required to plan a flight to a destination determined by your examiner. You're told where to plan your flight to in advance of your test day. Prior to your flight, your examiner might go over the plan with you and ask questions.

On my test date, the weather was fine at the airport where I was taking my test (Reid Hillview, CA), but the weather was questionable enroute to Fresno, my planned destination. When my examiner asked me if we could go, I told him that we could certainly take off and fly the first leg of the trip, but that I'd have to check weather again enroute to determine if we could continue or if we'd have to divert. He said that he liked this answer because it showed that I was willing to make use of in-flight resources instead of simply cancelling the flight.

At first I was thinking if there was so much as a cloud fragment in the sky that I should cancel. I figured that the conservative approach would win me points. But this wasn't the case. Being conservative is a good thing, but knowing how to get weather information in flight is even better.

The weather at Reid-Hillview was great and there was nothing in the forecast to suggest it would worsen. The weather toward Fresno wasn't great (low clouds), but it was forecast to improve. Along the route there was plenty of good weather and there were plenty of alternate airports. So this was definitely not just a "no-go" decision. My decision to go was based largely on forecasts and knowing that I had escape routes (other airports) if I needed them.

This was a good decision on my part that was based on a decent analysis of the current situation. That's what examiners are looking for.

My practical test went okay, but not great. I was very nervous. We took off and within minutes my examiner diverted me to another airport. A diversion consists of finding a suitable alternate airport on your chart, picking a heading you believe will get you there, flying that heading and determining how much time and fuel will be required to get there.

We diverted to South County airport. Not knowing the area, I decided to fly parallel to a nearby freeway. I knew South County was just off the

Figure 3: *SUCCESS!* Here I am (left), just moments after my checkride, shaking the hand of Mike, the man who gave me my wings. Mike dispels myths that FAA examiners are scary monsters.

freeway, so if I flew south, I'd find it. My examiner later told me that he would have preferred that I picked a more direct heading. But what the hell, he said, I found it.

Enroute to South County he had me do some of the required flight maneuvers and the oral portion of the test continued throughout. I demonstrated an emergency descent over South County and we did all the required landings. I'm quite proud of my landings nowadays (most anyway), but back then my landings were always questionable. These were no exceptions.

My examiner could have failed me for a few things I felt I did wrong. But he didn't. He told me later that he is usually able to discern between nervousness and incompetence. Good thing for me.

We made our final landing and I taxied the airplane to the tie-down spot. All the while he said nothing. I had no idea if I had passed or failed. I stopped the plane and shut down the engine. He started unbuckling his belt and still said nothing. He opened his door and said, "Well, it's a "pass," but with comments."

Despite my yearning to run joyfully screaming throughout the airfield, I sat and patiently listened to his comments. But this wasn't easy. Ever since I was 10 years old I've wanted to be a pilot. At that moment I had become one. I just couldn't wipe the smile from my face.

We went into his office and did the paperwork, which included the best endorsement any CFI ever wrote in my logbook: a successful checkride! (Yes, examiners are CFIs too.) When we were finished—smile still planted firmly on my face—we went back out to the airplane for a few pictures. He wished me well and told me to fly home safely.

My flight home from South County to San Carlos was amazing. The sun was setting and the San Francisco Bay Area never looked more beautiful. I steered my airplane so that I remained clear of San Jose's airspace. I called air traffic control to let them know where I was and to get a clearance home. I resisted embarrassing myself by telling ATC that I had just passed my checkride.

The radios were quiet and the skies were clear of other traffic. ATC cleared me to fly direct home right smack-dab through the center of San Jose's airspace. It was like all the other local pilots had landed in recognition of my success and let me have the entire sky to myself.

My smile never faded. I was on top of the world (or at least a thousand feet above the San Francisco Bay Area) and there was no stopping me.

But there's a funny thing about flying west just before sunset. The sun gets in your eyes. To make matters worse, it was quite hazy. Before I knew it, my smile was gone and I realized that the irony of me killing myself on my flight back home after a successful checkride was folklore in the making of which I wanted no part. But I honestly could not see where I was going. I knew that San Carlos was ahead of me, but you can't land at a runway you can't see!

So I relied upon my training. One of the things students are taught is to use all available resources. I took inventory of the resources available to me at that time:

First off, I had my radio. ATC was providing me with a service called *flight following*, during which they alert a pilot to oncoming traffic. (Most of the time.) So I knew that by listening to the radio I could get a sense of who else was out there. The San Francisco Bay Area is a radar environment near several major airports and special equipment called a *transponder* is required on all local airplanes to ensure that ATC can spot them. Yes, it's possible that a plane could have been up there without a transponder, and yes it's possible that radar fails, but I figured this was a good resource anyway.

So this eased my mind about running into an oncoming airplane. Further, I knew that anyone coming toward me would have wonderful visibility since the sun was behind them.

The next task was to find San Carlos and line myself up for the landing. I fired up my hand-held GPS unit (we'll talk more about GPS later) and got myself exactly where I needed to go. I also let the San Carlos tower know that I was flying in compromised visibility just so they'd know that I wouldn't automatically see all other airplanes near the airport.

Using these resources got me home where I found my smile waiting for me once again.

In retrospect, I should have landed as soon as I saw that my visibility was going to hell. There were plenty of airports around. It was bad judgement on my part to keep going, no matter how excited I was or how in-control I *felt* I was. Good judgement comes from experience. Experience, on the other hand, comes from bad judgement. I gained some experience that day.

"Checkride" is a word you'll hear over and over again throughout your training. Your CFI will tell you how examiners will want things done on your checkride. Other students will tell you tales of their checkrides, and you'll often commiserate about your fears of the fateful day.

But the day will come. And if you're prepared, you'll do fine.

ATTITUDE ADJUSTMENT

One of the things you can expect from your flight training is at least a slight change in attitude. There's a whole psychological aspect to learning to fly that I'm even less qualified to comment on than learning to fly itself. So I'll keep this very brief.

Consider these learning-to-fly facts:

- Flying is a skill that requires much in the way of physical/mental coordination, the ability to think clearly and overcome fears, and the ability to maintain a level head.

- Very few people learn to fly.

- Learning to fly is a challenge most people consider for a long time before they start their training. Most never start.

- Adults rarely take the time to learn something so totally new and foreign to them.

Collectively considered, these facts (and others) make learning to fly a life experience that really makes a difference. You're learning to do something most people only dream of doing, and many others fear too much to even consider. Once you get your license—and even during your training—you might find yourself awash in a sense of accomplishment the likes of which you've never experienced.

Perhaps this is why people in aviation are generally so friendly. You might even find yourself being extra nice to total strangers around the airport. I don't know what it is that makes this so. Maybe it's the sense of camaraderie that aviators share. Air traffic controllers are typically addressed as "sir" or "ma'am." And pilots and controllers alike are quick to bid one another a nice flight or a nice day.

Somehow these people just seem a bit more decent. Don't get me wrong: aviation is no substitute for professional psychotherapy, but a good sense of accomplishment goes a long way.

While leaving the airspace of a busy nearby airport one day, my CFI congratulated the tower controller on doing such a good job of handling the considerable traffic. The controller thanked her in return for our cooperation. It was a warm and fuzzy cockpit moment.

From that point on I took notice of the work air traffic controllers do. I now thank them for their help. And I'm confident that, silently, they also thank me for not running into another airplane during their shifts.

But even outside the airport environment I find some things seem different to me. I see a different sky than others do. They see a nice, clear day with beautiful white puffy clouds. I see an unstable atmosphere, unlimited visibility and the likelihood of convective turbulence. Others see a warm, hazy day and I see compromised visibility on a smooth flight.

And on occasion, when day-to-day things seem too much to handle, I remind myself that I can actually fly a flippin' airplane. How cool is that?

It works every time.

2

First Things First

STUDENT CERTIFICATE LIMITATIONS

As a student pilot, there are some restrictions placed on your flight activities that will be removed once you get your license. For example:

- Students pilots cannot fly more than 50 nautical miles from their home airport without a CFI's written endorsement in their logbook certifying that the longer flight is allowed. This rule is in place, I suppose, so that you won't get too lost or wander into unfamiliar territory.

- Students pilots cannot fly over an undercast (an overcast cloud layer as seen from above). The logic here is that in the unlikely event that you must make an emergency landing, you won't be able to see where to land!

- Students pilots cannot land at certain airports. Some airports like San Francisco International and Los Angeles International prohibit student pilots from landing or taking off. The reason here should be obvious. But this is not a big deal. Most private pilots won't land at these airports anyway because of the expensive landing fees incurred.

- Students pilots cannot (usually) fly solo at night. Some flight schools might allow you to fly solo at night, but not many. Although the airplane doesn't know the difference between daytime and nighttime operations, flying at night can be quite tricky. It's harder to see things in the cockpit and on the ground. It's also harder to see oncoming clouds.

- Students pilots cannot fly in strong winds. When your CFI endorses you to fly solo, she will specify weather conditions that must prevail for your flights. If the wind, for example, is above a limit she sets, you're grounded. While this is a very good and safe idea, don't be afraid to train with your CFI in windy conditions. Your CFI will know what's not safe. Getting practice in strong winds can only help you out later.

There will be other limitations imposed on your solo flight endorsement too.

After you pass your checkride all of these limitations *legally* go away, but you should self-impose some for a while longer. Winds are a great example. Gradually "up" the amount of wind you permit yourself to fly in, but don't jump the gun. If you're not sure you can handle the current winds, then you should play it safe and stay on the ground. Flight training is available to you even after your checkride. If you need some touch-up work on wind landings, night flying, or anything else, call up your old CFI and schedule some flight time together.

SETTING PERSONAL LIMITS

The FAA offers a big book called the Federal Aviation Regulations (FARs) that's chock full of rules. What it's not chock full of are safe margins for each pilot. What's safe for me might not be safe for you.

Construct your own set of rules and regulations based on the FARs. You can think of them as the MARs (My Aviation Regulations). In time you might choose to relax some of these restrictions as your proficiency in the cockpit grows. Some you will keep forever.

WEATHER LIMITATIONS

Weather affects all pilots, from students with less than ten hours logged to career captains with tens of thousands of hours under their belts. Weather also affects all airplanes. No airplane ever built has been tough enough to overcome serious weather. And no pilot, no matter how visually gifted, can see an oncoming airplane or mountain in zero visibility.

More than anything else, bad weather will be the determining factor in the "go/no-go" decision you make before every flight.

If you only remember a handful of things from your flight training, keep this high on the list:

Bad weather will kill you.

THE THUNDER ROLLS

To a non-pilot a thunderstorm means loud noises and a light show. To a pilot, a thunderstorm means much more. A thunderstorm can literally tear a small plane apart. You can forget about being able to control your airplane if you find yourself in the grip of a thunderstorm. The forces expelled can challenge a 747's ability to stay airborne. Your little Cessna or Piper doesn't stand a chance.

You're only chance, in fact, is to stay clear of areas in which storms exist or are forecast. The FAA maintains no regulation that keeps pilots certain distances from thunderstorms. (The FAA also doesn't require a fire extinguisher be on board general aviation aircraft, so consider the source.) So this is an area where you need to set your own regulation.

There are guidelines for how much distance to keep between yourself and a thunderstorm, but I prefer to maintain what I call an *airplane's worth* of distance. That is, if thunderstorms are anywhere along my route of flight, I stay out of the airplane.

I'm not being paranoid here. There are additional weather phenomenon associated with thunderstorm areas that can be hard to discern until you run right into them. Severe turbulence is only the beginning.

You'll learn more about thunderstorms and other dangerous weather during your flight training. Pay close attention.

FLYING BLIND

Visibility is everything when it comes to VFR flying. VFR stands for "visual flight rules" and it refers to the set of regulations that govern flight by reference to the horizon and other visual "clues." IFR (instrument flight rules), on the other hand, refers to the regulations that govern flight by reference to cockpit instruments, such as when flying through clouds. Pilots flying IFR must have an instrument rating, which you can and should get after you've earned your private pilot certificate.

The FAA's visual flight rules (VFR) define whether or not it's legal for you to take-off or fly when visibility is restricted. You'll go over these rules in depth during your ground training. But the basic rule is this: If ground visibility is reported as less than 3 miles, or the lowest cloud ceiling is 1,000 feet or less above the ground, you cannot legally fly under VFR.

Here's a catch: The weather might legally be VFR when you take off, but what happens if you encounter clouds or fog *during* your flight? One of two things is likely to occur:

- You will execute a 180-degree turn and go back to where the weather was clear, or

- You'll continue to fly into the reduced visibility until you've completely lost reference to the horizon at which point, if your name is Kennedy, you'll become the lead story on the evening news.

Clouds and fog aren't the only visibility compromisers either. Haze, smog and smoke, among other environmental particulates, can also reduce visibility to unsafe levels.

So what's unsafe? The FAA says no less than 3 miles, but this just isn't good enough. Later on I'll give you some examples why.

As a student pilot, your CFI will restrict your solo flights to times when visibility is reported at a given minimum, typically well higher than the FAA's legal minimums. But it's really up to you to analyze conditions for yourself. There will be times when your CFI isn't around. You'll have booked an airplane to go flying, and you'll see that the weather report looks "clear" and "legal" even though the sky tells a different tale.

When a discrepancy exists between what's forecast and what you see with your eyes, trust the worst of the two. At the very least remember this: you'll be flying in the sky, not in the forecast. Sometimes weather forecasts say bad things are coming and no bad comes. But as a student pilot you need to play your hand conservatively.

Also consider the time of day you fly. Evenings and mornings can mean terrible visibility if you're flying into the sun. (Remember the story about my flight home after my checkride?) Visibility can be reported as unlimited, but if the sun is directly ahead of your flight path, you won't see a thing. This is especially true if there is any other visibility hindrance such as haze, fog, etc. The sun will just light those atmospheric particles right up. A scratched up windscreen doesn't help much either, and those come standard on most rental aircraft.

Nighttime flight offers additional visibility concerns. Clouds are easy to see during the day, but not so easy to see at night. You could be flying in clear weather and before you know it, you're eyeball-deep in zero visibility. The best defense here is the forecast and weather observations from local airports, both of which we'll cover later. If clouds are reported in your area, pay attention. Clouds at night are often easier to see over cities than in rural areas because city lights illuminate lower cloud layers, making them more visible. But you can't always rely on this.

There are a few tricks to keep in mind for cloud avoidance at night:

- What's forecast and reported? If clouds are in the forecast, and especially if clouds are reported by local airports, then be careful. Choose a flight altitude that keeps you clear of the reported clouds or, better yet, choose a flight path clear of the entire area.

- Keep an eye on the wingtips of your airplane. Your airplane's wing tip lights will illuminate moisture. If you can see the air, then the air is moist. The easier it becomes to see, the more moist it is. Clouds and fog are moisture, so if your lights show nothing, then you're still in clear weather. But if you start to see a halo around the lights, make that 180-degree turn back to clear weather.

- Keep an eye on the horizon. If for any reason the horizon becomes obscured, turn back to where you know clear weather exists. An obscured horizon signals clouds, fog, or some other obstruction such as a mountain range.

Remember that VFR flying legally requires, by definition, reference to the horizon or other visual clues. Once those references are gone (or visibility becomes less than 3 miles, which is very tough to estimate at night), you are no longer flying in legal VFR conditions.

We'll talk more about emergency options to get yourself out of these situations later.

WINDS A' HOWLIN'

We touched on the significance of winds earlier, but we'll go into more detail here. There are two classifications of winds:

- **Surface** – Winds at the Earth's surface.

- **Aloft** – Winds above the surface.

Surface winds are a consideration during taxiing, take-offs and landings. (Taxiing is the aviation-fancy word for driving the airplane on the ground, usually to or from the runway.)

Pilots break surface winds down into two core components in order to handle them properly:

- **Headwind component** – How much of the wind is hitting you head on?

- **Crosswind component** – How much of the wind is hitting you from the side?

The direction and velocity of the wind and the orientation of your airplane determine the amount of headwind and crosswind you experience at any given time. As your airplane turns on the ground, these values change.

A strong headwind on takeoff has the effect of shortening the time it takes you to get airborne. During landing, a strong headwind reduces the amount of runway you need to stop the airplane. Landing and takeoff are the only times you'll appreciate headwinds; they slow you down enroute.

Crosswinds are usually more of a concern while you're near or on the ground. Crosswind take-offs and landings are an acquired skill. But until you acquire the skill, don't risk it. Instead, if you're scheduled to fly solo on a day with strong cross-winds, find a CFI to go up with you. It's good practice and later you'll be glad you became a crosswind master.

Even after you become comfortable with cross-winds, be mindful of wind gusts. If the crosswind is estimated at 10 knots but gusts are blowing above 10 knots, skip the flight if you're going solo. Gusting crosswinds can blow your airplane on its side, which would be terribly embarrassing.

A small plane that lands on anything but its wheels sounds like a thousand soda cans being crunched at once, and no one at the airport misses it.

Crosswinds were a real stumbling block for me during my training. It took me forever to get the hang of it. Eventually I became pretty good at dealing with them, though I still won't challenge the really strong ones.

Winds aloft are typically stronger than those at the surface. They are also typically less of an issue. Both of these *typically true* statements can also be false. Weather is a giant variable that seldom cooperates with human guesstimates.

Strong winds aloft can often go unnoticed by newer pilots. For example, let's say you have a 20-knot headwind. The net result is that your airplane is flying slower, but that's hard to perceive from the cockpit. If your airspeed is, say, 120 knots, then you're groundspeed—the speed at which you're actually traveling across the ground—is only 100 knots.

If the wind is coming from behind you, then you're actually going faster across the ground than shown by your airspeed indicator. (In this example, your groundspeed would be 130 knots.) More on groundspeed issues later.

Even when the wind is coming from your side you might not notice it much. It becomes apparent when you've planned to fly a given heading and you find yourself having to fly a different heading just to stay on course. (This, incidentally, happens on just about 110% of flights, so don't let it fluster you.)

But if the winds aloft are forecast to be very strong, take notice. When Mother Nature is blowing hard, she's trying to tell you something. We'll see how later.

PERSONAL PERSONAL LIMITS

Weather conditions should not be the only limits you place on your go/no-go decision. One of the thousands of acronyms you'll hear during your flight training is IMSAFE:

- I – Illness: Are you sick? A simple sinus infection can be a nightmare during flight.

- M – Medication: Are you on any medications that might affect your performance? Are you on any medication that invalidates your medical certificate?

- S – Stress: Are you stressed out about anything that's dominating your thoughts? Maybe you got your first credit card statement since starting your flight training?

- A – Alcohol: Are you drunk? Hungover?

- F – Fatigue: Are you tired? Could you use a nap?

- E – Emotions: Are you a mess emotionally? Did your lover just leave you? Did you just scratch your new car?

IMSAFE is designed to give you a quick checklist to consider before each flight. Consider it your personal preflight.

The NTSB (National Transportation Safety Board) has long since known that most aviation disasters are not the result of a *single* bad event, but a *series* of bad events. If you ever lose an engine, the difference between a *forced* landing and *crash* landing might be in the amount of sleep you got the night before. Adding a personal problem to a mechanical problem greatly reduces your chances of a happy landing. If you're in tip top shape, you're far more likely to live to tell the tale of the bad engine.

PRACTICAL LIMITATIONS

Weather and personal limitations are only two of the many things to consider when determining if a flight makes sense. Much of the emphasis in your flight training will be on decision making. Some decisions are more obvious than others.

LAX TO JFK BY CESSNA MIGHT NOT BE IDEAL

I figured that once I got my license I'd be flying myself everywhere. Silly me. You gain an appreciation for just how affordable commercial air travel is once you start renting and flying airplanes long distances.

I pay about $85 per hour for a Cessna 172. The first time I flew from San Carlos to Santa Ana and back, my total flight time was about 7 hours. At $85 per hour, this ended up costing almost $600. By contrast, United or Southwest would have taken me for about $120.

Now, if I had taken three others with me, the total costs would have been closer, but the airlines still would have won out. And I would have had to either take three pretty petite people, or stop for gas a few times. A Cessna 172 cannot hold the weight of 2 full fuel tanks and 4 full bellies. (We'll talk more about the weight limitations of an airplane later.)

Speed-wise, the difference between a 172 and a 737 is closer than you might think. Consider that commercial airlines want you at the airport a full hour before departure. If you check any bags, then you have to wait around for them to get to the baggage claim area after your flight. So we'll add another 30 minutes for that. Add another 20 minutes for the time it takes a big jet to taxi from the runway and deplane all of the passengers. And, of course the one hour flight time.

So the total trip on a big jet would cost us about 2 hours and 50 minutes of our day. It took 3 hours to fly to Santa Ana from San Carlos in a Cessna 172, 10 minutes longer.

Now if I owned my own plane, flying myself would make far more sense. Cost-wise it might still end up being cheaper flying commercial, but it's not nearly as fun.

TERRAINASAURUS REX

One of the other big disappointments of small aircraft is their performance. A trip from San Carlos to Mammoth Lakes would be a perfect weekend getaway if it wasn't for those pesky Sierra mountains that lie between.

Every airplane has a maximum altitude to which the airplane is capable of climbing. While big jets can easily reach altitudes in excess of 30,000 feet, a Cessna 172, for example, is doing great if it can get above 12,000 feet. And, as you'll learn later, weather conditions contribute to this considerably. Airplanes like colder weather. On hot days, they just don't perform as well. Air pressure plays a big part here too.

So even though we could, in theory, get our Cessna high enough to avoid the mountain peaks themselves, this is still not good enough. Mountain flying can be terribly turbulent with updrafts and downdrafts that are far more powerful than our little Cessna. If we were at 12,500 feet and found ourselves caught in a string downdraft, we could end up in pretty bad shape. We'd have to either be much higher or have a much stronger airplane that we knew could fight those nasty downdrafts. We'll cover this more later.

Also important to *always* consider, when flying in a single engine airplane is that our single engine might give out at some point. Believe it or not, this isn't the worst thing that can happen to you in flight! Light airplanes typically glide pretty well. But in order to prevent an emergency like an engine failure from becoming a disaster, you need to be able to glide some place that can serve as a suitable landing site. The only thing less suitable than mountainous terrain is probably the mouth of an erupting volcano.

So, pathetic as it sounds, light planes pretty much follow highways when traversing rugged terrain— or at least the ones with smart pilots at the controls do.

If you're thinking that a twin-engine airplane is the obvious solution, you'll be surprised to learn that engine failures in twins can be even more dangerous than a single-engine airplane. This is because a twin-engine airplane with only one engine active is much harder to control. When a single-engine airplane loses its engine, it starts to descend, but handles no differently. A twin, on the other hand, becomes a yawing beast that has lost 50% of its power, but a full 80% of its performance. So that crippled twin pilot has 20% of the performance he's used to, and his airplane is pulling either left or right very hard. For the record, this is why twin-engine airplanes have such large tail sections; it better enables the pilot to fight the yaw imposed by flight on only one engine.

AVOIDING WET WINGS

Flying over open water is only slightly better than the mountains if you lose your engine. Keep in mind that even if you can get the airplane down in the water—and remain conscious throughout the landing—you're still in deep water, so to speak, with a sinking airplane (or what's left of it). Unless your airplane is a seaplane, it was not designed to land in water. If you've ever belly flopped from a high dive, you know that water feels much like cement when hit hard.

The only safe way to fly over water is to ensure that you fly no farther out than the distance your airplane would require to reach the beach with a dead engine. This distance depends on the airplane's glide performance, your altitude, the winds and a few other factors your CFI will cover with you. Sandy beaches can make suitable emergency landing sites, providing you can reach them. Rocky beaches might not be great, but at least a water landing near shore is better than one five miles off the coast.

The FAA has something to say about flights over open water too. Pilots can't take airplanes more than 50 nautical miles from the nearest shore unless life preservers or an approved flotation device are on-board for each occupant of the aircraft. [FAR 91.509]

Okay, so we can't fly more than 50 nautical miles from shore. But 49 nautical miles is still a long way to swim, especially if you're not warmed up. Assuming the glide distance of a Cessna 172 in a wind-free sky, we would have to be at an altitude of just over 33,000 feet to glide 50 nautical miles without an engine. Keep in mind that 172s, on a (really) good day, *might* reach 14,000 feet.

This regulation also says you can't fly an airplane over water for more than 30 minutes or farther than 100 nautical miles from the nearest shore unless your flotation device collection is supplemented with enough life rafts to accommodate all occupants, a pyrotechnic signaling device for each life raft, a self-buoyant portable emergency signaling device and a life line.

Note that the self-buoyant emergency signaling device must be portable. The FAA doesn't allow one of those self-buoyant emergency signaling devices that are built in to, say, your house.

I've always wondered about the chances of getting a life raft out of the back of the airplane after a water landing. Think about it: you essentially just crashed your airplane. You're out in the middle of nowhere. The water's cold and the airplane is sinking. You're probably bruised up, or worse. Your passengers are freaking out because by this time they're convinced this was not part of the tour.

Hell, I find it difficult to get things in and out of the back of the airplane on the ground! (You might laugh now, but trust me when I tell you that the most dangerous aspect of general aviation is stepping in and out of the airplane.)

Luckily the FAA has considered the placement of the survival gear. This same regulation tells us that the gear must be *clearly marked* and *easily accessible*. That rules out the back of a 172.

Conventional wisdom has some pilots thinking that water landings are a good option in an emergency. While I'd rather land in water than in a forest full of trees, airplanes with landing gear sticking out just won't fare well in the water. Damage will occur; there's no way around it. Head for the shore. Even if you don't make it, you're closer than you were. We'll talk more about emergency landings later.

Engine failures over water are where that second engine on a twin can be a real bonus. If one engine goes, you might lose some altitude, but you can probably reach a nearby airport. Given that most open water is at sea level with few, if any, obstructions, altitude won't be an issue. Land your airplane, get out and kiss your second engine.

INVISIBLE WALLS

The last fun-limiting factor we'll discuss is airspace. I won't go into details here, because I'll cover it later, but airspace must be a consideration when determining if a flight is possible or practical.

Some areas are off limits to some or all aircraft. The military has reserved some space for their training operations and the government has reserved other spots for security reasons. Some restricted airspace changes from moment to moment, depending on certain events like presidential appearances or fire-fighting activities.

Restricted airspace falls into many categories ranging from simple avoidance *advisories* to absolute legal *forbiddance*. Airspace will be a big part of your training, so I won't spoil the fun here by saying too much.

For the purposes of this section, it's important to note that airspace restrictions might prevent a flight from being possible, or, at the very least, require rerouting.

So, if after reading about some of the restrictions on general aviation "freedom," you're still gung-ho to proceed, the following sections will help you determine the best type of training for you.

CHOOSING A FLIGHT SCHOOL, INSTRUCTOR AND TRAINING AIRPLANE

Aside from the military, there are three different training options available to aspiring pilots:

- **Part 141 Schools** – Part 141 schools offer structured programs that follow specific syllabi.

- **Part 61 Schools** – Part 61 schools typically use free-lance CFIs, each having her own way of teaching.

- **University** – Several universities offer degree programs for pilots.

"Part 61" and "Part 141" refer to which regulations govern the school and its programs.

One type of school doesn't always produce better pilots than the others. It's not uncommon, however, for career-bound student pilots to be told they should consider either a Part 141 or university program. Keep in mind, however, that commercial airlines don't tend to care where a pilot gets her training. It's *flight experience* they're after.

STRUCTURED PROGRAMS (PART 141 SCHOOLS)

The FAA governs the programs offered by Part 141 schools, so each CFI has little to do with what's taught or how it's taught. Programs are typically full-time, with the ground training taught in a classroom environment.

Part 141 schools like to boast that pilots can get their licenses with fewer hours than those attending Part 61 schools. For example, the FAA says a Part 141 student needs 35 hours of training before he can take his private pilot checkride, whereas a Part 61 student requires 40. Big deal, I say.

The difference in required hours is more dramatic for advanced ratings, like a commercial certificate. But here's the catch: airlines are looking for flight hours. So where's the advantage in getting your certificate and additional ratings with fewer hours? You'll still need to log those extra hours somewhere.

I met a 19 year old woman who was attending a popular Part 141 aviation school in Florida. She obtained her private certificate and her instrument rating in less time than it took me to get my private license alone. But the lion's share of her flight experience was during training activities. So while she had a more advanced rating than I had, my logbook showed many more flight hours under more diverse conditions. She is airline-bound, but might find that her fast-track training won't serve her as well as she'd like. Airlines want experience and experience comes from flying airplanes. So speeding your way through your training, thinking you're on the fast track to a career in aviation, might backfire if you end up with many advanced ratings and a logbook full of empty pages.

I spoke to a Part 141 school and asked what advantages they offered over Part 61 schools. I was told that their more structured program ensured their CFIs were top notch and well trained. Upon additional research I found that their CFIs made $14 per hour. CFIs at nearby Part 61 schools were making twice that. This left little doubt in my mind as to where the better CFIs were likely to go.

I would agree that Part 141 CFIs are more *consistent* in quality, but I'm not so convinced that the level of quality is better than that offered by their Part 61 counterparts.

Part 141 training is typically paid for up front, which can mean a considerable outlay of cash or credit. If you end up disliking the school, or choosing not to continue your training for any reason, getting money back might be tough. Make sure you consider your "outs" before you write any checks.

PAY-AS-YOU-GO (PART 61 SCHOOLS)

Most aviation training facilities are Part 61 schools. At these schools, training consists of the basic FAA requirements and anything else the individual CFIs deem appropriate or necessary. Typically there is no school-standard for training.

This can be good and bad. If you end up with a great CFI (as did I), your training can far exceed any programs certified "acceptable" by the FAA. Conversely, if your CFI stinks, you might just squeak by and never know the difference. More on this later.

Some Part 61 schools offer pay-as-you-go programs, meaning that you pay for the CFI and the airplane after each lesson. There are no up-front fees other than maybe a school or club membership, which is just a way for them to get some bucks out of you each month whether you fly or not. Membership typically entitles you to reduced rental rates, which should more than pay for the cost of membership each month. If they don't, the school is charging too much.

As previously mentioned, avoid schools that make offers too good to be true. There simply is no cheap way to learn to fly. One low, easy monthly payment might be a fine way to acquire a room full of tacky furniture, but not for something as serious as your pilot training.

In choosing a Part 61 school you want to make sure of two things up front:

- Location – Is the school convenient? If it's not, you might not find the time to get there. This is less of a concern for Part 141 training because there you won't be slotting lessons into your work day.

- Maintenance – How well are their airplanes maintained? Ask them who maintains their airplanes. If they do it themselves, ask about the mechanics' experience. If they use another company, ask pilots around the airport about the maintenance company. If the company has a good reputation, then this is a good sign. If not, then keep looking.

UNIVERSITIES

Universities that offer aviation degree programs are probably your best option if you're airline-bound and lack a pilot's certificate and a college degree. Airlines would prefer that you have both, so keep that in mind.

One advantage offered by university programs is access to non-aviation courses that can enhance a pilot's education. One commuter airline pilot that I spoke with received his certificate and degree from a university that also offered degrees in meteorology. The school's aviation program, in fact, required that pilots take meteorology courses. This not only looks great on a resume, but it's valuable training. Only senior airline captains that I talked to had as much weather knowledge as this young, professional pilot.

The quality of instruction at a university is likely to be pretty good. The faculty are, after all, education professionals. Universities are also more likely to offer additional resources required by full-time students, such as housing.

One advantage to university training that I've heard folks speak of is the total immersion in aviation one experiences while attending. You eat, sleep, work and play aviation. As such, your flight education might be more deeply entrenched into your brain because it was part of your life rather than part of your afternoon.

CHOOSING THE RIGHT PROGRAM

After reading the previous sections, you might already have an idea of which type of program is best for you. If not, consider the following:

- **Time** – Structured programs like universities and Part 141 schools are probably better choices for younger students that are seeking full-time aviation training. If you have a job, you'll need the flexibility that a Part 61 school offers.

- **Learning style** – If you prefer someone to "steer" you through your education, Part 61 training might not be for you. Part 61 students must actively participate in the direction of their training because you can't always rely on a freelance instructor to cover all the bases. Conversely, if you are a go-getter with regard to how you learn, the structure of a Part 141 or university program might frustrate you.

- **Money** – If money is tight, a Part 61 school is the way to go. (Unless you qualify for financial assistance that can pay for Part 141 or university training.) A Part 141 or university program will require a big chunk of change up front.

- **Commitment** – If you're not completely sure that aviation is right for you, consider a Part 61 school, at least at first. You can pull the plug on your training at any time without losing any advance payments you've made. The downside of this is that Part 61 students might be more likely to give up when they encounter frustrations.

- **Flexibility** – If you have a day job, then you'll need the flexibility of Part 61 training. You can train when you like and take any breaks that you need for family, health or other reasons. Another flexibility offered by Part 61 programs is the choice of CFI. If you get one you don't like, you choose another. This isn't usually an option in other programs. (More on choosing CFIs comes next.)

- **Education** – If you're airline bound, you'll want that four-year degree. Might as well combine your aviation training with your college education. If you have no interest in flying professionally, then university aviation training might amount to nothing more than a pile of student loan bills and a better understanding of the weather.

- **Goal** – If you don't plan to go beyond your private pilot certificate, or maybe your instrument rating, a university will be overkill for you. University programs typically include all ratings through commercial. Part 61 and Part 141 schools offer educations on a rating-by-rating basis.

Choosing either a Part 61 or Part 141 school for one rating doesn't mean you are locked into that choice for additional ratings. You might get your private certificate at a Part 61 school and then, after knowing that aviation is right for you, choose to get your instrument rating at a Part 141 school.

No single method of training can be considered better than the others over all. If you consider your personal situation, one method will likely seem best for you.

CERTIFIED FLIGHT INSTRUCTORS: THE GOOD, THE BAD & THE UGLY

Were your parents good parents? You probably have an opinion about this now that differs from the one you had as a kid. It's tough to determine when a person educating us is competent until we've learned the subject well enough to be able to reflect on the training. So with parents; so with CFIs.

There are some basic things you can determine up front about a CFI:

- **Do you get along?** – More than anything, if you just don't like your CFI, you'll get nowhere and hate the process all the while.

- **Does your CFI display confidence?** – A CFI rating is considered one of the most difficult aviation certificates to obtain, but that doesn't mean every person who gets one deserves one. Having no prior knowledge of aviation yourself doesn't preclude you from asking some good questions. If you get answers that make sense to you, then you might have found someone good. If you get nervous giggles and shoulder shrugs, then keep looking. If you get what seems like a load of garbage, it probably is.

- **Can you afford your CFI?** – CFIs charge different hourly rates. Find out how much up front.

- **Are your schedules compatible?** – If you have no common times free for training, then keep looking.

THE OLD AND THE NEW

Unless you're about 18 years of age, chances are that you'll find many CFIs younger than yourself. This seems a bit disconcerting at first, at least it was for me. How much could a 21-year old know about teaching anything, let alone a subject as complex as aviation? I just assumed that the more *mature* CFIs would be better choices. They typically had more flight experience and probably had more teaching experience too. They certainly had more life experience.

And with few exceptions I have found this theory to be true. This arguably irresponsible statement will no doubt infuriate many younger CFIs who read this.

But the difference between the young and the old isn't entirely due to age and experience. It's motive and goals. A 55-year old flight instructor that's been flying since back when flight attendants were *stewardesses*, is probably set career wise. For this person, the job of CFI is a end, not a means to an end.

Conversely, the MTV-generation CFIs are more likely airline bound and using your checkbook to amass the hours required to get there. This sounds horrible, I realize. But the truth of this situation has to be considered by those seeking flight instruction. This is not to say that all young CFIs are bad, or even that most are bad. *Some* are bad.

So what's the real issue?

There are several issues to consider: Many students have found themselves CFI hunting not because they didn't like a former CFI, but because their CFI was hired away by an airline. I've known students who went through 3 or more CFIs during their training for this very reason.

Getting hired is great news for the CFI, but it can lead to delays and inconsistencies in training for the student. When interviewing CFIs, ask them about their career goals. If they're going to the airlines, ask how long it will be before they start job seeking. If the answer puts their job search right in the middle of your training (any time in the forthcoming six months), interview some other CFIs.

This, however, isn't just about them leaving you. It's about quality of education. I'm a firm believer that once the hunt begins for a new job, it's hard to maintain interest in the present job. You might be prepping for your first solo flight while your CFI is prepping for an interview.

It's easy to argue that CFIs that are "almost there" with regard to airline careers will have more teaching experience. This might be true. You could benefit from this experience over the relative inexperence of a new CFI, but consider the possible disruption.

So what's left? There are basically two CFI categories left: Old Timers that have already done the airline thing, and CFIs that have no interest in anything but teaching. These are the rare and potentially most powerful categories. An Old Timer will bring a wealth of experience to the cockpit about which a younger CFI can only theorize. Someone who's only interest is teaching has probably undergone some more advanced education training, or at least has a better appreci-ation of the skill and art of educating.

At my flight school there were a few examples of both of these last two special categories (and countless examples of the first).

One is an Old Timer named John. There's something about John that immediately puts one at ease. His mild manner speaks volumes of his confidence as an aviator and an instructor. He just gives you the sense that he really knows how things work and that he'll make sure you really know, too, before your training is complete.

I took a progress test flight with John one day. (They call these test flights *phase checks*.) I could tell that John knew what was up from the moment we got together. He asked all the right questions and he had all the right answers when I did not.

After the flight, he talked with my regular CFI. He was honest and accurate. He told her I was so concerned about smashing into an oncoming airplane that I wasn't flying the airplane to the extent that I should be. Of course I argued this point 'til the cows landed, but he was right. I was hyper-concerned about midair collisions and it did consume too much of my concentration.

This was a very brave thing for him to say. After all, with the intense emphasis on safety in aviation, one would think that the last thing a CFI would say about a student was that he was trying to be "too safe." But this wasn't what John was saying at all. I wasn't being too safe, I wasn't being safe enough. My concentration was compro-mised. That was his report and he was right.

And then there's April in her early thirties. She might or might not be airline bound, but it doesn't seem to make any difference. She is so excited by teaching aviation that she expresses no other interests at all (except football). She has long since passed the minimum experience requirements that most airlines would require of her, but still she teaches. And the benefits to her students are enormous. Her longer-than-average tenure as a CFI has given her not only a wealth of hours, but a wealth of education experience.

With a CFI like this, a student can feel secure in knowing that not only will the FAA-required basics be taught, but that the "real" stuff will be covered too. I've seen students ask April questions for which she had no immediate answer. Often she researches the question in her off hours, or instigates take-no-prisoner debates with other CFIs until an answer is found.

When asked for CFI recommendations, I mention April and John. April will kick your ass all the way into the cockpit of a 737. Her voice of reason and preparedness will ring in your head on every flight you take. John will suggest a place that the two of you can fly for lunch. Along the way, he'll casually mention some aviation adage that will stick in your head forever and might save your life one day.

The other CFIs sit around the airport lounge and talk about who's hiring.

MY RIGHT-SEAT BUDDIES

I've had three different flight instructors (so far). CFI #1 was a nice enough guy. He seemed to know how to fly an airplane, but when I asked him what made an airplane turn, he asked another CFI to help him explain. I can be dense, but I'm not *that* dense. A good CFI has several ways of explaining everything. This guy didn't, so I moved on.

CFI #2 came along some two years later. I was discouraged by my first CFI and I wanted to make sure I found someone better before I started up again. I finally started training with CFI#2 on a friend's recommendation.

I was loving it at first. My training was going nicely and I felt like I was making real progress. But then came the snags. I found myself having the same problems over and over again. The trouble was that this CFI offered the same explanations over and over again. What he said was always sound advice, it just wasn't registering with me.

One time I got so mad I could have pushed him out of the airplane. He always had me reciting this mantra during each approach: "Airspeed, VASI, centerline. Airspeed, VASI, centerline." Over and over. The idea was to remind me to watch my airspeed, stay on the proper glide slope (VASI is a lighting system that helps pilots come down at just the right angle), and stay centered on the runway. (*Centerline* is the stripe painted down the middle of the runway.)

As always, I landed to the left of centerline. And, as always, he reminded me that I should try to stay on centerline. This made me *crazy* with frustration, "Where do you think I'm trying to land," I barked, "the freeway?" (There was a freeway paralleling the runway.)

Of course I knew I was supposed to land on the centerline, but for some reason I was have trouble doing so. My problem with him was that he didn't explore other ways of helping me gauge the landing other than reciting that same damn mantra, which, for the record, I still mumble to myself today.

I met CFI #3 when I started taking groundschool and still flying with CFI #2. She was teaching and I, low and behold, was actually learning. Her teaching style was one that worked for me. Concepts that had thus far eluded me, started to come into focus. I decided that I had to get this woman in the cockpit with me or I might be landing left of centerline forever. She agreed.

This was a bit awkward because CFIs #2 and #3 worked together and were friends. I really did like CFI #2 as a person, so I didn't want to offend him. So instead of dropping #2, I decided to train with both. I figured I could get the best of both worlds.

I can't begin to tell you how confusing this became. I had mistakenly assumed that flying was flying, and that every CFI would pretty much teach and approach it the same way. But each CFI had preferred ways of doing just about everything.

I started trying to sort the mess out by determining who was right and wrong on a conflict by conflict basis. As it turned out, they were both right on all accounts. I just couldn't understand that then. I even asked other experienced pilots to break the ties for me. But that resulted in even more opinions describing the way things should be done.

Designing an airplane is a science; flying one is an art. Don't let anyone tell you otherwise. Art is never *wrong*, it just sometimes looks funny.

I'm not talking about major discrepancies though. It wasn't like one CFI would tell me to land on the centerline and the other would insist on the freeway. Or that one would remind me to maintain a constant pitch attitude on take-off while the other preferred barrel rolls. It was the minor, style-related things that differed.

For example, CFI#2 wanted me to pull the power back at a certain point before landing so I could stabilize my descent early. CFI#3 also wanted me to pull back power, but she preferred not doing so until I was closer to the airport. Her argument was that it was easier to lose airspeed and altitude than it was to gain it back again if needed. Further, her way ensured that I maintained power until I had my landing clearance. Reducing power sooner sometimes required that I add power back again if the tower tried to squeeze other airplanes in ahead of me forcing me to fly out further before turning toward the airport. (This will all make more sense after you've learned about the special way in which airplanes fly to and from airports, and the tricks that tower controllers use to get ten airplanes into a space big enough for five.)

Statistics suggest that engine failures occur most often during power changes. If this is true, then maintaining power until the last moment makes even more sense.

But the major difference between the two instructors wasn't apparent to me until I started my instrument training. CFI#3 was teaching me

what I needed to know for instrument flying. Maintaining airspeed and power for as long as possible on an approach is an instrument thing. Those basics made instrument training easier to grasp.

CFI #2 was prepping me for my private pilot checkride. CFI#3 was prepping me for my instrument rating checkride. And in doing so, she also prepped me for my private checkride.

Both were great pilots; both were good instructors. One just worked better for me.

TRAINING AREA CONSIDERATIONS

The area in which you train makes a difference. Depending on where you live, you might not have a choice. But if you do have options, consider them carefully.

CORN FIELD INTERNATIONAL

I know a woman that learned to fly in a corn field, as she describes it. The simplicity of her training environment meant that she was able to get her license in fewer hours, but it also meant that her training was far from complete.

Eventually she moved from the corn field and now flies out of San Carlos, just 7 miles south of San Francisco International. Things are different for her now. The cockpit radio is no longer a chit-chat device for airborne communications about weekend barbecues and elk sightings. It's now a necessary means of avoiding airborne disaster.

The importance of navigation changed for her too. Navigation in congested airspace is necessary to keep pilots from straying into the paths of oncoming jumbos. Some busy areas like San Francisco and Los Angeles have airspace boundaries that are so chopped up and divided amongst local airports that it's like flying through a maze. You *have* to know exactly where you are at all times. If you don't, you could find yourself wandering into airspace reserved for someone else.

Eventually she learned what she needed to know and she does great now. But she still admits to feeling somewhat overwhelmed at times. Her aviation roots are in corn fields, but she now shares airspace with some pretty serious air traffic.

If you have the option of training out of a small, nontowered airport or a busier one with a control tower, consider your long term aspirations. If you plan to become a professional pilot, by all means choose the busy airport. If you don't plan to ever leave the vicinity of the smaller airport, then train there. (But I suspect you'll want to leave eventually!)

Even if you don't plan to fly professionally, there are great benefits to training at busier airports. You become more familiar with air traffic control, airport procedures, weather, airspace and you have fewer problems transitioning to the corn field, when necessary.

Another advantage to larger airports is that there are typically smaller airports nearby. This not only gives you the option to fly to more airports, but it helps you become equally comfortable with all types of airports. The corn field dilemma can go both ways: Some pilots trained in larger airports feel less comfortable when landing at airports without control towers governing everyone's moves. I'm one of them.

But it does usually take longer to get your license when you train out of a busier field. There's more to learn up front. A smart CFI is not going to let you solo in busy airspace until you've demonstrated that you understand and can identify airspace boundaries, and that you are comfortable on the radio. These are skills that corn field pilots spend very little time on before soloing or even getting their licenses. After all, if there's no airspace to consider and no air traffic controllers to talk to, how do you practice?

You need to learn it all eventually, regardless of where you train, but I think it's better to get it all in while you're still developing flying habits and while you still have a CFI sitting beside you. That way this stuff becomes second nature and not something that stresses you each time you enter busy airspace or land at Corn Field International.

WEATHER MATTERS

Bad weather cancels commercial flights, so you can imagine what it does to flight training in small planes. There are few inhabited places in the United States that don't have at least *some* good weather during the year. So consider the good-weather months for your region and plan your training accordingly.

San Francisco summers are typically foggy. This wreaks havoc on private pilot flight instruction. But the autumn and winter months can be wonderful. Even though the occasional storm can ruin a flight lesson, the bulk of the days are beautiful.

No time of year guarantees perfect weather, but some times are better than others. Consistency is key during flight training, so you don't want to cancel too many lessons due to weather.

When I first started my lessons, it was during California's En Niño storm fiasco of 1998. I had one lesson and then had to cancel my next four. By the fourth cancellation, the field I was flying out of, Gnoss Field, just north of San Francisco, was literally underwater.

I eventually gave up and decided to wait for better weather (and a better CFI).

So plan to start your lessons at the beginning of your area's good weather season. The preceding bad weather months can be a great time for groundschool and reading books like this one.

Figure 4: *SIMPLE, SAFE, STANDARDS* The Cessna 172 (left) is the world's most popular trainer. A fantastic safety record coupled with impressive specifications for a single-engine trainer make this airplane a staple of aviation. The Piper Warrior (right) is another great trainer, which sets the standard for low-wing trainers. The high-wing, low-wing thing can be like religion to some pilots. Some will swear by one configuration, while others swear by the other. [Photos: author]

TRAINING AIRCRAFT OPTIONS

There are many different types of training aircraft and each have their advantages. No flight school will offer them all, but every flight school will say that they offer the "best" options. Know what you want before you decide where to train.

ECONOMY CARS ARE HUGE

Training aircraft all share one common characteristic: they're small and uncomfortable. That bears repeating about 100 times, but I'll spare you. If you're a big kid, your airplane options are limited. If you're a heavy kid, your airplane options are limited too.

Each airplane has what is called its *useful load*. This refers to the amount of added weight the airplane can carry. Airplanes don't discriminate when it comes to this weight limit. Everything weighs something so everything is considered: fuel, oil, baggage, and even you and your CFI.

The trick is to find a training airplane that can accommodate the weight of you, your CFI and *full* fuel tanks. Full tanks aren't required for most training flights, but it's hard to control the amount of fuel you'll find in rental airplanes. Previous renters might have filled the tanks and then used only a little. Or they might have filled the tanks

thinking they were doing the next pilot a favor. It's very hard to get fuel out of an airplane, so if the combined weight of you and your CFI requires that you fly with less than full tanks, you'll find yourself with many last minute cancellations.

Your CFI will probably make an issue of this up front if it's a concern. But if the flight school has only one type of airplane, you might not hear an honest assessment.

The airplane that I liked to use for my training was a fairly standard Cessna 172. With full tanks, it could accommodate another 760 lbs. My CFI weighed 130 lbs and I weighed 185 lbs. So our combined weight of 315 lbs wasn't a challenge for this airplane at all, even right after Thanksgiving. (Figure 4)

There was another type of airplane at the flight school, called a Diamond Katana, which could carry only 313 lbs with full tanks. Had I trained in the Katana, I would have had to make sure the fuel tanks were not full before each flight. The combined weight of my CFI, myself and full tanks would have been well over the airplane's weight limit. (Figure 5)

If "impressive vertical size" is featured in your personals ads, then I'm afraid that comfortable training options probably don't exist for you. Make

Figure 5: *NO RELATION* One might think the Diamond Katana would be an obvious favorite of mine, given our shared name. But this fun little airplane is really better suited for folks a wee bit lighter than me. Flying it solo (without a passenger) is no problem for me, but if I bring along one of my beefier buddies, then full gas tanks are out of the question. [Photo: author]

Figure 6: *CIRRIOUS FUN* The Cirrus offers about as much fun as you can have in an airplane without joining the Mile-High club. Sleek looks, great performance and a cushy interior make this puppy seem like far more than a trainer. And it is far more: about twice the price per hour. [Photo: Cirrus Design Corporation]

sure you sit in whatever airplanes a flight school offers before you commit to anything. You might hate the cramped quarters so much that you'll decide flying isn't for you after all. You have to be comfortable when you fly or your concentration won't be where it needs to be.

TRIED AND TRUE VS. STATE OF THE ART

The Cessna 172 is a flight training standard for good reason. It offers a reasonable weight capacity, it probably offers the most cockpit room of any trainer, and it's got a great safety record. But some argue that it's antiquated. It's true that 172s made today differ only slightly from those made 30 years ago, but that's primarily because the 30-year old design still flies well.

Some newer trainers can appear pretty sexy at first glance. Diamond Katanas, for example, are sleek little airplanes reminiscent of the graceful simplicity of gliders. They truly shame the boxy contour lines of the Cessnas and Pipers design-wise. But, again, the airplane's limited useful load can be a problem.

Some Katana pilots also report that Cessnas and Pipers feel like tanks, by comparison, when flying. The feather-light Katanas just love to fly. This

makes for a very fun, effortless flight experience, but it's not an honest taste of *most* airplanes. You can reduce the power on a Katana and the airplane glides on and on. A powerless Piper Warrior, on the other hand, sinks like a rock. The Cessna 172 falls somewhere in between.

A relatively new kid on the block is the Cirrus SR-series aircraft. Here you have the sex appeal of the Katana married with the muscle of the 172 and the Warrior. Sitting in a Cirrus is an absolute dream, until you have to pay the rental bill. Currently, these airplanes can cost as much as twice the hourly rate of the previous models mentioned. (Figure 6)

Flight basics are flight basics, however, regardless of the airplane used.

The biggest differences between trainers will be:

- Instrumentation – Are the radios and navigation equipment in good shape? What types of navigation equipment are available? Some newer trainers, like the Katana and Cirrus, have on-board GPS (Global Positioning System) navigation units. GPS is great, but it's nothing that can't be easily added to other planes. Most manufacturers now offer *glass cockpit* instrumentation options on new

Figure 7: *PANEL PREFERENCE* Most trainers have instrument panels similar to the Cessna 172 panel shown above. The flight instruments, which we'll discuss later, are among the round dials. The radios are in the stack of equipment on the right. The yoke, which controls the airplane direction of flight, is mounted in front of the pilot, much like a car's steering wheel. [Photo: author]

A glass cockpit (below) looks wonderful—and really can increase flight safety if the pilot fully understands how to use the instrumentation—but is found far less often on training aircraft. The panel below is from a Cirrus. Note how the stick is mounted to the pilot's left. [Photo: Cirrus Design Corporation]

aircraft. A glass cockpit is one in which many traditional gauges have been replaced by computer displays. (Figure 7)

- **Wing Position** – Cessna wings are mounted on top of the airplane's body (called the *fuselage*) and Piper, Cirrus and Katana wings are

mounted on the bottom. This matters very little during training. You'll get used to either and it will be fine. Each have pros and cons with regard to visibility and other factors, but neither compromises safety when handled properly. (See previous figures for a comparison.)

- **Yoke vs. Stick** – Cessnas and Pipers have *yokes* to steer the plane, while the Cirrus, Katana and some other trainers have *sticks*. A yoke works somewhat like a car's steering wheel and a stick works like the joysticks found on video games. Yokes and sticks are also used to move the airplane's nose up and down, which affects altitude. More on that later. The stick might appeal to those with fighter pilot fantasies, but it matters little. You get used to one or the other. See them both in figure 7.

Truth be told, the glass cockpit instrumentation of more modern trainers offers a better glimpse of the way aviation is headed. But the more "antiquated" instrumentation is what dominates the general aviation industry for the time being. What's more, many FAA test questions specifically refer to this type of instrumentation.

So the bottom line is that there is only one significant difference between airplanes that matters for training purposes: Can it hold the weight of you, your CFI and full tanks? If not, look elsewhere or cut down on those pasta dinners for a while.

GROUNDSCHOOL: YES OR NO?

Much of what you need to learn about aviation is best taught outside the cockpit. Educators like to theorize that the cockpit is an example of the absolutely worst environment for education: it's uncomfortable, loud and filled with distractions. I agree. After many of my training flights I would sit with my CFI to talk about what we had done. Much of the time I felt as though we weren't even in the same airplane! She would remember things happening of which I had no recollection.

The cockpit is especially bad when you're trying to learn things that require some thought, like navigation. Here is where ground-school can be invaluable.

Groundschool isn't required by the FAA. The FAA requires that you pass your written exam, but they don't care how you go about preparing for it. Most CFIs are happy to cover the subjects taught in groundschool with their students. This isn't surprising considering that CFIs are usually paid hourly.

I found groundschool to be a great benefit. Mine cost about $200 for 16 classes. I thought this was a great deal. Classes were once a week and covered many topics that were missing from the tradi-tional aviation textbooks. This, in large part, is due to the instructor. Mine was such an aviation fan that she would often stray from lesson plans to tell us about all sorts of stuff we wouldn't have otherwise learned. This turned out to be a great thing in the long run. Every one of my fellow groundschoolers agreed.

A classroom environment is also a great place to argue points and ask questions. I usually found myself full of questions. Other students would often ask things that I hadn't thought of, so there was benefit there too. And totally unlike the cockpit, the classroom environment is relaxed and panic-free. Even in post-flight lessons with my CFI I found myself so mentally drained from the flight I couldn't really concentrate on what was being taught.

Groundschool also gives you the chance to take some practice FAA written tests. This helps you get used to the test questions and gives you a better sense of which subjects you need to work on. My groundschool instructor liked to discuss real-world situations that helped explain the point behind the various FAA questions. This really helped me put things into proper perspective.

Part 141 flight schools will include groundschool as part of their standard training. Most other flight schools will either offer groundschool classes themselves, or they can refer you to another school that does.

I think it's best to start groundschool about one month before you start your in-cockpit flight training. That first month of groundschool (4 classes) familiarizes you with the airplane and how the various controls work. It's great to have this head start before you're paying for airplane rental time. What's more, concurrent ground-school and flight training really helps to clarify things. Some of what you learn in one venue won't sink in until you experience it in the other.

There is an additional benefit to groundschool if you're planning to become a CFI. The CFI certif-icate requires a certain amount of groundschool instruction. You can have your groundschool sessions entered in your logbook to satisfy this requirement well in advance. Make sure you mention this to your groundschool instructor if he or she doesn't mention it to you.

INSTRUMENT GROUNDSCHOOL

As you now know, your private pilot certificate doesn't allow you to fly in the clouds. For this you need an instrument rating. But many non-instrument-rated pilots have been killed by inadvertently flying into instrument meteoro-logical conditions (IMC) and losing control of their airplanes.

I figured that as an extra measure of safety I would take an instrument groundschool even before I completed my private pilot training. I waited until I had finished my private pilot groundschool and passed my written exam so I wouldn't overload my mind. I also asked my CFI if we could concen-trate on more instrument cockpit training than was required for the private certificate. Essen-tially, this was the start of my instrument training.

The instrument groundschool was great because so much of aviation is orientated toward instrument flight. For example, most commercial flights are conducted under IFR regardless of the weather. Small regional commuters might conduct short-distance flights under VFR, but no jet service is flown VFR.

Additionally, the air traffic control system is in place primarily for airplanes flying IFR. ATC will provide assistance to VFR pilots whenever they can, but if the workload becomes intense, we VFR pilots are left to our own devices. During these busy times it's good for VFR pilots to understand what IFR aircraft are doing to ensure that we stay out of their way. When an IFR airplane is at the "PUPPY" intersection and cleared for the "Runway One Niner, ILS approach," you'll know what to watch for if you're in the area. Without the training you might hear only, "Puppy, blah, blah, blah."

Another huge benefit to IFR training is the advanced understanding you get of navigation systems. During primary flight training you are required to know enough about your navigation equipment to help you determine your position if you get lost. But primary training doesn't go into enough detail to get private pilots truly comfortable with their navigation equipment.

This is considered acceptable because your primary means of navigation as a VFR pilot is supposed to be visual. But with today's complex airspace and ever increasing air traffic, the more you know about your airplane systems the better. In many areas, the only way you'll know for certain when you're clear of restricted airspace is by the use of on-board navigation equipment. If you're not comfortable with the equipment, using it could become nothing more than a distraction. And we know where cockpit distractions can lead.

Instrument training also better acquaints you with runway markings and lighting systems. During primary training we learn about the runway markings and lighting that affect VFR flights. But airports are full of markings and lighting systems that are specific to IFR flights. Pilots unfamiliar with an airport's IFR resources might become confused.

Instrument training betters you as a pilot. It's not required as part of the basic private pilot license, but, as we've discussed, what is required simply isn't enough. It's up to you to advance your training.

FINANCING YOUR TRAINING

Flight training costs vary, but they never vary enough to be considered inexpensive. There are many financing options available to student pilots. Loans, grants, scholarships and even the good ol' credit card can get you through your training.

Let's first get an idea of some average monthly expenses.

ESTIMATING MONTHLY EXPENSES

Below is an estimate of monthly costs associated with training at a Part 61 flight school. As discussed, the total time required for you to complete your training might vary considerably from this estimate, depending on many factors. Costs for Part 141 training are easier to estimate because the school typically has a set fee for the courses offered.

The estimate assumes the following:

- Each lesson lasts two hours

- Your CFI charges $35 per hour

- The airplane rental is $80 per hour.

The national average for students to complete their training is 70 hours, which helps illustrate the overoptimism of the FAA's minimum requirement of 40 hours. I've assumed 84 hours in the estimate.

Month	No. of Lessons	CFI Time	Airplane Rental	Misc.	Monthly/Total Costs	Monthly/Total Hours
1	8	$560 (16hrs)	$1120 (14hrs)	$300	$1980/$1980	14/14
2	7	$490 (14hrs)	$960 (12hrs)	$50	$1500/$3480	12/26
3	8	$560 (16hrs)	$1280 (16hrs)	$40	$1880/$5360	16/42
4	6	$420 (12hrs)	$960 (12hrs)	$30	$1410/$6770	12/54
5	7	$560 (16hrs)	$1120 (14hrs)	$100	$1780/$8550	14/68
6	10	$700 (20hrs)	$1280 (16hrs)	$300	$2280/$10,830	16/84

The number of CFI hours vs. rental hours varies because you'll be spending more time on the ground with your CFI at first, as you're learning things for the first time, and toward the end as you prep for your tests. Somewhere in the second or third month you'll probably start soloing, so you'll start incurring airplane rental fees without CFI time. The miscellaneous column is for books, supplies, flight club membership dues and, at the end, the cost of your FAA written test and checkride.

Groundschool isn't factored into this estimate because it's not a requirement. Add another $200 for that, if you go that route.

CREDIT CARD FINANCING

Part 61 flight schools that charge by the lesson can probably be financed with just a credit card, assuming your credit limit is at least $2000 per month and you're not going overboard buying flight jackets, aviator sunglasses, fancy wrist watches and "My Other Car is a Cessna" license plate frames. (More on aviation accessories later.)

Your CFI might or might not accept credit card payments, however. Many CFIs are free-lancers that are not employed by the flight school. Check to see if this is the case at your school. If you can't pay your CFI with a credit card, you'll have to make sure you have the cash on hand or a checkbook handy.

There's an organization called the Aircraft Owner's & Pilot's Association (AOPA) that offers a credit card that can save you some money. We'll talk more about the AOPA as an organization later, but for now we'll focus on their credit card. It works like this: you get a 5% rebate on all purchases made through participating flight schools, pilot shops, etc. up to a maximum of $250 per year. Their website has more information. *(Visit **http://AirDiamond.com/sa** for a link.)*

Other cards might offer purchase incentives that are even better for you. If you're a frequent-flyer mileage junkie, what better way to rack up 10,000 miles in 6 months?

The point is that if you're going to use a credit card, make sure it's a card that's giving you something back. You'll be spending a lot of money, so you might as well get what you can out of it.

Don't underestimate your credit card as an option. Many credit cards offer rates and terms that are better than other types of financial aid.

FLIGHT SCHOOL FINANCING

You're more likely to find a Part 141 flight school that offers student financial aid than you are a Part 61 school. This is in part because of the higher up-front fees associated with going with a Part 141 program. One prominent school that I talked to said that a full 90% of its students relied on financing. Of all of the financing options, however, school-funded financing is least likely to offer you the best deal. Schools are not banks. But some schools will do almost anything to lock a student into a training contract.

SCHOLARSHIPS AND GRANTS

The FAA maintains a webpage that lists some grant opportunities that students can investigate. *(Visit* **http://AirDiamond.com/sa** *for a link.)*

Scholarships are also available.

Grants and scholarships are available to students at both Part 61 and Part 141 schools. The only exception are federal sources, which might require students to be enrolled in Part 141 programs.

PAYING THE PIPER

It's tempting to accept any financing that's offered to you simply because you'd also like to eat while you learn to fly. But choose your options carefully. Those juicy senior airline pilot salaries don't come to new hires. You're going to have to repay your debts on a very modest income at first. And if you are airline bound, keep in mind you'll need your private certificate, your instrument rating, your multi-engine rating and your commercial rating

before anyone will even consider hiring you. If you're going to be flying big jets, you'll need to tack on your ATP rating to that list.

The entire cost of the training you'll need to fly jets for a major airline is roughly equal to the cost of a 4-year degree at a university. This is why you should combine the two activities if it makes sense in your position.

Regardless, it's not going to be cheap.

SECURITY DOCUMENTATION REQUIREMENTS FOR TRAINING

The Transportation Security Administration (TSA) requires student pilots to provide flight instructors with some documentation before their flight training can start. The documentation required depends on the citizenship of the applicant.

These requirements govern *flight training* only. In other words, training that takes place in an airplane or flight simulator. You might start groundschool at any time without any documentation.

DOCUMENTATION FOR U.S. CITIZENS

If you are a citizen of the United States (or U.S. National or Department of Defense employee), take with you on your first day of flight training:

- An original or government-issued birth certificate for the United States, American Samoa or Swains Island, plus a photo ID, or

- A current, valid (not expired) United States passport, or

- An original U.S. Nationalization Certificate with raised seal, plus a photo ID, or

- An original U.S. Citizenship and Immigration Services (USCIS) or Immigration and Naturalization Service

(INS) form N-550 (or N-570 Certificate of Naturalization), plus a photo ID, or

- An original certification of birth abroad with raised seal or U.S. Department of State form FS-545 (or form DS-1350), plus a photo ID, or

- An original certificate of U.S. citizenship with raised seal, USCIS or INS form N-560 (or forms N-561 or N-581), with photo ID, or

- Department of Defense or Federal Agency written certification attesting to your U.S. citizenship or nationality, plus your government-issued photo ID.

For most student pilots who are U.S. citizens, that long, confusing list of requirements can be boiled down to a photo ID and birth certificate, or a valid passport.

DOCUMENTATION FOR NON-U.S. CITIZENS

Not surprisingly, student pilots who are not citizens of the United States have to jump through a few extra hoops. If you do not fall into the U.S. citizen category defined above, here's how it works for you:

- Fill out a form you can find online. *(Visit http://AirDiamond.com/sa for a link.)* Instructions for completing the form are on the website. Different categories are defined for pilot applicants. If you have never been licensed to fly an airplane, you are in Category 3. You might fill out and submit this form before you come to the United States for your training.

- You will need to have your fingerprints sent to the TSA. The American Association of Airport Executives handles finger-printing for the TSA. Contact them at 703-797-2550 for information on the procedure,

or find them online. *(Visit http://AirDiamond.com/sa for a link.)*

- When you arrive at your flight school for training, a photo of you will be taken and submitted to the TSA.

- You must provide your flight school with a current and valid passport and visa, if appropriate.

Assuming your documentation is in order, your training can start immediately, without TSA approval. Your flight school will submit the necessary documents to the TSA on your behalf. Your fingerprints will be submitted to the TSA by the agency that collects them.

Make sure you are ready to begin your training when you submit your documentation. After 180 days, your application expires if your training has not begun and you must start the entire process again.

DO THE RIGHT THING PROPERLY

In theory, any flight instructor you meet will be familiar with these security requirements and be able to guide you through the process. But there's no guarantee. These requirements went into effect in October, 2004. It might take a while for some flight instructors to get up to speed on the process.

If you meet with a flight instructor who doesn't inquire about your documentation, whether you are a U.S. citizen or not, do not start your flight training until you discuss the requirements with that instructor and have your paperwork ready to go. Your CFI must provide an endorsement in your logbook confirming your documentation was checked before training can begin. The last thing you need is the TSA coming after you because of a paperwork mishap. The responsibility for following the correct procedures is shared between you and your flight instructor.

Figure 8: *DEAR DIARY* Here's my first logbook. It's a good thing logbooks don't get airsick, because this poor thing has seen some pretty sloppy flying and some pretty bad landings. Student pilots are required to carry their logbooks on every flight. After you get your license, you can leave your logbook at home if you like. Licensed pilots are not required to carry one.

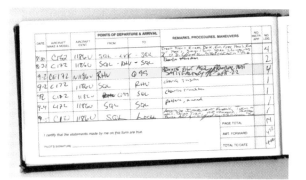

Figure 9: *WOO HOO!* It might look like scribble to you, but this highlighted line from my logbook is sheer art to me: it's my checkride entry! If you look carefully, you can see the word "satisfactory," as entered by my examiner. You might also notice from the right-hand column entries that by the time I took my checkride, I had landed a Cessna 172 over 400 times!

STUFF YOU'RE GOING TO NEED

Flight training requires more than a fat checkbook, some paperwork and a burning desire. You'll lug so much stuff to and from flight lessons that you'll wonder if you need that gym membership at all. The trick is know what you do and don't need, and when.

LOGBOOK

One thing you'll want to get before your first training flight is a pilot's logbook. This little book will go everywhere with you as a student. Every flight is logged, complete with a description of what you did on the flight. This is the official record of your training. Without the record of experience it provides, you can't get your license. (Figure 8)

There are several types of logbooks. As a student, you don't need the more complex books. Your CFI can help you choose a good one.

Due to the extreme importance of the information in the book, you should make copies of it regularly. Photocopies of the pages will suffice to prove your experience if you lose the book itself.

Electronic logbook programs are fine for licensed pilots, but each lesson logged in a student's book needs to be signed by a CFI, so electronic logbooks won't do. Even after you get your private pilot certificate and continue on with your instrument or multi-engine ratings, you'll still need a paper-based logbook. I'm a lover of technology, but I just don't see the benefit of electronic logbooks until you've completed absolutely all of your training. (And even then you'll need a CFI's signature to verify that you've received the every-other-year pilot check-ups we call *biennial flight reviews*, or BFRs.)

Entries in logbooks are based on the honor system. No one (except your CFI) verifies that entries are accurate and true. So be careful and honest about the entries you make.

Make sure that you enter absolutely every flight you make. They all matter, and some things you do during a flight might apply to more advanced ratings you'll seek later. For example, an instrument rating requires a certain amount of "hood" work. A hood is a view-limiting device designed to force a student to focus on cockpit instrumentation instead of looking outside the airplane. Only three hours of hood time is currently required for the private pilot certificate, but if you and your instructor do more hood work than that, you can apply the additional work toward your instrument rating.

Student pilots are required to carry their logbooks with them on all solo flights. If an FAA inspector happens to be at your airport and asks to see your logbook as you get in or out of a cockpit, you'd better have it. If you don't, you will be shot and killed by the inspector. Or worse, you'll have FAA paperwork to deal with.

BOOKS

The book you are now reading is undoubtedly the finest aviation book ever written, but there are others. A few books will be suggested by your instructor. Others you can pick up along the way.

The bible of aviation rules and regulations is referred to as the FARs (Federal Aviation Regulations). The Federal Aviation Regulations are commonly published combined with another aviation staple called the AIM (Aeronautical Information Manual). Together, the FAR/AIM provides the FAA's official aviation rules and regulations, complete with general information on the way aviation things are *supposed* to be.

Your instructor might also require that you buy a general pilot training textbook. Several are available and you'll probably be told which to get, so there won't be much of a decision here on your part.

Aviation books are covered in detail in the section, "Books" on page 64.

Figure 10: *HAL 8999* The E6B is a handy tool for flight training. Manual models (right) and electronic models (above) are available. Your CFI might have a preference as to which type you use.

FLIGHT COMPUTERS

Flight planning is easier with some sort of flight computer. A flight computer helps you determine time enroute, fuel requirements, wind correction angles and many other things too. What's more, use of a flight computer is a required part of your training.

When I first heard the term "flight computer" I envisioned some fancy device that could tell me where to go, how long it would take to get there and also make coffee. The basic flight computer, however, called an E6B (pronounced "ee-six-bee"), is basically a slide rule with a circular disc attached, usually priced less than $20. (Figure 10)

I was horrified by the sight of the E6B at first. It looked terribly confusing and I was certain it wouldn't make coffee. But it's actually a pretty handy device. I still can't get over all the tricky little calculations that can be done with it.

There are also electronic versions of the E6B. These look like glorified calculators and vary in price from about $30 to $90. They do all the same basic calculations as the slide rule version, but they're easier to master for some. Your CFI might insist that you use the manual kind, but the FAA doesn't care which you use.

 Fans of personal digital assistants (PDAs) like the Palm Pilot will be thrilled to learn of all the handy aviation software that's available for those devices. But be forewarned: you can't use any such devices while taking your FAA written exam. You can use an approved electronic flight computer on the test, but the rule is that such a device can't have any memory functions. A PDA is capable of storing user information, which disqualifies it.

Calculators with memory functions might also be questioned by your testing center. I took a standard calculator in for my test that had a basic memory function. The woman behind the counter insisted that I demonstrate clearing the memory before she'd let me take my test. I didn't even know how to clear the memory! I was lucky there was someone nearby that could do it for me.

SUNGLASSES, WRIST WATCHES AND OTHER COOL PILOT THINGS

Certainly you've seen them: aviator sunglasses that give any man that *Top Gun* sort of machismo look, and any woman...well, that *Top Gun* sort of machismo look. And those aviator wrist watches that feature so many dials and buttons that *telling* time becomes something for which one must *set aside* time. And those bomber jackets: who can resist?

WATCHING YOUR WATCH

When I started flying I didn't wear a watch. But I soon realized that I needed one, so watch shopping I went. I found watches that had

multiple time zones, stop watches, calendars and even altimeters! (An altimeter indicates your present altitude.)

I figured an extra altimeter might be a good back-up option in case my panel-mounted one ever failed. And having a timer would be a good thing too, since I knew there were certain things that needed to be timed during flight.

My logic on these accounts amused my CFI no end. It's hard enough to know the correct combinations of buttons to push to work those damn things while sitting still on the ground! Forget trying to do it in a cockpit. Remember, your eyes are *supposed* to be outside the cockpit, not focused on your gizmo-packed, superhero wrist watch.

"But what about the altimeter?" I wondered. Surely an altimeter-equipped watch would make a great back-up device?

There are several airplane "things" for which back-up devices are useful and practical. Somewhere just above keeping a back-up engine on hand would be a back-up altimeter in your wrist watch.

Altimeters, themselves, typically don't have a high failure rate. And if yours *does* fail, air traffic control is not going to trust altitude reports from your wrist watch. They'd rather know that your altimeter failed, period. That they can deal with, and so can you.

I ended up with a watch that had both an analog dial and a digital display that could show another time zone. No altimeter, no dictation device, no pager, and no built-in laser-controlled alien defense system. I figured I would set the digital time zone to Greenwich Mean Time (called *zulu time* in aviation), so that I would have at-a-glance reference for when I got in-flight weather updates, which are typically based on zulu time. But you know what? I never even look at my watch for anything but the current local time while I'm flying.

If you already wear a watch, chances are it's suitable for aviation. If you need to buy one—and all pilots should have one—get one that is easy for you to read. That's the only important requirement. All the other gadgets just serve to confuse the issue and I'm sure you'll find them of limited practical use.

HERE COMES THE SUN (GLASSES)

Sunglasses were another beast that confused me. What exactly *are* aviator sunglasses? As it turns out, "aviator" is simply a frame style. It has nothing to do with any advantages the glasses offer pilots. It's a look, and nothing more. On some, it's a good look. On me they looked ridiculous. My face is just too small for those huge lenses. Tom Cruise I ain't. But then, he can't fly an air... Come to think of it, he can do that too.

The next question that plagued me was polarization. Was it important? Was it better in flight? I asked around and got many different opinions. One person said polarized glasses gave him a headache. Others swore by them.

There is one real concern about polarization: Sometimes you can see moiré patterns through certain types of tinted glass. (It looks kind of like a rainbow pattern.) I see this effect when I look through the side windows of my car, but I don't see it through the windshield. I've never flown in an airplane with glass windows, so it's not been a problem there. (Most airplane windows are plexiglass.) But polarization can also be an issue on certain instrument displays. Some LED-type displays appear "off" at certain angles. That is, no characters are visible. This hasn't been a problem for me, but make sure you have the option to return your new shades if they don't work in the airplane you fly.

The last consideration was lens color. I wanted to make sure that I didn't get a color that would affect the colors I saw on aviation maps (called *charts*). I figured I might become disoriented if the chart colors appeared wrong.

I laugh about this stuff now, but these were real concerns of mine back then. I wouldn't recommend sunglasses that have a severe lens color, but any of the standard tints should pose no problems, provided you can get used to them.

I ended up with a pair of glasses that have polarized, neutral-colored glass lenses, wrap-around frames and a price tag of $250. They are great glasses, but I just dropped them the other day and scratched one of the lenses. Now they're less than great. When I buy another pair they'll be about $20 and I'll fly just as well.

So instead of getting the $800, gizmo-packed wrist watch, find one for $40 with an easily readable display. And instead of paying $250 for a pair of sunglasses like I did, buy a pair for $20 that are comfortable and look good on you. (Image is everything.) Then take the $990 you'll have saved and buy a hand-held GPS and a hand-held cockpit radio. Now *those* are good back-up devices! (We'll talk more about them later too.)

DRESS FOR THE OCCASION

No special apparel is required for aviation. Have cool clothes for hot days and warm clothes for cold days. Warm clothes are also nice for flights at higher altitudes. It's not uncommon to fly at altitudes where the outside air temperature is below freezing. During San Francisco winter months, the freezing level is often as low as 5,000 feet. Training airplanes are drafty. If it's cold outside, it'll be cold inside too.

Airplanes do have heaters, but some of us have heard so many warnings about the potential carbon monoxide dangers of cockpit heaters that we prefer to simply dress warmly.

Regardless of what you decide to buy to accessorize your training, don't buy anything until you find that you actually need it.

ADDITIONAL STUFF WE'LL LEAVE UP TO YOUR FLIGHT INSTRUCTOR

Your CFI might ask you to buy some additional stuff to aid in your training. Get an idea of what you'll need in your first few lessons. If money is a concern, ask your CFI to determine the things you need immediately and what can wait.

3

Diving In

THE SCARY STUFF UP FRONT

Your awareness of aviation started long ago. You've probably been flying on commercial airlines for years. You've read the news. You've heard about all sorts of aviation-related events, including flights gone wrong.

I've spoken with many students about their earliest flight training concerns. Most agree that crashing was high on the long list of fears and concerns. Ask rookie SCUBA divers what crosses their minds when entering the water, and you hear the word "shark" most often.

People have fears. So let's address some common ones here so we might put things in better perspective for you.

ENGINE FAILURES

Airplane engines do fail. Sorry to have to confirm an already overly popular concern, but it is real. That said, they fail *very* infrequently. When an engine fails, it signals the end of the flight, but not necessarily the end of the world.

A good portion of your flight training will focus on *emergency procedures*, which are the things we do when something goes wrong. Follow the procedures properly, and your chances of living to tell

the story of your troubled flight are greatly increased. Forget the procedures and luck becomes your only hope.

It's important to go over the emergency checklist procedures routinely with your CFI. After you get your license you'll want to review the procedures regularly on your own.

But don't just go through the motions; make sure you completely understand why it is you're supposed to do each item on the checklist. If some item makes no sense to you, ask your CFI to explain. Having a genuine understanding of each checklist item will do wonders for your pilot intuition if something does go wrong. (Figure 11)

All engine failures present an urgent situation, but the seriousness of the situation depends in large part on where you are when it happens. For example, an engine failure during taxi toward the runway is a completely different beast than one that happens moments after take off. One that occurs while you're sight-seeing along the sandy shores of Summer is quite different from one that happens late at night as you're flying over rugged terrain in the dead of winter.

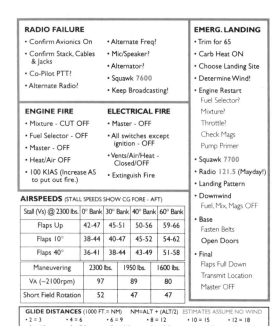

RADIO FAILURE	
• Confirm Avionics On	• Alternate Freq?
• Confirm Stack, Cables & Jacks	• Mic/Speaker?
	• Alternator?
• Co-Pilot PTT?	• Squawk 7600
• Alternate Radio?	• Keep Broadcasting!

EMERG. LANDING
• Trim for 65
• Carb Heat ON
• Choose Landing Site
• Determine Wind!
• Engine Restart
Fuel Selector?
Mixture?
Throttle?
Check Mags
Pump Primer
• Squawk 7700
• Radio 121.5 (Mayday!)
• Landing Pattern
• Downwind
Fuel, Mix, Mags OFF
• Base
Fasten Belts
Open Doors
• Final
Flaps Full Down
Transmit Location
Master OFF

ENGINE FIRE	ELECTRICAL FIRE
• Mixture - CUT OFF	• Master - OFF
• Fuel Selector - OFF	• All switches except ignition - OFF
• Master - OFF	• Vents/Air/Heat - Closed/OFF
• Heat/Air OFF	
• 100 KIAS (Increase AS to put out fire.)	• Extinguish Fire

AIRSPEEDS (STALL SPEEDS SHOW CG FORE - AFT)

Stall (Vs) @ 2300 lbs.	0° Bank	30° Bank	40° Bank	60° Bank
Flaps Up	42-47	45-51	50-56	59-66
Flaps 10°	38-44	40-47	45-52	54-62
Flaps 40°	36-41	38-44	43-49	51-58
Maneuvering	2300 lbs.	1950 lbs.	1600 lbs.	
VA (~2100rpm)	97	89	80	
Short Field Rotation	52	47	47	

GLIDE DISTANCES (1000 FT.= NM)   NM=ALT + (ALT/2)   ESTIMATES ASSUME NO WIND

• 2 = 3	• 4 = 6	• 6 = 9	• 8 = 12	• 10 = 15	• 12 = 18
• 3 = 4.5	• 5 = 7.5	• 7 = 10.5	• 9 = 13.5	• 11 = 16.5	• 13 = 19.5

Figure 11: *MAYDAY! MAYDAY! MAYDAY!* Each airplane you fly will have an emergency checklist for various situations like engine or electrical fires or dead-engine landings. Commit as much of these checklists to memory as you can and re-read them frequently. You don't want to be getting to know your airplane's emergency procedures for the first time right after something big has gone wrong during your flight.

Keep this *very* important concept in mind. Flight planning is your first line of defense against mechanical failures. While choosing your route, ask yourself how you feel about having to conduct a forced landing in the area. If the ground below is flat and abundant with highways, dirt fields, salt flats, sandy beaches or some other airplane-friendly landing spot, you're planning well. If you're planning routes over rugged peaks or large expanses of water, then you're reducing your options.

This is not to say that you'll never fly over rugged terrain or open water. But I want you to remember what we discussed about aviation

disasters being the result of a series of events. Eliminating a suitable emergency landing spot could certainly be an event in such a series.

BEST GLIDE

The most important first step after an engine failure is to get your airplane to a certain airspeed that's called *best glide* and point yourself toward the spot you plan to land. Best-glide speed is the airspeed at which your airplane flies the most efficiently with regard to drag. But more specifically, this is the airspeed at which your airplane will glide the farthest without engine power.

You reach best-glide speed by pulling back or pushing forward on the yoke, which in turns raises and lowers the nose of the airplane. The higher the nose, the slower the airplane will fly. Once stabilized at best-glide, you immediately start performing the emergency checklist procedures for your airplane.

The amount of time and distance your airplane will actually fly without power depends on several factors, including the aircraft model, the winds and, most importantly, the altitude you're at when the engine fails. The higher your altitude, the farther you can glide. For this reason I tend to plan my flights at higher altitudes.

Wind affects your glide distance too. If you have a 20 knot tail wind during your glide, all the better. Your airplane will fly farther. A head wind reduces your glide distance. So it's important to know the direction the winds are blowing along your route.

Let's take a look at a glide distance table for a Cessna 172:

Altitude (×1000)	3	4	5	6	7	8	9	10
Distance (Miles)	4	6	7	9	10	12	14	15

The numbers in the top row are thousand-foot altitudes. The bottom row is the number of nautical miles the airplane can glide under the following circumstances:

- **Airspeed at 65 knots** – This is the best-glide speed for this aircraft model. If the airplane is flying either faster or slower, the glide distance will be reduced.

- **Propeller "windmilling"** – When an engine fails, the propeller will either be frozen or continue to turn, driven by the force of the on-coming airflow. This is called *windmilling*. A frozen propeller increases drag and therefore reduces the airplane's glide range.

- **Flaps up** – Flaps are a part of the wing that are used to help the airplane descend. When they are down, they increase drag and will therefore reduce the airplane's glide distance. We will talk more about flaps later.

- **Zero wind** – The chart figures shown assume no wind. If the airplane is flying into the wind, the glide range is reduced. If flying the same direction as the wind, the glide range increases. It's important for pilots to always know the direction the wind is blowing for many reasons. This is one of the more important ones.

You can see from the table that altitude gives you an additional margin of safety. Your route might not be right over a perfect landing spot, but depending on your altitude and the winds, you might be able to reach it if it's within the estimated glide distance.

So it is possible to plan flight portions over water or unforgiving terrain, but make sure you're high enough to glide to safety if required.

PARTIAL POWER LOSS

The best news about engine failures is that they are very rare. What's even better is that most engine failures are not *total* failures. Most engine

failures reduce the engine's capabilities considerably, but do not totally disable it. This means you might still have enough power to get yourself down safely.

This is not to say that if you have a partial power failure over flat land that you should risk flying over mountains to get back to the airport. Use good judgement. If your engine starts to die, assume that total power loss is imminent and start looking for a place to land. Don't risk trying to get back to your airport if there's a suitable landing spot right beneath you.

Look at it this way: an airplane that's stranded out in the boonies with a partially disabled engine is a whole lot better than a pile of airplane wreckage two miles from an airport.

CHOOSING A SUITABLE LANDING SPOT

I was amazed to learn of all the places that make suitable emergency landing spots. But this is one of the hardest things for a new student to estimate from the air. *Everything* looks too small to land on from the air, including most runways! But after a while you'll get a better sense of what will work.

During your flights, ask your CFI about different spots you see. This helped me get a much better sense of what would and would not work, and why. For example, once I saw a small road that I though would be perfect. If figured that if it was wide enough for two-lane traffic, that it was wide enough for my Cessna. And it would have been perfect, too, if it hadn't been for the telephone wires that ran right along side it. These were the sorts of things that my CFI helped me think of ahead of time.

Suitable, however, can mean different things. Shallow water is more suitable than deep water, but a sandy beach is more suitable than any water. (Unless your airplane is a seaplane!) But a sandy beach littered with unavoidable giant rocks or sunbathers becomes less suitable than the shallow water. And the shallow water becomes less suitable than the deeper water if the shallow water is known for its appeal to big wave-worshipping surfers.

Further, suitable might depend on other factors too, such as time of day. A highway might make a great landing spot at three in the morning, but bumper-to-bumper rush-hour traffic will hinder your heroic landing. And regardless of the time of day, you have to watch for those roadside wires and concrete overpasses.

Always keep one thing in mind when picking your spot: the idea of the emergency landing procedures is to get you and your passengers down safely. *Emergency procedures have nothing to do with preventing damage to the airplane!* This is simply not a priority in an emergency. Land your airplane anywhere that will enable you to walk away. Forget the airplane! Your insurance company would much rather replace the airplane than face wrongful death lawsuits brought on by the families of your passengers.

DOING WHAT YOU CAN AS PILOT IN COMMAND

Short of getting an aircraft mechanic's certificate and doing a thorough inspection of every engine before you fly, there are still some things that you, as pilot-in-command (PIC) can do to help avoid engine failures.

The first thing you can do is check the airplane's maintenance logbooks. Every airplane has a maintenance logbook, as required by the FAA, that details each inspection and service performed on the airplane. While much of what's written in the logbook will seem like a foreign language to us as lay pilots, you can at least see if the airplane is due for any inspections.

Checking logbooks is especially important if you're renting an airplane from a company that's new to you. If you rent from the same place all the time, you'll have a better sense of when

inspections are due. Some places even provide a bulletin board or some other easy means for you to see airplane maintenance schedules.

After you're certain the airplane is up to date with regard to inspections, you'll want to check the *squawk sheet*. The squawk sheet is a daily log of things found wrong in the airplane by other pilots. (Assuming it's a rental aircraft used by others.) Some items can be very minor, such as a torn seat, but others should give you a very real sense that something might be wrong: "Oil pressure gauge pegs at full power." This item could describe a faulty oil pressure gauge or an engine that's about to ruin someone's flight.

This happened to me recently in a rental aircraft. I noticed the gauge had pegged when I applied full power for take-off, but my excitement to fly overpowered my good sense to abort the take-off. I hoped that it would get better.

I continued to fly out and the gauge continued to be pegged all the way to the high side. I knew from my training that you don't mess around with the oil in aircraft engines. But most of the training I had received focused on low-pressure indications, not high ones. Could this just be a faulty gauge? Maybe so, but I wasn't the one to make that determination.

I radioed back to the tower that I had a high-pressure indication and wanted to return to the field. They must have agreed that it was a situation to be reckoned with because they cleared the airspace and runway of other traffic and offered me my choice of either runway with an immediate clearance to land.

This got my attention. Having airspace and runways cleared for them is something that I knew many pilots had experienced as their final aviation event.

I knew that there was a possibility that my engine could quit and that I'd have to glide down. Turning back to the runway I had just taken off from would have been great, except that the 17-knot headwind I encountered on take-off was so strong that I was afraid I wouldn't be able to get the airplane down with a 17-knot tail wind. (Landing with a tail wind is very difficult because the airplane is traveling so fast across the ground. We'll talk more about that later.)

I opted to circle around the airport and come in on the more wind-friendly runway.

I thought back to my training and started going through the mental process of things I could be doing at that moment: I maintained a reduced power setting so as not to stress the engine any more than needed. I kept myself very close to the airport while circling in case gliding became my only option. And, most importantly, I flew the airplane without letting the circumstances distract me. This last one, as it turned out, was the only one that mattered.

"Skyhawk 73T: Do you require emergency services standing by?" the tower asked as I was turning toward the airport. I was really wishing my passenger hadn't heard that. The tower was essentially asking me if I thought there was a chance I was going to crash. Knowing I was well within gliding range to the airport at that point, and that the airplane remained flyable, I assured them I would be okay.

I landed without incident and the engine never did quit. I was cleared to taxi back and a fire truck followed me the entire way.

When I got back into the office of the place that rented me the airplane, I entered in the squawk sheet: "Oil pressure gauge pegs at full power." This simple sentence described a situation that prompted ATC to clear the airspace, give me clearance to any runway I wanted, and have a fire truck standing by on the runway waiting for me.

The rental office didn't ground the airplane. It was out flying again the very next morning without ever having been inspected by a mechanic. What amazed me more than the company allowing it to continue to fly was that the subsequent pilots, some of who were instructors, agreed to fly the airplane.

As it turned out, the oil pressure gauge was defective. Did I overreact? Let's put it this way: If you're concerned about overreacting to an instrument's warning indication, then eventually all that a pegged gauge will mean to you is that a gauge needs to be replaced.

Read the squawk sheets for your airplane before you fly. An engine that exhibits any odd behavior, be it a strange sound, vibration, power variation, or unusual gauge reading is an engine that's trying to tell someone something. Be the someone who listens.

The final thing that you can do as pilot-in-command is a thorough preflight check, which involves, among other things, a visual inspection of the outside of the *entire* aircraft. If the slightest thing seems out of the ordinary, refuse the airplane, or at least ask a mechanic if the problem is serious.

When in doubt, check the pilot's operating handbook (POH) for the airplane. The POH is the absolute authority as to the proper operation of a given airplane. You'll see references to it all the time throughout this and other aviation texts. Ask your CFI where to find the POH for your airplane.

If the POH describes an oil-leaking *feature*, then the oil leak you see might be okay. But if no such feature is mentioned in the POH, assume the oil leak is a sign of something gone wrong.

"Old" is not an excuse for leaking when it comes to airplane engines. "Old" is only an excuse for *ugly* as it applies to airplane interiors. It's hard to come by rental aircraft in pristine shape. With experience you'll get a better sense of which issues are really issues at all. Until you gain that experience, however, assume that *all* issues are issues.

During your preflight checks, make notes of things that don't seem perfect on your airplane. Then ask your CFI about each one. If you're told the defect isn't important, ask why. Asking "why" really furthers your education and really forces your CFI to think his answers through before he speaks.

Following all of these precautions doesn't guarantee a fault-free engine. But if your engine does fail during flight and you make it home, you'll want to make sure that it didn't fail because of some oversight on your part.

POP! BANG! OFF FALLS A WING

The gist of the previous section was that engine failures were survivable if good flight-planning practices were followed and good common sense prevails once the engine stops humming.

This section will be very brief: If your wing falls off, you're dead. That's the bad news. The good news is that wings don't typically fall off. Is it possible? Sure, anything is possible, but the possibility of your wing simply falling off is so low that it's safe to say you can forget about it ever happening to you.

A fire-fighting aircraft did lose a wing in Northern California in 2002. There was video footage of it all over the news. Just as it started its water drop, the right side wing ripped away from the fuselage. This was the only time I have ever heard of such a thing happening. I never found out why it did happen.

If you encounter severe or worse turbulence and don't follow your airplane's recommended safety procedures for rough air, all bets are off with regard to wing stability.

TURBULENCE

There are several categories and types of turbulence. "Air pocket" is not one of them, so forget you ever heard the term. My mother once described an air pocket as a chunk of the sky that had no air in it. The airplanes fly into it and drop hundreds of feet because there is no air to keep them flying.

Amusing theory, but I don't believe it's even possible on our planet. But my mother was a master of amusing theories. Cars were supposed to be flying by now, by the way, in case you missed her memo back in the '60s.

Later, we'll talk about what the "air pocket" drop effect really is, but for now we'll concentrate on turbulent conditions that are actually possible within the atmosphere of Planet Earth.

BUMPY AIR CLASSIFIED

The FAA classifies turbulence as *light, moderate, severe* and *extreme*. Most turbulence encountered is light. Sometimes it becomes moderate, and rarely is it ever worse. If you fly into moderate or worse turbulence, blame yourself for not using the weather resources available to you that could have helped you avoid such things.

Rough air is also typed as *turbulence* or *chop*. I'll let you read through the AIM to see if you can actually understand the difference between the two. They basically say that chop has a rhythmic aspect to it, whereas turbulence is more random.

I guess chop is more danceable. Whatever. Bumpy air is bumpy air.

The funniest thing about the definition of turbulence in the AIM is that it's biased toward commercial aviation. For example, the AIM says that in moderate or worse turbulence that food and beverage service is to be terminated. So, should you ever encounter such bad air, immediately snatch the peanuts from the trembling hands of your passengers and tell them that "party time is over!" as you yank the soda cans from their tray tables.

Rough air is no fun. I have always hated it and I probably always will. My gut starts to tense up as soon as the airplane starts to bounce. Don't feel like you're a wimp just because you hate it too. The idea is to get yourself out of the bad air, if possible. And if not, to get yourself through it without losing your lunch.

BUMPY AIR EXPLAINED

Without going into too much detail, most turbulence you'll encounter is caused by updrafts. There you are flying along and all of a sudden you fly through an updraft. For that moment your airplane is thrusted upward. But that doesn't last forever, so you sink again on the other side.

Surface heating and mountain slopes are the two main causes for updrafts.

Another type of weather phenomenon that can cause bumps is *wind shear*. Wind shear is defined as a sudden change in the direction of wind, usually caused by the passage of a weather front. Here, the airplane drops and rises because of increasing and decreasing headwinds.

If an airplane is flying along at a given airspeed and experiences an immediate drop in airspeed, it will drop. An airplane can't slow itself down that fast, but if a 30-knot headwind wind suddenly becomes a 30-knot tailwind, the airplane effectively loses 60 knots of airspeed. That's a big drop that might reduce the airplane's airspeed to one at which the lift generated by the wings is no longer strong enough to keep the airplane flying. The airplane drops and the passengers scream—you guessed it—"Air pocket!"

But the airplane won't fall all the way to the ground, provided it's more than a few hundred feet *above* the ground. Eventually the airplane drops to a spot where the wind is once again behaving and lift becomes sufficient to remain airborne.

We'll learn about lift and airspeed later.

These are the two basic reasons for the turbulence that you will experience in your training. The causes for each type are numerous: storms, mountains, certain cloud types, etc. Basically, turbulence is caused by an abrupt change in atmospheric conditions at that moment in that spot. You'll learn more about this as you study aviation weather.

ROUGH AIR PROCEDURES

Severely rough air can damage your airplane. But if you adhere to the procedures prescribed for flying your airplane in rough air, you should be fine.

Every airplane has an airspeed defined for it called *maneuvering speed*. This is the speed at which abrupt movement of the yoke (forward or back, or side to side) will not damage the airframe. This is also the speed at which you'll perform flight maneuvers like steep turns, hence the name maneuvering speed.

The actual maneuvering speed for any flight depends on the airplane and the weight the airplane is carrying at the time. The heavier the airplane, the faster it can travel through the bumpy air. Most airplanes define their maneuvering speed for maximum weight. So if your maneuvering speed is listed as 85 knots, keep in mind that it will be slower than that if you're flying at anything less than the maximum weight for your airplane. Your CFI can help you calculate this speed for each flight.

MID-AIR COLLISIONS

Somewhere below fear of engine failures for student pilots lies the fear of mid-air collisions. This fear is intensified once you realize that there is no magical FAA-blessed device that keep airplanes from flying into one another. I began my training assuming that every airplane would have some magical gizmo that would alert me to oncoming traffic—radar or something like it. But the only such gizmo on most general aviation aircraft is known as the "pilot."

Many larger airplanes do have collision avoidance systems, but it's safe to assume that no trainer aircraft will sport such hardware for the foreseeable future. The systems are still far too expensive for most general aviation budgets. And the potential liability makes the general aviation market a scary place for manufacturers of such devices.

Once upon a time a popular aircraft manufacturer offered a new feature on an airplane model with retractable landing gear. The device warned pilots when they were about to land while their landing gear was still up. What a godsend. One time it didn't work properly, or maybe the pilot ignored the warning. Regardless, a lawsuit was filed against the airplane maker and the feature never found its way onto another aircraft.

Once I realized that traffic avoidance was really up to me, I became very nervous about it. Students are taught the FAA's preferred way to use their eyes (called a *scan*) to see and avoid other traffic, but I've never seen a pilot stick to this method for more than a few seconds at a time. Traffic avoidance is one of those things that makes a new student pilot feel very uneasy.

Mid-air collisions do occur but, like engine failures, they are rare. There are things you can do to reduce your chances of hitting other aircraft.

MAPPING THE SKY

If you had a device that could render an accurate image of all of the other air traffic near your airplane, you'd be able to easily avoid airborne fender benders. But since you don't have any fancy device to generate this image for you, you have to learn to "visualize" nearby traffic yourself.

Your eyes are your primary and best tool for this purpose, but there are other resources too:

- **Radios** – Not only will you use your radios to transmit your location to others, but other pilots will use the radio to transmit their location to you. Even if the conversation doesn't involve you directly, listen to what pilots are saying to each other and ATC. When they report a position, visualize where that position is with regard to your position. If they're nearby, take notice. Get on the radio and report your position, if necessary. If you've got radios, use them. Monitor the frequencies of nearby airports and air traffic controllers. Listen for departing and landing airplanes.

- **ATC Services** – You can also make good use of your radios by involving ATC in your flight. *Flight Following* is a service by which ATC will monitor your route of flight and issue traffic and other advisories to you as needed. This doesn't alleviate you from the responsibility of traffic avoidance yourself—and there are times that ATC will be so busy they'll refuse you the service entirely—but when available, this is a great second set of eyes that can see much farther than you can.

- **Passengers** – Four eyes are better than two. Before each flight advise passengers to keep their eyes peeled for traffic. If you've got kids aboard, make a game of it: how many other airplanes can they spot? If this raises their level of hyperactivity above your tolerance threshold, revert to the "Who can count to one million in their head?" game.

- **Charts** – Even though charts don't map real-time traffic, they are very useful for traffic avoidance. Charts depict areas of military training activities and other areas where increased traffic is likely. They also depict airspace boundaries, which are critical for traffic avoidance. If you wander into or even too near the boundaries of busy nearby airspace, you might find yourself in big trouble. Funny thing about jets: they fly very fast. They can approach and eat you long before you ever see them. We'll learn to read charts later.

- **Navigational Equipment** – Your airplane will likely be equipped with all sorts of electronic navigation equipment. Such equipment alone can't keep you from hitting other traffic, but it can help you more accurately determine your position. This is important not only for avoiding airspace and terrain, but for reporting your position to ATC or other pilots. I once had what I thought was a close call over the ocean near Half Moon Bay California. I reported my position as I approached the field for landing. But shortly thereafter another airplane reported himself in the very same position as me. I called him back to verify, but he insisted this was where he was and that he didn't see me either. It was quite an erie feeling. I wasn't sure quite what to do, and I was concerned that the sound of crunching soda cans was imminent. Knowing that he was turning toward the field, I turned out over the ocean. I flew a complete 360-degree turn but he was no where in sight. A moment later he announced he was on final approach for landing. As it turned out, he was not at all where he reported to be. But this situation turned out okay. Sometimes the opposite (and worse) situation occurs where airplanes report themselves as being in different places when they are, in fact, right on top of one another.

Always know exactly where you are and use your eyes, radios, charts, passengers and navigational equipment to help you maintain this awareness. Throughout your entire flight know the correct answer to the ATC request: "report position." It will help you maintain a better visual sense of the skies around you.

FLYING BLIND (OR OTHERWISE) INTO THE CLOUDS

Flying into clouds isn't a fear that students typically have at first. It's one that comes after some actual flight experience. Flying into reduced visibility can be just as bad as any of the worst situations caused by any of the preceding fears in this section.

Once you lose your visual references, you're less than two minutes away from a total loss of aircraft control, according to FAA statistics. The best solution to this problem is to simply avoid flying into bad weather. But if you do inadvertently encounter bad weather, you need to have a plan of action ready to go to get yourself back into the clear.

Do not rely on passenger input in a situation where you're in the clouds, and *do not* rely on your own intuition either. Without visual references your body will play tricks on you. You might think you're turning when you're not turning, and you might think you're climbing when you're flying level or even descending.

This phenomenon, called *spatial disorientation,* is tough to describe to anyone who's never experienced it. But there are times on the ground you might feeling something similar. Say you're sitting on a train that's beside another train on an adjacent track. The other train starts to move forward and you have a momentary sense of moving backward. The disorientation happens for only a few seconds because other "clues" will clear things up: You'll look out the opposite window and see that you are not moving. Or, you'll see that passengers are still boarding. Within a moment or two, you're able to mentally negotiate the disorientation away.

But once you enter a cloud or fog in an airplane, there might be no visual references to clear things up and your body will become confused. We underestimate the impact our vision has on our physical awareness. But if you think about it, you rely on your vision to "tell" you what's going on quite a bit. Virtual reality rides in amusement parks rely on this principle. Without a video screen to watch, riders would simply feel as though they were being tossed about. The images on the screen are what tell us when we're moving up, down or turning.

In an airplane, the only "video screen" is a windscreen full of either white or black, depending on the time of day. There is no visual clues as to the airplane's actual movement. You're body starts conjuring up assumptions about what's going on and your mind begs you to react accordingly. This is very hard to overcome for most pilots. We don't often have reason to disbelieve our bodies. We "feel" like we're turning so we straighten out the yoke only to put the airplane in a turn going opposite the direction we thought we were turning. Then we feel like we're climbing so we lower the nose until things "feel" right again. A quick glance at the airspeed indicator shows that we're picking up speed fast. But why? It must be broken, we rationalize.

This is the sort of mess pilots find themselves in. During training for an instrument rating, you'll learn to rely on your cockpit gauges for your "visual" clues. But until you've completed that training, you need to stay clear of reduced visibility.

The first thing to do if you ever fly into zero visibility is to get your eyes on your attitude indicator. (Figure 12) This instrument becomes the "visual horizon" with which you will determine the actual attitude of your airplane. Without your attitude indicator, you'll have no easy way of determining which way is up.

There's another reason that we say to immediately get your eyes on this instrument. It's the first step in your *plan of recovery*. When something goes wrong and a person doesn't have a plan in place to handle it, panic ensues. Once panic sets in, all hope of recovery is jeopardized. By thinking of this as your first step toward recovery, you remind yourself that recovery is only a few more steps away. With your eyes on your "new" horizon, you can complete the remaining steps.

Figure 12: *ARTIFICIAL HORIZON* These three attitude indicators show the airplane in a climb (top), flying level (left), and in a descent (bottom). Though is seems as though the little orange airplane wing is moving, it's actually the plate behind the wing that moves up and down as the "real" airplane climbs and descends. The dial also rotates to show the airplane in a turn. This is why we say to get your eyes on the attitude indicator is you ever fly into the clouds. It's the only instrument in your cockpit that gives you a sense of both your vertical and lateral movements.

FAA training teaches you that after flying into a cloud you should execute an immediate 180 degree turn to get yourself back to the good weather behind you. This is good advice because it makes total sense. Behind you there was clear weather. You know this because you were just there.

But what happens if you do panic? In such a situation the simple act of turning around might become mentally impossible.

I always monitor a local ATC frequency during my flights. It helps me maintain a sense of what's going on around me and it also ensures that help is but a microphone-button click away.

Keep in mind that the 180-degree turn is your best bet—and you do nothing during that turn to distract you, such as talking on the radio!—but if you can't make the turn you need to ask for help.

Click that microphone button and announce that you are a "VFR pilot in IMC." This will get ATC's attention better than even, "Look! A UFO!" IMC stands for *instrument meteorological conditions*, which means less-than-VFR visibility. Any visibility less than 3 miles is IMC. Visibility greater than 3 miles is considered VMC, or *visual meteorological conditions*.

ATC can spot you on radar (if available in your area) and help you get out of the mess. There are other non-radar options that ATC can offer too. Your CFI will go over them with you. The idea is to let ATC know that your already bad situation will likely become disastrous without some help.

ATC can assist you only with heading and attitude *suggestions*. They cannot physically prevent you from diving or climbing so steeply that you lose control. This is why keeping your eyes on your attitude indicator is so important. If you're diving or climbing, you'll see it.

Regardless of the method you use to get yourself back into the clear, *do not take your eyes off of the attitude indicator*! If you need to adjust a radio or piece of navigational equipment, do so by glancing at it momentarily, but immediately get your eyes back on the attitude indicator and keep them there.

This important topic goes far beyond the scope of this section. Your flight training will include lessons during which you'll fly "under the hood," which means that you wear special goggles (called *foggles*) or some other view-limiting device that is supposed to simulate zero visibility. But take it from someone who has flown in real zero visibility: the foggles don't give you a total zero visibility experience. However bad visibility seems with them on, remember that a real cloud is worse. Ask your CFI if you can ride along on an instrument training flight that will be flying through clouds. That'll give you a better sense of what to expect.

POPULAR WAYS TO KILL YOURSELF IN AN AIRPLANE

When I first started taking flight lessons I was eager to find out as much as I could about why airplanes crashed. I searched through the NTSB's aviation accident statistics website to learn what I could. *(Visit **http://AirDiamond.com/sa** for a link.)* One causal phrase popped up far more than any other: "pilot error."

Pilot error accounts for the vast majority of aviation accidents. Your airplane has far more to fear from you than you do from it. Keep that in mind.

But equally important to remember, as mentioned, is that most aviation accidents happen as the result of a series of events gone wrong.

For example, one famous commercial airliner crash near San Diego, California started out as an urgent situation of one kind and ended up a disaster of another. Based on a panel light indication, the flight crew believed they had a landing gear problem. The captain elected to circle until he could solve the problem. While focused on landing gear issues, the airplane ran out of fuel and crashed. This crash was the result of a series of things gone wrong, with pilot error being the most devastating of all.

The point here is to keep yourself aware of circumstances. If something goes wrong, keep in mind that focusing too intently on the problem at hand might result in others things going wrong too. No matter how bad the current situation, your primary responsibility is to fly the airplane. Everything else is secondary. The pilot's mantra is "aviate, navigate, communicate."

An airplane with stuck landing gear has options. An airplane without fuel has none. An airplane that has stuck landing gear and then runs out of fuel is an airplane destroyed by its designer or maintainer, and its pilot.

FUEL EXHAUSTION

The idea that a pilot could simply run out of fuel seems ridiculous to most student pilots. How could anyone be so stupid? But there are a few major differences between *training* flights and *private* flights that make the possibility of fuel exhaustion far easier to appreciate:

- **Tank levels** – Most training flights start out with full fuel tanks. Training flights last about an hour, so students don't typically see airplanes with low fuel levels.

- **Flight planning** – Training flights of any significant distance are planned with fuel consumption in mind. You know before you depart how far you'll go and how much fuel is required. It's part of the training and planning.

- **Student focus** – Students are in learning mode whenever they take a lesson. Without the distractions of passengers, scenery or navigating unfamiliar areas, they can remain more focused on the flight itself. Carefully watching the gauges is one of the benefits of this type of focus.

Now let's relate those situations to the real world. If you own your own airplane, you probably won't find it with full tanks at the start of each flight. This is especially true if you fly to several destinations in a day. What makes matters worse is that the fuel gauges on most airplanes can't be trusted. FAA regulations require that the gauges accurately show *full readings* and *empty readings* only. Anything in between is a manufacturer's best guess. This means that if your gauges show your tanks to be one quarter full, you might have a half

a tank left, or you might be much closer to empty than you think. This is why all preflight inspections require you to *visually* check the fuel tanks.

Additionally, precise flight planning typically happens less often as pilots gain experience. Student pilots like to have trips mapped out to the letter, but more experienced pilots are happy to rely on their charts and navigational skills. So finding a way home presents no challenge, but a bad guess on fuel requirements can drain tanks dry on the way.

I've been fortunate enough to never run my tanks dry. But I do confess that there have been a few times where I've failed to keep an eye on the gauges as closely as I should have. One flight in particular gave me a bit of a scare. I estimate four hours of flight time when I take a Cessna 172 up with full tanks. This is a bit conservative, which is fine by me. The rental airplanes I fly usually have full tanks when I get them, so this is a flight-time estimate that's become quite familiar to me.

This one day I did my preflight and noted that I had only half-full tanks. This wouldn't be a problem because I only planned to be up for about an hour. My passenger and I took off into absolutely perfect flying conditions. It was one of those days that flying was made for. He asked if we could go farther than we had planned—about an hour farther out. I figured it was okay because these planes fly for four hours before needing fuel. I had failed to remember that I left with half tanks. About fifteen minutes into our flight extension I looked at my gauges and my heart jumped. It was then that I remembered I left with only two hours of fuel aboard, not four. I was lucky enough to realize this in plenty of time.

AVOIDING FUEL EXHAUSTION

My CFI always liked to say there is no excuse for fuel exhaustion. That said, fuel exhaustion happens all the time.

The only accurate way of planning consumption is by considering *time*. Airplanes burn *gallons-per-hour* not *gallons-per-mile*. Know the fuel-burn rate of your airplane and use that number to estimate the requirements of your flight. If your airplane burns 10 gallons per hour and you'll be flying for 2 hours, then you'll need 20 gallons at least. You actually need more, but we'll discuss why later.

Keep in mind that wind plays a factor here. Head winds increase the amount of time it takes to get places. If those winds are strong, yesterday's 60-minute trip might take 90 minutes today.

Airplanes that crash because of fuel exhaustion are listed in the NTSB accident archives under the "pilot error" category.

WEATHER ENCOUNTERS

Pilots without instrument ratings cannot legally fly into instrument meteorological conditions (IMC). As mentioned, without instrument training, a pilot cannot maintain control of an airplane in IMC.

But pilots take chances. Sometimes those chances are weather related. The desire to fly is strong. If a flight is important to a pilot, that pilot might decide that even though weather isn't forecast to be great, it might be good enough. This sort of thinking is dangerous. Weather is unpredictable and unforgiving. Storms almost never divert their courses just to avoid Cessnas.

It usually goes like this: the pilot determines the weather is good enough to fly. The flight takes place and enroute the pilot encounters bad weather. Instead of immediately turning back to good weather, as previously discussed, the pilot starts hoping things will improve. Things don't improve and all of a sudden the pilot is left without options.

The NTSB has determined this to be the basic cause of the crash that killed John F. Kennedy, Jr. Upon reaching reduced visibility, Kennedy lost his sense of the horizon, his body started playing tricks on him, and a CNN feature story soon followed.

AVOIDING BAD WEATHER ENCOUNTERS

The best way to avoid entering bad weather is to stay well clear of it. Do this by checking forecasts before you fly and, on longer trips, get weather updates enroute. Get enroute updates regularly if questionable weather is expected along your route or at your destination. Knowing in advance where the bad weather is enables you to make other plans. Finding out that you can't land at your destination airport once you arrive in the local area might require that you divert to another airport far away. Such a diversion might take you out of the "bad weather" accident category and into the "fuel exhaustion" category. Both are still the result of pilot error.

DISTRACTIONS

Throughout your training your CFI is supposed to cause in-flight distractions to see how you handle things. The truly ironic thing about this is that CFIs tend to be distracting by nature, so it's sometimes hard to determine when they're actually trying.

There are many possible distractions that can pop up in flight. Some might be as benign as dropping the pencil you were using. Others can be as serious as a mechanical malfunction. Regardless of the severity, however, your primary responsibility as pilot-in-command is to continue to fly the airplane safely. This means dividing your time appropriately between your regular aviator duties and the problem at hand. Do not obsess over the problem. If you disregard your flight duties, the recovery of your dropped pencil could necessitate the recovery from a spiral dive too.

Have I mentioned that most aviation accidents are the result of a series of events?

Not all distractions come from inside the cockpit. ATC, for example, can spew so much information at times that a new pilot can quickly become overwhelmed trying to digest it all.

One day I was flying north from San Carlos and needed to fly through San Francisco International Airport's airspace. Permission is required to fly through airspace like this, so I had my radio tuned to the appropriate frequency and was listening for a break in the on-going communications that would allow me to ask for my permission.

While awaiting my turn, I heard things like:

ATC: *United 2133, turn left heading 210.*

PILOT: *Left 210, United 2133.*

ATC: *Southwest 532, descend niner thousand.*

PILOT: *Descending niner thousand, Southwest 532.*

ATC: *American 2412, cleared for the visual, one-niner right.*

PILOT: *Cleared visual, one-niner right, American 2412.*

There was a lot of stuff going on, but eventually a break came and I announce:

PILOT: *Norcal Approach, Skyhawk 1186 uniform, off San Carlos, request Bravo transition enroute Gnoss.*

Norcal Approach is the name of the agency that controls the San Francisco area airspace. Bravo is the type of airspace that surrounds busy airports like San Francisco. (More on that later.) And Gnoss is the name of a small airport north of San Francisco, which was my destination that day.

Okay, so I'm expecting one of those easy-to-understand instructions that ATC was tossing out to the Big Boys. But instead I get:

ATC: *November 1186U, cleared into Class Bravo, maintain VFR at or below one thousand five hundred, stay south and west of the Bayshore freeway, San Francisco altimeter 30.02, traffic eleven o'clock, 2 miles southbound, altitude indicates 2000, report in sight.*

I about fell out of the airplane. "Huh?" was about the only reaction my brain could muster at that moment, and that controller—not to mention every other pilot in the area at that time—was expecting me to read back the instructions. Lucky for me, my CFI was aboard to respond while I recovered from my deer-in-the-headlights panic.

This qualified as a bona fide distraction. In the time it took me to disbelieve what I was hearing, I was not flying the airplane to the best of my abilities, and not looking for traffic as I should have been. This was *number one* in a possible series of disaster events. There was no *number two*.

AVOIDING DISTRACTIONS

Distractions are, by nature, unexpected. So there's no way to avoid them all. But with experience you'll start to gain a sense of which distractions are more likely and how to avoid them.

Pens and pencils, for example, are always falling on the floor. So have a number of them easily accessible. And when initiating a radio call to ATC, have a pencil and some paper ready to jot down what they say. If you miss something, don't panic. Simply ask them to repeat it.

Passengers can also be quite distracting. I tell mine during my preflight briefing that I am unavailable for cockpit conversation during take-off, just before and after landing, and anytime I'm talking on the radio. I let them know in plenty of time when it's time for them to keep quiet. That way I can concentrate on the most critical aspects of the flight, take-off and landing, with all the focus I need. I've never had any passenger tell me that this seemed unreasonable.

The best way to handle the unavoidable distractions is to do so calmly, using common sense. If you encounter a mechanical malfunction, assess the situation and act accordingly. For example, if your attitude indicator fails on a perfectly clear afternoon flight, don't panic. You don't need it.

If your airspeed indicator fails, rely on familiar power settings to estimate your airspeed. For example, if you know that reducing your engine power to 2000 RPM gets your airplane to 85 knots, then work it that way. On your approach, reduce power as you're accustomed to doing and listen for the stall warning horn. (The stall warning horn is a device that sounds when you get too slow for the airplane to remain flying.)

If your CFI doesn't stress knowledge of the airspeeds that certain power settings give, ask for it to be included in your training. It's great to know, especially when you move on to more advanced ratings.

If your engine fails, rely on the emergency procedures that you've had ingrained into your head. If they don't feel ingrained, practice them with your CFI until they are.

But remember, regardless of how severe a distraction seems, you must continue to fly the airplane! The difference between an emergency and a disaster lies in the way the pilot handles the emergency.

FLYING BEYOND YOUR CAPABILITIES

Every pilot has limits above which her capabilities are seriously reduced. Can you land an airplane? Of course you can. Can you land one in a 10-knot crosswind? Probably. What about a 25-knot crosswind?

At what point does "Of course!" become "No way!"?

You need to know your limits before you overstep them. If crosswind landings aren't your forté, then choose a maximum crosswind that you're comfortable with and use that as your limit. Book some time with a CFI during windier conditions to improve your skills. Don't do it alone.

Also set some minimum visibility requirements. The FAA says it's legal for you to fly in 3 miles visibility, but you'll be surprised by just how bad 3 miles visibility really is. Let's crunch some numbers:

An airplane traveling 120 knots (with no wind) is moving at 2.3 miles per minute. Now let's assume that an airplane flying the opposite direction is also flying at 120 knots. With only 3 miles visibility, this leaves the two pilots with less than 40 seconds to take evasive action to avoid a midair. And if one or both of those planes is traveling faster than 120 knots, the time decreases.

Another concern is airplane performance. High performance airplanes require more from a pilot than do trainers like the Cessna 172 or Piper Warrior. Everything happens faster in a high performance airplane and these planes are typically less forgiving when pilots do stupid things. You might be a real Cracker Jack behind the yoke of a 172, but a Mooney cruising at 180 knots might reduce you to an airborne bumbling buffoon.

And what about the runway? Not all runways are the same. Some long, well maintained runways offer the pilot little or no challenge. But some are short, while others are made of grass or some other soft surface. Many have obstacles on either end that can challenge landing or departing pilots. There are techniques for dealing with airport challenges like these, but if you're not in practice, you're better off avoiding fields like these. Again, book some time with a CFI and practice some short- and soft-field takeoffs and landings, or practice the techniques yourself at a bigger field before the skill becomes a real world necessity.

LISTEN TO THE LITTLE VOICE

The desire to fly at every chance you get will be a strong one. You'll probably find yourself successfully mentally negotiating otherwise unfavorable situations just to get yourself airborne. This is obviously dangerous and has killed many pilots.

You must determine your personal limits ahead of time and stick to them. During preflight isn't the time to decide if the crosswinds look to be too much for you. It's like grocery shopping while you're hungry: a very bad and potentially expensive idea.

Of course you want to improve your piloting skills, but adverse conditions can turn on you if you're not ready to handle them. Get a CFI to go up with you and practice. Just because you get your license doesn't mean you can't book additional time with a CFI to smooth out the rough edges.

There's an old saying in aviation that it's better to be down here wishing you were up there than to be up there wishing you were down here.

THE STUDENT AS THE TEACHER

When I started my flight training I expected to be told what I needed to do every step of the way. But unless you're attending a Part 141 flight school or an aviation university, this just isn't a realistic expectation. CFIs know how to fly airplanes, but this doesn't automatically make them great instructors. Some are, mind you, but many aren't.

The onus for a good aviation education is on you as a student pilot. You must guide your own training to ensure that you learn all that you can, and all that you need, to be a good pilot. Passing the FAA exams isn't enough. Keep in mind that every pilot whose "pilot error" has ever crashed an airplane also passed the FAA tests.

So how do you know what you don't know?

Without already knowing how to fly, it's tough to know what you still have to learn. But it gets easier with time. This book, for example, might be your first introduction to the entire process. You should talk to other student pilots too. What have they learned? Search Internet newsgroup archives and read, read, read. Read everything you can get

your hands on. If three different authors agree that checking the airplane's oil before each flight is a good idea, and your CFI says it's optional, then you have grounds for questioning your CFI.

THE CFI's ROLE (AND PROBABLE GOALS)

The FAA requires your CFI to cover everything that's required for you to pass your checkride. And most good ones will do just that. The great ones will go a step beyond and the bad ones will fall short.

Your CFI might or might not follow some sort of syllabus. Mine did not. I didn't know what to expect from lesson to lesson. This was frustrating at times because I never knew how close to "finished" I was. On the other hand, my own curiosities often lead my training into areas not preplanned by my CFI. In the end, I got an aviation education that was uniquely *mine*.

It's important to realize that most CFIs are not CFIs by career. As previously mentioned, many are amassing the flight time required to get airline jobs. This is fine until a student loses his CFI in the middle of his training.

I don't want to make CFIs seem like villains. But keep in mind that these are, for the most part, *aviation* professionals, not *education* professionals. If something doesn't sit right with you, keep asking until you get an answer that satisfies you. If your CFI cannot provide answers that work for you, move on.

Your CFI is there to ensure that you don't kill yourself while you teach yourself to fly. In the meantime, any good advice they might offer is icing on the cake.

TAKING THE BULL BY THE YOKE

At first you're pretty much at the mercy of your CFI's good and bad training ideas. But in time you'll develop your own curiosities about aviation and you should explore each and every one.

I am one that must experience everything first hand in order to fully appreciate it. There's a long list of things that you *never* do as a pilot, but for me this just served as a checklist of things I wanted to try.

As an example, conventional wisdom has it that if your engine fails shortly after take-off, you never turn back to the airport to land. The reason is that you lose so much altitude and airspeed in the turn that getting back to the airport successfully is unlikely.

Okay, I could *almost* accept this. But I figured that there had to be an altitude at which a turn-back *would* work. So I asked my CFI if we could dedicate a lesson to experimentation. I wanted to pull power, turn the airplane around at various bank angles and see how much altitude I actually lost. (We did this at a safe altitude, of course. Even I wasn't dumb enough to want to try it just after take-off!)

We experimented and I saw what I needed to see. In a 30-degree bank turn with the engine idle, we lost about 400 feet in a 180 degree turn. So if I lost my engine just after take-off, it's true that I wouldn't be able to make it back. But if I was up to 1,000 feet, my chances improved greatly.

The good that came from that day's lesson was that I understood, first-hand, *why* a pilot shouldn't turn back just after take off. This is the sort of thing that adds to your experience as a pilot. With any luck, you'll never need to draw on the knowledge.

If you ever feel uncomfortable with any type of flight maneuver, ask your CFI to devote some extra time to it. If you want to fly at night, spend some extra time on night flights with your CFI. Flying at night can be quite different. The more experience you have the better. The first time you preflight an airplane in the dark you'll see what I mean.

Your CFI should guide you to the point where you're ready to take your checkride, but it's up to you to make sure that you get to the point where you feel like a competent pilot. Every CFI is different and every CFI teaches aviation from a different perspective. Talk with other students and pick their brains about what they've learned. If you're having trouble getting the hang of a certain maneuver or flight concept, other students can often offer invaluable advice based on their experiences. At the very least, you might find that you're understanding more than you thought!

STAYING FOCUSED & ENTHUSED

Learning to fly takes a while and it's sometimes hard to stay focused throughout your training. At first it's pretty easy because you're so starved for information that you hang on your CFI's every word. But once you're passed the solo stage, it's easy to start getting restless. By that point you know how to fly the plane and it's all you want to do!

What makes matters worse is that students commonly reach certain stages in their training where they become so discouraged that they want to quit. It happens at different times to everyone, but the first such episode frequently happens around the 10 hour mark. By that time you've gotten a sense of how things are supposed to work, but you might not have mastered every-thing yet. Sometimes it feels as though you'll never get it. This is common; most every student feels this way at one point or another.

My first frustration was landing the airplane. I just wasn't getting it at all, even after 20 hours. Each of my landings seemed worse than the rest. I was discouraged because I figured that I should have at least been improving over time, but it didn't seem as though I was.

My CFI tried to assure me that all students go through "funks" during their training. But I wasn't buying it. I saw other students doing well.

What made it harder for me was that I was spending so much time and money and I felt I was getting no where.

But I plodded through the funk. I took the time to investigate other resources of information for my troubles that I thought might help. This was a good idea. Internet newsgroups were a real savior to me during these times. It was nice to read about other students going through the same stuff and coming out on the other end, pilot's license in hand. Even better, hearing all those other piloting stories renewed my enthusiasm for flying.

Bad landings weren't my only problem, however. Radio communications, navigation and a few required flight maneuvers also taxed my brain. I got myself through each frustrating moment by remembering that so many other students had done it. If something wasn't registering with me, I just had to figure out a new ways to learn the information.

Flying a plane has it challenges, but if you can read this book then chances are you can learn to fly an airplane. There will be tough times during your training. There will be times when you'll feel so frustrated by the process that you'll want to scream.

But if you make up your mind that you're going be become a licensed pilot, then you will.

EDUCATIONAL RESOURCES

Take advantage of every aviation educational resource you can get your hands on. Aviation is better studied than taught. You'll get more out of it if you pursue the knowledge rather than rely on your CFI to feed your brain. A CFI offers only one opinion, one set of experiences and one perspective. Your CFI will not know the best way of doing everything.

Make your goal to learn more about aviation than your CFI knows. Toward the end of my private pilot training my CFI and I were able to debate aviation issues and swap ideas and suggestions. I certainly didn't know nearly as much as she did, but there were some things that I had learned that she didn't know. There's no better way to learn than to teach. Learn all that you can so that you can teach it to others and, as a result, *really* learn it.

BOOKS

Pilot supply shops usually have a pretty good selection of aviation books. You'll find some aviation books at general book stores, but I find the books in these stores to be more focused on aviation history and stories rather than training. Pilot shops are also more likely to sell the books' most recent editions. Your average bookseller probably doesn't appreciate why they need to stock this year's Federal Aviation Regulations manual when they still have plenty of last year's on the shelves.

Must-have reading includes:

- Federal Aviation Regulations/Aeronautical Information Manual (FAR/AIM)

- Ground Study Manual

- Airport Reference Guide

- Practical Test Standards Guide (PTS)

Each of these books is described below.

FAR/AIM

The FAR/AIM contains FAA regulations and other information useful to aviators. The FARs are updated annually and read like typical legalese. They are cryptic and dull as often as they're cut-to-the-chase clear and concise. You are expected to know many of the regulations by heart, so you might as well read them.

Figure 13: *FAR AIM* The Federal Aviation Regulations are often published with the Aeronautical Information Manual. Reading an actual regulation often makes it easier to understand than just reading various interpretations of the regulation in books. The AIM is full of great information and I think it's very well written.

Some regulations are actually interesting to read. For example, do you ever wonder why flight attendants require that your seat belt be fastened for taxi, take-off and landing? Or why they actually show you how to use it on each and every flight? These are FAR requirements that apply to you, too. [FAR 91.107] And do the federal aviation regulations really say that "no person may tamper with, disable, or destroy any smoke detector installed in any aircraft lavatory"? You'll find those very words in FAR Part 135.

I found it fascinating to learn just how many regulations apply to commercial flights and my flights too. Everything from oxygen requirements to the need for flotation devices. If commercial jets never flew above 15,000 then they wouldn't need to tell you about oxygen at all. (This is the altitude at which all aircraft occupants must be provided with oxygen.) If you climb above 15,000 feet you'll be briefing passengers on the use of oxygen too.

The AIM portion of the book includes some of the best aviation writing you'll ever read. It's clear (for the most part) and right to the point. Many topics that I first learned about from other aviation texts never made sense until I read the AIM's explanation.

I found the FAR/AIM to be most fun to read (if that's possible) while I was a passenger on commercial flights. Whenever a flight attendant would bark that "federal aviation regulations require..." I'd look it up. I often wondered if those

regulation-savvy flight attendants had ever even read the regulations themselves! Regardless, for some reason they were more enjoyable to read when I was sitting on an airplane.

The FAR/AIM is also available as a CD-ROM. This is a handy addition to the printed text because it permits searching. It's sometimes hard to figure out which part of the FARs contains the regulation you're after.

The FAA offers pilots a searchable copy of the FARs online. *(Visit **http://AirDiamond.com/sa** for a link.)*

GROUND STUDY MANUAL

The ground study manual is the bible of your flight education. It covers all aspects of flight training and is typically quite large in size. (Get your FAA medical certificate *before* you've been hauling this thing around for a while and develop back problems.) What you're reading now is not the same thing as a ground study manual. I do address many of the same topics, but the things you'll read about throughout these pages are the topics that *I* think are most important. Ground study manuals cover it all, as mandated by the FAA, but typically won't prioritize anything for you.

Several companies publish ground study manuals. Your CFI will probably have a preference as to which one you buy. If you're planning to attend a groundschool course, don't buy anything until you find out which book is used in the class.

AIRPORT REFERENCE GUIDES

Every airport is different. Some have one runway, some have many. Some have specific approach and departure procedures with which pilots must comply, while others just use conventional procedures. Airport reference guides offer answers to pilots' questions so that unfamiliar airports can be safely used.

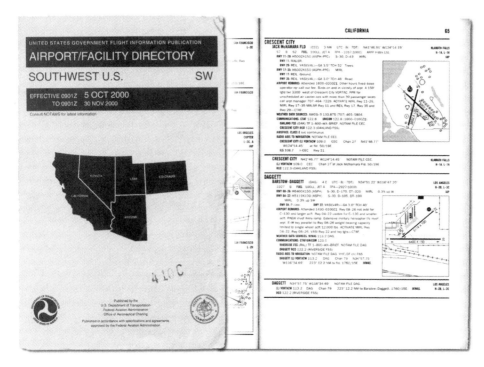

Figure 14: *TOURIST GUIDE* The Airport/Facilities Directory is useful, but somewhat tough to understand at first. Much of the information is encoded, requiring frequent trips to the directory's legend. Some airports have diagrams, but most do not.

Every 56 days the FAA publishes a booklet called the *Airport/Facilities Directory*, more commonly known as the "A/FD." It's chock full useful airport information, but it lacks one important quality: *readability*. For the sake of space, much of the information within the directory is encoded. This makes for quick scanning of the information, but for those not familiar with the code, the pages just look like a mess. (Figure 14)

A/FDs are published for different regions of the U.S. They are only a few bucks, so it's a good idea to keep a current copy with you. You can buy them from just about any pilot supply store.

On the premium end of airport directories is the *Pilots Guide*, which is what I use. (Figure 15) This directory, published by Optima Publications, takes the basic data you'd find in the A/FD, makes it readable, and adds additional information and graphics. Pilots Guide directories are currently available for the Southwestern states, the North-

western states and for California (an entire directory is required to cover the state's many airports). Visit the Pilots Guide website to learn more about the directory and to see when additional directories will be available for other parts of the nation. *(Visit **http://AirDiamond.com/sa** for a link.)*

This directory costs considerably more than the A/FD, but it's worth the cost. (It's something like $40.) When you buy the directory you are also buying a year's worth of updates. The company automatically sends new and revised pages when they become available, usually a few times within the year.

My second choice for a directory is the Flight Guide. *(Visit **http://AirDiamond.com/sa** for a link.)* The advantage of this directory is that it's smaller in size than the rest and has coverage for the entire U.S. I prefer the lush graphics and

122 - PALM SPRINGS

Palm Springs Int'l. Airport

LOCATION
2 nmi east of Palm Springs.

On Los Angeles Sectional and L3-L4 Charts.

See also Palm Springs TRSA Map in *General* Section at the front of this Guide.

From other airports:
12 nmi W of Bermuda Dunes	PSP	115.5✓	224°	5 nmi
19 nmi E of Banning	TRM	116.2✓	292°	21 nmi
19 nmi S of Yucca Valley	PDZ	112.2✓	081°	55 nmi

FREQUENCIES AND ARRIVAL INFORMATION

| ATIS - 118.25 | Monitor ATIS prior to calling Approach Control, Tower or Ground. |

| PALM SPRINGS APPROACH - 126.7 W-N (0600 - 2300 - local time) - 118.85 NE-SW | Call Approach while still outside the TRSA. (See Approach Map and |
| Los Angeles Center - 128.15 (2100-0600) | Approach Notes opposite page.) |

| PALM SPRINGS TOWER - 119.7 (0600-2300 local time) | Call Tower prior to entering Class D Airspace (below 3,000' MSL & within 4.1 nmi.) (See Apch. Map opp. page.) |

Winds at Palm Springs usually favor the use of Rwys 31 and the information below is based on that condition. Although not required, pilots are encouraged to call Approach Control for TRSA services. Approach will generally assign a discrete transponder code and give instructions as follows:

COMING FROM:	**EXPECT INSTRUCTIONS TO:**
Northwest (Banning, Morongo Valley)	Fly east-bound along Interstate 10, then enter downwind or base for Rwys 31L or 31R as advised by Tower. (See Approach Note 4 on opposite page.)
Southeast (Cactus City, Oasis, Thermal)	Continue approach for straight-in, Runways 31L or 31R. (See Approach Note 3.)

| PALM SPRINGS GROUND - 121.9 | Remain on Tower frequency until instructed to change to Ground. |

Figure 15: *PILOTS GUIDE* The Pilots Guide offers a far more pilot-friendly overview of airports. Graphics and photos are common and the layout of the guide is more in line with how pilots actually use an airport directory: arrival and departure information are grouped separately. The only drawback to this directory is that many parts of the country are not yet covered in the company's various editions.

photos included in the Pilots Guide, but if I was in an area not covered by the Pilots Guide, this is the directory I'd use.

Other companies also provide airport directories, but you'll be hard pressed to find one better than these two.

For those handy with a Web browser, have a look at AirNav. *(Visit **http://AirDiamond.com/sa** for a link.)* It offers a listings for U.S. airports that are particularly useful if you need to see some data for an airport that's not within your printed directory. This site offers a great wealth of information, but its online nature makes it tough to take with you on flights. You can print listings, but you might find enroute that you need to go to an airport for which you didn't print a listing. There are wireless devices that would allow you to

access the site from the cockpit, but I have yet to see one such device that is convenient enough to use that it would not cause undue distraction.

PRACTICAL TEST STANDARDS (PTS)

The PTS is a small booklet that standardizes the way in which FAA examiners are supposed to conduct checkrides. Until the PTS came about, each examiner conducted tests in his or her own way, which could be unfair to students.

The PTS will be of limited use to you at first, since most of what it covers won't make any sense until you've completed that portion of your training. But you'll want to pick up a copy several months before your checkride. It gives you a great checklist, of sorts, to make sure you've covered everything with your CFI.

ASA reprints the guide for sale. You can purchase these guides in pilot supply stores.

ORAL TEST PREP GUIDES

There are texts that claim to prep students for the question and answer portion of the checkride, but these books might give you quite a scare. I got one and just about dropped dead when I read some of the content. Many of the topics were so technically deep that I had no idea how to answer them. The book simply went into far more detail than did any of my other educational texts. My CFI warned me not to let the book discourage me and she was right. My actual oral test didn't go into anywhere near the same level of detail as the prep guide. But the books do provide a nice "cliff-notes" review of your training, which is handy prior to your checkride.

ADDITIONAL AVIATION BOOKS

I read many aviation books during my training. One book was supposed to help me make better landings, while another aimed to improve my navigational skills. A third was supposed to fine-tune my radio communications while a forth offered basic flight tips. There are all sorts of them out there. As your training progresses you might find yourself yearning for a bit more information on a particular topic. Aviation books are great for that.

I particularly liked the writings of authors Richard Collins and Barry Schiff. They're both legends in the aviation training community for their extensive histories of books, videos and magazine articles. Collins provides a "real world" practicality to his works, which I like. Student pilots can find themselves so immersed in flight theory that it's hard sometimes to get an idea of the challenges flying an airplane *actually* presents. Collins' irreverent sense of humor is downright hysterical at times. Schiff offered not only a wealth of personal experience, but he speaks as a pilot who obviously loves flying airplanes.

Perhaps the best thing about reading so many different books is that you hear the same topics discussed from many different perspectives. So much of aviation is open to interpretation and opinion. Hearing different explanations for the same things really helped me grasp exactly what the topic was all about.

All of the books mentioned here can be purchased from most pilot shops. If you don't have a pilot shop in your area, check out one of the many online pilot shops and book sellers.

TRAINING VIDEOS

Training videos and DVDs are easy to come by in the aviation world. If you like watching and learning by watching, then this might be a good way to go. My professional background is in multimedia communications, so one would think I would be a real fan of video-based training. But, for the most part, I'm not. I have a few fundamental problems with video training tools.

First off, I find that most companies producing video training materials lack the skills required to produce good video. This makes for training tapes that lack professionalism and in some cases even come across as humorous in their deliveries. Secondly, studies show that people tend to "vege out" when watching television, which as a medium, offers no challenge to the viewer. We're used to watching T.V. for entertainment, not for education. We tend to simply watch the images and not absorb too much.

Interactive CD-ROMs and DVDs address this to an extent. But I still question whether the content will be engaging enough to prevent the computer user from popping open a Web browser window and surfing off into oblivion.

Books require the reader to move through the content at her own pace. If the reader isn't ready to receive more information, the reading stops. With videos, the viewer might be momentarily mentally saturated, but the video rolls on with the viewer possibly missing important bits of information.

One great advantage to video and CD-ROM/DVD media is the ability to demonstrate topics by use of animation. Sadly, however, some companies fail to take advantage of this great opportunity.

Now this is all opinion on my part. Others might swear by video training. I did appreciate aviation videos while I was sweating away on my exercise machine. But to me this was more entertainment than education. The videos held my interest, but they were simply driving home points that I'd already read in books or learned in groundschool. If I had relied on the videos as my sole source of information, I would have missed much.

Many flight schools have video libraries that are available to students. If yours does, by all means check out some videos. You might find yourself chuckling at some of the more absurd deliveries, but some tapes might offer explanations that work for you.

INTERNET SITES

I'm a big fan of the Internet. I think that amidst all of the advertising and SPAM some really useful information can be found. You just have to know where to look. Visit my site at ***http:// AirDiamond.com/sa*** for links to the sites below.

AVIATION WEBSITES

There are several good aviation websites out there. I'd recommend a visit to see what each offers. Some sites are commercial and others are provided by aviation enthusiasts who just want to help out.

Here's a partial list of some nice sites:

- **FAA** – The FAA's website is full of all sorts of information. You can find various publications, studies and an online version of the FAR/AIM.

- **NTSB** – The first thing I did at the National Transportation Safety Board's website was to search the aviation accident database to learn

why airplanes crash. As morbid as this sounds, it was a great experience. You can also see accident statistics from years past. If your friends are hesitant to get into an airplane with you, pull up this site and show them the accident statistics for railroad travel, by comparison. That'll sober them up!

- **DUATs** – Two different DUATS (pronounced *doo-watts*) websites offer weather information, though they do so in slightly different styles.

INTERNET NEWSGROUPS

Internet newsgroups are a great resource for information and communication with other students and pilots. These groups are publicly accessible to anyone. If your Internet service provider doesn't allow access to them, get a new Internet service provider. Some popular aviation newsgroups are:

- **rec.aviation.student** – This newsgroup is a great place to ask questions and get a feel for what other students are learning. The group includes student pilots from all over the world, though the majority are from the U.S. Each of these students is likely learning from a different CFI, so you get to hear about teachings of many different styles. One really fun thing about this group is that students commonly announce their first solos and the outcomes of their checkrides. It's a great way to get a feel for a typical checkride long before you ever take yours.

- **rec.aviation.piloting** – Here you'll find licensed pilots. But students are certainly encouraged to ask questions. This is where I find the majority of the really juicy debates. Pilots are seldom at a loss for an opinion on any aviation subject, and you'll read them all here.

- **rec.aviation.owning** – Airplane owners gather here. If you've got the itch to buy your own plane, this is a great place to ask some questions. Common topics are the "renting vs. ownership" dilemma, and the "which plane is better" debate, which is always fun.

I often read things in the newsgroups that I'd never heard before. Arguments and debates on various aviation topics are always plentiful and it's great to hear all the differing viewpoints. I would take some of these topics to my CFI and we would discuss them further. If you can engage your CFI in a few good debates you might find your training sessions far more stimulating.

None of these newsgroups is moderated, however, so you have to decide for yourself if what you're reading is *worth* reading, but it's pretty easy to sort through the nonsense. When in doubt, ask your CFI if what you've read makes any sense.

SAFETY SEMINARS

The FAA sponsors many safety seminars throughout the country. Most are free. Once you get your student medical certificate, you'll be on the FAA's mailing list. They send out events calendars monthly.

Topics are varied, but you'll probably find at least a few that interest you each month. The seminars are typically a few hours long and are offered at local airports, flight schools or hotels.

Flight schools and other local aviation companies might also offer seminars of their own. Ask around at your school to find out.

OTHER PILOTS

By now you can tell that I'm a big fan of getting different viewpoints on subjects. It's not that I don't ever trust any one person's opinion, it's just that no one person can know everything. This is why conversations with other pilots can be wonderful educational experiences.

I'm not just talking about conversations with old-timers, either. Other student pilots can be great resources, as previously mentioned. But

if you can get an audience with some old-timers, by all means pick their brains for all you can. The one thing that experienced pilots can offer is experience. And experience is everything in aviation.

Pilots love to tell stories of their most frightening flights or their close calls. Students quickly amass such stories for themselves too. It's sometimes funny to think back on your most frightening moments as a student once you've logged a few hundred hours. What you experienced as serious, extreme, life-threatening turbulence at 15 hours, becomes "light chop" at 150 hours.

There is one danger to discussions with other pilots, however. Over time, pilots tend to develop some bad habits. Your CFI might insist that you do something a certain way for good reason. But when bring these things up to other pilots, you might hear all sorts of opinions on why what your CFI is asking of you isn't necessary. Don't let other pilots contaminate the good habits your CFI is trying to get you into.

BUZZWORD-LOVING ACRONYM HELL (OR BLAH FOR SHORT)

There are so many acronyms in aviation that it's comical. It seems like everything that is defined by more than one word is referred to as an acronym. We'll cover some of the more common ones here so that you'll be able to keep up with those airport lounge conversations from the start.

VFR VS. VMC VS. IFR VS. IMC

There are two basic types of flights: VFR and IFR. As a reminder: VFR, which stands for "visual flight rules" refers to the FAA regulations that govern flight by reference to the horizon or other visual clues that help determine the airplane's attitude and position. IFR (Instrument Flight Rules) refers to the regulations that govern flight by reference to cockpit instruments, such as while flying through clouds.

Two other terms, VMC and IMC, are often used interchangeably with VFR and IFR to describe the same thing, but there is a distinct difference between the terms. VMC and IMC refer to weather conditions, not flight rules.

VMC stands for "visual meteorological conditions." During VMC, the current visibility is presumed good enough for flight by visual references. Both VFR and IFR flights are legal in VMC. IMC stands for "instrument meteorological conditions." During IMC, only IFR flights are legal. IMC, by definition, means that there is not enough visibility to fly by visual references.

In summary, VFR and IFR refer to the regulations governing a flight and therefore the way in which the flight is conducted. VMC and IMC refer solely to the current visibility.

IFR and VFR also refer to different types of flight plans. A flight plan is a report that is made to ATC that defines various aspects of your intended flight, including your aircraft number, route of flight and number of persons on board.

You will hear references to flights that are on IFR flight plans. This means that the flight is being conducted under IFR and the pilot is instrument rated. A VFR flight plan means the flight is being conducted under VFR and the pilot might or might not have an instrument rating. All VFR flights must be conducted in VMC, but IFR flights can be flown in either VMC or IMC. Pilots must be instrument rated to conduct IFR flights, regardless of whether current conditions are determined to be VMC or IMC.

Dizzy?

BRAVO! ROMEO & JULIET WIN THE OSCAR FOR LAST TANGO IN QUEBEC!

A disclaimer: the following explanations are compiled from the assumptions of many individuals. I can't promise you that the reasons given are accurate, but the net result is the same.

Once upon a time, airplane radios were of such poor quality that it was necessary to use unique sounding words to represent individual letters of the alphabet. This was so "B" didn't sound like "E" or "D" or some other similar sounding letter. The phonetic alphabet was devised to reduce such airborne communications breakdowns.

Each word in the phonetic alphabet starts with the letter it represents. For example, the letter "A" is represented by the word "alpha." "B" is "bravo" and so on. The words that were chosen have few if any other rhyming words in the English language, so confusion was kept to a minimum even over scratchy radios. (Figure 16)

Two numbers were also replaced with words. Rumor has it that this was because some non-English speaking wartime allies were unable to pronounce the numbers properly. So 3 was replaced with the word "tree" and 5 was replaced with "fife." Few pilots actually use tree and fife today, but they are still considered preferable by the AIM.

Most popular of all the number changes, however, and still used by pretty much all pilots today is the word "niner," which is used in place of the number 9. Legend has it that this replacement was because of the German word for "no," which is pronounced the same as the number 9 in the English language. Though I wonder just how many U.S. fighter pilots were actually speaking German over the radios during the war to necessitate such a clarification.

Regardless of the true origins for all of these alphanumeric replacements, the phonetic alphabet is still used in aviation today and you need to know it.

One game that I used to play to help me memorize the alphabet was to speak out license plates that I saw driving to and from my lessons.

THE PHONETIC ALPHABET	India (in'-dia)	Tango (tan'-go)	4
	Juliet (jul'-ee-et)	Uniform (un'-ih-form)	5 (fife)
	Kilo (kee'-low)	Victor (vik'-tor)	6
Alpha (al'-fa)	Lima (lee'-ma)	Whiskey (wis'-kee)	7
Bravo (bra-vo')	Mike (mike)	X-Ray (ex'-ray)	8
Charlie (char'-lee)	November (no-vem'-bur)	Yankee (yan'-kee)	9 (nine'-er)
Delta (del'-ta)	Oscar (os'-kar)	Zulu (zoo'-loo)	0 (zero)
Echo (ek'-oh)	Papa (pa'-pa)		
Foxtrot (fox'-trot)	Quebec (ka-bek')	1	
Golf (golf)	Romeo (ro'-mee-oh)	2	
Hotel (ho-tel')	Sierra (see-er'-a)	3 (tree)	

Examples:
"N1186U" is spoken "november one one eight six uniform"
"Class B airspace" is spoken "Class Bravo airspace"
"Runway 9" is spoken "runway niner"
One exception: When runways parallel one another, the words left, right and center are used to identify them. For example,
"runway 13L" is spoken "runway one tree left" not "runway one tree lima."

Figure 16: *FONETIK ALFABET* Aviation-speak requires pilots to memorize and use the phonetic alphabet. Though daunting at first, it's not tough to master.

RADIO COMMUNICATIONS

English is considered the international language of aviation, but this doesn't mean that what you'll hear over the radios will sound like any English you've heard before.

There are a number of aviation-specific phrases used to simplify radio communications that you should know. In the AIM you'll find what's called the "Pilot/Controller Glossary." This great resource defines most of what is said between pilots and air traffic controllers. It's important that you understand the lingo. Take some time and read through it.

Explaining all of the phrases here wouldn't make any sense. They'll mean more to you once you actually need to use them. Throughout the rest of this book you'll learn some as they apply to what we do. I'll let you and your CFI cover the rest of them together.

But here's something important to remember: if you're flying solo and a controller says something that you don't understand, ask for clarification. Don't feel intimidated! "Say again please" is a perfectly acceptable response when necessary.

One on of my early solo flights I was cleared for landing and told by the control tower that "traffic in position is a Cherokee." I knew that "in position" referred to an airplane that was sitting on the runway ready to take off. And I knew what a Cherokee was. But I was dumbfounded as to why I needed to know that a Cherokee was about to take off. Was there something special about a Cherokee that I didn't know? Are they likely to explode on the runway? Do they take off vertically? After it takes off, will it turn back and try to shoot me down? Why should I care?

So I piped up on the radio, "I'm sorry sir, I don't know why you're telling me about the Cherokee." The controller explained that he was required to alert pilots that had been cleared for landing if there was traffic on the runway.

I'm sure the other pilots on the frequency at that time got a kick out of my ignorance at that moment, but at least I learned. And I never forgot it again. As embarrassed as I was for admitting my ignorance, at least I was able to make my landing without the distraction of wondering why he told me about the Cherokee. And we know where distractions can lead. (Have I said this enough already?)

If you are *ever* unclear about an ATC instruction, ask for clarification.

Sometimes an ATC instruction requires a "read-back." In other words, the controller expects the pilot to repeat the instruction for confirmation. I have looked far and wide for an official FAA document that explains when a read-back is required, but I cannot find one. I have spoken to many experts within the FAA that all agree there is no such beast.

As a rule of thumb, I read back only instructions that are specific to my airplane. I don't read back advisories that pertain to other aircraft too. For example:

TOWER: *Skyhawk 1186U, turn left 20 degrees and descend 3,000. San Francisco's airspace is busy at the moment, so expect delays.*

PILOT: *Turning left 20 degrees, descending 3,000, 1186U.*

The controller gave me two instructions that pertained to me directly, and offered what was basically an advisory that affected many aircraft. I read back the instructions only.

Or, the one I'll never forget:

TOWER: *Skyhawk 1186U is cleared to land, traffic in position is a Cherokee.*

The clearance to land is specific to me, but that Cherokee in position has nothing to do with my airplane. That was simply an advisory. The proper response would have been:

PILOT: *Roger, cleared to land, 1186U.*

We'll cover read-backs more when we actually start dealing with ATC communications.

KNOWING POPULAR AIRPLANES HELPS

Air traffic controllers are expected to know a lot about many different types of airplanes. For example, knowing how fast an airplane can fly helps controllers sort out the order in which they should arrange airplanes for landing. They're not likely to ask a twin-engine cruising at 160 knots to follow a Cessna doing 70 knots.

But the challenge for new pilots is that ATC often instructs us to follow other airplanes. This can happen on take off, but is even more likely during approach to landing.

One day I heard: "Cessna 1186U, follow the Mooney turning base." Okay, I knew what "follow" and "turning base" meant, but what the hell was a Mooney? I assumed it was an airplane and not a flying cultist, but what did one look like? And what about a Lancair, Trinidad, Duchess or an experimental?

Coming from my Cessna-centric student perspective, I was amazed at how many other airplanes were out there. Apparently everything wasn't either a Cessna or a Piper.

Spend some time at your local airport and take a close look at all of the airplanes. These are the airplanes you are most likely going to be asked to find when you're in the air. You might also want to get a book on different airplane models too. The idea is not to become so familiar with each model's nuances that you could pick it out in the dark from 20 miles away, or argue the merits of the v-tail Bonanza vs. the t-tail version. The idea is to get a general sense of the basic physical structure of the airplane so that you can pick it out from other nearby airplanes. (Figure 17)

For example, most Cessnas are high-wing airplanes, meaning that their wings are on top of the airplane. Pipers (Cherokee, Warrior, etc.) are low-wing airplanes. Wing location is perhaps the easiest thing to identify from a distance. The number of engines is another easy one. If you're told to "follow the Cessna" and you see a low-wing airplane, that's probably not the Cessna. (For the record, some twin-engine Cessnas are low-wing aircraft, but most controllers will refer to such airplanes as a "twin Cessna.")

Some airplanes, like Mooneys, have other easily identifiable features. Mooneys are known for their unique looking tail fins, which appear to be on backwards by comparison to those on other airplanes. (Figure 18)

Airplanes classified as "experimental" can look like anything. Experimental airplanes are typically kit airplanes built by their owners. These airplanes are not certified for production by the FAA, thus the experimental status. I used to think that anything considered experimental must be an odd looking duck with 3 wings, 4 tails and 2 cockpits. I was surprised to learn that most look quite normal by airplane standards. But when a controller calls out an experimental airplane to you, such as when she wants you to follow one in the traffic pattern, it's anyone's guess what it might look like. Ask if you're in doubt.

It's important to be able to recognize airplane models during the enroute portion of your flight too. If ATC is providing any traffic advisory services they will call out other airplanes to you.

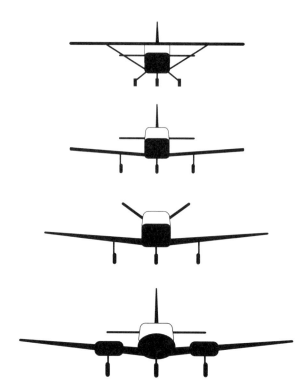

Figure 17: *THE USUAL SUSPECTS* At most training airports you're likely to see a handful of different types of airplanes. It helps to know a bit about the shape of each type. From the top left, we see a Cessna 172, known for its high wing and wing struts. Below that is a profile that could be a Warrior, Cherokee or a variety of other low-wing aircraft. Next is the V-tail Bonanza. This is the only airplane with such a tail design, so it's easy to spot. Twin engine airplanes are often referred to by ATC as simply a "twin," but they might be called by name. The one shown here could be a Piper Aztec, a Piper Seneca or a number of other twins. If you see a twin with a T-tail, meaning the rear wing (called an elevator) is mounted on the top of the tail, then you might be looking at a Duchess.

It's important that you positively identify the airplanes called out to you because once you say that you see them, the sole responsibility for collision avoidance becomes yours.

Figure 18: *TELL TAIL SIGNS* There's no mistaking the backward looking tail section of the Mooney (above). Another unique tail section belongs to the Beechcraft V-tail Bonanza (upper right). Some Bonanzas have conventional T-tail configurations, so the "V" isn't a given. Tail-draggers (middle right) lack a nose wheel, but have tail wheels (or skids) in the back. Tail-draggers popular at training airports include the Piper Cub, Pitts, Citabria and some older Cessnas. You'll also see several different models of high-performance single-engine airplanes, such as the Piper Malibu (bottom right). It can be tougher to recognize these in flight because their profiles aren't that different from those of other single-engines. But as you gain experience you'll recognize them by their profiles as well as performance: they're fast. [Photos: author]

4

Meet the Major Players

There are a few agencies and organizations that become familiar to every pilot. Sometimes a given agency can seem like a friend and at other times a foe. But keep in mind that they are each in place to serve you as a pilot. Without pilots, there is no need for any of the supporting agencies mentioned here. So don't let anyone push you around; it's all about you, baby!

FEDERAL AVIATION ADMINISTRATION (FAA)

The FAA is the public face of aviation. These are the folks that make and enforce the regulations that we, as pilots and aircraft passengers, must obey. The FAA is also the source of the strict safety regulations that govern the design and manufacture of aircraft registered in the United States.

But the FAA isn't always seen in a favorable light by pilots and the public alike. Some of the criticisms lobbed at the FAA are justified, though some are born of ignorance for what's going on behind the scenes.

We'll get into some of the juicy details below.

THE FAA CONTROVERSY

Up until 1996, the FAA was charged with the safety *and* promotion of civil aviation in the United States. (The FAA does not govern military aviation.) Think about this for a moment. To be responsible for safety means to ensure that guidelines are established and followed and that potential dangers are avoided by whatever means necessary, regardless of expense. Promotion, on the other hand, means to do whatever is possible to encourage growth by making progress in aviation easier and more affordable.

Forcing an airline to add collision-avoidance equipment to each of its airplanes at a cost of $50,000 per airplane might certainly be the interest of aviation safety, but not aviation promotion. The airlines could argue that the expense would necessitate fare hikes, which would discourage aviation as an affordable means of transportation. On the other hand, the postponement or prevention of important safety equipment or regulations goes against the safety portion of the charter.

In 1996, "promotion" was dropped from the FAA's official mandate, but old habits die hard. There are long-standing friendships between FAA and airline personnel. It can be hard to pass any sort of legislation that you know will adversely affect a friend's business.

But "friends" of the FAA also include private pilots. Would collision avoidance hardware installed on each and every aircraft in the United States make our skies safer? Sure it would. But is it fair to force private pilots to bone up $5,000 to install the hardware on their airplanes? Is $2,000 fair? At what point does a force purchase become fair?

Therein lies the great FAA controversy. This delicate balance between "safe" and "affordable" leaves the FAA with few close friends.

REGULATIONS

A popular saying in aviation is that FAA regulations are written in blood. Even more morose, however, is that the FAA is referred to by many in Washington as the "tombstone agency."

The essence of these criticisms is that the FAA adopts new safety measures only after someone has died. This goes back to the safety/promotion paradox. The FAA doesn't want to unduly hinder aviation until they are forced to do so, usually by public pressure.

This leaves us with a love/hate relationship with the FAA similar to the one many have with law enforcement. Speed limits are a great idea so long as they don't apply to us when we're in a hurry. The same applies to aviation regulations.

Regardless, the FAA regulations are the bible by which we fly. Chances are that you won't find them too restrictive. On the contrary, you'll probably find yourself at times thinking they don't go far enough. For example, if one of the worst things that can happen in flight is a cockpit fire, then why aren't we required to have a fire extinguisher on board? Is a $20 fire extinguisher too much of a financial burden to someone with a $100,000 aircraft? If an instrument rating makes pilots safer, then why aren't all pilots required to

get one? And if a flight plan would have helped authorities find JFK Jr.'s downed Piper faster, then why aren't flight plans required on VFR flights?

The reason is the same: *undue restrictions.* Instrument ratings take time and cost a lot of money to obtain. Forcing every pilot to have one would discourage potential students from pursuing aviation and would be seen as an outrage by current pilots who fly safely in fair weather every day.

So what about fire extinguishers and VFR flight plans? Who knows why they aren't required. Fire extinguishers are a minimal expense and filing a flight plan is free. One day the FAA might be forced to address these issues.

WHEN GOOD PILOTS DO BAD THINGS

Sometimes you run a red light because you think you can make it and get away with it. Sometimes you make an illegal u-turn because you didn't know better. Pilots are drivers with wings, so few of us are immune to the temptations drivers face to twist the rules for sake of convenience.

You are expected to know and abide by the regulations that govern your flight. From the FAA's perspective, it's as simple as that. But sometimes pilots get themselves into trouble without even trying.

Some infractions seem so minor that if you get caught in violation of one, you might find yourself flabbergasted that what you did mattered at all.

As mentioned, student pilots are required to have their log books with them on every flight. But licensed pilots are not so required. If an FAA inspector comes out to your airplane during your training and asks to see your log book, you'll find yourself with some explaining to do if you don't have it.

Brought to the fore more recently is the impact of temporary flight restrictions (TFRs). An area that is legal for civil aviation flight one day, might result in an F-16 escort the next day. TFRs are used to temporarily secure the skies around large public gatherings, like sporting events, or any other place officials feel that civil aircraft could pose a threat. Since the events of 9/11, many nuclear facilities have been surrounded by TFRs. Time will tell if the "temporary" nature of these restrictions will become permanent. You'll read more about TFRs later in "Transportation Security Administration (TSA)" on page 100.

Your best defense against violating regulations like these to is become familiar with how FAA regulations affect the flights you take, and to learn where to find out about all the temporary restrictions that might be in effect when you fly. We'll cover all of this throughout this book.

PUBLICATIONS OFFERED

The FAA offers a number of publications of interest to pilots. The FAR/AIM is certainly the most visible FAA publication, but other documents are great resources too.

Currently, the follow documents (and more) are available online. *(Visit **http:// AirDiamond.com/sa** for a link.)*

FEDERAL AVIATION REGULATIONS (FARS)

The FARs are the one FAA publication that pilots fear most. Though they are available online, you should get a printed copy from a pilot supply store. You'll need it for ready reference during your lessons.

AERONAUTICAL INFORMATION MANUAL (AIM)

You'll usually find a copy of the Aeronautical Information Manual at the back of the FAR book you buy. The AIM conceptualizes many aviation subjects so pilots can better understand them. The AIM does not include regulations, though it does reference and expound upon many of the regulations found in the FARs.

The types of subjects you'll find in the AIM include an overview of airport runway and taxiway markings, a list of which airports in the U.S. are considered ports-of-entry for general aviation aircraft, what to do if you're intercepted by military aircraft, an overview of ATC services available to pilots, what to do in an emergency and so on. The list of topics is vast, and the writing is great. Read the AIM, you'll learn a lot from it.

PILOT/CONTROLLER GLOSSARY

Once you start talking to air traffic controllers you're going to find that they know some pretty big words. They also know some pretty small ones that you thought you knew, but come to find that you don't know at all—at least in the context in which ATC uses them.

The Pilot/Controller Glossary is a very important document that you must read. It defines the standard phrases that pilots and controllers are to use when talking to one another.

For example, you don't say, "understood," you say, "*Roger.*" And you don't say "okay, I'll do that," you say "*Wilco.*" (Will comply.) And when ATC tells you that there are *numerous targets* in your vicinity, they are alerting you that other aircraft are nearby. They are not suggesting that you arm your weapons.

This sort of thing might not strike you as being terribly important up front, but the sooner you start using the correct language, the easier it will be for you later.

Air traffic controllers are bound by a set of regulations like we are. They are permitted to say certain things and not permitted to say others. Knowing the lingo really helps pilots understand what the heck a controller is trying to say.

Here's an example of what I mean. A pilot was headed to San Carlos airport, flying under VFR (visual flight rules). The clouds were rolling in so he knew he had to get home. He contacted the control tower and the conversation went like this:

PILOT: *San Carlos tower, Cessna 1186U, inbound.*

TOWER: *1186U, San Carlos is currently IFR. State your intentions.*

PILOT: *Uh... I want to land.*

TOWER: *1186U, San Carlos is currently IFR. State your intentions.*

PILOT: *Uh, I'm going to land safely?*

TOWER: *1186U, San Carlos is currently IFR. State your intentions.*

Can you imagine how this poor pilot was thinking he had entered the ATC twilight zone? What drug was this controller smoking?

The pilot could see that clouds had developed near the airport, but visibility was still okay. So why wouldn't the controller let him land?

The problem was that the cloud coverage made it impossible to fly in and out of the airport under VFR because VFR requires that airplanes remain a certain distance away from the clouds. (More on that later.) Even though visibility was fine, the clouds were too close to permit legal VFR flight.

There is, however, a condition called *special VFR* under which a pilot might be granted permission to land at an airport so long as she can remain clear of the clouds and forward visibility is at least one mile. [FAR 91.157]

This pilot was well aware of the concept of special VFR, but he didn't understand why the tower hadn't suggested it. The tower controller didn't suggest special VFR because controllers are not allowed to suggest special VFR to pilots. Pilots must ask for it. The controller's phrase "state your intentions" was his way of prompting the pilot to ask for a special VFR clearance to land. It was not intended to drive the pilot insane.

CONTRACTIONS (7340.1)

The FAA uses more contractions than I've ever seen in my life. Weather reports are full of them, but you'll be hard pressed to find any FAA document that doesn't at least include a few. This FAA document champions the use of contractions to the extent that it actually claims: "Without them, written communication becomes cumbersome."

Well, *IM NT SO SUR ABT THT.*

Contractions are also used to identify aircraft—you might think it's called a Piper Warrior, but it's actually a P28A.

This publication offers some background on contractions and provides lists that enable you to find out what a contraction is and decode ones you don't know.

Keep this document in mind when you start getting weather briefings.

AIR TRAFFIC CONTROL (7110.65)

This document describes the basic procedures air traffic controllers should use when handling various situations with aircraft. Why should you read it? Because it will offer you a sense of how things appear from the controller's perspective. The more we know about each other's reality, the better for us all.

This document isn't a must-read, but you might find it interesting to browse.

Ever wonder what an air traffic controller is supposed to do when an airplane is hi-jacked? This document tells you.

NOTICES TO AIRMEN (NOTAMS) (7930.2)

NOTAMs (pronounced, "no-tems") are advisories to pilots as to non-standard situations at airports or with navigational equipment.

The FAA publishes NOTAMs on its website, but this offering is of limited use. The point to NOTAMs is that they are up-to-the-minute advisories. Pilots typically learn of NOTAMs when they get a weather briefing, which we'll cover later. Your weather briefing should include all of the NOTAMs on the FAA's site that might affect you, limiting this online archive's usefulness for flight planning.

AIRWORTHINESS DIRECTIVES

When a defect is found in a particular type of aircraft, the FAA issues an *airworthiness directive* (AD) to alert mechanics, aircraft owners and pilots to the danger and the need for a fix or modification to the aircraft. ADs are regulations, not suggestions, so aircraft owners *must* ensure that their airplanes are in compliance with all applicable ADs.

ADs can require modifications as simple as the addition of a placard that alerts the pilot to the proper use of an aircraft component, or as serious as AD number 99-08-02 R1, which requires the inspection of the center fuel tank on all Boeing 747s to "prevent ignition sources and consequent fire/explosion in the center fuel tank." This particular AD was made effective on 5/11/1999, almost three full years after TWA flight 800 blew up over the Atlantic Ocean. The cause of the disaster is believed to be an explosion of its center fuel tank.

The FARs might be written in blood, but it's certainly not fresh blood.

Some ADs are one-time corrections and others are recurring, requiring aircraft mechanics to recheck the situation each time the airplane is in for an inspection.

One infamous recurring AD that was issued for the Cessna 172 instructs mechanics to check the front seat rails, which affix the front seats to the floor. In some cases the seats have broken free of the position locks in the rails and lurched backward, causing the pilot to lose control of the airplane. This is a serious concern for all.

In 2001, this defect cost Cessna $480 mil. when a Florida jury found the company guilty of not voluntarily recalling and fixing seat rails they knew to be defective. A pilot and two passengers were severely burned when, upon approach to landing, the pilot's seat flew backward causing him to pull back on the yoke, which, in turn, caused the airplane to slow to a speed at which it could no longer fly and it crashed. (We call this a "stall," a topic we'll discuss later.)

The FAA maintains a library of ADs, some of which date back to the 1940s. Make sure that you read all of the ADs for the airplane you fly so you'll have some sense of the history of the airplane's shortcomings.

ADVISORY CIRCULARS

When the FAA feels as though pilots need to be alerted to certain safety considerations, or offered some "guidance," they issue an advisory circular. These documents are not regulatory in nature, so pilots are not bound to follow the suggestions contained therein.

Advisory circulars range from recommendations of the type of fire extinguisher that should be used on an aircraft, to the effects of facial hair on the effectiveness of oxygen masks.

NATIONAL AERONAUTICAL CHARTING OFFICE (NACO)

In the year 2000, the FAA officially took over the responsibility for publishing aeronautical charts (maps) from the National Oceanic & Atmospheric Administration (NOAA). The National Aeronautical Charting Office was set up within the FAA to handle the task.

You'll purchase charts for the areas in which you fly. VFR charts are more commonly called *sectionals* because they depict a section of airspace. Sometimes you'll only need one, but in some areas you might need a few.

Regions that include the nation's busiest airports have special charts, called *terminal area charts*, that show greater detail than sectionals, but cover a smaller area. If you fly in one of these areas— Miami, Chicago, New York, etc.—you'll need both a sectional and a terminal area chart.

Charts can be purchased in pilot supply shops or through online resellers. They cost about $7 each. All charts have expiration dates after which the charts should no longer be considered safe for navigation. Some companies offer subscription services that automatically send you updated charts as they're published. This is a nice idea for those that live nowhere near pilot supply stores. Those that do, might prefer to just buy charts as needed rather than waiting for the mail to arrive.

I find it useful to buy at least two copies of each chart I use. Charts are double-sided and I find that unfolding and refolding the chart in flight can be one of those cockpit distractions we've talked about. I get the second copy set up as needed and just switch charts at the right time. Much easier. It also gives me a back up in case I lose one.

I have taken old charts that cover most of California and pieced them together on a wall in my home. This provides me with a great at-a-glance view of an area much larger than any one chart depicts. You can also put a string up on the wall with measurement markers that will permit you to easily measure the distance between points on different charts, which is much tougher to do when the charts are on a table. But remember, you cannot rely on these charts for navigation once they've expired! You must have current versions in the cockpit with you.

AIR TRAFFIC CONTROL (ATC)

The voice on the other side of the radio often intimidates student pilots. I think the misconception many students have is that we inconvenience these aviation professionals who have better things to do than offer direction to measly student pilots. After all, there are *real* airplanes up there with *real* pilots. Why bother with lowly students?

This was my feeling as a student. Then one day I had a conversation with a 30-year Delta Airlines captain with one of those perfect voices for cockpit-to-cabin flight updates. He also had some good things to say. I asked if it bothered him (and other pro pilots) to hear students taking up more airtime on the radio because of the extra help they needed.

"Absolutely not!" he said. "I want every pilot that's anywhere near my airplane to get all the information he needs. If I hear a student getting clarification of some ATC instruction, I'm glad to know he had the wherewithal to ask. What bothers me is diverting my flight path because some general aviation pilot didn't follow instructions."

He went on to say that during his airline training, he was taught to intentionally slow down ATC communications that had become frantic. "Folks start talking so fast on the radio—presumably in the interested if brevity—that you hear a lot more 'say-agains'. A repeated instruction takes more time than one spoken a bit slower, but clearly."

Is he correct? Let's just say his is one of the many aviation opinions you'll hear. Let's also say that this man has been flying airplanes for over 35 years, is one of the most senior pilots at Delta, and serves as an examiner of other Delta pilots.

From that day on, I saw ATC in a different light. They are not perfect, but they are the best friend I have when I'm flying. And they are there for *me*. They don't want me to ramble on the radio, but they also don't want me in the flight path of a 777.

Figure 19: *ATC WHO'S WHO* An ARTCC, or Center, is the ATC overseer of a large geographic area. Busy local areas, like Chicago, Los Angeles and New York, will have approach facilities to help aircraft get in and out of the area safely. Here, EastWest Center is about to tell the airplane on the left to contact Westland Approach. The airplane on the right is already within the airspace of Eastland Approach and will soon be told to contact the Pinky Airport Tower for landing clearance. "Hand-offs" like these are the way that ATC "moves" aircraft between sectors. Airports outside an approach facility's boundaries fall under the jurisdiction of the ARTCC for the area. So if a pilot was to contact ATC after leaving the area of one of the small (green) airports in the middle of the image, that pilot would contact EastWest Center directly.

Some controllers will be very helpful and others will be idiots. They are human. In fact, it's fair to say that controllers are just like pilots in that regard.

CONNECTING THE ATC DOTS

The term "ATC" is used by pilots to identify pretty much everyone on the other side of the radio that's not another pilot. But the ATC system is complex and involves the cooperation of several different micro-organizations that fall under the larger ATC umbrella.

Each ATC organization is responsible for a given "chunk" of the air above us, which they call *sectors*. Sectors vary in size considerably. Smaller sectors are usually subsets of larger sectors. (Figure 19)

The smallest ATC controlling entity is an airport's *control tower*. A control tower is responsible for the airspace that surrounds the airport. Each airport's airspace differs in size. (We'll talk about airspace in depth later.)

In busier metropolitan areas there is usually another ATC entity called an *approach facility*. These folks are responsible for getting air traffic in and out of the local area. They usually oversee departures and arrivals from several airports.

An example of an approach facility is *Norcal Approach*, which controls the airspace around the San Francisco Bay area. Major airports within their jurisdiction include San Francisco, Oakland and San Jose International airports. Southern California Approach, referred to as *So-Cal Approach*, watches over departures and arrivals for Southern California airports, including Los Angeles International, Burbank and Orange County. Approach facilities are often referred to as "departure" for airplanes leaving the area. In

Figure 20: *VOICES IN THE SKY* Twenty air route traffic control centers cover the continental United States. Airplanes are handed off between the centers throughout their flights. Centers also hand off airplanes to, and accept airplanes from, approach control facilities and control towers. For example, a flight leaving Miami International enroute to JFK would first talk to Miami Internationals' tower, then be handed off to Miami Departure, then Miami Center, Jacksonville Center, Washington Center and on to New York Center, Kennedy Approach and finally JFK's tower.

other words, when entering the San Francisco area you might be told to contact *Norcal Approach*, but when departing you'd contact *Norcal Departure*. The controllers and frequencies are the same, but the approach/departure designation helps controllers keep track of who's going where.

Approach facilities also track aircraft transitioning their airspace, but not intending to land.

Once an aircraft flies outside the sectors controlled by an approach facility, it enters airspace controlled by an *air-route traffic control center* (ARTCC). More commonly referred to as a *center facility*, or simply *center*, these folks oversee aircraft flying over larger areas between approach facilities and towers. To give you an idea of the scale of the airspace controlled by a given center, there are only 20 centers covering the entire continental United States. (Figure 20)

Center facilities also oversee all of the nooks and crannies between approach facilities, when radar coverage permits.

ATC LINGO

You'll hear various ATC facilities referred by several different names. Usually names are truncated for the sake of brevity. The trick is that different people delete different parts of the name and expect everyone else to know what they are talking about. This usually isn't a problem because most pilots know the approximate boundaries of the various ATC facilities near them, so nicknames seem pretty obvious.

An air-route traffic control center is usually referred to by it's location name or simply by "center," if the aircraft is no where near the center's boundaries. For example, Seattle Center might be referred to in any of the following ways:

ATC: *Skyhawk 1186U, contact Seattle Center.*

ATC: *Skyhawk 1186U, contact Seattle.*

ATC: *Skyhawk 1186U, contact Center.*

The basic "Center" designation is more likely if the aircraft is no where near the facility's boundaries with another Center facility, which would cause confusion. For example, the southern end of Seattle Center's airspace borders the northern end of Oakland Center's airspace. Controllers talking to aircraft in that area are more likely to be specific about which center they are referring to.

Approach facilities are similarly nicknamed. San Francisco's Norcal Approach is referred to several different ways:

ATC: *Skyhawk 1186U, contact Norcal Approach.*

ATC: *Skyhawk 1186U, contact Norcal.*

ATC: *Skyhawk 1186U, contact Approach.*

Again, the nickname used depends on the aircraft's location. Aircraft well within the Norcal Approach control sectors are more likely to hear "Norcal" or "Approach." Aircraft flying into the area will likely hear controllers refer to "Norcal Approach" or "Norcal" for clarification.

Airport control towers are usually referred to by the airport's name: For example:

ATC: *Skyhawk 1186U, contact San Carlos.*

ATC: *Skyhawk 1186U, contact San Carlos Tower.*

You won't typically hear anyone refer to an airport's control tower as simply "tower" unless you're communicating on the ground. For example, a controller monitoring the airport's ground operations might tell you to "contact tower" to get permission to depart.

WHO'S YOUR ATC DADDY?

So there you are flying at 7,500 feet somewhere above some place. You want to contact ATC, but how do you know who controls the airspace you're flying in?

During flight planning, pilots should note the various ATC agencies that control the airspace they'll be using. I'll show you how to find that out later. But if you ever find yourself without any idea of who to contact, anyone can help you. If you contact one agency and ask for help, they will either help you or give you the frequency to use to contact the appropriate agency.

BUTTING HEADS WITH ATC

There will be times where you find an ATC instruction to be either unnecessary, inconvenient or unsafe. There are ways of dealing with each situation.

ATC is not the final authority governing your flight. You are *always* the final authority as to what your airplane does. This in mind, you'd

better have a good reason for deviating from an ATC instruction. And the *only* good reason in the eyes of the FAA is safety. If ATC tells you to turn left and that left turn would put you right into a cloud, you might refuse the instruction, but explain why. For example:

ATC: *Cessna 1186U, turn left heading 090.*

PILOT: *Cessna 1186U unable to maintain VFR at 090. Suggest 010.*

Here, the pilot has refused the instruction, explained why and suggested a possible solution in one statement. ATC will not fight you on this. They will appreciate the input. They don't want you flying into the clouds any more than you do. They will either approve your suggestion, make an alternate suggestion or have some other airplane move to avoid you (assuming the turn was for traffic avoidance).

Always visualize the outcome of an ATC instruction before you comply. If you have doubt about the instruction, confirm ATC's intention. With experience you'll get a sense of what ATC is likely to tell you to do before they say anything. If you know that a standard instruction to approach your airport is to "fly over the field at or above 1,200 feet" and one day you hear, "fly over the field at or below 1200 feet," you could say, "confirm at or *below* 1200 feet?" This is usually enough to jog the controller's memory to correct the instruction or confirm it.

If you feel that an ATC instruction is either unnecessary or simply inconvenient, you might query the controller about it, but don't argue. For example, ATC might clear you for a certain type of approach into an airport, but not necessarily the approach you'd prefer.

TOWER: *Cessna 1186U, report over the field at or above 1,200 feet for right traffic, 30.*

PILOT: *Could Cessna 1186U get a straight-in to 30?*

The controller will either approve your request or deny it. She might or might not explain why it was denied. For example;

TOWER: *Cessna 1186U straight-in approved, report 3 mile final.*

Or you might hear:

TOWER: *Cessna 1186U, unable to offer straight-in at this time.*

The controller is not trying to be difficult. There's probably a good reason why you can't fly the straight-in approach. Most likely because there is other traffic in the area that would conflict. (Don't worry about the difference between different approach types for now.)

I've heard pilots argue with ATC about the stupidest things. One woman was furious because the tower had sequenced a Cessna 172 ahead of her Mooney. "Sir," she said in a venomous tone, "you should do some research on your airplanes. I'm far faster than that 172!" She was correct in that she was faster. But she was also sequenced behind the 172 and there was nothing wrong with that. She simply had to slow her speedy airplane down a bit. In this case, the controller not only denied her request to land ahead of the 172, but suggested that she not argue with ATC instructions in the future.

CONTROLLED AIRSPACE VS. UNCONTROLLED AIRSPACE

Controlled airspace refers to airspace that is controlled by ATC. Airspace not controlled by ATC is called *uncontrolled airspace*. Don't confuse this concept with airspace for which there are no rules or regulations. *All* airspace within the United States is controlled by FAA regulations even if it is not controlled by ATC. Uncontrolled airspace is called *Class Golf*. All other U.S. airspace is controlled.

Within ATC's controlled airspace is a more restrictive type of control called *positive control*. Positive control means ATC is in *absolute* control over what airplanes do in that airspace. In the United States, the airspace at and above 18,000 feet that is designated as *Class Alpha* is considered positively controlled airspace. All airplanes in this airspace must be in constant radio communication with ATC and be on IFR flight plans so ATC knows exactly where they're headed. These flights are monitored and controlled continuously by ATC.

Can a pilot in Class Alpha airspace deviate from an ATC instruction in the interest of safety? Yes. Pilots can *always* deviate from ATC instructions in the interest of safety, no matter what type of flight it is and no matter what type of airspace the flight is in at the time.

The very nature of airspace "control" simply means that the area is visibly on ATC radar. It does not mean an airplane's every move is determined by ATC. In fact, in *Class Echo* airspace—the controlled airspace which covers the majority of the United States—VFR airplanes aren't even required to talk with ATC. You can fly anywhere you like without intervention from anyone. (Of course you must adhere to applicable FAA regulations during your flight.)

The other controlled airspaces are Class Bravo, Class Charlie and Class Delta.

BIG BROTHER, BIG BOTHER...OR NOT?

ATC has no way of electronically identifying you in the air unless you first identify yourself. Radar can detect that an airplane is present at certain location, and can determine its altitude if the airplane has certain equipment, but it cannot determine exactly which airplane it is or who is flying it. (Figure 21)

This helps illustrate that ATC's primary function is air traffic control, not policing. They are not air-traffic cops waiting to write you up for speeding.

Figure 21: *SKYBALLS* Air traffic controllers often sit in darkened rooms, side by side, in front of radar terminals. As airplanes cross different sectors in the sky they are handed off to the next controller. So when you are told by ATC to contact another controller on a new radio frequency, chances are the new controller is sitting right next to the old one.

In fact, most FAA regulation infractions go unpunished. The infractions that do result in punitive actions have usually also resulted in an accident.

Once you get passed the notion that ATC is there to spy on your every move, you can start taking advantage of the real reason they are there: flight safety. There are many services ATC offers that are of great benefit to pilots. And, for the time being at least, ATC services in the United States remain free of charge to pilots.

ATC SERVICES & RESPONSIBILITIES

ATC's primary responsibility is the safety of IFR traffic. This doesn't mean, however, that there aren't services available to VFR pilots. You'll regularly hear that ATC services are available to VFR pilots on a "work-load permitting basis." This means if ATC gets too busy with IFR traffic, we VFR pilots are on our own. But most controllers will try to accommodate everyone if they can do so safely. After all, if the skies are busy, the controllers would rather be in contact with everyone. This way if someone gets in the way, they can move one airplane rather than several.

I've never been denied any ATC services, though I have been asked to wait for a few minutes from time to time. When this happens to you, there's no reason to panic. Emergency services are *always* available to everyone. If ATC denies you a requested service, it shouldn't prevent your flight. If the safety of your flight *requires* an ATC service, then your flight shouldn't be flown.

FLIGHT FOLLOWING

Flight Following is the best service that ATC offers to VFR pilots. It works like this: you identify yourself to ATC and request the service, they identify you on radar, and then they give you traffic alerts along your route of flight. If another airplane's route of travel might intersect yours—or even if it's close—ATC alerts you to the other airplane's position and suggests actions if you cannot see and avoid the airplane on your own. The word "suggest" here holds relevance. ATC is not responsible for traffic avoidance on your VFR flight. Only you can determine the actions to take. They can and will help when they can, but the ultimate responsibility for traffic avoidance when flying in VMC is with the pilot.

Here's a typical Flight Following example:

PILOT: *Norcal Approach, Skyhawk 1186U, request.*

This is the standard opening to ATC for VFR aircraft. We identify ourselves and let them know we're after some help. "Norcal Approach" is the local controlling agency for this pilot's area.

When the controller gets the chance, she will respond:

ATC: *November 1186U, go ahead.*

ATC typically refers to private airplanes by their complete tail numbers rather than by model. After we initially identify ourselves, they remember what kind of airplane we are. Our complete tail number is N1186U, hence the "November." All U.S.-registered airplanes' tail numbers start with "November."

Then we respond with our request:

PILOT: *Skyhawk 1186U is a 172/U over Sunol Golf Course at 3,500, request Flight Following enroute Stockton.*

Translated this means: "Skyhawk 1186U is a Cessna 172. We're currently flying over the Sunol golf course at 3,500 feet. We would like you to keep an eye on our flight progress and issue traffic advisories on our way to Stockton airport."

"172/U" is spoken as "one seventy-two, slant uniform." The *uniform* designation identifies the navigation equipment on board this particular airplane. Your CFI will go over the different suffixes with you.

We need to let ATC know about all this airplane-specific information so that they can suggest the best courses of action. For example, knowing we're a 172 enables them to estimate how fast we can travel and how fast we can climb. If another airplane is headed right toward us, they will know that telling us to quickly climb an additional 5,000 feet isn't practical since the 172 doesn't climb that quickly. Instead, they'd have us turn. If we were a

Figure 22: *SQUAWKING 5370* Once we get a squawk code from ATC, we enter it into our transponder. From that point on, ATC can positively identify us on their radar screens. Below you can see the result of a pilot pushing her IDENT button: the blip brightens and stands out from the rest.

jet, they'd know that we could climb well, we'd be traveling very fast, and that they need to warn other light airplanes near us to avoid our "wake," which can really shake up a small airplane.

ATC will likely respond with:

ATC: *November 1186U, squawk 5370 and ident.*

The squawk code will be a 4-digit number that no other nearby airplane is currently using. We enter this number into a piece of equipment called a *transponder*. A transponder receives the ATC radar's interrogation and responds with this unique code, thus positively identifying us amongst other aircraft.

When controllers asks us to *ident*, they want us to push a button on our transponder that makes our "blip" on their radar screen brighten up for a moment (or stand out in some other manner), making it easy for them to positively identify which blip is us. You can see the IDENT button in the upper left corner of figure 22.

After we enter the squawk code, and press the IDENT button, ATC will eventually let us know if they have positively identified us on radar:

ATC: *November 1186U, radar contact 2 miles east of Sunol, altitude indicates 3,500.*

PILOT: *Roger.*

This confirmation of our position means Flight Following has begun. "Roger" simply means we understood the communication. They tell us the altitude they see so that we can verify our equipment is accurate.

At this point you might hear nothing from ATC for a while. But you have to keep your radio on and your ears open because you never know when the advisories will come:

ATC: *November 1186U, traffic one o'clock, 5 miles, westbound, altitude indicates 4000, type unknown.*

Here we're told that an unknown type of aircraft is headed our way. It's currently 5 miles away, a little off to the right of our nose, and is flying west. It's at 4,000 feet according to the information received by its transponder.

ATC reports traffic as if the sky was a clock face and we were at the center of the dial. One o'clock means we look ahead and slightly to the right. Nine o'clock means we look off our left wingtip.

So we start looking for the airplane. If we're flying at 3,500 and this other airplane is flying at 4,000, why do we need to worry at all? Altitudes are estimates based on equipment that must be calibrated properly by a mechanic and set properly by the pilot. The possibility that both airplanes could be reading several hundred feet above or below their actual altitudes is *very* real. Further, as mentioned, larger aircraft generate wake vortices that can literally turn a small plane like our 172 upside down.

The key elements in this ATC advisory are:

- we don't know what type of aircraft it is

- it's only reported to be 500 feet above us

- it's headed our way

This is serious and we must first find the airplane before we can be sure that we can avoid it.

We start looking for the oncoming traffic in the general vicinity in which ATC reported it to be. But we also expand the search if we don't immediately spot the plane. Everything is an estimate, including the position reported by ATC. If after 15 seconds or so we don't see the traffic we report back to ATC:

PILOT: *Skyhawk 1186U, negative contact.*

This tells ATC we can't see the airplane and we need additional advisories or suggestions. At this point ATC might suggest that we turn to a certain heading. That would go like this:

ATC: *November 1186U, turn left 20 degrees, vectors for traffic.*

PILOT: *Turning left 20 degrees, 1186U.*

"Vectors for traffic" is ATC's way of letting us know why their having us turn.

If we see the airplane we say:

PILOT: *Traffic in sight, 1186U.*

ATC: *Roger.*

If the other airplane has turned away or for some other reason no longer poses a threat, ATC will say:

ATC: *November 1186U, traffic no factor.*

This means it's not likely that the airplane will affect us anymore. But keep in mind there *is* another airplane out there somewhere. Finding it wouldn't hurt. Especially since airplanes can turn and this one might turn back again.

Our response would be:

PILOT: *Roger, 1186U.*

This back-and-forth goes on for the duration of the Flight Following service. If you leave your current controller's airspace you will be directed to contact the next controller:

ATC: *November 1186U, contact Stockton approach on 113.35.*

PILOT: *113.35, 1186U.*

We tune in the new frequency and report:

PILOT: *Stockton Approach, Skyhawk 1186U, level 3,500.*

ATC: *1186U, roger, Stockton altimeter 29.96.*

"Level 3,500" tells the new controller that we're flying level at 3,500 feet. If we were climbing to, say, 5,500 feet, we'd say, "currently 3,500, climbing 5,500." If we were descending we'd say, "currently 3,500, descending 2,000."

We don't have to repeat any of the other specifics about our airplane or our Flight Following request because this information was communicated by our previous controller. Our new controller already knows who were are and where we're headed.

The Stockton controller gives us a new altimeter setting because this setting, which we'll talk more about later, changes from area to area. An accurate setting is required to ensure the altitude we're reading is accurate.

Eventually Flight Following stops because radar service is lost or we've reached our destination. If ATC initiates it, it goes something like this:

ATC: *November 1186U, radar contact lost, squawk VFR.*

This means we're no longer on Flight Following because radar contact was lost for some reason. We've either traveled beyond the range of the controller's radar, or our equipment has malfunc-

tioned. "Squawk VFR" means to set our transponder to 1200, which is the standard setting for aircraft flying under VFR without using ATC traffic advisory services.

ATC might also terminate Flight Following by instructing us to contact our destination airport's control tower:

ATC: *November 1186U, radar service terminated, contact Stockton tower on 123.45.*

If we cancel Flight Following for whatever reason, we'd say;

PILOT: *Skyhawk 1186U would like to cancel Flight Following.*

ATC: *November 1186U, radar service terminated, squawk VFR.*

Flight following is a great service. Use it whenever you can. It not only keeps you comfortable talking with ATC, but it's a great safety resource too. Search and rescue operations are far more effective for downed airplanes that were using Flight Following because ATC knows exactly where the aircraft was when it went down. If ATC isn't in contact with you and your airplane goes down, it might be hours before anyone even realizes you're missing, let alone determines where you went down.

CONTROL TOWERS

Services provided by tower controllers include taxi, take-off and landing clearances, traffic advisories for the local area, weather reports for the field, and other stuff too.

Towered airports have a designated airspace surrounding them that is either Class Bravo, Class Charlie or Class Delta. The horizontal and vertical size of the airspace varies for each airport depending on terrain restrictions and IFR approach requirements. There are standards, but there are exceptions too. Your CFI will cover the various sizes with you.

As a VFR pilot you can leave any tower-controlled airspace at any time without a clearance from anyone, but *entering* a tower-controlled airspace always requires a clearance. The clearance requirements vary for each type of airspace.

Classes Charlie and Delta share the same clearance requirements: You must hear the controller say your airplane's tail number. This sounds like an odd little word game, but it's only one of many you'll encounter in aviation, so bear with it.

For example:

PILOT: *San Carlos tower, Skyhawk 1186U, over Crystal Springs, inbound.*

The following responses constitute a clearance to enter the airspace:

TOWER: *Skyhawk 1186U, report at or above the field at 1,200.*

TOWER: *Skyhawk 1186U, stand by.*

The second response is actually a legal clearance to enter the airspace even though it doesn't sound like one. If the controller says our tail number the clearance is issued. I used to think of this quirky rule as a trick pilots played on controllers. Could we stump the controller into saying our tail number when he didn't really want us to come in? Rest assured, however, controllers know the rules too. If you hear your tail number, you're cleared into either Class Charlie or Class Delta airspace.

Clearance to enter Class Delta is granted directly by the control tower. Clearance to enter Class Charlie is granted by the local air traffic control facility. This is because Class Charlie towers (and Class Bravo towers, as discussed below) are too busy to handle all of the traffic that enters their large airspaces, especially considering that much of that traffic is just transitioning the airspace with no intent to land at the airport.

Clearance to enter the airspace, however, isn't a clearance to land. Approach and landing each require a specific clearance. By announcing you are *inbound* in your initial call, you tell the tower your intentions. If you didn't plan to land, but merely wanted to fly through the airspace, you would have asked for a *transition* instead of stating you were inbound:

PILOT: *San Carlos tower, Skyhawk 1186U, over Crystal Springs, request Delta transition, Sunol.*

This tells the tower that we want to fly through the airspace, but that we're not planning to land. Stating our current location (Crystal Springs) and a point on the other side of the Delta airspace (Sunol) defines our proposed route of flight for the controller. This important information enables the controller to ensure that the area will be clear of traffic before he sends us through. If it's not clear, he might deny the transition or require that we take another route.

A similar request to transition Class Charlie airspace would be made to the local controlling facility and not the tower. For example, San Jose International Airport in the San Francisco Bay Area is a Class Charlie airport. If all we want to do it fly though their airspace, we'd contact Norcal Approach, the airport's controlling facility:

PILOT: *Norcal Approach, Skyhawk 1186U, over Wood-side, request Charlie transition, southbound.*

If Norcal Approach didn't want to us to come into the airspace yet, their response would be something like:

TOWER: *Traffic calling over Woodside, stand by.*

Our tail number was not used in the transmission so we're not cleared to enter the airspace. In this case we must circle outside the airspace until we hear our tail number or decide to go somewhere else.

In cases like this, keep your ear on the radio. If the controller is very busy it might take some time to get back to you. If you badger him, it might take even more time! If it genuinely seems as though you have been forgotten, which is possible, a friendly reminder is in order. If you're low on fuel or become so while circling, politeness must be reinforced with assertiveness:

PILOT: *San Carlos tower, Skyhawk 1186U, over Crystal Springs, inbound, minimum fuel.*

The phrase *minimum fuel* is recognized as meaning that you need priority. It also means that you were in idiot to have stayed out so long before coming home, so don't rely on it as your ticket to rockstar treatment by controllers. If my fuel reserves were getting that low and I was having trouble getting into an airspace for landing, I'd consider another nearby airport before I had to declare minimum fuel.

For Class Bravo airports, the clearance requirements are more restrictive. This is because Class Bravo airports are the busiest airports in the country and traffic must be closely monitored. Typically you won't be asking for landing clearances at Class Bravo fields because the landing fees are significant. But you will have reason to transition the airspace.

Some Class Bravo airports don't even allow student pilots to land. And some flight schools won't allow their students to even transition Class Bravo airspace without a CFI on board. Both of these restrictions help emphasize the seriousness of Class Bravo airspace. If you make some boneheaded maneuver in Class Delta airspace, you might inconvenience another pilot who has to fly around you. But if you do the same in Class Bravo, you might necessitate the diversion of a Qantas 747 that's been enroute for 15 hours from Sydney, not to mention the many other flights that would have to be resequenced to allow the 747 to re-enter the approach.

As with Class Charlie, requests to enter Class Bravo airspace are not made to the airport's control tower. They're made to the local controlling agency. The controlling agency for Los Angeles International Airport is called "So-Cal Approach," so the call would go like this:

PILOT: *So Cal Approach, Skyhawk 1186U, request.*

ATC: *November 1186U, go ahead.*

PILOT: *Skyhawk 1186U, over the Van Nuys VOR, request "Hollywood Park" Bravo transition, enroute John Wayne.*

A VOR (each letter pronounced) is a navigational facility that pilots can use to determine their position. "Hollywood Park" is a predefined route of flight through the area that VFR pilots are expected to fly. The route is shown on the local terminal chart. Mentioning John Wayne airport as your destination lets ATC know what you plan to do once you get on the other side of the Bravo airspace.

ATC's response to this request will or will not include the *very* important distinction between clearances to enter Class Bravo airspace as opposed to those required to enter Classes Charlie and Delta. If ATC comes back and says something like, "Roger 1186U, transition to Queen Mary approved" you are *not legally cleared!* Here we have another one of those ATC word games. But it's an important one. To enter Class Bravo airspace legally, you must hear what we call "the magic words." The words are "cleared to enter Bravo airspace" or something to that effect.

A legal clearance would sound like this:

ATC: *November 1186U is cleared to enter the Los Angeles Bravo airspace, "Hollywood Park" transition approved, maintain VFR at 8,500 feet.*

If you get what sounds like a clearance that does not use the magic words, here is what to say:

PILOT: *So-Cal Approach, verify Skyhawk 1186U is cleared to enter Bravo.*

This will jog the controllers memory that you're rightfully seeking the magic words.

Tower controllers are responsible for their immediate airspace only. Areas beyond the towered airport's airspace boundaries, both horizontal and vertical, are controlled by someone else. Once you fly outside this area, the tower has no further interest in you.

In some cases tower controllers might initiate transitions to adjacent airspaces for you. For example, if your local airport is right next to Class Bravo airspace and your route of flight requires transitioning the Class Bravo airspace, your control tower might contact the controlling agency directly, alert them that you're on your way, and get your squawk code for you. (Remember, the squawk code is the 4-digit number you put into your transponder so ATC can keep track of exactly who you are.) This is handy because you not only get your squawk code up front, but if the clearance transition will be denied you'll hear about it before you depart.

But is this an actual *clearance* to enter the Class Bravo airspace? No! Until you hear the magic words by the controlling agency, you are not ever cleared to enter Class Bravo airspace. Tower controllers from Class Delta or Charlie airports cannot issue clearances to enter Class Bravo airspace. No controller can issue a clearance to enter an airspace for which they are not directly responsible.

TO TWO FOR FOUR

We don't say "climbing to 5,500" in our ATC communications. This is because "to" sounds like "two." "Two, five thousand, five hundred" is actually 25,500 feet. It's not likely any controller would expect a Cessna 172 to be jetting its way to 25,500 feet, but this can be a real danger for some aircraft.

If United flight 1322 is "leaving thirty-five thousand, descending to niner thousand" are they dropping to 29,000 feet or all the way to 9,000 feet? "To niner thousand" is exactly how the altitude 29,000 feet is spoken. A savvy controller that's not eyeball deep in other airplanes would probably figure this out, but there is room for confusion.

We also don't say "for" for the same reason. If a radio frequency change is in order and we're told to go to "135 for [static] Stockton"? Was that 135.0 or 135.4?

Aviation accidents have happened because of communications mishaps less likely than these.

Omit those two confusing little words (to and for) from your radio vocabulary and your intent will be clearer. You are not "climbing *to* five-thousand feet," you are "climbing five-thousand." You are not "descending *to* one thousand, five-hundred feet," you are "descending one thousand, five-hundred." ("To one thousand, five-hundred feet" is how you'd speak 21,500 feet.)

MEET THE VOICES ON THE OTHER SIDE OF THE RADIO

ATC specifics are better experienced than explained. Many control towers and controlling facilities are happy to provide tours of their facilities. In fact, they've dubbed these orientation tours "Operation Raincheck." Ask your CFI or flight school if they are aware of such tours. If not, call the facilities yourself. Your CFI can help you find the phone numbers.

Seeing the controllers in action serves several purposes. Most importantly, you see that these are real people. I went on a tour of Oakland Center one day. Oakland Center is the agency responsible for enroute traffic in and out of Central and Northern California and the Western part of Nevada. This is a major ATC center responsible for thousands of commercial flights per day.

I was allowed to put on a set of headphones and listen in while a fantastic controller directed an impressive number of commercial flights in and out of the area. He had that authoritative, professional-sounding air traffic controller voice, but he wore cut-off jeans and a sleeveless David Bowie t-shirt. His Teva sandals were off at his feet.

Between mission-critical calls to commercial aircraft he asked about my training. Comments like, "I think flying in small planes is rad; I've always wanted to..." were interrupted by "United 2111, descend one-two thousand, contact Norcal on 135.5." Then immediately we'd be back to, "...learn to fly. I think I'll start lessons this summer because..." then: "Delta 566, contact Salt Lake Center on 124.3."

You get the idea.

Every time I hear a controller now I think of him. Maybe he'll read this book during his flight training.

An ATC visit also clues you into the challenges controllers face. An ATC-savvy pilot can really increase the efficiency of airborne communications. If you know what a controller needs from you, you'll not only help expedite communications, but you're more likely to get the clearances you want. Further, controllers can help you better understand some of the nuances of flying through your local area. If you've always wondered why they ask you to do a certain thing, you can ask and learn.

A trip to a local airport's tower is also a great idea. The controllers there can be of enormous help to a student. You will undoubtedly have many questions about the way things work. I found it a great benefit to just sit and listen to communications with other airplanes. You get to hear other pilots say and do the same stupid things you've said and done, and you get to see why you shouldn't ever say or do those stupid things again. Things look very different from the tower's perspective.

Knowing how ATC works makes you a better pilot by enabling you to help controllers do their jobs more efficiently. Conversely, good controllers have also taken the time to go up in planes to learn what we go through.

A good relationship with ATC is a good thing. Do what you can to establish one for yourself. They are there to help and they can be truly helpful.

FLIGHT SERVICE STATIONS (FSS)

Once upon a time there were centers at airports all over the U.S that were equipped with knowledgeable aviation professionals whose sole purpose was to provide in-person weather briefings and other useful flight information to pilots. The advent of technology and shrinking FAA budgets resulted in the closing of most of these facilities, but some are still in place. The surviving flight service stations are available by phone, and, in most places, on the radio in your airplane. Some still provide walk-in services to pilots, but given the facilities' remote locations, most pilots opt for the other contact options.

SERVICES OFFERED

The array of services offered by flight service stations vary for VFR and IFR flights. We'll focus on services available to VFR flights.

WEATHER PROS

By far the most important service offered by an FSS is a professional weather briefing. There are many automated and Internet-based weather reporting services, but there's no substitute for the analysis of a weather professional that's been interpreting weather data for years—a consideration that's especially important for student pilots.

You can also rely on an FSS to provide you with enroute weather updates over your airplane's cockpit radio. This is valuable because most Cessnas and Pipers still lack airphones and

Internet connections. It's great to know how the weather at your destination airport is holding out while you still have plenty of time to make alternate landing plans if the fog has moved in. And if it has, the FSS is a great resource to help you decide where to go instead.

FLIGHT PLANS FILED, OPENED AND CLOSED

Flight service stations are also the place where you file, open and close your VFR flight plans. You'll typically *file* your flight plan on the ground, *open* it shortly after you take off, and *close* it either on the airplane's radio just before you land, or over the phone after you land.

You can also rely on the FSS to amend your flight plan if needed. If you change your route of flight or want to revise your arrival time, call them up on the radio and make the change. The FSS computer system is nationwide, so regardless of which FSS you used to file your flight plan, you can amend or close it with any other.

After taking down flight plan information, an FSS briefer will usually remind pilots to close their flight plans upon arrival at their destination airport. This is serious business. If you fail to close your flight plan and the FSS is unable to verify your arrival, search and rescue operations ensue. After all, if you don't arrive when you say you will, they must assume the worst.

Officially you're not considered overdue until 30 minutes past the arrival time you estimated in your flight plan. One FSS official told me that they actually start making phone calls to find you at 20 minutes past your estimated arrival time. This is phase one of the search. A quick call to an airport's control tower or business office can often verify that aircraft has landed safely and its pilot simply forgot to the close her flight plan. This accounts for some 80% of overdue pilots.

If there is no control tower or business office to contact, things become more complicated.

By 30 minutes past your estimated arrival time the search intensifies. Local law enforcement might be called to drive to the field and look for your airplane. Flight service personnel will also call airports along your route of flight to see if you've landed elsewhere. This portion of the search operation usually finds 80% or so of those pilots still missing after phase one of the search.

Eventually, after all the "easy" options have been exhausted, local authorities will initiate a search and rescue operation. This is great if you actually went down, but terrible if you simply forgot to close your flight plan.

I find it helpful to include the words, "CLOSE PLAN!" in big letters at the bottom of all of my navigation logs and at the end of my post-flight checklist. (A navigation log is a piece of paper that defines your route of flight. We'll get into this in the navigation section.) Some airplanes also have reminders posted in the cockpit.

Most amusing to me—and maybe most effective—is when I see the reminder, "Have you closed your flight plan?" posted above the urinals at an airport restroom. I suppose the theory is that this is one of the first places pilots are likely to go after landing. (I'm not sure how they handle this in the Womens' restroom. Back of the stall door?)

Another memory aid I've heard pilots mention is putting their wrist watches on the wrong hand. Eventually the watch bothers them enough, they wonder why they've...and, bang!, they reach for that phone.

This brings up an important point. The process of search and rescue starts out with just a simple few phone calls, but ends up many hours later with aircraft physically hunting for you. If you realize two hours after you land that you forgot to close your plan, don't run and hide. Call an FSS *immediately* and let them know you're okay. They might have words for you, but rest assured that the words will be far worse as time goes on.

Keep in mind these people are assuming an aircraft has crashed and that its occupants might be injured or dead.

So the good news is that if you file a flight plan and your airplane goes down, someone will eventually come to find you. The bad news is that if they do so because you forgot to close your plan, you could be in big trouble. The FAA will determine what punitive actions are warranted, if any. If you forget to close your plan on a recurring basis, the FAA might "forget" that it ever issued you a pilot certificate in the first place.

As mentioned, if you're on Flight Following and your plane goes down, search and rescue will commence immediately. Flight plans are a great safety measure, but nothing beats Flight Following for quick action.

So why bother with flight plans at all if you plan to use Flight Following? Flight plans are a sure thing. Flight Following is available on a workload-permitting basis. While chances are you'll probably get Flight Following when you ask, there is always the chance you won't. Your flight plan will be there as a back up, or if the radar contact required for Flight Following is lost for whatever reason.

Keep in mind that *radar contact* is not the same as *radio contact*. It's possible to be lost on radar and still be accessible by radio (and vice-versa). If ATC loses you on radar but can still communicate with you over the radio, they obviously won't send out search and rescue teams.

PILOT REPORTS (PIREPS)

One valuable service offered by flight service stations is actually dependant on the cooperation of pilots. PIREPs (spoken "pie-reps") are first-hand accounts, made by airborne pilots, of weather conditions aloft. There is no better source for weather data. If an airplane just reported

moderate turbulence with cloud bases at 3,000 feet in a given area, you can forget the forecast for clear, smooth air.

CONTACT OPTIONS

You can contact a flight service station either by telephone or cockpit radio. All flight service stations share one toll-free number, 800-WX-BRIEF. ("WX" is aviation speak for weather.) You can reach an FSS on this number from anywhere in the U.S. Your call will be automatically routed to the FSS nearest your area. If the one nearest you is too busy, the call will go somewhere else.

Once airborne, your airplane's radio is your only contact option. (The FCC says you can't use your cellphone in flight.) There are two frequencies that are considered *standard* FSS frequencies, meaning that you should be able to reach an FSS on one frequency or the other:

- **122.2** – If you don't know a local radio frequency to use to contact the FSS nearest your current location, try 122.2. This should reach a nearby FSS, though reception might not be ideal. Navigation charts often show local FSS frequencies to use in a given area, but those little numbers can sometimes be hard to find on a busy-looking chart in a bouncing airplane. If you do see any other frequencies on your charts for your area, assume they will work better than 122.2.

- **122.0** – This frequency is reserved for filing PIREPs and getting enroute weather updates. Don't use this frequency for other FSS stuff, such as dealing with flight plans. You can, however, use it to learn the appropriate "regular" FSS frequency for your area. Refer to the folks monitoring this frequency as *Flight Watch*, though they are regular FSS briefers sitting, in most cases, right beside the folks on the standard frequencies.

Sometimes an FSS antenna is located far from some areas that the FSS services. In these cases, the regular contact frequency, 122.2, might not work well or at all. To solve this problem, land-based lines are used to connect the main FSS antenna with remote transmitters and receivers. These remote facilities are either part of VORs or stand-alone antennas called *Remote Communications Outlets* (RCO).

Contacting an FSS over an RCO and *some* VORs is easy. The frequency to use is listed on the charts. You dial it in and announce yourself to the FSS. That's it. (Figures 23 and 24.) The hardest part of using an RCO is actually finding one on the chart. The little boxes that represent them can be hard to spot.

Using some VORs for FSS contact is a little more complicated because two different radio frequencies are used. Pilots use one frequency to talk to the FSS and another frequency to listen to the FSS. The "listen" frequency is the VOR frequency itself.

First off: *you never transmit on a VOR's frequency.* This means that you will always transmit to the FSS on a frequency listed at the top of the VOR box.

The only thing left to know is how you'll hear the FSS speak back to you. If the VOR frequency is underlined, as it is in figure 24, you use the frequency at the top of the VOR box for two-way communications. Easy.

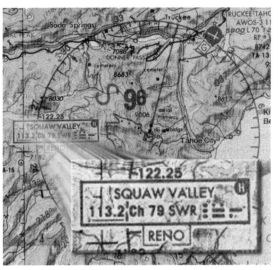

Figure 24: *VOICES IN THE VOR* The large circle on this aviation chart segment represents the location of a VOR. The inset box shows the VOR identification information, but also shows that the Reno FSS uses this VOR to communicate with pilots. The radio frequency at the top (122.25) is used by pilots for two-way communications with the FSS. When the VOR frequency is underlined, as it is in this image (<u>113.2</u>), it means that pilots cannot hear the FSS on that frequency and should use the frequency listed at the top of the box for two-way communications.

If the VOR frequency is *not* underlined, as is the case in figure 25, then you must configure your radio to listen on the VOR frequency itself.

This dual-frequency process requires one brain cell more than many pilots are willing to use. As a result, some pilots won't contact an FSS unless they can do so by using a single frequency.

Figure 23: *RCO* A Remote Communications Outlet is a stand-alone antenna. It has a single frequency that pilots use for two-way communications with the local FSS. The name of the local FSS is listed below the box on the chart. Here we see the Fall River Mills RCO, which can be used to contact the Rancho FSS on frequency 122.4.

Figure 25: *FSS RECEIVE* When a VOR frequency is *not* underlined, it means that pilots should use the VOR's frequency (109.6 in this image) to hear the FSS and they should use the frequency listed at the top of the VOR (122.1 in this image) box to transmit to the FSS. The "R" printed after the frequency at the top means that the FSS can hear pilots (they *receive*) on that frequency, but they cannot use it to talk back to pilots.

It's easy to remember if you think that "underline is easy," meaning that if you see that underline, the VOR is one of the easy ones.

The "R" at the top of the VOR box always confuses pilots. Do *they* receive on that frequency or do *we* receive on that frequency? Don't worry about it! Just remember that pilots always transmit on the frequency listed at the top of the box.

SPEAKING FSS

There is no wrong way to contact an FSS, but there are *preferred* ways. If you call up and say, "Uh…Flight Service? This is…uh…Cessna 4956D. Anybody there?" you will get a response. Granted, there might be a room full of FSS briefers (not to mention other pilots) chuckling at your technique, but no one is going to ignore you because you didn't use some magic words.

Magic words, however, can expedite things considerably. FSS briefers monitor many different frequencies at once. They sit in front of a panel of lights, each representing one radio frequency. A light blinks when a pilot talks over the light's frequency. The problem is that the light stops blinking when the pilot stops talking. So if you call up and say, "Hey, pay attention to me!", by the time the briefer looks up at the panel to figure out what frequency the whiny pilot's using, the light has stopped blinking.

Here's where magic words come in to play:

PILOT: *Oakland Radio, Skyhawk 1186U on 122.2*

Now the briefer knows exactly where to find you. If you're using a VOR or RCO, you should specify the frequencies and facilities you're using:

PILOT: *Rancho Radio, Skyhawk 1186U, transmitting 122.1, listening Fort Jones VOR. (Figure 25)*

You could say the Fort Jones VOR's frequency (109.6) instead of referring to it by name, but these FSS professionals are quite familiar with which frequency goes with which facility.

The FAA has started phasing out FSS dual-frequency communications over VORs, so these situations will become increasingly rare.

Announcing yourself over an RCO or a single-frequency VOR is even easier:

PILOT: *Rancho Radio, Skyhawk 1186U, Fall River Mills RCO. (Figure 23)*

PILOT: *Reno Radio, Skyhawk 1186U, Squaw Valley VOR. (Figure 24)*

When you announce just a facility's name, the FSS assumes you are transmitting and receiving on a single frequency.

As mentioned, frequency 122.0 is reserved for Flight Watch. As such, it's not necessary to announce a frequency when making these calls. The FSS would like you to announce your position though:

PILOT: *Reno Flight Watch, Skyhawk 1186U over Clear Lake Reservoir.*

This not only makes them aware of your position, but if the 122.0 frequency is not strong in that area, they might suggest that you switch to another frequency that will work better.

This brings up an important point about contacting an FSS: Do not give up just because you don't get a response on a listed frequency. Look for other frequencies and try them. If you can't get a FSS frequency to work, try calling Flight Watch on 122.0. If you can't reach either, ask ATC for assistance. They will likely know a frequency that should work in your area.

Spend some time with your CFI getting up to speed on the use of the radios in your airplane. It will not only help you when contacting an FSS, but when debugging a radio irregularity or failure. I have had several situations in which I could not contact who I needed to contact on my radios. Never has the problem actually been a failure in my radios. Usually I had dialed in the wrong frequency or set up my radios incorrectly. Once it was a failure on the part of the ground facility's receiver. Assume a radio failure as a last resort if you can't get a hold of who you need.

FSS VS. ATC: WHAT'S THE DIFFERENCE?

The difference between an FSS and ATC can seem vague at first, but the distinctions are many and significant. First off, an FSS has no authority over any aspect of your flight. They cannot prevent you from flying, nor can they direct your flight enroute.

An FSS can *recommend* that you not fly or suggest routes if you ask them to. For example, if a VFR pilot calls an FSS for a weather briefing and the weather is not forecast to be VFR, the FSS might say that "VFR flight is not recommended." (They will never, however, say that VFR flight *is* recommended any sooner than they'd say that IFR flight is not recommended on beautiful days!)

An FSS recommendation to stay on the ground is not binding to a pilot, but you're well advised to heed the warning. These are weather professionals. They know what they're talking about.

ATC, on the other hand, can and does restrict flights. As mentioned, ATC might deny clearance to a pilot wanting to fly into an airspace. Additionally, it is ATC who will close an airport due to fog or other safety restriction. All ATC actions are, of course (in theory), in compliance with FAA regulations.

Another difference between the agencies is pilot participation. Pilots are never required to contact an FSS for anything. If you never file a VFR flight plan and never check the weather, then you might never have occasion to call one. But if you fly into a towered airport or ATC-controlled airspace, then you must contact ATC and follow their instructions unless flight safety prevents you from doing so.

Some services are available from both agencies in varying degrees. An FSS can provide you with detailed weather, whereas ATC might provide only basic weather data, if any, depending on the equipment available to the controller. This ability varies throughout the country. Further, if you ask a controller for a weather forecast, she'll certainly refer you to an FSS. Weather forecasts are not the responsibility of ATC.

Typically, you will open and close flight plans with an FSS, though there are times when ATC will do this for you. One day I was leaving San Carlos for a flight northward through San Francisco's Class Bravo airspace. Just after departure I was cleared into the Bravo airspace before I had a chance to open my flight plan. I asked the San Francisco controller if I could go off frequency for a moment to open my plan with the FSS, but of course he refused. (I figured that he would.) Having me out of immediate radio contact was too dangerous in a busy airspace like that. Instead, he opened my plan for me.

In some cases an FSS might act as a go-between for a pilot and ATC. This is more common for IFR pilots seeking departure clearances, but it might happen to a VFR pilot too. In these cases, for whatever reason, the pilot and ATC are not able to connect via radio. An FSS can communicate with pilots over RCOs and some VORs, so they might be able to reach pilots in areas that ATC cannot. In these cases you will hear the FSS phrase instructions "ATC clears..." or "ATC requests..." An FSS cannot issue a clearance for anything. They can only relay ATC clearances.

I've heard of two separate occasions where an FSS saved the day when airplane radios went dead enroute. In each case the pilot pulled out a cellphone, dialed 800-WX-BRIEF, and had the FSS relay ATC instructions.

Cellphone use is forbidden in airplanes by FCC edict, not by the FAA. In an emergency, you use any resource you have at your disposal. (Yes, a radio failure in a busy airspace is an emergency worthy of breaking an FCC regulation.) The FCC doesn't have the authority to take your pilot license away and the FAA will commend you for having the wherewithal to use your cellphone to ensure flight safety.

FSS: USE IT OR LOSE IT!

Funding for public services is always subject to the chopping block. We've seen it happen to flight service stations in the past and it could happen again. We'd fly in a very different world without FSS assistance.

You'll grow to appreciate them more as you gain more flight experience, but even as a student pilot you'll learn to love them. As mentioned, FSS weather briefings are the most reliable source that students can use. Online services offer raw weather data, but offer no experienced interpretation of that data. FSS briefers are the specialists that really know how to make the data useful. They understand pilot needs and concerns, and they understand weather.

Remember the FSS while enroute too. File those PIREPs every chance you get. You'll not only help justify the need for the FSS, but you'll also help other pilots who can use the information. Everyone wins.

Another win-win proposition is the filing of flight plans. It costs you nothing to file a plan and it also helps justify the need for the FSS. So when you call for a weather briefing, file a plan. It's the safe thing to do.

Seek out and visit your nearest FSS. They're more than willing to offer orientation tours, which they've dubbed "Operation Take-Off." Like an ATC visit, you get to see how things are done, which helps you in the air.

If you ever find yourself tapping on the top of the instrument panel mid-flight because there's nothing else to do, call up the local FSS and let them know how your ride is going.

During the development of this book I called my local FSS many times to ask questions. During one call, which lasted more than 30 minutes, I spoke with three different briefers, all willing to help solve some mysteries I had stumbled upon.

On another occasion I actually made an appointment and went to visit the Oakland Flight Service Station. I sat for three hours with three different employees, each friendly, knowledgeable and genuinely interested in getting me the information I needed. My final question to them that day was whether there was anything they wanted student pilots to know about their operation. Their operations manager replied without hesitation:

"Yes," he said. "Make sure they know we're here for *them*. "Service" is our middle name."

TRANSPORTATION SECURITY ADMINISTRATION (TSA)

The newest player on the aviation field is the Transportation Security Administration, more commonly known as the TSA. Set up after the attacks of 9/11, the TSA is responsible for the security of all the nation's transportation systems including rail, sea, highway and, of course, air. Even city bus and commuter light rail and ferry systems are now under the watchful eye of the TSA.

Most people will have direct involvement with the TSA only when they pass through metal detectors at airports. But as a pilot, you'll be watching the TSA even more than the TSA is watching you. This is because the TSA issues what are called *temporary flight restrictions* or TFRs, which define time periods during which general aviation aircraft are not permitted to fly in certain areas.

Common TFRs include areas in which a prominent public figure is to appear, or areas near an outdoor sporting event. At times of heightened national security levels, entire metropolitan areas might be under TFRs. For example, it was a long while after the attacks of 9/11 until general aviation aircraft were permitted to fly freely over New York City. And some restrictions over Washington D.C. remain in place today. Though dubbed "temporary," some TFRs remain in effect for quite some time.

It's very important to know if any TFRs will affect your flights. Your CFI can show you how to learn about TFRs in your area. The penalty for flying through some TFR areas might be a slap on the wrist, but a violation of others might result in a military aircraft escort to a nearby airport where you can be sure trouble awaits.

But another very important reason to honor TFRs is that they are, as named, *temporary*. If general aviation pilots violate TFR areas to an excess, some of the nation's most wonderful flight areas might become permanently off limits to us. Many people don't have the love for flying that you and I have. Each time a general aviation pilot initiates a breach of national security, we move inches closer to permanent restrictions.

5

About Your Airplane

During you're flight training you'll be learning so much about your airplane and its capabilities that you'll swear they're training you to *build* airplanes rather than fly them.

I used to run car comparisons through my mind regularly: If I don't need to know how much weight my car can tow, why do I need to know how much weight my airplane can hold? If I don't know how much oil my car burns in an hour, why should I care how much my airplane burns?

Arguments abound as to what's really important for a pilot to learn about an airplane. But think of it this way: it can't hurt to know as much as possible. When something goes wrong, knowing all that you can could be the difference between solving the problem in the air and a forced landing.

Rest assured, at some point in time something *will* go wrong. This is not meant to spook you, but prepare you. Airplane systems fail sometimes. By far, however, most failures amount to little more than an inconvenience.

That said, the difference between an inconvenience and a disaster often depends on the pilot's understanding of what went wrong and how to best deal with it. When you drive in the snow and your car starts to lose traction and slide, your

instinct might be to use the brakes. But an informed pilot (er... *driver*) knows better. There are many such situations in aviation.

We learn all that we can so that we can trust our instincts and know when we *cannot* trust our instincts.

An in-depth understanding of your airplane's flight capabilities and limitations can keep you out of potentially dangerous situations like airspeeds that are too slow or too fast, airplanes that are overloaded and fuel reserves that *should* have been adequate.

YOU LIFT ME UP

Before we can discuss much about anything to do with airplane performance, we have to first understand why an airplane flies.

An airplane (or any object for that matter) must somehow overcome gravity in order to fly. Nature supplies a force called *lift* to counter gravity and make flight possible. As the force of lift increases, it eventually overpowers gravity, which is a constant source, and the airplane flies.

Airplanes climb, fly and descend by increasing, maintaining and reducing lift, respectively.

As air passes over an airplane's wings, lift is generated. The majority of the lift an airplane generates is the result of Newton's third law of physics that says for every action there is an equal and opposite reaction. Have a look at figure 26. Air encounters the front of the wing and the wing's shape diverts the air downward. The diverted air flow is called *downwash*.

What's equal and opposite to downward? Upward, which is the effect the downwash has on the wing. The air moves down, the wing moves up. Newtons third law would make it seem as though any sturdy flat surface could be used to generate lift. And it can. The difference between an airplane's wing and a sheet of plywood is that the airplane is also aerodynamic, balanced and has an engine to propel it.

Additional lifting magic lies in the shape of the wing as seen from the side. (Figure 26, again.) Wings are designed in a shape that's called an *airfoil*. The sleek airfoil design helps generate additional lift using magical methods that I'll let your CFI explain. The majority of the lift, however, is credited to Newton's law. This airfoil stuff is just icing on the lift cake.

As more air passes over the wings, more lift is generated. At some point, the force of the lift generated by the increasing airflow overpowers gravity and the airplane flies. The way to move *more* air over a given wing is to increase the speed of the air. You could do this in a giant wind tunnel, but wind tunnels make longer trips less practical. Instead, we need a way to move the airplane *through* the air, thereby increasing the airflow over the wings. If you're thinking *engine*, you're on to something.

GETTING FORCEFUL WITH EVIL FORCES

In order to get an airplane to fly, we need to overcome gravity. Gravity wants to keep us planted firmly on the ground. If you think about it, the real cause of all airplane crashes (other than

Figure 26: *LIFTING THEORIES* There are a few theories as to how airplane wings generate lift. One experts seem to agree on is Newton's third law, which says for every action there is an equal and opposite reaction. As an airplane wing forces air downward, the wing is forced upward. Hash out other popular theories with your CFI.

midair collisions) is gravity. If anyone ever tells you that flying isn't safe, you assure them that flying is perfectly safe. It's gravity that's dangerous. Gravity *occasionally* takes an airplane down, but it takes stumbling children in playgrounds down every day. We don't hear about it on the news only because monkeybar mishaps are not within the jurisdiction of the NTSB.

Gravity is evil. (Until it's time to land, of course.) Gravity is also relentless. Keeping an airplane airborne is a constant fight to overcome this wicked force. Succeed and the airplane flies. Fail and the airplane falls.

Gravity has a partner-in-crime that's just as intent on preventing airplanes from flying: *drag*. The drag I speak of here has nothing to do with stiletto heels and feather boas. This drag is caused by friction in our atmosphere. Drag wants us to remain still. When we move, drag sees to it that we don't move far without continued effort.

The relationship between lift, gravity and drag is central to what fixed-wing aviation is all about. (*Fixed-wing* simply means that we use wings to generate lift as opposed to some other means, like a rotor blade or hot air.)

Figure 27: *PUSH ME, PULL YOU* The odd-looking thing we know of as an airplane, is a device designed to manipulate thrust, drag, lift and gravity in order to fly. Thrust moves us forward, drag pulls us back. Lift raises us, gravity pulls us down. These are the "4 forces" you'll hear about repeatedly throughout your training.

We need to move air over the wings to generate lift and overcome gravity, but we must first overcome drag in order to get that air moving. Luckily, as if by design, an airplane's engine provides a drag-fighting heroic force called *thrust*. Think of thrust as lift's partner in fighting the two evil forces. Together, they keep us airborne.

Thrust gets us moving, which moves air over our wings, which produces lift, which makes our airplane fly. When thrust overpowers drag, the airplane accelerates. This, in turn, moves more air over the wing and generates more lift. When lift overpowers gravity, the airplane climbs. When the forces are equal, the airplane maintains airspeed and altitude. When drag overcomes thrust, the airplane slows. This reduces the airflow over the wings and, in turn, reduces lift. As lift is reduced the airplane loses altitude.

The heart and soul of your airplane's ability to generate lift lies in its ability to overcome drag. We rely on the thrust generated by our engine to overcome drag, but, as we already learned, losing our engine doesn't mean that we come crashing down.

So how can an airplane continue to fly without an engine if we rely on the engine to overcome drag?

Without engine power, you need to find an alternate source of thrust to overcome drag, or your airplane is going to slow to the point where it can no longer remain airborne.

Here, we can use one of nature's evil forces to our advantage. By pushing the nose of the airplane down just a bit, we allow gravity to grab a hold and propel us, however gradually, toward Earth. Before long, we're moving air over our wings and once again generating lift, which further retards our descent. We're essentially using gravity as a source of thrust, but this brilliant idea won't work forever. For gravity to work as a "thrust generator," the airplane must be pointed downward. A downward-pointed airplane eventually flies to the same destination every time.

So by losing an engine, you lose your source of thrust, but that's all. By using gravity as an alternate source of thrust (in other words, gliding), you can slow your descent and bring your airplane down safely.

You might recall (or not) from high school physics class how perpetual motion isn't possible. Scientists tell us this because friction impedes an object's motion and friction is *everywhere* to one degree or another. Roll a ball and it eventually stops. Swing a pendulum and it eventually stops. The denser the atmosphere, the sooner the object stops moving.

On Earth, objects require a fairly constant source of thrust to remain in motion. This is because of the density of our atmosphere. It's easy to consider density and how it affects thrust and drag by comparing air to water. Swing your hand through the air and you meet *some* resistance.

Swing your hand through water, however, and you'll get some serious exercise. Water is much denser than air.

So wherever there is atmospheric density, there must be a source of thrust to overcome friction in order to keep objects moving.

Density, on the other hand, makes "lift" possible. Without at least *some* density in our atmosphere, an airfoil would have no effect. You could angle a wing any way you wanted, but it would never produce any lift, regardless of the speed at which the air traveled over the surface.

Think back to the arm-swinging exercise for a moment: If you angle your hand (like a wing) while you swing it through the water, you can raise and lower your arm pretty easily, even at slower speeds, by adjusting the angle of your hand. But if you swing your arm at the same speed through the air, and you adjust your hand to the same angles, you'll see no effect at all.

In denser atmospheres, lift can be generated at slower speeds. In less dense atmospheres, increased speed is required to produce lift. If an atmosphere had no density at all (I suppose this would be a lack of atmosphere, or a vacuum), lift would be impossible, regardless of speed.

It's important to remember that our discussion on atmospheric densities assumes a constant level of gravity. You'd have to be a pretty big idiot to spend much time sorting out how to generate lift in a zero-gravity environment.

Objects moving in outer space have significantly less friction to overcome because space lacks our dense atmosphere. This enables objects to travel much further on a smaller burst of thrust before they ultimately slow and stop. This is why, for example, the Star Trek series seems to run on forever.

But space travel, like multi-engine flying, requires an advanced rating. So we won't cover it here.

Let's come back to Earth for a review:

To fly, we need to overcome the two evil forces of nature: *drag* and *gravity*. Our engine provides the *thrust* we need to overcome drag, which affords us forward motion. That motion moves the airflow over our wings that we require to generate *lift*. The lift enables us to overcome gravity.

It's so very simple it's a wonder no one thought of it before me.

So now, when your FAA examiner asks you to explain the four forces that affect flight, you'll do so while imagining captains Kirk, Picard and Janeway twirling in stiletto heels, arms extended, feather boas dancing wildly in the dense atmospheric wind.

CONTROL ISSUES

Airplanes need to move in three dimensions. Conveniently, aircraft manufacturers equip airplanes with dohickies called *control surfaces* that make this possible.

Control surfaces enable pilots to manipulate an airplane's *attitude*. When we say "attitude" in aviation we refer to the airplane's position in three dimensional space, not its cranky disposition. For example, is the airplane level? Pointed upward? Banked left? Upside down? Control surfaces make attitude adjustments possible by temporarily changing the shape of the airplane, thereby affecting the way the airplane interacts with the on-coming airflow, which we call the *relative wind*.

The control surfaces found on most trainers are illustrated in figure 28. They are:

- **Flaps** – Typically found inward on the airplane's wings, the flaps' primary purpose is to enable a steeper decent angle without an increase in airspeed. (You'll see how shortly.) Flaps are raised and lowered by an electronic motor or a manual hand lever,

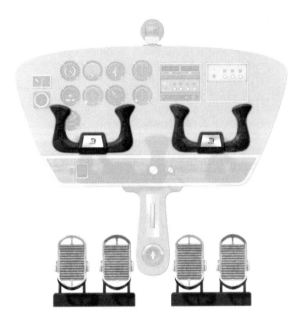

Figure 28: *THE REAL AIR TRAFFIC CONTROLLERS* Ailerons are controlled by turning the yoke left and right. They move opposite one another: as one goes up, the other goes down. Moving the yoke forward and back swings the elevator up and down. The rudder is controlled by the foot pedals and the flaps are either controlled by an electronic switch or a manual level, depending on the airplane model. The flaps, unlike the ailerons, move up and down in unison.

Figure 29: *CONTROL SURFACE CONTROLLERS* An airplane's yoke(s) and foot pedals are used to control the ailerons, elevator and rudder. The yoke rotates left and right like a steering wheel to control the ailerons, and forward and backward to control the elevator.

depending on the airplane model. Flaps always move in sync with one another. Technically, flaps are not considered a control surface because they do not change an airplane's attitude. But they fit nicely into this discussion.

- **Ailerons** – Working opposite one another (one flips up when the other flips down), ailerons (pronounced *ale'-eer-ons*) bank and turn the airplane. They're usually located alongside the flaps nearer the wing tips. Ailerons are controlled by turning the airplane's yoke (the airplane's "steering wheel") left and right. (Figure 29)

- **Rudder** – The rudder is attached to the airplane's vertical fin, which is called the *vertical stabilizer*. The rudder *does not* turn an airplane, but it does help an airplane turn properly. (Explained later.) The rudder is controlled using the airplane's foot pedals. The foot pedals are also used to steer the airplane when you're on the ground. (Figure 29)

- **Elevator** – The elevator is the flap-looking extension found on the rear of the airplane's horizontal stabilizer (the little wing at the back). Elevators force an airplane's rear either up or down, oppositely forcing the airplane's nose up or down for climbs and descents. The elevator is controlled by pushing the yoke forward (elevator down) and backward (elevator up).

A control surface is usually connected to the device that determines its position (yoke or foot pedals) by either a wire cable, metal rod, or both. No fancy connections are used here for good reason.

Using the most basic means of connecting flight controls to control surfaces, manufacturers reduce the likelihood that a control surface will become inoperable in flight. If your engine fails, your control surfaces continue to work. If your electrical system dies, your control surfaces continue to work. (Your flaps might be driven by an electric motor, but remember they are not actually control surfaces.)

Of all the airplane system failures that are possible, the loss of a control surface in flight can be the hardest to successfully overcome. This is not to say it's impossible to land an airplane with a control surface failure, but I'd personally rather land with a dead engine or electrical system. If a pilot safely lands an airplane after an engine failure, other pilots congratulate her on a job well done. If a pilot safely lands an airplane without the use of ailerons, that's one damn good (and lucky) pilot!

Recall the U.S. military spy plane that was forced to land in China in March of 2001. While the rest of the world was debating who was to blame for the accident, the aviation community was simply in awe of the pilot's ability to land the plane with so much structural damage.

THE CONTROL SURFACE PURPOSE

The forward profile of an airplane is designed to minimize the surface area of the airplane that hits the on-coming airflow. This is a basic aerodynamic principle: the less surface area to interfere with the on-coming airflow, the more efficient the design. Car manufacturers employ similar design concepts in the interest of fuel efficiency and performance.

When an airplane is flying straight and level (not turning and not climbing or descending), control surfaces are *almost* in their neutral positions. I say almost because center-of-gravity factors and various turning tendencies that affect trainer airplanes force the pilot to usually deflect one or more control surfaces slightly just to remain straight and level. But for the purpose of this discussion, let's assume that in straight and level flight, the control surfaces are in their neutral positions. (Figure 30)

Figure 30: *STRAIGHT AND LEVEL* With no control surfaces deflected, this airplane flies straight and level. This configuration is also referred to as 'clean' because there is minimal interference with the relative wind.

Figure 31: *CONTROL SURFACE DEFLECTION* The downward deflected right aileron (left) pushes the right wing up. The opposite happens on the other wing. Later we'll discuss how this turns the airplane.

When a control surface is moved, it temporarily changes the forward profile of the airplane. The oncoming airflow (relative wind) collides with the extended control surface and the control surface (with the airplane attached) and the relative wind each deflect to a certain degree. (Figure 31)

Airplane control surfaces work very much the same way a boat rudder works. When a boat rudder turns one way, the collision of the oncoming water with the rudder surface deflects each in opposite directions. The water is deflected one way and the boat's rear section is deflected in the opposite direction.

THE SURFACE VS. THE WIND

The balance of power in the battle between the relative wind and an airplane's control surfaces shifts as the airflow increases and decreases. The word we use to refer to these airflow velocity changes is *airspeed*. As airflow velocity increases, so increases our airspeed indication, and vice versa.

Control surfaces on slow moving airplanes, like those on slow moving boats, are less effective than they are when the vehicle is traveling fast. This is why large ships require the assistance of tug boats when moving through harbors; the ship is traveling too slowly for the rudder to have any useful effect.

As a vehicle picks up speed, the control surfaces become more effective, requiring less deflection to do their jobs.

Let's look at this more closely.

At slow airspeeds, the weaker relative wind is easily deflected by the control surface, hardly affecting the airplane's flight path at all. (Recall the large ship in the harbor.) When flying slowly, pilots must use exaggerated control inputs to get the airplane to respond.

As airspeed increases, the increasingly powerful relative wind eventually overpowers the control surface and the control surface must either yield (move) or break under the pressure. This is what changes the airplane's attitude. This is also what can cause control surface failures at excessive airspeeds. More on that later.

When the airplane's airspeed decreases, thereby decreasing the strength of the relative wind, the balance of power shifts back again. The airplane's weight and moment, and gravity eventually overpower the relative wind, making the control surfaces less effective.

If your airspeed declines enough so that the control surfaces have no effect whatsoever, they are said be *stalled*. Don't confuse a stall of this type with an engine stall. We typically don't use the term "stall" in aviation to describe a failed engine.

During your training you will practice flying your airplane as slowly as possible during a flight maneuver that's (not surprisingly) called *slow flight*. The purpose of slow flight is to get you used to the way the airplane's control surfaces behave with minimal airflow. Airplanes are harder to control when they fly slow and they tend to fly slow nearest the ground, during take-off and landing, when mistakes are least forgiving. This is why slow flight training is so important.

FREEWAY HAND FLYING

When I was a kid, I used to put my arm outside the car window, hold my hand at about a 20-degree angle to the horizon, and pretend my hand was an airplane wing. (Okay, I admit I still do this sometimes.) When the car was moving slowly, my hand would lie "grounded" on the top of the car door because the combined weight of my hand and arm overpowered any lifting force that my inefficient "handfoil" could generate.

But on speedier highways, my hand could fly! This was enormously cool and could entertain me for hours. As the car accelerated, my hand could eventually generate enough downward airflow deflection (lift) to overcome gravity.

As the car slowed, the amount of lift my hand was generating was reduced to the point where gravity won out. My hand would fall back down on the car door. If the car continued to accelerate, I would eventually have to reduce the angle at which I held my hand so it wouldn't fly all the way up to the car roof. Given a constant car speed (think airspeed), I could adjust the angle of my hand to determine its "altitude."

For the record, this variance of angle is called *angle of attack*. You'll hear more about that in ground-school and we'll talk a bit more about it later.

At the start of the hand/airflow conflict, my hand was the victor, forcing the relative wind to yield. But as the relative wind picked up speed (strength), the downward-deflected air from the bottom of my hand (lift) became stronger than gravity and my hand flew.

Airplanes work the same way: as the speed (strength) of the relative wind increases, the air colliding with the control surface becomes stronger, eventually overpowering the control surface's tendency to resist, thereby forcing the airplane to turn, climb or descend.

SPEED HIGHS

So what happens to a control surface if the relative wind becomes *too* strong because the airplane is flying too fast? The technical term is *structural damage*. For every airplane model there is an airspeed that manufacturers warn against exceeding. This is known as the airplane's *never-exceed* speed.

Airplanes have a series of specific airspeeds that are relevant for one reason or another: The never-exceed speed is one. The maximum speed at which flaps can be extended is another. The slowest airspeed at which the airplane can fly is another.

Collectively these are called *v-speeds*. I'm guessing that "V" stands for velocity. They are notated by a large V in front of one or more smaller characters that define the v-speed's meaning. Never-exceed speed is notated as V_{NE}. You'll see other v-speeds throughout the rest of this book.

Typically you'll never reach V_{NE} unless you're in an over-enthusiastic descent. The engine in your trainer simply won't have the power to get you there on its own. But if you're flying at full throttle

and you point your airplane's nose downward, you're adding gravity to your thrust arsenal, so V_{NE} becomes a concern.

If you exceed V_{NE}, you can break a control surface, or worse.

SPEED LOWS

At the opposite end of the dangerous-speed index are what we call the *stall speeds*. Just like an individual control surface can stall, so too can an entire wing. When you hear someone say that an airplane stalled, they are usually referring to a wing stall.

There is a minimum amount of airflow that must pass over the wings to keep an airplane airborne. If during a flight, the airplane slows to the point where this minimum amount of airflow isn't possible, the wings *stall*. A stalled wing produces no lift.

The nice thing about training aircraft is that they are designed to automatically recover from wing stalls with almost no effort on the pilot's part. For example, if your airspeed gets too slow and your airplane stalls, the airplane's nose drops and the airplane starts a descent. Can you guess what happens next? The airspeed increases, which is exactly what you need. When the airspeed climbs above stall speed, the wings once again generate lift and the stall is broken. This typically takes only a few seconds.

It's possible to stall one wing before the other. This can be dangerous and can lead to what we call *spins*. An airplane in a spin can be hard or impossible to recover. You aren't required to practice spins during your training, but you are required to understand how they can happen and how (in theory) you are supposed to recover from them.

There are a few types of spins, but luckily the most common is also the easiest to recover from. (Figure 32) The basic theory behind spin recovery

Figure 32: *SPIN* When one wing stalls before the other, it drops and the airplane might enter a spin. In this image the airplane's left wing stalled and dropped and the airplane entered the spin. This is the most common type of spin. Discuss spins and spin recovery with your CFI.

is to apply full *opposite* rudder to the direction of the spin, relax pressure on the yoke, and then, after the spin has stopped, gently pull back on the yoke to return to level flight.

Let's think about this for a moment. What good would opposite rudder do? Have a look at figure 32. That airplane is spinning to the left. If the pilot applied full right rudder, try to visualize what the airplane would do. It would "kick" itself out of the spiral pattern.

But why relax the yoke when we're already falling so fast? If an airplane is spinning, it is also stalled. (An airplane cannot spin unless it is stalled.) Pulling back on the yoke will do nothing but ensure that the airplane remains stalled. We want the airplane to take advantage of its native design to help break the stall. This happens only if we relax the yoke pressure and just let the airplane "be."

After the spinning stops, you'd *gently* pull back on the yoke to get the airplane back to level flight. If you pull back too quickly, you might enter another stall if your airspeed is too slow, or damage the elevator if your airspeed is too high.

The most important thing I can tell you about spins is that more student pilots were getting killed each year practicing them than there were pilots killing themselves by unintentionally entering them. This is why the FAA ceased requiring spin training for private pilots. If you want to experience a spin, have an aerobatic instructor take you up. Chances are a normal CFI hasn't had much experience with actual spins. Things can go wrong. You might as well have someone in the cockpit that will consider any unforeseen circumstance as "fun."

As mentioned, an airplane cannot spin if it is not stalled. This is why it's important to always maintain an airspeed well above your stall speed, especially when flying within a few thousand feet of the ground, which is common when you're setting yourself up to land. Your CFI will (or should) drive this point down your throat so I'll spare you here.

You'll practice stalling your airplane throughout your training. The idea to stall practice, however, is not to teach you how to stall an airplane, but to teach you how to safely recover from a stall. I went through the first 20 or so hours of my training wondering why it was so important for me to learn how to stall an airplane. When would I ever want to stall an airplane? I suppose I should have asked sooner.

AILERONS

Ailerons lift one wing while lowering the other. In essence they "roll" the airplane around an imaginary line that extends from the tip of the airplane's nose backward. This line is called the airplane's *longitudinal axis*. (Figure 33)

Odd as it might seem, ailerons are what pilots use to turn airplanes. This concept confuses more than a few student pilots who assume that the rudder (described later) does all the turning. In fact, you don't need a rudder at all to turn an airplane.

Figure 33: *LONGITUDINAL AXIS* Extending from the airplane's nose backward, is the longitudinal axis. The ailerons rotate the airplane around this imaginary line.

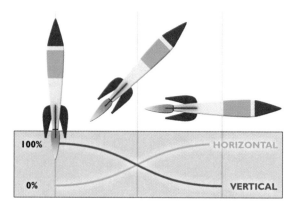

Figure 34: *LIFT SHIFT* A rocket's sole source of lift is the thrust generated by its engine. As the rocket tilts, part of that vertical lift is diverted sideways and pushes the rocket off in a new direction. The rocket starts to climb more slowly because of that loss of vertical lift. As the rocket continues to tilt, the remaining vertical lift is diverted sideways. The rocket is now traveling horizontally very fast, but will eventually tumble back to Earth because it has no more vertical lift to counter gravity.

So how does raising one wing higher than the other turn the airplane? The credit goes to lift. Only this time the lift isn't vertical, it's horizontal. Recall our discussion on how a wing's downwash helps propel the wing upward. So what happens to that downwash if the wing is tilted? Sidewash! This isn't an actual aviation term, but it helps illustrate what's going on when an aileron raises a wing.

Let's use a rocket as an example of how lift can shift from being vertical to being horizontal. A rocket uses the thrust of its engine as its only source of lift. But what happens if you turn a skyward-rocketing rocket slightly sideways? As you can guess, it starts to drift off to one side. This is because some of that vertical lift has been diverted to horizontal lift. (Figure 34)

The amount of lift the rocket engine generates is finite, so as some lift is diverted sideways, less is available to propel the rocket vertically. As the rocket starts to turn, it also starts to climb at a slower rate.

If you continued to tilt the rocket, it would continue on an increasingly horizontal path. Its vertical climb speed would also continue to slow as more and more lift was diverted horizontally.

Eventually the rocket would become horizontal. At this point there would be no vertical lift at all. The rocket would be traveling horizontally at maximum speed, but it would also start falling back to Earth because without any vertical lift, there is no force to overcome gravity.

Now let's relate this to an airplane. As the ailerons lower one wing and raise the other, the airplane, like our rocket above, tilts. What was once downwash lifting the wing has now become that "sidewash" we mentioned. The more the airplane tilts, the more downwash becomes sidewash.

Remember that "sidewash" is technically referred to as the *horizontal component of lift*. This horizontal lift "slides" the airplane one way or the

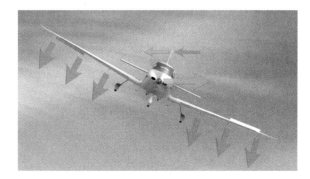

Figure 35: *TURNING TAILS* As the horizontal component of lift shoots off to the left (large blue arrows), sliding this airplane toward the right, the vertical stabilizer (tail section) hits the oncoming sideways airflow (small blue arrow) and resists the slide. The result is that the nose slides more and the airplane turns.

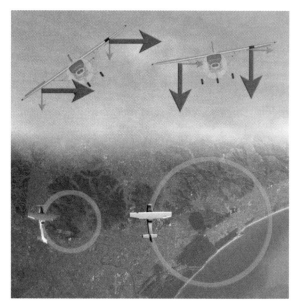

Figure 36: *HORIZONTAL COMPONENT OF TIGHTER CIRCLES* As ailerons are deflected, part of the vertical lift is diverted horizontally, thereby requiring additional power to maintain airspeed and altitude. The more the ailerons are deflected, the more lift is diverted and the tighter the airplane's turning radius becomes. The large arrows in this image show the balance of lift shifting from vertical (right) to horizontal (left). If the airplane were turned completely sideways (90° bank), there would be no vertical lift left at all.

other, depending on which wing is up. If the right wing is up, the airplane slides to the left. This continued process turns the airplane.

Okay, so now we have a sideways moving airplane. This still doesn't explain why it turns. But think about that big ol' tail sticking up at the back of the airplane we call the vertical stabilizer. What do you imagine happens when the airplane starts moving sideways? The oncoming airflow (relative wind) hits the tail, which creates some resistance and causes the back end of the airplane to slide sideways *less* than the front end. The net result is that the nose of the airplane is pointed in the direction of the turn and the airplane turns. (Figure 35)

The official answer to "What turns an airplane?" is *the horizontal component of lift*. The more complete answer is, "The horizontal component of lift shifts the airplane sideways. The vertical stabilizer resists the sideways movement and the nose of the airplane shifts faster. This turns the airplane."

Like a rocket's engine, the lift an airplane wing generates is finite. As we divert some of it sideways to turn, we lose some that we depended on to keep us aloft. The steeper the

bank, the more of an issue this becomes. In order to maintain our altitude, we need to pull back on the yoke.

If we don't manipulate the yoke to compensate for the loss of vertical lift in a turn, we'll lose some altitude. We won't come crashing down to the ground, but we might fail our checkride. You are expected to maintain altitude within certain tolerances during all flight maneuvers to demonstrate that you understand the connection between horizontal and vertical lift.

A 45-degree turn yields a much tighter turning radius than does a 20-degree turn, but it also requires more back-pressure (pulling back) on the yoke to maintain the same altitude. (Figure 36)

Adding back-pressure increases lift, but anytime you increase lift, you also increase drag. Knowing that thrust overcomes drag, you'll need to add some power when you turn if you want to maintain altitude and airspeed. If you don't add power you'll start to lose airspeed. When you start to lose airspeed, you'll start to lose lift. When you start to lose lift, you'll start losing altitude. To maintain altitude you'll need to pull back on the yoke, which increases drag. To compensate for the added drag, you'll need to add power.

So no matter which way you look at it, you need to do what you need to do. If you know what to do ahead of time, you'll be able to maintain your altitude and airspeed gracefully. Otherwise you'll be playing catch-up.

During your training you'll practice a maneuver called *steep turns* that demonstrates these concepts.

Summarizing ailerons:

- Ailerons work opposite one another: one goes up as the other goes down.

- Airplanes turn because of the horizontal component of lift, which is created when the ailerons bank the airplane.

- As horizontal lift increases, vertical lift decreases.

Ailerons are a great example of a control surface that you wouldn't want to lose. Can you turn an airplane without using the ailerons? Yes, using the rudder, but it's not an efficient thing to do. It's kind of like walking your dog by pushing on his tail.

But didn't I just say a page or so back that the rudder *doesn't* turn the airplane? I was actually telling you the truth. Only the horizontal component of lift can turn an airplane. The trick lies in generating horizontal lift by using only your rudder. After you read the next section you'll know how.

Figure 37: *VERTICAL AXIS* The rudder rotates the airplane around its vertical axis. This affects the airplane's attitude, but it does not, in and of itself, turn the airplane.

RUDDER

Let me be the first to say to you, "More right rudder!" You'll hear this phrase from your CFI more times than you can imagine. You'll hear it in your sleep.

The rudder rotates the airplane around another imaginary line called the *vertical axis*. (Figure 37)

If the wings generate the lift that moves an airplane up and down, and the ailerons are used to turn the airplane left and right, what's left to do? Who needs a friggin' rudder?

While it's true that you could fly much farther ignoring your rudder than you could ignoring some other control surface, your flight wouldn't be very efficient with regard to aerodynamic sleekness. This is because single-engine prop airplanes have mysterious left-turning tendencies, which I'll let your groundschool instructor explain. (Okay, they're not really mysterious.)

So you have an airplane that's trying to turn slightly left and a rudder-fearing pilot whose compensating by using slight right aileron. The net result is increased drag. Use of the rudder enables pilots to offset the airplane's natural left-turn tendencies.

Let me clarify something. When I say "left-turning tendencies," I really mean "left-yawing tendencies." Yaw describes the alignment of the airplane's longitudinal axis to the airplane's flight path. Refer back to figure 33 to imagine the airplane's flight path in relation to its longitudinal axis.

For example, let's say that the airplane is flying straight ahead, but it's cocked to the left. Here we'd say it is yawed to the left. The application of right-rudder would fix this. By applying the rudder we rotate the airplane around its vertical axis, thereby realigning its longitudinal axis. (Figure 38)

It's a bit confusing to grasp at first, but keep in mind that anytime you manipulate an individual control surface, you are rotating the airplane around one axis to realign another axis. For example, let's say you deflect the ailerons to turn to the left. You are rotating the airplane around its longitudinal axis to realign its vertical axis. When you apply right-rudder to compensate for left-yawing tendencies, you are rotating the airplane around its vertical axis to realign its longitudinal axis.

I've heard commercial airliner pilots joke that they haven't used the rudder in years. This isn't actually truthful, but rather a joke underscoring the reduced need for constant rudder control in multi-engine airplanes, which lack the left-turning tendencies suffered by single-engine prop planes.

During a turn, the rudder helps you align the airplane with the arced flight path. Because of the airplane's natural tendency to yaw to the left, you'll find that you sometimes don't need

Figure 38: *RIGHT RUDDER!* The airplane on the left is yawed and no rudder correction has been applied. On the right, the pilot has applied proper rudder correction to (rudder circled) realign the airplane's longitudinal axis. A yawed airplane flies less efficiently because the relative wind hits the side of the fuselage, increasing drag.

any rudder deflection on shallower left turns. You just reduce the amount of right-rudder pressure you were using to keep the airplane flying straight. (Figure 39)

What's really odd to me is that sometimes I need right rudder even in a left turn! This happens when the left turn is shallow enough so the left-yawing tendencies of the airplane are still overbearing. This is most noticeable during a climbing left turn. (The airplane's left-turning tendencies are increased during climbs.) Conversely, when you turn right, you need even more right-rudder. (Figure 40)

Can the airplane fly without this yaw correction? Sure it can, but less efficiently because the relative wind is now not only hitting the front of the airplane, but the side too. A sideways-cocked airplane isn't very aerodynamic and can, in some

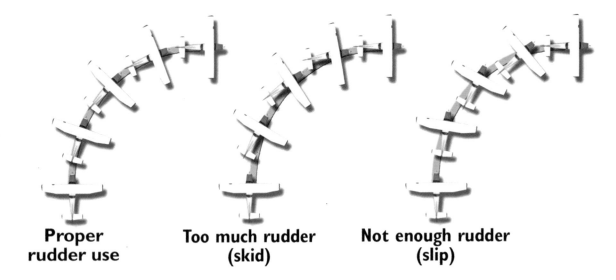

**Proper
rudder use**   **Too much rudder
(skid)**   **Not enough rudder
(slip)**

Figure 40: *CLEAN TURNS* When proper rudder pressure is applied, the airplane's longitudinal axis is aligned with the flight path (left). If too much rudder is used, the airplane's tail "skids" out. This is called a skidding turn (center). When a pilot fails to apply enough rudder, the airplane's tail "slips" inside the flight path, putting the airplane into a slipping turn (right).

cases, be unsafe. So when I say that you can get away without using the rudder, don't assume I'm saying you don't really need your rudder. You can also fly with your eyes closed, but I don't recommend that either.

JUDGING PROPER RUDDER USE

So how do you know when you're using the rudder properly? Old-timers will tell you that if you *fly by the seat of your pants*, you'll know all you need to know. This is because it's possible to "feel" when an airplane is out of proper yaw alignment, especially in a turn. During a turn, you and your passengers shouldn't feel any sense of sideways pressure at all.

If the rudder is used properly, you feel nothing more than an increase in downward pressure against your seat. This increased pressure is caused by yet another evil natural force: *centrifugal force*. Centrifugal force wants the airplane to continue flying in the direction it was flying before the turn started.

As we've discussed, you need an opposing force to counter each of these evil forces of nature. As luck and physics would have it, we have an opponent to counter centrifugal force. The horizontal component of lift takes on centrifugal force while your remaining vertical component of lift handles the ever-evil gravity.

But only with proper rudder use can the horizontal component of lift hit centrifugal force squarely on the jaw, thereby negating its side-pulling effect.

If while turning you feel yourself forced sideways one way or the other, then centrifugal force and the horizontal component of lift are not in balance. When the two forces are in check, you and your passengers feel no sideways force at all and sarcastic comments from your CFI about rudder use are minimized for the duration of the turn.

Imagine driving at 50 mph and turning on a flat surface. You'd feel a strong pull toward the direction in which you were originally driving.

Figure 39: *RIGHT RUDDER, MAYBE!* The airplane's left-turning tendencies make the application of right rudder for the top airplane's right turn absolutely necessary. The pilot of the bottom airplane has applied no rudder pressure at all. The airplane's natural left-turning tendencies have aligned the longitudinal axis with the turn arc.

Your car might even skid. But if the turn were to happen on a banked roadway, like a highway on-ramp that was designed for the posted speed limit, you wouldn't feel the sideways force at all (unless you were traveling faster than the posted speed limit). The forces would be in balance, which makes the turn possible and safe. By using your rudder to keep the airplane properly aligned with the turning flight path, you can keep the forces in balance aloft too.

For those of us less attuned to "feel" and more attuned to gauge readings, there are flight instruments that can help. One is called a *turn & slip indicator* and the other is simply called a *turn coordinator*. Your airplane will have one or the other. The premise of these instruments is simple: keep a ball that is floating in liquid centered. If the airplane is yawed, the ball will be displaced. (Figure 41)

For the purposes of this discussion we're going to focus on the turn coordinator. Use of the turn and slip indicator is similar, but that instrument lacks the cool little airplane.

When the wings of the little airplane are aligned with either of the two angled tick marks on the turn coordinator, as shown in figure 41, the airplane is said to be in a *standard rate turn*, which is an 18-20 degree turn in most training airplanes. The word "standard" here applies more to aircraft flying under IFR than it does to you and me. VFR pilots use bank angles steeper than standard all the time. A "normal" turn for us will be about 30 degrees and a "steep" turn will require a 45-degree bank.

IFR pilots limit themselves to this somewhat shallow bank angle to keep the possibility of spatial disorientation to a minimum and so that turns can be timed accurately. The "Two Minutes" indication on the turn coordinator's dial means that a 360-degree turn at standard rate will take two minutes. So a 180-degree turn would only take one minute. A 90-degree turn would take 30 seconds and so on. There are legitimate reasons for an IFR pilot to know how long a turn will take, but you'll learn about that during your instrument training.

It's easy to know which rudder pedal to use by remembering the phrase "step on the ball." For example, if the ball is to the right, step on it with the right rudder pedal until the ball centers.

TURNING AN AIRPLANE USING ONLY THE RUDDER
Here's the section I teased you about earlier. You can use a rudder (only) to turn your airplane, but it requires some brain flexing to understand why it works.

Figure 41: *TURN COORDINATOR* A turn is said to be coordinated when the ball (circled) remains centered throughout. In this image, the pilot must "step on the ball" with the right rudder to coordinate her turn. The airplane object is actually an indicator that tilts left and right. When level, it indicates the airplane is flying straight ahead. When the airplane's wing tip aligns with the lower tick marks, the airplane is in a standard rate turn. The "2 MIN" indication on the dial tells us that a 360-degree turn at standard rate will take 2 minutes to complete, though the exact timing can vary somewhat for each airplane.

Figure 42: *RUDDER TAKING TURNS* A rudder can be used to turn an airplane without the use of ailerons. As the rudder rotates the airplane around its vertical axis, one wing is "pushed" forward while the other is "pushed" backward. The net effect is that the forward wing is "faster" and therefore generates more lift. Meanwhile, the opposite wing slows and generates less lift. The difference between the lift generated tilts the airplane on its longitudinal axis just like ailerons do. The horizontal component of lift takes it from there.

Think back to our conversation on lift. We know that in order to generate lift, there must be a certain amount of air flowing over the airfoil generating the lift. As that airflow decreases, lift is reduced. As the airflow increases, lift increases.

Okay, here's where the minor nuances of airflow over control surfaces really hits the old noggin with some impact. When you deflect the rudder one way or the other, you rotate the airplane around its vertical axis. This pushes one wing forward and pulls one wing backward. Airflow increases over the "forward" wing, which, in turn, increases the lift generated by that wing and the wing goes up. Airflow and lift decrease for the "back" wing so that wing drops.

And what happens when one wing is up and the other is down? We get that good ol' horizontal component of lift and the airplane turns. (Figure 42)

So, should pilots use the rudder turn the airplane? No, the rudder should be used only to adjust the airplane's yaw. Can a rudder be used to turn an airplane? Yes.

WHEN YOU SLIP YOU FALL

There are situations in which you'll purposefully want to displace an airplane's yaw to create additional drag. Our little airplanes don't have air brakes, so increasing drag is our only way of dropping airspeed and, optionally, altitude quickly.

Figure 43: *SLIP IT IN!* The pilot on the left is using a side slip to drop airspeed and altitude on her final approach. (Winds are not an issue.) She has applied left rudder and just enough right aileron to cancel the effects of the left turn that would otherwise be caused by the "fast" right wing. There's a strong crosswind on the field in the right image, as indicated by the arrows and the very small windsock to the right of the 30 runway numbers. To compensate, this pilot is using a forward slip. Left ailerons are used to counter the force of the crosswind and opposite rudder is applied to straighten out the airplane's longitudinal axis. This slip can be maintained all the way through touchdown. The upwind wheel (left) will touchdown first.

Flap deployment increases drag, but flaps are not meant to be lowered and retracted quickly. What's more, lowering flaps at higher airspeeds can damage the flaps and the mechanism that controls them.

For a momentary "burst" of drag, pilots of small aircraft perform what we call *slips*.

There are two types of slips: *side slip* and *forward slip*. A side slip is usually used to quickly drop airspeed and, optionally, altitude. A forward slip is usually used to compensate for a crosswind during landing. Either can be used in just about any situation at the pilot's preference. (Figure 43)

Remember them like this: During a side slip, the airplane's longitudinal axis (nose to tail) is aligned sideways. During a forward slip, the airplane's longitudinal axis is aligned forward.

The idea behind a side slip is to rotate the airplane around its vertical axis in order to turn the airplane's fuselage into a giant air brake. Side slips are handy during an approach to landing when you can't use your flaps, or when you're above the speed at which it's safe to use your flaps, and you need to lose altitude and/or airspeed quickly.

To enter a side slip, you apply rudder in one direction while applying just enough aileron in the *opposite direction* to counter the turn tendency caused by the rudder. (Remember from figure 42 how the "fast" wing will raise and initiate a turn.)

So if you use right-rudder, you'd turn the yoke to the left. This turns the airplane's fuselage somewhat sideways into the relative wind, thereby dramatically increasing drag.

You'll notice during slips that the ball of the turn coordinator is not centered. This is exactly what you want for a slip, and it helps illustrate how a non-centered ball during "normal" flight is less efficient. Whenever you see the turn coordinator's ball to one side or the other, you're in a slip or a skid, whether it's intentional or not.

So, when you're CFI is barking, "more right rudder!" it's because you're flying with the side of your airplane's fuselage facing into the relative wind.

Keep an eye on the airspeed indicator during side slips. You'll be amazed at how quickly it drops. You'll eventually need to reduce or remove the slip, or push the nose forward to maintain a safe airspeed.

You'll most likely use side slips intermittently, meaning that you'll enter one for 15 seconds or so and then release it. You won't enter a side slip and maintain it all the way to the ground. If you ever use a side slip near the end of an approach make sure you remove the slip before you touchdown on your main landing gear (the ones under the wings). The main landing gear is fixed in position, so if the airplane is in a side slip when you touchdown, the gear will hit the runway sideways. The gear could collapse if you hit hard enough.

Keep in mind that side slips are an option when you need them, but you might go many, many flights without ever using one. If you find that you frequently need them during approaches— the term used for the final phase of flight that precedes landing—you might want to reconsider how you set up your approaches. If you prepare for an approach properly, a side slip shouldn't be necessary.

Forward slips are used to counter crosswinds on landing. Crosswinds make it tough to keep the airplane properly aligned with the runway: you get yourself centered on final approach and then the wind blows you left or tight. The strength of the crosswind determines the amount of forward slip required.

To enter a forward slip, you'd apply as much aileron as necessary to counter the drift of the crosswind and keep the airplane centered on the runway. Effectively, you are turning into the wind to the same degree the crosswind is blowing the airplane sideways, thereby nullifying the drift influence of the wind. But since you are technically in a turn, however slight, one wing is high and the airplane's longitudinal axis is no longer aligned with the runway. This is where the rudder comes into play. Apply enough *opposite* rudder to straighten out the nose. So if you're turned to the right, use left rudder. Maintain this attitude right through touchdown.

During a forward slip the airplane flies straight ahead with one wing higher than the other. You'll touchdown on the low wheel first, which is the idea. This was very hard for me to grasp at first. My equilibrium just wanted that airplane to fly wings-level. It takes some getting used to, but it sure beats trying to find another runway that has no crosswind. (More on crosswind landings in "Crosswinds making you cross" on page 235.)

It's hard sometimes to keep the differences between the two types of slips straight. So let's summarize them for comparison:

- Side slips are primarily used to reduce airspeed and/or altitude at any stage of a flight.

- Forward slips are primarily used to counter crosswinds on landing.

- Side slips use the rudder as the primary control surface. Ailerons are used, as necessary, to keep the airplane flying straight ahead.

- Forward slips use the ailerons as the primary control surface. Rudder is used as necessary to keep the nose of the airplane aligned with the runway.

- Side slips turn the airplane's fuselage (longitudinal axis) sideways, thereby increasing drag and reducing airspeed. Wings remain level.

- Forward slips raise one wing, effectively turning the airplane into the crosswind. Rudder is used to align the fuselage (longitudinal axis) with the runway.

- Side slips must be removed prior to touchdown to avoid landing gear damage from the sideways impact.

- Forward slips are maintained throughout approach and touchdown to prevent the airplane from drifting off the runway.

Practice both types with your CFI. If your airport doesn't have significant crosswinds, find one that does and practice.

So you can see that the "useless" rudder actually has many uses. The coolest pilots avoid aviator sunglasses and use their rudders properly.

Summarizing the rudder:

- The rudder rotates the airplane around its vertical axis.

- The rudder helps coordinate turns by aligning the airplane's longitudinal axis with the turning flight path.

- The application of at least some right-rudder pressure is required most of the time in single-engine training airplanes because of their left-yawing tendencies.

If you lost your rudder during flight, you'd be in much better shape than if you'd lost your ailerons. And now, if you ever do lose your ailerons, you'll remember there's still a way to turn the airplane, albeit less efficiently.

Just be aware of the rudder's real purpose so if you ever do have to get along without it, you'll know what's been compromised. And keep an occasional eye on that ball in the turn coordinator. Keep it centered and your CFI will be so amazed that she'll not know what to do with herself.

ELEVATOR

The elevator is well named, doing exactly what you think it would do. It makes the airplane go up and down. Technically, we know that an increase or decrease in lift is what makes an airplane go up and down, but the elevator helps us control the airplane's attitude so that we can, in turn, increase and decrease lift.

The elevator helps rotate the airplane around its *lateral axis*. (Figure 44) I say "help" because an increase or reduction in power will also rotate the airplane around the lateral axis to a degree. When you decrease power, the nose drops. This is also a rotation around the lateral axis.

The elevator is located on the rearward edge of the horizontal stabilizer, which is the smaller wing at the tail section of the airplane. Some airplanes, like the Piper Warrior, have what's called a *stabilator*, which is a horizontal stabilizer that rotates as a single unit. There is no separate elevator. Functionally, stabilators work the same as elevators. We'll use the term elevator to refer to both throughout this section.

Recalling our discussion on how an airplane's flight controls rotate the airplane on one axis in order to realign another axis, the elevator rotates the airplane on its lateral axis in order to realign its longitudinal axis up or down. (Figure 45)

Figure 45: *GOING DOWN?* The elevator forces the tail section of the airplane up or down, which forces the nose oppositely. The rotation takes place around the airplane's lateral axis (the one that goes through the wings, not shown here), and realigns the airplane's longitudinal axis, shown here as a blue line.

Figure 44: *LATERAL AXIS* Extending from wing tip to wing tip is the airplane's lateral axis. The elevator rotates the airplane around this axis to climb and descend. The absolute position of the lateral axis depends on the airplane's center of gravity, which varies from flight to flight.

When the elevator is raised, the rear of the airplane is forced downward, which raises the nose. This increases the amount of surface area on the underside of the wings that directly hits the relative wind. The degree at which a wing encounters the relative wind is called the airplane's *angle of attack*. (Figure 46)

The higher the nose, the higher the angle of attack. And the higher the angle of attack, the higher the *potential* for lift and the higher the drag.

I say "potential" because without adequate power (thrust), higher angles of attack just produce additional drag.

Remember, drag is lift's evil nemesis. Where there is lift, there is drag. When lift increases, drag increases. If sufficient thrust is available to overcome the added drag brought on by the increased angle of attack, lift is increased and the airplane climbs. If there is not adequate thrust to overcome the added drag and enable the airplane to climb, the airplane simply loses airspeed.

This is a good time to think back to our discussion on stalls. You'll often hear about your airplane's *stall speed*, but then you'll also read that an airplane can stall at any speed. This baffled me to no end during my training. There are two *absolute* situations at which your airplane will stall. One is when your airspeed drops below a certain level (stall speed). No matter what your angle of attack the airplane will stall. The second situation is when your angle of attack has exceeded a certain degree, which is called the airplane's *critical angle of attack*. At that point, the airplane will stall no matter what your airspeed.

It's helpful to consider a wing's critical angle of attack like this: Do you expect a wing to generate lift when it's level with its flight path? Sure. Do you expect a wing to generate lift when it's at a 90 degree angle to its flight path? Of course not. It

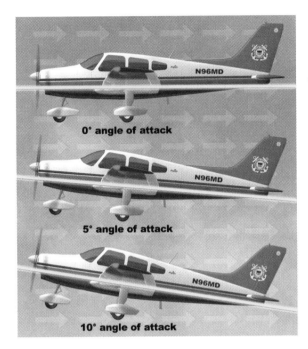

Figure 46: *ATTACK ANGLES* This airplane is shown at three different angles of attack, the angle of the bottom airplane being the greatest of the three. At greater angles of attack, the bottom of the wing encounters (and diverts down and back) more of the relative wind, thus increasing both lift and drag.

would be nothing more than a huge air brake at that point. So somewhere between "level" and 90 degrees must be the magical breaking point. That magic angle is the critical angle of attack.

Keep in mind an airplane's performance characteristics—including its critical angle of attack—take into consideration the airplane as a whole. So when Cessna says that a 172's critical angle of attack is *x* degrees, they say so assuming that the 172 will not be hot-rodded with the jet engine from an F-16. Considering the *available thrust*, the 172 has a given critical angle of attack. If the 172's engine was far more powerful, the airplane's critical angle of attack would be greater. Consider the many fighter jets that can climb vertically. They wouldn't be able to do so with the engine of a 172, regardless of wing design.

Think back to our freeway-hand-flying topic back on page 109. Given a constant airspeed (the speed of the car), we could generate more and less lift by gradually changing what we now know as the angle of attack of our hand. If we increase our angle of attack toward 90 degrees, our hand eventually "stalls" and drops because the drag caused by our hand's increasing vertical profile has overcome the lift produced. (I'm not sure what the actual critical angle of attack is for a hand!) Our lift-to-drag ratio has gone completely in favor of drag. We're generating no lift at all.

Get that car going 200 mph and your hand will "fly" at a much greater angle before stalling.

THE ELEVATOR'S PARTNER

Think of the elevator as a control surface with a full-time partner. This partner is the throttle control. Most of the time you make a significant change in the position of the elevator, you will also make a throttle adjustment.

For the purposes of this discussion, I want you to think of the throttle as the "thrust controller." Push it forward and it generates more thrust. Pull it back and it reduces thrust.

The partnership comes from the fact that changes in the elevator's position usually require either an increase or decrease in thrust.

When you push the yoke forward, thereby lowering the elevator, you force the airplane's nose downward. Gravity soon kicks in as a secondary source of thrust and the airplane's airspeed increases. To maintain your current airspeed, you reduce power (thrust) by pulling back on the throttle. If you don't reduce power, the two forces of thrust will cause your airplane to gain airspeed. If you ever look at the airspeed gauge on your airplane and wonder how the airplane could ever reach those higher numbers. Push the nose down without decreasing power and you'll find out.

The opposite happens when you pull back on the yoke. By raising the elevator, you increase lift and drag, which means your current power setting will probably be inadequate. The pee-shooter prop engines on most trainers are so meager that full-power settings are usually required for all climbs.

So, if a climbing airplane slows, does that mean we're somehow losing thrust? Technically no. We just "repurpose" thrust during climbs. Think back to what happens when an airplane turns. Part of the vertical component of lift generated by the wings becomes horizontal lift. It's still there, but it's now doing a different job. The same concept applies to thrust. When an airplane is flying straight and level, 100% of the engine's available thrust is being used to propel the aircraft horizontally. But when you point the airplane upward in a climb, a portion of the horizontal thrust becomes vertical thrust. With less available thrust to propel the airplane horizontally, it slows. Conversely, when the airplane's nose is pointing downward, the engine's vertical thrust is helping to drive the airplane down.

Summarizing the elevator:

- A downward-deflected elevator lowers the airplane's nose. A reduction in power is usually required to keep the airplane's airspeed from getting out of hand.

- An upward-deflected elevator raises the airplane's nose. An increase in power is usually required to keep the airplane's airspeed from falling too low.

Losing your elevator will make flight tough, but not necessarily impossible. As a substitute, you'd have to rely on power settings to climb and descend. You know that a faster airplane wants to climb and a slower one wants to fall. Use that knowledge to your advantage in case you ever have to fly without the use of your elevator. (Also ask your CFI to demonstrate how the elevator's trim tab can help too.)

Figure 47: *TAKING OFF SOFTLY* This airplane has just departed from a grass airstrip (soft field) using partial flaps. The left (port) flap can be seen in this image just above the landing gear.

A malfunctioning elevator stuck either up or down is very bad news. Most airplanes would not be able to overcome a mess like this. You might recall the Alaska Airlines jet that went down in the seas north of Los Angeles back in 2000. That crash was cause by an elevator that was stuck in a down position. The airplane entered a nose dive from which recovery just wasn't possible.

The elevator is a great control surface to check thoroughly during your preflight inspection.

FLAPS

Flaps are not considered control surfaces because they do not control an airplane's attitude, nor are they required for flight. But I figured this was a handy place to talk about them.

Flaps extend from the rear of the wing surface and remain flush with the wing when retracted, or flip downward when deployed. When deployed, flaps change the "shape" of the wing, from the perspective of the relative wind. (Figure 47)

There are many different types of wing flaps and I've yet to know why it's important for student pilots to understand the differences between them all. We'll leave that torture to your groundschool instructor.

Figure 48: *FUN WITH FLAPS* Flaps increase lift and drag at the same time. The more the flaps are lowered, the more drag they introduce. Use of full flaps (left) enables an airplane to descend at a steeper angle without gaining airspeed. When flaps are lowered just a bit, say 10° (right), they increase the wing's ability to generate lift without introducing too much drag. This flap configuration might be used when the airplane is taking off from a grass or dirt runway (what we call a *soft field*) because the pilot wants to get the airplane out of the muck as soon as possible.

Flaps can be lowered in varying degrees, which controls the effect they have. When deployed at lesser degrees, flaps increase lift and introduce only a small degree of additional drag. Some airplanes use small degrees of flaps for take-off. (Figure 48)

When deployed at higher degrees, the lift-to-drag ratio flips and the flaps introduce more drag than they do lift. This is the idea behind the use of full flaps when an airplane is inbound to land.

The FAA wants you to remember that flaps are used to *steepen descent angle without increasing airspeed*. This notion is right out of the FAA written test.

Technically the FAA's statement is true, but it's vague. Exactly *how* do the flaps steepen the descent angle without increasing airspeed? And why do I care? Further, the FAA explanation doesn't take into consideration the use of flaps on takeoff by some aircraft. But let's explore what they mean by steepening descent without increasing airspeed. (Get out your falsies, readers, it's time to get back to the drag bar.)

Flaps deployed at higher angles increase drag considerably. Increased drag reduces the effect of the available thrust. Reduced thrust means reduced airspeed and less airspeed means less lift. When airplanes lose lift they descend. With absolutely no lift at all, an airplane would fall vertically like a rock. So by reducing lift with flaps, the airplane leaves level flight and descends at an angle somewhere between level flight and falling like a rock. (Figure 49)

But how do we steepen the descent angle without increasing the airspeed?

If while flying level you push the nose downward, you'll enter a descent. But you'll also pick up airspeed. It's like coasting down a hill without using brakes. The more you push forward, the steeper your angle of descent and the faster you'll go.

The important difference between a simple nose-down descent and a descent that uses flaps is that while you are in a nose-down, airspeed-increasing descent, you are *not reducing lift*. In fact, the increase in airspeed increases lift! You'll find yourself having to push down on the yoke harder

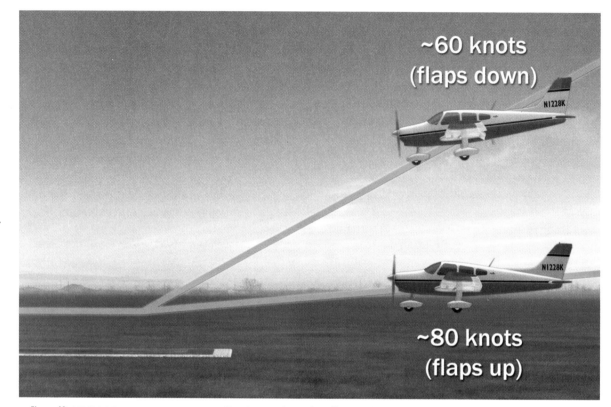

Figure 49: *HIGH OR LOW, FAST OR SLOW* Flaps increase drag and enable an airplane to descend at a steeper angle while still remaining relatively slow. Without flaps (and the increase in drag they provide) an airplane must come in at a shallower descent angle because a steeper angle would increase airspeed. Steep descent angles are preferable because they enable the airplane to maintain altitude for as long as possible and they help keep the airplane clear of ground obstacles that lie in the approach path. Slower airspeeds are preferable (unless there's a strong crosswind) because you want the airplane traveling as slow as safely possible when it touches down. Flaps also enable an airplane to fly at a slower airspeed before it stalls, so flap-less landings require some additional airspeed as a safety margin. You can land an airplane without flaps, and you should practice doing so. But under ordinary circumstances flaps can enhance safety, so use them.

and harder because the airplane will be fighting to stay airborne. And staying airborne is exactly *not* what you want to do when it's time to land.

So by forcing the nose down, you achieve only one of the functions of flaps: You increase your angle of descent. But the by-product is that you increase airspeed and, therefore, lift.

Don't get me wrong: if you force the nose down you *will* descend. It's not like the added lift will overpower you and force you to remain airborne

forever. But you will also pick up airspeed, which you don't want when you're setting up to land. If you've got a lot of altitude to lose and want to pick up some time, go ahead and start a descent this way. But if you keep this angle all the way to the runway, you might find that you're trying to set the airplane down at 140 or so knots, when typically we touch down at 50 or 60 knots.

Fully deployed flaps *first* increase drag, which reduces airspeed. The airspeed reduction, in turn, reduces lift. This is why flaps, as the FAA says, can

KNOTS VS. MILES PER HOUR CONVERSION

Common Speeds	Knots Per Hour (MPH / .8688)	Miles Per Hour (knots *1.151)
Lift off	55	63
Cruise Flight	110	127
In the Pattern	85	98
Final Approach	60	69

Figure 50: *FLAP FLIPPER* Most Cessna trainers have flap-position switches located toward the bottom of the instrument panel on the passenger side. The "stair stepped" position settings enable the pilot to choose flap settings by "feel" without having to actually look at the switch. Cessna aircraft have electrical motors that actually move the flaps; these switches control those motors. Piper flap levers look (and work) like parking brake levers found in some cars. As you pull up on the lever, the flaps deploy. Piper flap levers are physically connected to the flaps by rods and cables.

steepen your angle of descent without increasing airspeed. The airplane descends, but it doesn't gain unwanted airspeed. In fact, once those flaps are deployed, you'll need to force the nose down just to maintain airspeed.

There is a consistent relationship between lift, drag and the various flap positions. When flaps are retracted, they cause no additional lift and no additional drag. (Okay, the mere presence of their mechanical linkages probably adds a little drag, but forget that for now.) When flaps are lowered only slightly, say 10 degrees, they generate more lift than they do drag. Drop them down to 20 degrees and you're getting something near equal parts lift and drag. Extended to 30 or 40 degrees, flaps generate almost no lift at all, but add lots of drag. The ratio changes with each flap position. Cessna 172 flap positions are 10, 20, 30 and sometimes 40 degrees. If we had an enormously powerful engine that could generate enough thrust to overcome the massive drag imposed by flaps set to 40 degrees—and we had flaps that could withstand the force—then we could consider 40 degrees of flaps to generate lift too. (Figure 50)

Don't ever forget the role that thrust plays in relation to drag and lift. Given enough thrust, you can always overcome drag. (Remember that rocket whose engine generates 100% of its lift?) When an airplane manufacturer (or me) says that *x* degrees of flaps means a certain amount of lift or drag, we are considering the airplane as a whole,

As mentioned, some airplanes use flaps for takeoff, usually extended to shallower positions, like 10 degrees. This helps increase lift and only slightly increases drag, which the engine is capable of overcoming. The Cessna 172 pilot's operating handbook (POH) recommends that flaps be extended to 10 degrees for soft-field take-offs. This added boost of lift enables the airplane to overcome gravity sooner and therefore less stress is endured by the landing gear as the wheels roll over the soft or rocky ground. There is added drag, but it's not too much for the engine to overcome. Extend a departing 172's flaps to 30 degrees or more, and you'd better have a very long runway with lots of wonderful scenery, because you won't be flying anywhere. The 172's engine is simply not powerful enough to overcome the drag imposed by 30 or more degrees of flaps on takeoff.

The only safe way of testing this theory is during flight. While flying with your CFI at a speed safe for flaps, lower your flaps to 30 degrees or more. Then pull back on the yoke and try to climb. You'll swear the yoke is directly attached to the airspeed indicator. As you pull back, you gain a slight amount of altitude, but you lose all of your airspeed.

This would be a different situation if you could press a magic button and double your engine's power. Then you could climb because the available thrust would more easily overcome the flap-added drag. (You might also find that your flaps rip right off of your wings because they are designed to withstand only a certain amount of relative wind resistance.)

You simply can't separate the relationship between thrust and drag.

Flaps are raised and lowered by an electrical motor on some training planes, such as the Cessna 172, while others, like the Piper Warrior, use a manual lever.

Can you land an airplane without the use of flaps? Certainly. And you should practice doing so with your instructor in case the day comes when you need to make a flapless landing.

One day I was flying a Cessna 172 and the airplane's alternator died. (That's the device that charges the airplane's battery.) My destination airport had no maintenance services, so I had to fly for a while until I could land somewhere else to have it fixed.

The first thing to consider after any airplane system failure is: *What did the system do and how do I compensate for its absence?*

The alternator charges the airplane's battery. Without it, I knew I was running my electrical system off of the airplane's battery and that meant I would lose electrical power within 30 or so minutes. (Your airplane's POH can help you determine how long you can expect your airplane's electrical system to remain on while running on battery power. Ask your CFI to help you determine this.)

I had been on Flight Following with ATC, so I wanted to let them know what was up. I radioed to them that I had lost my alternator and I was headed toward a certain airport for repairs. There was no reply. The radio display started flickering so I knew that power was fading fast.

I turned off all unnecessary electrical equipment, including my navigation equipment and radios. I left my transponder on so that I would continue to "blip" on ATC radar screens for as long as possible. (Transponders use a lot of power, so if you ever find yourself in a serious electrical system emergency, consider that.)

I checked my charts and headed for the nearest airport that offered aircraft repair services.

Flying a partially disabled airplane, I wanted to maintain as many options as possible until I was absolutely certain that I could reach the airport. What caused the alternator to fail? I didn't know. Was my electrical system about to burst into flames? I didn't know that either. My intent was to get the airplane safely on the ground and let someone qualified sort it all out.

The best source of "options" for a pilot is altitude. Altitude gives you time and distance (in the case of an engine loss), and affords you a choice of directions to fly. If you're flying at 2,000 feet with 3,000 foot hills to the north, east and west, then your flight direction choice has been made for you. So I knew that I wanted to maintain my altitude for as long as possible until I knew with absolute certainty I could reach my airport.

By the time I reached the airport and tried to lower the flaps, I got about 5 degrees worth before the battery died completely.

No flaps for me.

Another failure and another decision to make: *What did the system do and how do I compensate for its absence?*

Flaps steepen the angle of descent without increasing airspeed, as we know very well by now. Could I emulate this?

Let's consider the effect of flaps step by step:

- Flaps increase drag, which slows the airplane.

Okay, how could I slow the airplane without flaps? I had the obvious choice of reducing power, which I did. But even with a power reduction I was flying too fast to lose the altitude that I needed to lose to get down to the airport in a reasonable amount of time. I needed to increase drag even more.

A side slip was the answer. Using a slip I was able to steepen my descent angle without increasing my airspeed. But there was one remaining very important thing that flaps do that I needed to consider:

- Flaps increase lift, which allows the airplane to fly slower without stalling.

So without the added lift generated by lowered flaps, I knew my airplane would stall at a higher airspeed. The answer was to come in for my landing faster than normal to ensure I had a speed buffer.

The landing went fine and the repairs were made. It's funny how a pilot's "urgent descent" could so quickly become a mechanic's routine alternator swap.

Later, in "The Electrical System" on page 138, I'll admit what I did wrong during this approach and landing.

Your CFI will go over stalls and stall speeds with you in detail. This is very important stuff. Make sure you understand it.

So in summary we know that:

- Flaps increase drag.

- Flaps increase lift. (Anything that increases lift also increases drag.)

- Flaps reduce the speed at which the airplane can fly before stalling.

Keeping these three things in mind will make it easier for you to fly and land without the use of flaps in case you ever need to. Remember, pilot training is all about what to do when something goes wrong.

AIRPLANE SYSTEMS

The term *system* refers to your engine, your electrical wires and devices, your fuel tanks and lines, and stuff like that. The FAA would like you to know some really "nuts and bolts" stuff about these systems just in case you ever have to change a spark plug at 10,000 feet.

That sarcasm is somewhat unfair, but to many student pilots it's understandable. I couldn't for the life of me figure out why I had to know the difference between airplane carburetor types or where in the fuel line the primer injected fuel. Who cared? All I wanted to know was when I'd get to solo.

Well, some of this stuff turned out to be good to know. The purpose of some of it, however, still remains a mystery to me. Some of this stuff, more importantly, can save your life.

We'll cover some of the high-level topics in this section that you're going to need to know. This stuff is not only required by your FAA written and oral tests, but each time you go to a new place to rent airplanes, you'll probably have to fill out a form that shows that you know this information for each type of airplane you plan to fly.

Let's start off with a quick review of what makes flight possible:

An object needs only two things in order to fly: a source of thrust and a source of lift. Thrust moves it forward and lift moves it upward. If an airplane engine fails, thrust is provided by gravity pulling the airplane toward the Earth. An airplane's lift is generated as air moves over the airfoiled wings. So even without an engine's power, an airplane glides because it still has the two things required for flight, albeit to a lesser degree.

It's important to recognize that in this *very* simple explanation of what's required for flight, there is no mention of anything invented by humans. This is no coincidence. Humans didn't invent flight, we just adapted it to work for our own flightless bodies. After all, birds fly without the benefit of human engineering. In fact, the airfoil design that enables an airplane's wings to generate lift is borrowed from the wings of nature's feathered flyers.

Thrust and lift is all an airplane needs. Engines, radios, navigation equipment: it's all just for decoration.

I downplay the importance of airplane systems because it's important to always remember that these systems are in place to make flight *easier and safer*, but not to make flight *possible*. If you lose one system, you can and will deal with it. This is what being a pilot is all about: what to do when something goes wrong.

"Primitive" best describes the various systems found on most aviation trainers. This stuff is not rocket science. In fact, you'll be hard pressed to find many differences between the systems on trainer airplanes built today and those built 50 years ago. Sure, there have been tweaks along the way, but for the most part the beast remains the same.

Think of it this way: the better a pilot you become, the fewer airplane systems you *require* for safe flight. A lesser pilot might panic if a radio fails. A decent pilot, on the other hand, should be able to safely land an airplane with a dead engine.

This is not to say that *real* men and women only fly with broken airplanes! Airplane systems enhance flight safety. As such, they should be fully functional on each and every flight.

Airplane systems were not designed, however, to compensate for a pilot that wasn't paying attention in flight school. Learn the various systems and understand them. That way when a system fails in flight, you'll know what's required to compensate for the inconvenience of its loss.

What did the system do and how do I compensate for its absence?

If you can't answer this question for each of the systems on your airplane, you need to do some more reading before you fly again.

Ask yourself periodically during flights what you would do at that moment if an important airplane system failed:

If the engine died right now, where would I land?

If I lost my electrical system now, what would I do?

The reason you must reconsider these questions throughout your flight is that the answers will change. That vast grassy meadow below won't be there in 30 minutes. And while your radios don't do you much good when your flying isolated out in a corn field, losing them just as you enter O'Hare's busy airspace is an issue that needs immediate attention.

The first part of this book describes a good pilot as one for whom the cockpit presents no surprises. This largely applies to systems failures. You don't typically get a warning when a system is about to go, but it shouldn't matter. If you've already considered what you'd do at that moment if you lost a given system, an actual failure becomes nothing more than a prompt to get you into action.

SYSTEM CONTROL

Not surprisingly, the controls and monitoring equipment for each of the various aircraft systems that we're about to discuss are located inside the cockpit, as shown in figure 51 on page 132.

At the center of aircraft control is what we call the instrument "six pack." Centered on the instrument panel right in front of the pilot, these six gauges are the primary instruments a pilot uses to control the airplane's direction of flight and altitude. (Figure 52)

Now let's take a closer look at each system.

Figure 52: *THE SIX PACK* The gauges in the six-pack are collectively known as the flight instruments. Clockwise from upper left: airspeed indicator, attitude indicator, altimeter, vertical speed indicator (VSI), directional gyro (DG), turn coordinator.

THE ENGINE

> **[SYSTEM OVERVIEW] THE ENGINE**
>
> - PRIMARY PURPOSE: Source of thrust.
>
> - INTERRELATED SYSTEMS: The airplane's vacuum system is driven by the engine. The electrical system's alternator, which provides electricity during flight and charges battery, is also driven by the engine. (All explained later.)
>
> - TYPICAL FAILURE: Many engine failures cause only a partial power loss, meaning that the engine still runs, but generates less thrust.

I was taught and tested on the fact that my Cessna 172 had a Lycoming 320, 180-horsepower engine. I imagined that this was important to know for the many times I would go into my local airplane parts store in search of replacement bolts or other airplane engine "thingies." Or maybe the knowledge would simply make me more engaging in those airport lounge bull sessions: *Yeah, those Lycoming 320s: there's nothing like 'em!*

Hell, I don't even know what kind of engine my car has!

But guess what? There was information here that turned out to be useful. My engine was rated at 180-horsepower. Other Cessna trainers at my school had 160-horsepower engines. My 180-horsepower engine cruised a few knots faster and could carry more weight. The speed boost wasn't going to amount to much enroute time savings, but the ability to carry more weight was significant. But the differences between the two engines became most apparent when I flew one of the 160-horsepower airplanes. Just knowing that they were less powerful than the airplane I was used to made me more conscious of performance considerations.

Now when I consider flying an airplane I've never flown before, I find out about the engine. If it's a 160- or 180-horsepower model, it gives me a better sense of the type of performance I can expect. If the rating is 320-horsepower, I know that it might be a monster I am not prepared to tackle. Pilots who are used to 320-horsepower engines benefit from being able to anticipate the limitations of a 160-horsepower engine before they take off.

Figure 51: *COMMAND CENTRAL* Airplane systems are controlled using the various levers, gauges, gadgets and switches found in the cockpit. This instrument panel comprises only those controls that are required for a basic understanding of the various airplane systems. Actual instrument panels typically have more instruments and gauges, though once you understand the basics, a few more knobs and buttons won't throw you.

There's another benefit to knowing engine models, and it comes in the form of an audio waveform. I know what the Lycoming 320 180- (and 160-) horsepower engine is *supposed* to sound like when things are running properly. So if I get into an airplane with that engine and things sound odd, I know something might be wrong.

Did I learn enough about an airplane engine to fix it? Certainly not. I couldn't even change the oil. But when I started to think about it, I realized that while I didn't actually know what kind of engine my car had, I did "know" the engine in the sense that I could predict its performance and sense when something wasn't quite right. I always took that knowledge for granted because I get road-side towing assistance from my automobile club. If something goes wrong, help is always a toll-free call away.

OIL TYPE AND QUANTITY

[NEED TO KNOW] OIL SYSTEM

- Type of oil used
- Minimum safe oil level
- Oil level on-board before every flight
- Check oil pressure regularly during flight!

I don't ever check the oil in my car. Why would I? The oil-change people put it in there and I certainly didn't take it out. It must still be there. Right? I figure if the oil light comes on, I'll stop at a service station and let someone else deal with it.

Funny thing about the sky, however, is that service stations are never around when you need one. (Starbucks cafes are also rare, if you can begin to imagine.) The unfunny thing about airplane engines, however, is that when they run out of oil *very* bad things happen.

You must check the oil in your airplane before every flight!

This is no joke. I haven't been flying that long and I have already seen several engines fail as the result of no oil. (Other people had the planes at the time, by the way!) Checking the oil is easy. Learn to do it, and do it before *every* flight. If the airplane needs oil, add it before you take off. Don't wait until after your flight. This is where knowing the proper type of oil for your airplane comes in handy. You'll find yourself adding oil to airplanes all the time. This isn't one of those once-in-a-while tasks.

Knowing how much oil your airplane takes is less significant. You can usually see the quantity listed on the oil cap, or read it in the pilot's operating handbook (POH). What is very important to know is the *minimum* quantity of oil your airplane requires to fly. This will also be in the POH. Never fly an airplane that has an oil level below this quantity. If you fly to airports that have no services available, keep a few bottles of oil on board so you can get home again if you're low.

Another good time to check the amount of oil in your airplane is *after* each flight. An airplane that burns oil rapidly might be crying out for maintenance. An airplane that was burning one quart every five flight hours last month and is now burning one quart per hour is *definitely* crying out for maintenance.

The type of flying you do also factors into oil burn. Airplanes tend to burn more oil in training situations and during traffic pattern work than they do on long flights where engine power settings remain fairly constant.

During your flights you'll want to keep an eye on the oil pressure gauge. If you get a high or low reading, find an airport and land the airplane as soon as you can. The problem might be as simple as a faulty gauge, but it could be very serious. Don't ever take the oil system in your airplane for granted. (Figure 53)

Figure 53: *OIL IS PRESSING* Oil is an airplane's blood. If the oil dries up, or if for any reason the system loses oil pressure, you'll lose your engine if you continue your flight. Keep on eye on the oil pressure gauge throughout all phases of your flight.

If your engine runs dry of oil during a flight, your engine will fail. It's that simple.

CARBURETOR TYPES

> **[NEED TO KNOW]   CARBURETOR**
> - Does your plane have a carburetor, or is it fuel-injected?
> - Proper use of carb heat to counter carburetor icing
> - Weather conditions conducive to carburetor icing

Learning how carburetors work also tried my patience during my training. I didn't care what a carburetor was, let alone how one worked.

But the benefit in learning about carburetors comes less from knowing what they are and how they work, and more from understanding what causes them to fail. Ice is the villain here. Carburetor icing can choke an engine to the point where the engine quits. This is one of those engine failures that you can fix enroute if you know what to look for. Carburetor-equipped

Figure 54: *CARB HEAT* The left hand lever in this image is used to turn the carb heat on (pushed in) and off (pulled out). I'll talk about the two larger levers in a moment.

airplanes have a control, called the *carb heat,* that enables warm air to enter the carburetor and melt any ice that might have formed.

Turning on the carb heat is a very easy fix, but you have to know what symptoms to look for to recognize carburetor icing, hence the training. A typical first symptom is a rough running engine. This is easy to appreciate on the ground, but when your engine starts coughing at 5,500 feet, your mind and heart might start racing. A mental run-through of all the possible causes will help you quickly resolve the matter before the tears start flowing. The application of carb heat should always be on your rough-running engine mental checklist.

I won't go into the specifics about how carburetor icing forms—your CFI will cover this with you—but it can happen in weather conditions as warm as 70 degrees fahrenheit, so you need to be aware of it.

Newer airplanes tend to have fuel-injected systems that don't require carburetors or carb heat controls. Theses systems have "gotchas" all their own, however, so don't think you're in the carburetor clear just because you fly some fuel-injected fury. Further, it's unlikely that you'll be able to avoid flying carburetor-equipped airplanes forever. If that *still* isn't enough reason to get up to speed on carb icing issues, remember that the FAA will test you on it.

FUEL SYSTEMS

> **[NEED TO KNOW]** FUEL SYSTEM
> - Gravity feed system, or pump? Use pump when?
> - Left, right or both selector? Switch how often?
> - Fuel type (Probably 100LL)
> - Fuel quantity during entire flight (calculated)
> - Airplane's fuel burn rate (gallons per hour)

Here we have another one of those subjects that I figured was more useful information for the grease monkey than for me. And again I was wrong. It turns out there are important things to know about your fuel system besides where the gas goes.

Fuel tanks for most airplanes are mounted inside the airplane's wings, so you can assume there will be at least two. Some airplanes have additional tanks, including wing-tip-mounted "tip tanks," which can sometimes look like artillery. (Figure 55)

Some planes, like the Cessna 172, use a *gravity-feed* fuel system, which means the airplane relies on gravity to deliver fuel from the tanks to the engine. (You see, gravity isn't all bad!) Gravity-feed systems are only possible when the airplane's wings (and tanks) are positioned higher than the engine.

In low-wing airplanes, like the Piper Warrior, gravity doesn't cut it. These airplanes rely on fuel pumps to get the fuel from the tanks to the engine. The Warrior has an engine-driven pump and an electrical pump, which is used as a back up. The electric pump is turned on for takeoff and landing so if the engine-driven pump fails, fuel continues to flow during those critical phases of flight.

Figure 55: *FILL 'ER UP!* Airplane fuel tanks are usually located inside the wings (above). Not only is this a clever storage location, but it keeps the fuel close to the airplane's center of gravity, so as fuel burns, the airplane remains balanced. Some trainer airplanes have a single fuel tank located in the fuselage behind the seats.

Airplanes are also equipped with fuel tank selector switches so pilots can choose which tank to use. The fuel tank selector switch on a Cessna 172 includes positions for the left and right tanks individually, but also includes a handy "both" position that uses fuel from both tanks at once. Some switches in other airplanes lack the "both" position, requiring the pilot to switch fuel tanks enroute.

The 172 makes fuel management very easy: keep the tank selector switch set to "both" and remember that if you ever find yourself flying a 172 upside down you can expect your engine to quit because gravity can no longer feed fuel into the engine. But if you ever find yourself flying a 172 upside down during your training you've got bigger fish to fry.

Pilots flying airplanes other than the 172 have more to remember with regard to fuel management. Piper Warriors, for example, have no "both" option on their fuel tank selector switches. Their low wings also require the use of fuel pumps. Piper pilots must understand the proper use of the their fuel systems *completely* and pay extra careful attention to fuel management during flights.

Many a pilot has forgotten to switch tanks enroute only to hear the heart-stopping sputter of an engine gone thirsty. During the cruise portion of your flight, your airspeed and altitude are usually high enough that this momentary loss of power poses no real threat. Once a tank with fuel is selected, the engine usually comes back to life in a few seconds. (The oncoming airflow forces the prop to spin, which, in effect, is like push-starting a car.) You might have to manually restart the engine, but if you have enough altitude, this can be done safely. You might lose nothing more than some altitude during the ordeal, but talk about flight distractions!

A dry tank can be downright deadly, however, during takeoff and landing. You're close to the ground and you're flying slow. You just don't have any altitude or airspeed that you can afford to lose. If the engine cuts out on takeoff, you'll lose the power you need for the climb and your airplane might drop to the ground. A dry tank is less serious on landing *if* you have enough speed and altitude to glide in without power. But if you botch your landing and have to take-off again (called a "go-around"), and your selected tank is dry, expect to make the evening news.

Some pilots flying airplanes without the "both" switch position make a habit of switching tanks every 30 minutes or so in flight. It becomes part of their enroute checklists. (We'll talk about checklists later.)

This tank-switching exercise keeps the pilot "in the groove," so to speak, with regard to fuel management and also helps keep the weight on the two wings balanced. Forty gallons of fuel weighs 240 pounds. (Airplane fuel weighs approximately 6 lbs per gallon.) A full tank on one side of the airplane and an empty tank on the other might hinder your ability to fly the airplane with your usual flawless precision.

Knowing how much fuel your airplane uses is important for two reasons: First, you'll know how long your airplane can fly, and second, you'll know how much your airplane will weigh with full tanks. Fuel weight will mean more to you after we've talked about airplane performance and limitations.

Finally, you need to the know the type of fuel your airplane uses. There are only a few types of aviation fuel:

- 100 – Green in color, used in older engines.

- 100LL – Light blue in color, most common in today's airplanes.

- Jet – Clear in color, used in turboprop and jet aircraft. Smells like kerosine because it basically is kerosine.

Trainers commonly use 100LL (pronounced: *one hundred, low-lead*) fuel, which is found pretty much anywhere aviation fuel is pumped. The POH for your airplane will specify what type of fuel is required. Sometimes more than one type of fuel can be used, but *only* if the POH says it's okay. Automobile fuel and aviation fuel are not the same thing, though some airplanes are capable of running on automobile fuel. If your airplane can use standard automobile gasoline, you'll know about it. If you have to guess, the answer is most likely no. Read the POH to be

Figure 56: *THE GLASS GAUGE* A glass wand can accurately measure the amount of fuel in a tank.

sure. FAA regulations require that a POH be on-board the airplane for every flight. Now you know one of the reasons why.

Aviation fuel is usually only a bit more expensive than automobile gasoline. This is a dangerous statement to make in a printed publication, however, given the volatile nature of fuel prices. The differences aren't extreme, however.

It's very important that you check the fuel in your airplane before each flight and after each refueling. You're checking for three things:

- **Fuel quantity** – Fuel gauges in airplanes do not reliably represent the actual quantity of fuel in the tanks. FAA regulations require that fuel gauges accurately show full and empty readings only. Manually check your levels before each flight and use fuel-burn calculations to determine how much you'll burn enroute. Use the fuel gauges only to verify your visual check and your calculations. If you're enroute and your gauges get lower than you think they should be, land when you can and do a visual check. It's possible your calculations could be off or the tanks are leaking. Many pilots check fuel levels using special hollow glass wands that have numbers on the side that correlate to fuel quantities. (Figure 56) Dip the wand into the tank, hold your finger on the end and pull the wand out. The suction created holds fuel in the wand. You can see how much was in the tanks by reading the numbers. Clever.

- **Fuel type** – After each refueling, you must visually check the fuel to ensure that the proper type was pumped. You can test this by color and smell. Jet fuel smells like kerosine, so it's easy to detect. Your CFI will explain the best way to test your fuel as part of your preflight training.

- **Fuel quality** - As part of your preflight inspection you'll check for water or contaminants in the fuel tank, either of which can cause your engine to cough or stop completely.

ENGINE SETTINGS

The engines found on most trainer airplanes are simple in nature and have only one control for adjusting power and one gauge for determining the current power setting.

Usually mounted toward the bottom of the instrument panel to the pilot's right is the throttle, which is used to change engine power settings. The farther in the throttle is pushed, the higher the power setting. The tachometer is the gauge pilots use to determine the current power setting. (Figure 57)

Some airplanes have engines that work a bit differently because they have what is called a *constant-speed propeller*. On these airplanes there is one knob that determines the engine's manifold pressure and another that determines the actual RPM speed of the propeller. The airplane shown in figure 57 has what is called a *fixed-speed propeller*. On these airplanes the throttle directly controls the rotational speed of the airplane's propeller.

Your groundschool instructor can explain more about the differences between the two engine types. Though fixed-speed propellers are more common on training airplanes, constant-speed propeller trainers do exist, so you need to become familiar with how they work.

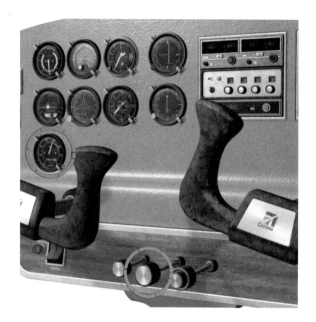

Figure 57: *THE GO TEAM* The throttle (circled) is the black knob that extends outward from the wooden portion of this instrument panel. (The red knob to the right of the throttle is called the mixture control. We'll discuss it later.) Also circled is the tachometer (close-up below), which is used to determine power settings. The farther the throttle is pushed in, the higher the RPM setting.

THE ELECTRICAL SYSTEM

[SYSTEM OVERVIEW] ELECTRICAL SYSTEM

- PRIMARY PURPOSE: Supplies power to avionics (radios, navigation equipment, etc.), electric flight instruments and electrically-driven motors, such as the Cessna 172's flap system.

- INTERRELATED SYSTEMS: The engine drives the electrical system's alternator, which provides electricity during flight and charges the airplane's battery.

- TYPICAL FAILURE: A failed alternator will prevent your airplane's battery from charging during flight. Eventually, all electrical power will be lost as the battery drains. Electrical system failures are typically limited to a single component, such as a failed radio.

If you've ever assembled a personal computer or a home entertainment monstrosity, you know how confusing electronic systems can be: One component seems to be malfunctioning, but after hours of swapping cables, flipping switches and testing, you find that the trouble was caused by something else entirely. Airplane electrical systems can be equally confusing. But regardless of the system, the more familiar you are with the components, the faster you can isolate and fix problems.

The most surprising thing I learned about aircraft electrical systems during my training was that many older airplanes still flying today don't even have one! It really made me sit and think about what the system actually does. It powers lights, radios, navigation equipment and, in some cases, motors, such as the Cessna 172's flap mechanisim. As nice as this stuff is, none of it is really needed for daytime flying unless you're flying through an area for which regulations require that you have radios and such.

But to further emphasize a point I made earlier: an airplane will not fall out of the sky just because its electrical systems fails. I think it's important to keep this in mind because humans have a tendency to panic when their lives are at risk. A pilot should be able to discern between times when her live is actually threatened and times when it has simply been inconvenienced.

An electrical system failure is an inconvenience. It is not a reason to panic.

FLIGHT INSTRUMENTS IN THE ELECTRICAL SYSTEM

On most trainer aircraft there is only one electrically-powered instrument— the turn coordinator, which was introduced back on page 116. The turn coordinator is located in the lower left corner of the flight instrument "six pack."

If an airplane has no vacuum system (described later), it might have more electrically-powered gauges. You'll need to check the airplane's POH to know for sure.

ELECTRICAL EQUIPMENT

The equipment that's powered by the electrical system differs somewhat for each airplane model. Communication and navigation equipment is always electrically powered. If you lose your electrical system, you'll lose the use of these components, hence the beauty of hand-held units you can purchase for backup, which I'll talk about later.

An engine needs battery power to start up, but once it starts, the engine provides its own electrical power to keep running. So even if your entire electrical system fails, your engine won't quit.

Some flight gauges, like the turn coordinator, are electrically powered, but the information provided by these gauges is also provided, to varying degrees, by engine-driven gauges. (We'll talk about engine-powered systems later.) So if your

electrical system goes, the non-electrical gauges continue to provide enough information to enable you to safely complete your flight.

System redundancy like this is not just a happy accident. Aircraft manufacturers assume that equipment will fail, so they design redundancy into every aircraft system. Airplane safety depends on this redundancy. If your electrical system goes, you have engine-driven gauges to pick up the slack, but you have lost the margin of safety that redundancy provided. The airplane might still be flying perfectly well, but when any aircraft system fails, you need to find a suitable airport and have someone take a look at it.

Conversely, if your engine quits, you lose the gauges it powers, but you'll still have the information provided by the electrically-powered gauges, such as the turn coordinator, and gauges powered by a third system that we'll talk about next.

Aircraft lights are also electrically powered. Most airplanes have cockpit lights that illuminate gauges, and exterior lights that enable others to see you in the dark. Losing your lights during the day isn't a big deal, but losing them at night is a very different situation. You know that the airplane will continue to fly fine without them, but without radios and lights, how will anyone else know you're there? Making matters worse, if the nearest airport's runways have pilot-controlled lighting (the pilot turns the lights on with his radio), you'll have no way of illuminating the runway to see where you should land.

Let's hope if you ever lose your electrical system at night that it's on an evening of a full moon.

•

As with all other airplane system failures, the first thing to do if you lose your electrical system is ask yourself:

What did the system do and how do I compensate for its absence?

You'll realize that during daytime flights there really isn't much to do other than find a nearby airport that offers aircraft maintenance and land. You just need to be extra careful about your maneuvers near the airport area because you aren't in radio contact with anyone.

The "what to do?" question for night flights should be answered before you depart. For night flights to be safe, electrical system redundancy is really a necessity. You can and should provide this redundancy because it's not likely that your airplane has a back-up electrical system. A handheld, battery-powered radio can be used to announce your position and intentions to other pilots or a control tower. A handheld GPS unit can help if you're flying in unfamiliar territory by providing a means of navigation.

Flashlights are also on the must-have list for night flights. It's best to have a few of them on board, with back-up batteries for each. Even if your electrical system is working properly you'll need handheld lights to conduct your preflight inspection, read navigation charts and find things in the cockpit. Most internal light systems on airplanes are inadequate for chart reading, especially in rental aircraft. We'll talk more about this stuff later in the book.

So what else goes out when the electrical system fails? The flaps in a Cessna are electrically powered, so without electricity they cannot be used. Back in the section on flaps I told the story of how I lost an alternator one day and ended up landing with only a few degrees of flaps because my battery went dead while I was lowering

> **[NEED TO KNOW]**   ELECTRICAL SYSTEM
> - Which flight instruments are electrically powered?
> - Which other devices are electrically powered?
> - Which devices draw the most electrical current?

them. In retrospect, lowering the flaps was a stupid thing to do in that situation. What if I had messed up the landing and had to do a go-around? If I had gotten the flaps to 40 degrees when the battery died, I would have had no choice but to land on the first attempt. The 172 can't climb well with 40 degrees of flaps. If I had botched the landing, I would have been in a very serious situation with very few options.

When the battery is dead, the flaps don't go up any better than they go down. So if you fly an airplane that has electrically controlled flaps, and you lose your alternator, consider *carefully* if you want to lower those flaps for landing.

Fuel gauges are often electrically powered, so don't be alarmed if your failed electrical system all of a sudden looks like a fuel crisis too. This is a good example of why we calculate fuel levels based on flight time and not gauge readings.

Go over your electrical system in detail with your CFI. Learn which devices draw the most electrical current. That way, if you ever lose your alternator, you'll know which devices are going to drain your battery the fastest and you'll be able to make better choices regarding which devices to switch off. (HINT: That transponder isn't as innocent as it looks!)

THE PITOT-STATIC SYSTEM

Figure 58: *THE PORT AND THE TUBE* The static port is a very small pinhole in the airplane fuselage takes samples of the static air around the airplane (above). If this tiny hole ever gets clogged by ice, dirt, bugs etc., none of the pitot-static instruments will work properly. The pitot tube (below) is usually mounted below one of the wings. Air enters the tube through the ram air hole (lower right). By comparing the pressure of this air to static air samples gathered at the static port, the airspeed indicator determines the airplane's speed.

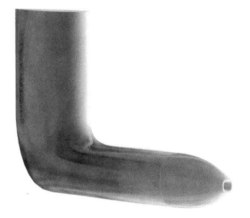

The pitot-static system takes continuous samples of the atmosphere surrounding the airplane. (*Pitot* is pronounced "pee'-toe.") An individual air sample is of limited use on its own, but by comparing two subsequent samples, the pitot-static instruments are able to detect and display changes in altitude and/or airspeed.

The pitot-static system gathers air samples through two sources. One is called the *static port*. Usually located on the side of the airplane's fuselage, the static port is only slightly bigger than a pin hole. (Figure 58) Part of your preflight inspection will be to ensure that this tiny hole isn't clogged. Many airplanes also have an alternate static air source that's usually located inside the cockpit.

The second air source used by the pitot-static system is called the *pitot tube*. This tube is usually mounted on the underside of the airplane's wing, but might also be near the nose section of the fuselage. The sole purpose of the pitot tube is to measure what's called *ram air pressure*, which is used to determine the airplane's airspeed. The difference in pressure between the static air and the ram air enables the airspeed indicator to determine the airplane's airspeed.

Though each pitot-static instrument provides different information, they each work off the same principles. A clog in the static line (including the static port itself), affects *all* pitot-static instruments. A clogged pitot-tube only affects the airspeed indicator. We'll talk more about the effects of clogs throughout this section.

The pitot-static system can be complicated to understand, but if I was able to get the hang of it, you will too. Some of the stuff we're going to cover here isn't usually taught until a pilot is going for his instrument rating. But you know what? An instrument rating should be "required equipment" for every pilot, so let's not shy away from some of the topics covered during that training just because the FAA thinks they are unnecessary for VFR flight. Learning this stuff now will not only make you a safer VFR pilot, but it will make your instrument training that much easier.

ATMOSPHERIC PRESSURE CHANGES

Before we get into each of the pitot-static instruments, we first need to talk about changes in atmospheric pressure, which is the foundation on which the pitot-static instruments are based.

Atmospheric pressure is an odd thing to conceptualize because we don't usually perceive it as we go about our daily activities. But if you've ever had your ears clog while flying in an airplane, driving down a mountain, or while SCUBA diving, you've experienced a change in atmospheric pressure.

Atmospheric pressure decreases as altitude (or elevation) increases. Air trapped inside a container will expand as the pressure outside the container decreases, as it does at higher altitudes. For example, if you fill a balloon with air on the ground and take it up in the airplane, the size of the balloon will actually expand as you gain altitude. Eventually the increasing pressure of the air inside the balloon will prove too much for the thin skin and the balloon will pop. (Figure 59)

Airplane have air-tight containers that are affected by atmospheric pressure changes. They include special compartments inside the pitot-static instruments and, potentially, the clogged sinus cavities of you and your passengers.

Take a sealed bag of potato chips up with you in one of your training flights and you'll see this phenomenon in action. During a climb to a high enough altitude, the bag will plump up like a balloon. The bag's rotund stature isn't the result of an increase in the volume of air in the bag—we

Figure 59: *BALLOON BULGE* Air trapped inside this balloon expands as the pressure of the surrounding air decreases. The volume of air inside the balloon, however, remains constant. If air was to leak out of a balloon during a flight, allowing it to shrink back to its normal size, the descent would further shrink the balloon to a size smaller than it was before the flight. If absolutely no air leaked out during the flight, the balloon would return to near its normal size during the descent.

know that we didn't blow any new air into it. It plumps because the air inside the bag remains at a sea-level pressure while the air pressure outside the bag decreases as altitude increases.

The decreasing outside pressure effectively "sucks" the bag outward. You could also say the increasing pressure inside the bag (relative to the air outside) plumps the bag outward. Regardless of how you look at it, it's the difference between the two air pressures that causes the bag to bloat.

If you've ever opened your luggage after a flight to find that some plastic tube of facial cream has exploded, moisturizing everything from your toothbrush to your underwear, you can thank the air that was trapped inside the container when the plane was climbing.

Descending yields the opposite effect: trapped air contracts as the "outside" air increases in pressure. If the container is strong enough, it holds its shape but you might hear a "whoosh" of air enter the container the moment you open it on the ground. If it's not a strong container, it will collapse somewhat. You might have noticed that plastic containers you've taken on commercial flights are squeezed after you land.

But if the container expands during the climb and contracts during the descent, why wouldn't it be the same size after landing that it was before take off? During the enroute portion of the flight any containers that are not absolutely air-tight will leak air and equalize themselves to the new, surrounding lower air pressure. Air escapes during the climb or during the flight and once the descent begins, the container starts to contract.

So now imagine your poor, clogged sinus cavities. You're flying at 8,000 feet and your sinus has adapted to the pressure. Then you descend. The air trapped inside your sinus starts losing the battle with the higher-pressure outside air that's trying to get in. If your sinus is totally blocked, this can become very painful. I don't have to tell you if you've already experienced it.

SCUBA divers are also familiar with this concept. Divers must "equalize" their ears on the way down to keep the pressure inside and outside the sinus the same. If a diver's sinus is blocked and the equalization cannot take place, the dive is aborted. An aborted dive is a drag (fear not: no thrust references are forthcoming), but at least a diver can abort the dive before it's too late. When flying, you often don't know that you have a sinus problem until it's time to descend. Aborting the descent isn't a long-term solution.

So why isn't there any pain on the way up? Your clogged sinus cavity has a magical way of letting air out much more easily than it lets air back in

again. Think of a clogged sinus as a doggie door that only opens one way. Rover gets out, but he can't get back in again.

Now back to the pitot-static system.

We know that the pressure at 10,000 feet is going to be less than the pressure at sea level, but how do we know when we're at 10,000 feet? If we had a sample of the air pressure at sea level, we could take a sample of the outside air pressure and determine our altitude based on the pressure difference. If we took frequent outside air pressure samples, we could even determine if we were climbing or descending and how quickly. And if we could compare the airflow hitting our airplane head-on (ram air pressure) with air that was not hitting us head on (static air pressure), we could determine how fast we were flying.

I know you're thinking that I'm brilliant for having come up with such ideas, but I must confess that the concept of comparing air pressure samples wasn't my idea. The pitot-static instruments found on every airplane are based on this very concept. I'm just one of the many poor slobs that was forced to understand it. Now it's your turn.

INSTRUMENTS IN THE PITOT-STATIC SYSTEM

The gauges in the pitot-static system are:

- Altimeter – Measures the airplane's altitude above sea level (upper right).

- Vertical speed indicator – Measures how many feet per minute the airplane is climbing or descending (lower right).

- Airspeed indicator – Measures the airplane's forward speed through the air (upper left).

Figure 60: *NOT HIGH, NOT LOW* Between the center of a high pressure system and the center of an adjacent low pressure system are areas of increasing (or decreasing, depending on how you look at it) atmospheric pressure. If a "high" exists over Northern California and a "low" exists over Washington, then Oregon will experience something in between the two. Pilots flying between the two locations will have to adjust their altimeters many times along the way.

THE ALTIMETER

An altimeter (pronounced "al-tim'-eh-tur") measures how high the airplane is flying above sea level. It does so by comparing the current outside air pressure with a sea-level air sample that is locked in an air-tight container inside the instrument. By measuring the difference between the two air pressure samples, the altimeter can determine the airplane's altitude. The greater the difference, the greater the altitude.

Simple, right? If only it was that simple.

The trouble is that atmospheric pressure changes depending on where you are in the skies above Earth at a given moment. You've heard meteorologists mention areas of high and low pressure. Well, every place that lies between these two areas has a pressure level somewhere between the high and the low. So if there's high pressure over California, and an adjacent low pressure system is over Washington State, Oregon will be in an area of gradating "medium" pressure. (Figure 60)

Therein lies the problem. The altimeter depends on the outside air pressure to determine how high the airplane is flying. But if that air pressure changes, how is the altimeter to know?

PITOT-STATIC
ALTIMETER

FAA REGULATIONS

A functional altimeter is required for all flights. You cannot fly legally without one. [FAR 91.205]

ERRORS

- Altimeter settings too low indicate higher than true altitude.

- Altimeter settings too high indicate lower than true altitude.

- Clogged static port/system causes altimeter to "freeze" at altitude where clog took place.

The altimeter below indicates an altitude of 7,500 (seven-thousand, five-hundred) feet. The large white hand indicates hundreds of feet. The smaller white hand indicates thousands of feet. The black hand with the white tip indicates tens of thousands of feet. The knob is used to adjust the barometric scale, which currently reads 31.02. The striped flag located just above the number 5, disappears when the airplane is above 10,000 (one-zero thousand) feet.

It doesn't know. And unless the pilot makes a setting adjustment to the altimeter, which we'll cover in a moment, the altimeter will indicate a change of altitude even if the airplane is flying perfectly level.

For example, imagine that your airplane is tied to a string that keeps you flying at exactly 1,000 feet above the ground for your entire flight. In an area of high pressure your airplane's altimeter might indicate 950 feet, while in an area of low pressure it might indicate 1,050 feet. The changes in atmospheric pressure "trick" the altimeter into indicating the airplane's altitude has changed.

If you're flying through areas of increasing lower pressure, the altimeter will indicate increasingly higher altitudes. So why does the altimeter assume the airplane is flying higher just because the atmospheric pressure drops? Remember that we discussed how atmospheric pressure drops as altitude increases? The poor, brainless altimeter's only way of determining how high the airplane's currently flying is to take an outside air pressure sample. If the outside air pressure lowers, the altimeter assumes—and indicates—that the airplane is flying higher.

Without any way to compensate for atmospheric pressure variances, an altimeter would be of limited use. An altimeter's air-tight, sea-level air sample represents atmospheric pressure of 29.92. This magic atmospheric pressure value is known as *standard pressure*. Remember this number because many calculations in aviation depend on standard pressure.

If we only flew through areas of standard pressure, we'd be fine with an altimeter that could not be adjusted. But standard pressure, despite its name, doesn't imply normal or typical pressure. It's a mathematical model. Don't apply too much importance to it. Your local area isn't atmospherically defective just because it's rarely "standard"!

Figure 61: *KOLLS-MAN WINDOW* Pilots use the altimeter's knob to enter the current altimeter setting into the Kollsman Window, which is named for its inventor.

To make altimeters useful, they have a feature called a *Kollsman Window* that enables pilots to compensate for pressure variances. Pilots use a knob near the Kollsman Window to dial in the local atmospheric pressure. (Figure 61)

The local pressure is more commonly referred to as the *altimeter setting*. Once properly set, the altimeter's *indicated* altitude will equal the airplane's *true* altitude. (See sidebar "Altitude vs. altitude" on page 146.)

Altimeter settings are given as four-digit numbers. The decimal after the first two numbers isn't usually spoken. So an altimeter setting of 30.11 is spoken "three zero one one." This means the local atmospheric pressure is showing as 30.11 inches of mercury on a barometric scale. (We'll leave the tedious barometric scale discussion to your groundschool instructor.)

The fact that we include hundredths of an inch in an altimeter setting suggests just how sensitive these instruments are. A variance of one inch in an altimeter setting equals approximately 1,000 feet of altitude difference. So if the local pressure settings during a flight go from, say, 29.92 to 30.92, your altimeter will be 1,000 feet off if you don't reset it properly. If the pressure goes up to only 30.42, you'll have a 500 foot error.

ALTITUDE VS. ALTITUDE

There are a number of different altitude *references* in aviation, but there are only two *real* altitudes:

- **True Altitude (Mean Sea Level)** – This is your height above sea level. True altitude is more commonly referred to as an *altitude MSL*, such as "6,000 feet MSL." Altimeters indicate MSL altitudes. An ATC directive to climb and maintain 9,000 (niner-thousand) feet means that you are requested to climb to 9,000 feet above sea level. If you were departing an airport along the coast, this would mean 9,000 feet worth of climbing. But if departing mile-high Denver International, you'd only need to climb 3,600 feet or so to reach 9,000 feet MSL.

- **Absolute Altitude (Above Ground Level)** – This is your height above the ground below. You'll rarely hear anyone use the term "absolute altitude." Instead, you'll hear references to *altitudes AGL*. For example, pilots are requested to remain 2,000 feet AGL above national forest reserves. If a given forest reserve's elevation was at 4,000 feet, this would mean pilots should fly no lower than 6,000 MSL over the area to maintain a vertical distance of 2,000 feet AGL.

The remaining altitude references depend on atmospheric and other conditions:

- **Indicated Altitude** – This is the altitude indicated on your altimeter. The accuracy of this indication depends on the accuracy of your altimeter setting. When your altimeter is set correctly, your *indicated* altitude equals your *true* altitude.

- **Pressure Altitude** – Pressure altitude is what you see on your altimeter when you set it to 29.92, regardless of what the actual local altimeter setting is at the time. Many of the aircraft performance charts found in POHs use pressure altitude when defining an airplane's performance limitations. This provides a standard reference for measuring performance. Pressure altitude will equal true altitude only when the local altimeter setting is 29.92.

- **Density Altitude** – The only problem with pressure altitude for determining aircraft performance is that pressure altitude doesn't take into consideration temperature variations. Airplanes perform better in cooler air than they do in hot air. Density altitude is pressure altitude adjusted for the current outside air temperature. This is the most important altitude to consider if you fly in or out of high elevation airports on hot days. We'll talk more about this altitude reference in the aircraft performance section too.

You'd typically have to fly a considerable distance in VFR weather to see a pressure variance of a full inch. A large pressure difference in a short distance indicates you'll either be crossing between two different weather systems (where clouds and/or turbulence is likely), or that the winds that day are very, very strong.

A note about pressure and winds: Winds typically blow from areas of high pressure to areas of low pressure. The closer the areas are—or the bigger the difference in pressure between them—the stronger the winds will be. A cyclone is an example of a weather system in which areas of differing pressures are very close to one another.

So let's consider some real dangers of having the wrong altimeter setting. First, there's terrain clearance. You definitely want to have an accurate setting when you're flying anywhere near obstacles

like mountains, radio towers or tall buildings. But another concern is other aircraft. If everyone is using the proper altimeter setting, everything should be fine. But if someone's altimeter is way off, things can become dangerous.

Say you're flying eastbound at 5,500 feet. You've left an area reporting an altimeter setting of 29.11, and that's what you have set in your altimeter. You're heading into an area reporting 29.61 but you haven't reset your altimeter. Your altimeter continues to indicate 5,500 feet, but your *true altitude* is slowly climbing to 6,000 feet because you're gradually working the stick back to maintain that indicated altitude of 5,500. (We'll talk about why the true altitude went up instead of down in a moment.)

As (bad) luck would have it, someone else is flying westbound at 6,500. She's leaving the area of 29.61 pressure and is headed your way. She too has failed to reset her altimeter. As she works her stick to maintain 6,500 feet, her airplane is actually descending to—you guessed it—6,000 feet.

ATC sees you heading for one another and asks you to report your altitude. You report 5,500 feet. Then ATC asks the other plane to report her altitude. She reports 6,500 feet. No one's concerned because the airplanes have 1,000 feet of vertical separation.

A quick note: if the two airplanes are equipped with altitude-reporting mode-C transponders, which is typical for most training airplanes, ATC would have suspected a problem beforehand. But you can't always rely on ATC to catch your mistakes.

Whenever you're flying and you hear that another airplane in your flight path is *anywhere near your indicated altitude*, assume you are both at the very same altitude and maneuver to avoid the other aircraft. Don't expect everyone's altimeter to be set correctly and to be accurate. Even when an altimeter is set correctly it can be somewhat inaccurate. Although an altimeter is required on VFR flights, there is no FAA regulation that requires it be inspected regularly for accuracy. (Inspections are required for airplanes that are used for IFR flights.)

The FAA written test wants you to understand some math involving the altimeter. The test will give you two altimeter settings and ask you to determine the difference in feet between the two settings. Just remember that one inch equals 1,000 feet and take it from there. The difference between 29.92 and 30.92 is 1,000 feet. (30.92-29.92 = 1 inch and 1 inch equals 1,000 feet) The difference between 30.88 and 28.38 is 1,500 feet. (30.88-29.38 = 1.5 inches and 1.5 inches equals 1,500 feet) The FAA has thus far kept the altimeter math questions pretty simple, never requiring any sophisticated calculations. But who knows what can happen in the future.

The FAA also wants you to know how a change in altimeter setting will affect the instrument's altitude indication. Will the indicated altitude go up or down? There's an old aviation saying that says, "high to low, look out below." What this means is that if your altimeter setting goes from a higher number to a lower number, then your altimeter will indicate a higher altitude than you thought you were flying.

And this is precisely where the jaws of most students drop. (And those dropped jaws don't usually close again until well after the students have received their instrument ratings.) But don't panic, just try to visualize what's happening.

Let's say that you keep your airplane flying level (connected to that 1,000 foot string) but you lower your altimeter setting from 30.11 to 29.61. Immediately your altimeter will read 500 feet higher than it did before, even though you really haven't climbed or descended at all. But your instinct as a pilot wanting to maintain his altitude will be to drop the nose to lose that 500 extra feet. Hence, the "look out below." (Figure 62)

The "high to low" trick also works for air temperature. If you travel from a hot area to a cooler one without resetting your altimeter, your altimeter will gradually indicate higher altitudes.

The flip side of "high to low, look out below" is "low to high, clear the sky." When traveling from an area of low pressure (or temperature) to one of higher pressure (or temperature), your altimeter will indicate a decrease in altitude. To compensate, you'll pull back on the stick, which causes you to climb, hence the "clear the sky" reminder. The better reminder, of course, would be to reset your altimeter, but that's not as catchy sounding.

But forget trying to remember everything you've just read. Instead, spend some time in your airplane playing with the altimeter. You'll get the hang of it there better than anywhere. Pretend that ATC has given you new settings and try to

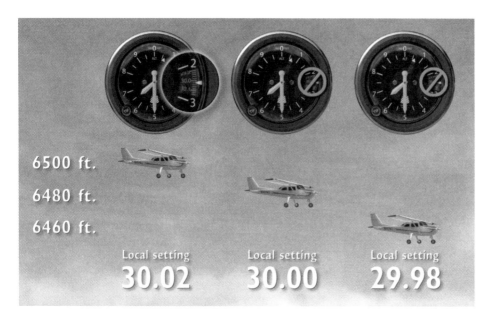

Figure 62: *HIGH TO LOW, LOOK OUT BELOW!* This airplane is flying into an area of decreasing pressure and the pilot has not readjusted the altimeter setting. As the pilot manipulates the yoke to maintain the indicated altitude of 6,500 feet, the airplane descends. Altimeters show an increase in altitude when they fly into areas of decreasing pressure because they "assume" that reduced outside air pressure means the airplane is climbing.

anticipate the effect the new setting will have on the gauge reading before you dial it in. Once you dial it in and see the new reading, imagine what you'd do to compensate. Pull up or push forward?

If you rent airplanes, ask your flight school if you can spend a half hour or so in the cockpit of an airplane that's not being flown. I'm sure they'll be happy to oblige. Do this at least once a month until you have a few hundred flight hours under your belt. Understanding the cockpit is much easier when you're not prepping for a flight. Play with everything, not just the altimeter, but remember that as soon as you turn on the electrical system, the rental clock is ticking. The altimeter doesn't require any electricity to work, so you can play with that for free.

Keep in mind that these "high to low" and "low to high" warnings assume a pilot will make yoke adjustments to maintain a constant altitude—you reset your altimeter setting and either raise or lower the nose to return to your original altitude. But an altimeter setting change alone doesn't change an airplane's altitude. You can play with

the altimeter setting all day long and not ever climb or descend. You change the airplane's altitude with the yoke, and you use your altimeter as an indicator of when it's time to do so.

It's vital that you always have an accurate altimeter setting. There are several sources from which you can obtain one. Air traffic control is a great source. ATC typically provides altimeter settings when you're using one of their services, such as flight following. Ask for the local setting if they don't offer it first. You can also get a local altimeter setting from automated weather advisory services found at many airports. We'll cover these later.

If a local setting isn't available, use the closest setting available. It might not be totally accurate, but if everyone's using it, then at least the error will be consistent between airplanes in the area. (It's kind of like getting away with bad fashion in that sense: If everyone is wearing socks with sandals, no one notices.) If everyone is using the same altimeter setting, regardless of its accuracy, then you only have terrain clearance to consider. And you shouldn't ever be flying close enough to terrain that an incorrect altimeter setting would pop the tires.

Properly setting your altimeter should be part of your pre-flight and in-flight checklists. If your airport doesn't have a control tower or an automated weather reporting system, adjust the altimeter until it indicates the field's elevation. Then you'll see the proper local altimeter setting in the Kollsman window. If you hear other airplanes asking for airport advisories inbound to your airport, let them know the current setting.

During your flights, check your altimeter setting every 50 miles or so, if ATC doesn't automatically provide you with new settings. If ATC provides a new altimeter setting that seems drastically different from your current setting, ask them to confirm the new setting before you dial it in. Mistakes happen more often than do severe atmospheric changes.

Like all other pitot-static instruments, altimeters are prone to errors caused by clogged static lines. The terrible thing about clogged static lines is that it can be tough to immediately spot the problem. This is because the pitot-static instruments connected to a clogged static line simply maintain their current indications as long as the airplane remains in straight and level flight. It's only when you change your altitude or airspeed that the problem becomes apparent.

Before we talk about what a stuck altimeter does during a climb or descent, let's theorize the effect first. By "stuck" we mean that air is trapped in the lines of the pitot-static system. We know that trapped air wants to expand during a climb. But we already have that sea-level air sample that's trapped in there too. So now we have two containers of trapped air that are both expanding as we climb. So which one wins? Actually, neither wins since both expand at the same rate.

The net effect of this is that a stuck altimeter retains the reading it showed when the system clogged, regardless of subsequent altitude changes. This might seem insignificant, but take a moment to imagine the feeling you'd get while looking at a stuck altimeter as you climb or descend. You'd quickly lose any sense of your true altitude, especially at night. It's said that IFR pilots learn to rely on their instruments, but VFR pilots do too, albeit to a lesser extent.

So what clues are there that your pitot system has a clog? The best indications are absolute, extreme precision flying on your part! If your pitot-static instruments are showing that you're maintaining your altitude and airspeed without any variance at all, chances are the system is clogged. Even the best pilots (and autopilots!) have to make minor adjustments to maintain straight and level flight.

When you identify one stuck pitot-static instrument, you must assume that the other pitot-static instrument readings are also erroneous. The first thing to do is switch over to your alternate static source, if one is available in your airplane. If not, there's still another option, but it's far less graceful. Smashing the glass face plate on the vertical speed indicator (described next) will allow air into the pitot-static system. Doing so will make the instrument inoperable, but this is okay because it's the least important pitot-static instrument.

Once new air enters the system again, the gauges correct themselves. Their readings, however, will be slightly higher than they were while using the outside static air source. I'll let your groundschool instructor explain why. The difference is negligible, but the FAA wants you to be aware of it so you can impress your friends at parties.

THE VERTICAL SPEED INDICATOR (VSI)

There are times when you'll want to know how fast you're climbing or descending. The vertical speed indicator (VSI) displays this information for

PITOT-STATIC
VSI

FAA REGULATIONS

A VSI isn't required on any flight, VFR or IFR.

ERRORS

• Calibration errors might cause a climb or descent indication when the airplane is on the ground. Factor these errors into your in-flight readings.

• A clogged static port causes the VSI to read "0" because there is no difference between subsequent air samples.

The VSI shows climb and descent speed in hundreds of feet per minute. Climbs are shown when the indicator tip is above the zero. Descents are shown when the indicator tip is below the zero. A climb rate of 650 feet per minute is shown below. A maximum of 2000 feet per minute can be accurately shown on this particular VSI. When the indicator rests over the zero, the airplane is flying level.

you. When you start a climb, the VSI starts comparing new air pressure samples to those taken moments before. By measuring the ongoing difference between the recurring samples, the instrument can estimate the vertical speed at which the airplane is traveling.

The VSI works just like the altimeter except that it compares two on-the-fly air pressure samples as opposed to one on-the-fly sample and one sea level sample. VSIs aren't adjusted in flight. We need to adjust the altimeter because it has that sea level air sample in it. But the VSI's air samples are all coming from right outside the airplane in the same atmospheric pressure.

There is a lag associated with VSI indications. This is because the instrument needs several seconds to get the hang of what's happening. The altimeter compares two air samples and the gauge reaction is fairly instantaneous. But the VSI must compare a number of samples in order to get any sense of consistency. Are we climbing? Descending? Or just encountering some bumpy air?

The VSI takes about eight seconds to display an accurate vertical speed reading. It can, however, show the *trend* of your vertical movement immediately. For example, the moment you pull back on the stick the VSI will show you in a climb. It just won't accurately display how fast you're climbing until eight seconds have passed. Trend information is useful for keeping the airplane level. If you're flying level (or think you are) and your VSI starts pointing up or down, you'll know that you're actually not flying level. (But at least you'll know your static system isn't clogged!)

Turbulent air can make a VSI dance. Don't try to chase a VSI if you're flying through bumpy air, you'll just drive (fly?) yourself crazy.

So why would you ever care how fast you were climbing or descending? You already know you're not going to get any speeding tickets for climbing too fast in a Cessna 172. But "too fast" isn't the concern here. Too slow, on the other hand, can be dangerous.

Climb performance is best measured on the VSI. If you've calculated terrain clearance that requires a 500 foot per minute climb after take off, the VSI will deliver the good or bad news. If you aren't getting the climb performance you need, you'll know it before you scrape the snow off a mountain top.

A reading of *500 feet per minute*, by the way, simply means that in a minute's time you will have climbed or descended 500 feet.

The VSI helps on the way down too. You'll calculate your descents based on a certain descent rate. Typically, this is 500 feet per minute. Based on this number (and another number called *groundspeed*, which we'll cover later), you can determine how far away from your destination airport you need to start your descent. After all, reaching your airport doesn't do you much good if you're still 10,000 feet above it! The VSI can help you remain on track with regard to descent rates. Passengers also appreciate shallow descents. Anything above 500 feet per minute might stir some delicate stomachs.

A clogged pitot-static system will result in a nice, clean reading of "zero" on the VSI. This is because the air sample comparisons no longer show any difference at all. The stuck air in there now is the same stuck air that was in there eight seconds ago. Even during a climb or descent the instrument shows no activity. A perfect VSI reading that lasts more than a few seconds is the best way to determine your static system is clogged. If in doubt, gently pull back on the yoke. If it still reads "zero," you know you have a problem that your alternate static source might be able to solve.

As mentioned, if your airplane has no alternate static source and you need one, break the faceplate on the VSI to let air into the pitot-static system. Do this, of course, only if it's absolutely necessary. If you're simply flying around the airport area on a perfectly clear day, you might not find a clogged pitot-static system to be life threatening. That said, if you're ever in doubt about your safety, break the faceplate.

THE AIRSPEED INDICATOR

As its name implies, the airspeed indicator displays the airplane's current *indicated* airspeed.

The airspeed indicator is the only instrument that makes use of the pitot tube as well as the static air port. You'll remember that the pitot tube measures ram air pressure. This means it's measuring the air pressure of the air that's "ramming" the front of the airplane. By comparing the ram air pressure to the static air pressure, the instrument determines airspeed.

Keep in mind that the pitot-tube is not some sort of wind-milling device that gets blown by the on-coming airflow and determines airspeed that way. I used to assume this. But come to think of it, if it were a wind-milling device, couldn't we also use it as a back up electrical generator? Why don't airplanes have wind-milling devices that can be used as back-up electrical generators? I'm betting it has to do with excess drag, but I don't really know. If you find out, let me know.

Back to our story:

The airspeed indicator actually has access to atmospheric air samples through three different sources. One is the static port that you just learned about. The other two sources are on the pitot tube itself. One is the ram air hole on the front of the tube. The second is a small hole in the back of the pitot tube, called the drain hole, which enables water that enters the front of the tube to drain without clogging the line. (Figure 63)

The airspeed indicator works on the same sample-comparison concepts used by the altimeter and VSI. Like the VSI, the airspeed indicator compares two on-the-fly air samples:

AIRSPEED VS. AIRSPEED

Like altitudes, there are a number of different airspeed references in aviation:

- **Indicated Airspeed (IAS)** – This is the speed indicated on your airspeed indicator. Though this is not your *true airspeed* (below), it is most commonly used for reporting purposes, such as when ATC asks for your current airspeed. The difference between indicated and true airspeeds isn't usually significant.
- **Groundspeed (GS)** – This is the speed at which your airplane is traveling over the ground. This is different than TAS or IAS because air moves. If you're flying into a 20-knot headwind, your groundspeed will be 20 knots less than your indicated airspeed. Vice-versa when you have a tail wind. The difference between GS and IAS/TAS can be quite significant, due to wind.
- **True Airspeed (TAS)** – This is your "real" airspeed, or how fast your airplane is actually flying through the air. TAS takes CAS (below) and adjusts it for current atmospheric conditions, including altitude and temperature.

The following airspeed references are less commonly considered by private pilots:

- **Calibrated Airspeed (CAS)** – The pitot-static method of determining airspeed is prone to certain errors. These errors vary at different airspeeds and airplane configurations. A CAS chart is published in the airplane's POH to show these errors at different airspeeds. The difference between IAS and CAS is usually pretty small, maybe a few knots at most, so you needn't be too concerned with it.
- **Mach** – Mach speed references are based on the speed of sound, which is dependant on the current air temperature. You'll hear Mach references used in communications between airline pilots and ATC. No one will ever expect you to report your airspeed in terms of Mach numbers.

Figure 63: *PITOT DRAIN HOLE* The drain hole located at the rear of the pitot tube enables water that enters the tube through the ram air hole to drain without clogging the tube.

one from the pitot-tube and one from the static port. The pressure difference between the two is used to determine airspeed.

That covered, let's get right into the instrument's errors and limitations. First we'll focus on the concept of *indicated* airspeed as opposed to *true*

airspeed. We'll also give these two speeds the nicknames IAS and TAS, respectively, which is how you'll usually see them referenced.

Indicated airspeed (IAS) is what you see on the airspeed indicator. True airspeed (TAS) is the airspeed at which the airplane is *truly* flying.

We'll get into the difference between the two in a second, but first we have to cloud the waters a bit more by introducing yet another airspeed. *Calibrated airspeed* (CAS) is indicated airspeed adjusted for certain instrument and installation errors. In other words, the pitot-static system ain't perfect. There are erroneous airspeed readings at different airspeeds. The errors, however, are so slim that they're hardly worth considering at all.

So we know that CAS is IAS adjusted for installation errors. But this still leaves us wondering about the mysterious TAS. If we account for installation errors, what more do we need to account for to get our real airspeed?

Atmosphere.

PITOT-STATIC
AIRSPEED INDICATOR

FAA REGULATIONS

An airspeed indicator is required for all flights. You cannot fly legally without one. [FAR 91.205]

ERRORS

- IAS does not account for installation/equipment errors or atmospheric conditions.
- Clogged pitot-tube reads "zero" airspeed.
- Clogged static port increases airspeed with a decrease in altitude and vice-versa.
- Clogged drain hole and ram air hole causes airspeed indicator to behave like an altimeter.

The white arc on the dial shows the safe speed range for having flaps extended. The larger green arc is the normal operating speed range. The yellow arc shows speeds that are only safe in smooth air. The red line shows the speed that should never be exceeded. There are special names for some of these speeds; we'll cover them in the performance section.

Specifically, atmospheric pressure and temperature. Once again atmospheric concerns come to bite us in the elevator, so to speak. TAS is CAS adjusted for atmospheric pressure (altitude) and temperature.

Let's try to understand why atmosphere is an issue to airspeed. Pressure decreases with altitude; we already know this. At 10,000 feet, air is less dense than it is at sea level. Less dense air should mean less resistance, or less drag. Right?

It does.

This is why airplane POH performance charts might show slight increases in TAS at some higher altitudes. Some, that is, but not all. There is a point of diminishing returns. Recall our discussion of how the less dense air inhibits the engine's ability to generate thrust. There's a slight point in the altitude/performance curve where the lack of drag affords the airplane a slight advantage in terms of airspeed. Above that point, however, the engine starts gagging for air, which reverses the effect.

Ever wonder why commercial airplanes like to fly at higher altitudes? The decrease of atmospheric drag, which leads to better fuel economy, is one of the big reasons. (Crazy student pilots at lower altitudes is another good one.)

So what about that ram air pressure hitting the pitot tube? Wouldn't that also be decreased at higher altitudes? It is. So the airspeed indicator shows slower airspeeds at higher altitudes than the airplane is actually flying. In fact, the only time that IAS and TAS will be the same is at sea level under standard atmospheric conditions.

Atmospheric pressure also decreases in higher temperatures. If it's warmer at 10,000 feet than it should be (according to the standard temperature scales on which the POH performance charts are based), then the air is even less dense, meaning that it's at a lower pressure than it would be at standard temperature.

The POH for your airplane will have charts that show IAS/CAS/TAS comparisons at various altitudes. The difference is typically very small, but it's yet another thing you're expected to understand.

By considering these sorts of things, however, you gain a better understanding of how atmospheric pressure affects all things in aviation and how all things in aviation are interrelated. For example, if the pressure at 10,000 is less than it is at 1,000 feet, what happens to the pressure at 40,000 feet? You'd be correct to guess that it's way, way less. So the airspeed indicator would indicate an even slower airspeed at 40,000 feet. (If you ever get your Cessna or Piper up to 40,000 feet, let me know if I was correct.)

Before you start thinking that those big jumbos flying up there at 40,000 feet are doing so with useless airspeed indications, be aware that their airspeeds are determined as percentages of the speed of sound.

The speed of sound is referred to as *Mach 1*. So an airplane flying at Mach .8 is traveling at 80% of the speed of sound. The actual speed of sound is dependant on the current temperature. So an airplane flying at Mach .8 one day might be flying at 500 knots, while Mach .8 the next day might be 550 knots. An instrument called a *Mach indicator* (or *Mach Meter*) takes care of airspeed monitoring for those high-flying aircraft. When they're flying near the ground, they rely on good ol' airspeed indicators, just like you and I do.

Let's take our discussion on decreasing pressure a bit further before we get back on topic. As atmospheric pressure decreases, so decreases an airplane's ability to generate lift. So it would stand to reason that eventually an airplane wouldn't be able to climb anymore. Right? After all, it's the density of the air that's used as the lifting force. Without atmospheric density, lift isn't possible.

This is where an airplane's *service ceiling* and *absolute ceiling* come in. A service ceiling is the maximum altitude to which that airplane can climb and still maintain a climb rate of 100 feet per minute. An absolute ceiling is the maximum altitude to which an airplane can climb. Every airplane has service and absolute altitudes. Keep in mind that these are *maximum* altitudes, not *promised* altitudes. The service ceiling on one of the Cessna 172s I fly is listed as 14, 200 feet in the airplane's POH. Yeah, right! Maybe I could climb that high if I filled the tanks with helium instead of avgas.

So what determines the absolute ceiling at which an airplane can fly?

First let's revisit the concept of gravity, the force of nature that hinders our climbs. We need lift to overcome gravity. Gravity is a constant force, so one might think that if you overcome it at sea level you should be able to climb forever.

But as altitude increases, and the density of the surrounding air decreases, our ability to generate lift also decreases. Less dense air means that there is less drag. And, as we've learned, where there is less drag, there is less lift, and vice-versa. We can't increase the outside air's density to satisfy our needs, so our only option is to move more air over the wings. To do this we need more thrust. But we can't generate more thrust because our engine is already maxed out and the thinning air has already made it less efficient.

So it would seem as though we have only two options. One is to put a more powerful engine on the airplane, and the second is to somehow get the same level of performance from our current engine at altitude that we do at sea level. The first option usually isn't an option, but the second option is called a *turbocharger*.

A turbocharger compresses the air that enters the engine so the engine "thinks" it's at (or nearer) sea level, and performs accordingly. Turbocharged airplanes get the extra pep they need at altitude to be able to climb even higher. If you look at the performance specs for an airplane that is available with and without a turbocharger, you'll see that the turbocharged model has a higher ceiling, though it might not necessarily be able to fly any faster than the standard model.

So we've solved the problem. With more power we could move more air over our wings, thereby generating more lift. But every airplane has a finite amount of power, with or without a turbo-charger. And this is why every airplane has a service ceiling.

If you remember one thing from this section, remember that airplanes hit their "glass ceilings" when there isn't enough available power to over-come the thinning atmosphere. Atmosphere thins for two reasons:

- Increased altitude

- Increased air temperature

So now imagine yourself sitting on a runway ready to take off. You have a full payload of fuel and friends. The airport's elevation is 7,700 feet and it's 97 degrees fahrenheit outside on a beautiful summer day. Are you going to need more power or less power than normal to achieve the performance you're used to at your little home airfield by the sea?

Way more.

The higher elevation means decreased air density. But that whopping high air temperature is really what will do you in. Mix the two together and that little airplane simply is not going to want to fly that day. The most immediate thing you'll notice is a much longer takeoff roll and far less climb performance. As you continue to climb, you'll also find your airplane pooping out at a far lower altitude than normal. Consider this your first discussion on what's called *density altitude*. We'll talk more about it later.

Figure 64: *HOUSE HUNTING* This little spider is only inches away from finding a nice, cozy home in the ram air hole of this pitot tube. If he "moved in," he would certainly cause erroneous airspeed indications if he didn't clog the tube entirely.

Now back to the airspeed indicator.

Clogs in the pitot-static system are perhaps most dangerous and confusing as they apply to the air-speed indicator. Erroneous airspeed indications can prompt pilots into doing some dangerous things. Since there are three air sources feeding the airspeed indicator, we have to consider the effects of clogs in some or all of those openings.

A clogged pitot tube is easy to recognize: the airspeed drops to zero because the ram air pressure has also dropped to zero. Most in-flight pitot clogs are caused by ice or bugs, though the likelihood of a bug clog decreases with altitude. But it's not unlikely to find bugs in the tube while you're still on the ground. (Figure 64)

Most airplanes have a heater element in the pitot-tube that can be used to melt ice (and even roast bugs!). A switch is located in the cockpit. If you suspect a bug in your tube during you preflight ground inspection, turn on the pitot heat to see if you can coax the little bugger out.

PITOT-STATIC SYSTEM BLOCKAGE ERRORS

The table below shows the effects that blockages (ice, bugs, dirt, etc.) in the pitot-static system have on the pitot-static instruments. The results shown assume a total blockage of the various air ports, but keep in mind that pitot-static system blockages might be only partial or might occur intermittently.

		Altimeter	VSI	Airspeed Indicator
1	Static Port: Clear Pitot Ram Air: Clear Pitot Drain: Clear	Normal	Normal	Normal
2	Static Port: Clogged Pitot Ram Air: Clear Pitot Drain: Clear	Freezes	Indicates zero	Airspeed remains accurate at the altitude where the blockage occurred. Airspeed reads lower at altitudes higher than where the blockage occurred and higher at altitudes lower than where the blockage occurred.
3	Static Port: Clear Pitot Ram Air: Clogged Pitot Drain: Clear	No effect	No effect	Airspeed drops rapidly to zero.
4	Static Port: Clear Pitot Ram Air: Clear Pitot Drain: Clogged	No effect	No effect	No effect
5	Static Port: Clogged Pitot Ram Air: Clogged Pitot Drain: Clear	Freezes	Indicates zero	Airspeed slowly drops to zero as trapped ram air "bleeds" out of the pitot drain hole.
6	Static Port: Clogged Pitot Ram Air: Clear Pitot Drain: Clogged	Freezes	Indicates zero	Same as #2.
7	Static Port: Clear Pitot Ram Air: Clogged Pitot Drain: Clogged	No effect	No effect	Works like an altimeter: Indicates no speed changes at blockage altitude. Shows a speed increase as the airplane climbs and vice versa.
8	Static Port: Clogged Pitot Ram Air: Clogged Pitot Drain: Clogged	Freezes	Indicates zero	Freezes

Only the airspeed indicator is affected by pitot system blockages. A clogged static port, on the other hand, affects all pitot-static instruments. A stable "zero" indication on the VSI might be your first clue to a clogged static port. In situation #5, the airspeed indicator slowly drops to zero because the trapped ram air pressure starts to escape through the pitot tube's drain hole. The airspeed drops to zero quickly in situation #3 because the ram air pressure is cut off at the source, but it is not trapped in the system. This is the same effect to the airplane as if it were sitting still on the ground. If you suspect a blockage in the pitot tube, turn on the pitot heat for a while and see if it clears. If you suspect a static port blockage, switch to your alternate static source.

If your airspeed indicator suddenly drops to "zero" in-flight, or starts acting erratically, turn the pitot-heat on for a few minutes and see if that works.

The pitot heat element is electrically powered, so if you lose your electrical system, you can forget about any bug barbecues.

Check your pitot tube for clogs during your preflight inspection and you should be fine. The likelihood of a bug getting inside the tube during flight is pretty slim. Always check your airspeed indicator when you first start your takeoff roll. Something could get in there between the time you perform your preflight inspection and the time you take off.

At the back of the pitot tube is the drain hole. If this clogs at the same time your pitot tube's ram-air opening clogs, your airspeed indicator starts playing a horrible trick on you. It behaves like an altimeter. If you climb, your airspeed indication goes up. When you descend, the indication goes down too. This is exactly the opposite of what happens normally. When you climb, your airspeed should decrease. And when you descend, your airspeed should (or at least could) pick up.

So why the reverse? Because with both holes clogged, there would be air trapped inside the pitot tube lines. And what happens to trapped air as altitude increases? It expands. The increasing pressure of the expanding air fools the airspeed indicator into thinking the airplane is flying faster. This, after all, is the very basis on which the airspeed indicator functions.

A static port clog is your final concern with regard to the airspeed indicator. And once again, we're going to theorize what will happen rather than just say what will happen.

An airspeed indicator works by comparing a ram air pressure sample to a static air pressure sample. Let's say that the pitot tube is fine, but at 6,500 feet the static port clogs. Okay, so we

have ram air pressure continuing to enter the system and we have trapped static air that was sampled at 6,500 feet.

As long as we remain straight and level, we probably won't notice anything since 6,500 foot air is 6,500 foot air, regardless of when it was sampled. But we want to climb, so we add some power and pull the nose up.

What's going to happen to our trapped 6,500 foot static air pressure sample as we climb? It's going to expand as the surrounding air pressure drops. The ram air pressure will seem to be weakening by comparison to the ever expanding trapped static air. So the airspeed indicator will think the airplane is slowing down.

Consequently, when the airplane descends, the airspeed indicator assumes the airplane is speeding up because the ram air pressure will increasingly overpower the trapped static air pressure.

The problem with a clogged static port is that airspeed indicator readings can seem believable even when they're wrong.

So how do you ever know what's gone wrong, if anything? Cross check! Now that you understand the relationship between the altimeter, VSI and airspeed indicator, you know that if one is acting oddly, you need to check to see if the others are acting oddly too. Your best friend in these situations can be your VSI. If you see that perfect "zero" reading, assume system-wide trouble. Switch to your alternate static source and see what happens.

If you don't have a VSI and can't ascertain whether or not your static system is clogged, you can cross-check your pitot-static indications with the indications on gauges run by the vacuum system, which is described next. Once again, systems redundancy can save the day.

One final note that applies to all instruments: If an instrument in your airplane has failed, cover it up with a sticky note or anything that you have that will fit. Some folks carry those plastic soap dishes with the suction cups on them for just this purpose. It becomes second nature to scan your instruments and act upon the readings you see. If one of those readings is false, your corrective actions might not be appropriate.

THE VACUUM SYSTEM

As soon as you see how dirty the insides of most trainer airplanes are you'll realize that an airplane's vacuum system has nothing to do with housekeeping. Driven by the airplane's engine—thereby not dependant on the airplane's electrical system—the vacuum system generates suction that drives the mechanical gyros found on a few cockpit instruments.

Because the vacuum system is powered by the airplane's engine, if you lose your engine you can forget about using your vacuum-driven gauges. Luckily, your turn coordinator, being electrically powered, is not affected by an engine failure.

Gyro-based instruments help you determine your airplane's three-dimensional position in space. The gyros spin at very high speeds (something like 18,000 RPM) and in doing so, behave like toy tops spinning on tables. When a top spins it wants to remain upright. If the table is tilted, the top tends to lean to remain that upright attitude. There is a dull technical term for this phenomenon, and yes, you're expected to know it: *rigidity-in-space*. Your groundschool instructor will go over this in more depth.

Gyro-based instruments in airplanes work the same way a toy top works. (They're just far more expensive.) The gyros in these instruments want to remain upright regardless of the airplane's attitude. This is how we determine if we're in a descent, climb or banking left or right. When we pitch up or down, or bank, the gyros remain in position. We effectively rotate around them. By connecting the gyros to various dials, we can read indications of our pitch (up/down) and bank (left/right) degrees.

Notice I said that the gyros are *driven by* vacuum suction, not *powered by* vacuum suction. This is because the vacuum system supplies no electrical power to anything; it is not an electrical generator. It supplies a source of air suction and that's all. The advantage to this method of driving the instruments is that it offers a system that's independent of the airplane's electrical system. Sure, the gyro instruments could all be electrically-powered—the turn coordinator is an electrically-powered gyro instrument. Powering them electrically would probably even make them more reliable, but it would mean that if you lost your electrical system you'd also lose too many vital instruments.

Some airplanes lack a vacuum system and rely solely on electrical power. While this might seem like it wouldn't be legal, it is. Neither of the two gauges driven by the vacuum system are required for VFR flights, so if the vacuum system fails, it's not considered a big deal for airplanes operating under VFR.

IFR flights are a different story. The vacuum-driven gauges *are* required for IFR flight. So those vacuum-lacking airplanes are not legal for IFR flight unless they have a back-up electrical system, which some do.

Figure 65: *SUCTION GAUGE* Keep an eye on the suction gauge to ensure that adequate vacuum suction is available to your gyro-based instruments. The acceptable range is defined in your airplane's POH. Suction that is too low or too high can cause erroneous readings on the gyro instruments.

The problem with vacuum systems is that the suction provided by the system must be within a certain range in order for the gyro instruments to function properly. There is a cockpit gauge to help you determine if the suction is adequate. It's called, oddly enough, the *suction gauge*. (Figure 65) Your airplane's POH will identify the acceptable range of suction for your system. If your indication is near the low or high end of that range, have the system checked. If it is below or beyond that range, you can't rely on the gauges.

Most vacuum systems will gradually lose their ability to generate suction before they fail completely. Though this might seem to be a benefit, it's actually a concern. A totally failed vacuum system simply doesn't work. The gyros do nothing and it's easy to recognize the failure. But a partially failed system is dangerous. The gauges appear to work, but can be slowly drifting. A pilot following them faithfully can find herself sideways before she ever realizes something is wrong. Obviously this is far more dangerous during IMC flying than it is during VMC. (Remember, IMC means *instrument meteorological conditions*. In other words, low-visibility IFR flying.)

We'll discuss some good ways to identify system failures in a little while.

So why not just do away with the vacuum system and install two independent electrical systems? While some aircraft manufacturers have gone this route, most have not. Regardless, your pilot training requires that you understand the vacuum system, no matter how obsolete you might find it. Keep in mind that if the FAA governed culinary training, there'd be test questions on butter-churning equipment and technique.

INSTRUMENTS IN THE VACUUM SYSTEM

Two cockpit instruments are based on gyros that are rotated by vacuum suction: the *attitude indicator* (above) and the *heading indicator* (below). As mentioned, the turn

coordinator is based on an electrically-powered gyro, so it's not part of the vacuum system.

THE ATTITUDE INDICATOR

If you were stranded on a desert isle and could only take one cockpit instrument with you, which one would it be? Most pilots, if not first recognizing the absolute absurdity of the question, would choose the attitude indicator. This is because the attitude indicator (also called the *artificial horizon*) is the only cockpit instrument that provides both pitch and bank information. A single glance at the attitude indicator can tell you to what degree you're climbing, descending or turning.

Of course a glance out the window can tell you pretty much the same thing, assuming you're flying in VMC like you're supposed to be. In truth, the all-important attitude indicator, preferred by islanders everywhere, is of limited use to the VFR pilot. We could get along fine without it. VFR training encourages pilots to judge climbs, descents and turns based on visual references to the horizon. If you spend too much time watching instruments, your CFI will smack you. Cockpit instruments show a lot of useful information, but they don't show oncoming 737s.

That said, there are good reasons to keep the attitude indicator in your visual scan. One is that it helps you fly more precisely. For example, if you know you're supposed to climb at an airspeed of 85 knots, you have two choices: you can yank back and forth on the yoke until your airspeed stabilizes at 85 knots, or you can pull back on the yoke until your attitude indicator shows the exact climb gradient that will yield an 85-knot airspeed. Both methods work, but the first way just looks tacky. By moving the stick back until the attitude indicator shows, say a 10-degree pitch-up, you can sit back and wait for your airspeed to adjust to exactly 85 knots. Stuff like this is the essence of

VACUUM
ATTITUDE INDICATOR

FAA REGULATIONS

Attitude indicators are not required for VFR flights.

ERRORS

- The miniature airplane on the instrument's display must be manually set to determine level flight. This should be checked periodically throughout your flights. Your VSI lets you know when you're flying level.

- Older attitude indicators might "tumble" if your airplane reaches banks in excess of 90 degrees.

Straight and level flight is shown on the attitude indicator below. The orange indicator in the middle of the display represents the airplane's wings and nose. The white tick marks along the outer edge rotate as the airplane turns, indicating 10, 20, 30, 60 and 90 degree bank angles. The tick marks just above and below the orange indicator dot indicate degrees of pitch. The attitude indicator is the only flight instrument capable of showing both pitch and bank information.

pilot coolness and the basis for instrument training. There's just too much to do during an IFR flight for you to be "chasing" airspeeds.

The other thing that's important about keeping the attitude indicator in your visual scan is that you subconsciously remember it's there. And there is a time when the attitude indicator can save a VFR pilot's life. If you're ever flying along and all of a sudden an unforecast cloud mass engulfs your little Cessna 172, you become what's known as a "VFR pilot in IMC." As far as ATC is concerned, this is akin to being a child with a loaded AK-47, safety-lock off.

At that moment you'd better start following the same flight practices as an IFR pilot or you're going to die. (Notice I said an "unforecast cloud layer." This is because I assume you checked weather before you left to make sure there were no clouds in your flight path.)

The moment your outside visibility goes to zero, you get your little eyeballs on that attitude indicator and you keep them there! You glance *momentarily* at the heading indicator (described next) to determine your reciprocal (opposite) heading and you *gently* turn your airplane around.

The FAA wants you to remember that if you ever fly into a cloud, you are supposed to initiate a 180-degree turn to return to clear skies. Easier said than done. As soon as you lose outside visual clues you're going to be hating life. Your instinct might be to turn the airplane, but you might turn too tightly in desperation to end the nightmare as soon as possible. You'll turn the yoke and get the airplane into some obscene 40-degree bank and you'll wait.

But the funny thing about lift...remember lift? The funny thing about lift is that even in a cloud you're going to lose some during a turn. To compensate, you'll need to pull back on the yoke. But how much? If you can't see the horizon, how do you know how far back to pull?

Some pilots will instinctively pull back too much just like they banked too much. This maneuver—usually only performed once by a pilot—leads to what's called a *graveyard spiral*. This is one maneuver you usually don't hear pilots boasting about in airport lounges unless you're clairaudient.

So how then do you safely control your rate of turn and pitch without reference to the horizon? By referencing the *artificial horizon*, otherwise known as your attitude indicator. Once you lose your outside visual references, your attitude indicator becomes the center of your universe. Lock your gaze on it and don't let up until the skies are clear again.

So, recovery from the *unforecast* cloud layer becomes:

STEP 1.   Eyes *immediately* on the attitude indicator.

STEP 2.   Glance at the heading indicator (shown next) to determine your reciprocal heading. (In other words, the heading that will get you going the opposite direction you're currently headed.)

STEP 3.   Eyes back on the attitude indicator.

STEP 4.   Pull the stick back and turn so the attitude indicator shows a 5-degree climb and a standard rate turn. (A standard-rate turn is the bank angle for your airplane at which the wings of the turn coordinator align with the angled tick marks, as shown in figure 66.) Use your best judgement on which way to turn based on your surroundings.

STEP 5.   A 180-degree turn at standard rate is going to take about 1 minute. That in mind, *occasionally* glance at your heading indicator until you can roll out on the proper heading.

STEP 6.   Keep your eye on the attitude indicator and continue to fly straight until you're clear of the clouds.

Figure 66: *TURN BACK* The moment the horizon disappears, gently pull back on the yoke until the attitude indicator shows a 5-degree climb and turn the airplane in a standard-rate turn until you have reversed your direction of travel. A standard-rate turn is the bank angle for your airplane at which the wings of the turn coordinator are aligned with the gauge's angled tick marks (below).

So why the 5-degree climb? One reason is that it helps you maintain altitude since you'll lose some in the turn. But it also *forces* you to think about your pitch angle and this might be the more important reason. Without this kind of focus, you're more likely to get yourself into a very steep climb or a descent, neither of which you want.

You'll practice turns like this with your CFI. Please don't consider this information to be any sort of IFR training. This is not IFR flying. This is VFR recovery from IMC. IFR flying is about getting from point A to point B safely, regardless of visibility. What we're talking about here is recovery from a situation that will otherwise kill you.

Think you can handle flight through the clouds without IFR training? If you do, then I strongly encourage you to arrange time to go flying with an instructor during IMC. Nothing in aviation training is quite so sobering as seeing how you'll react when you lose reference to the horizon.

At the very least, ask your CFI to play a little game with you. (As if CFIs need any encouragement to play games.) Tell your CFI you would like to establish yourself in straight and level flight and then close your eyes and see how long you can maintain that attitude. I had never heard of this exercise before my checkride. My examiner asked me to try this during the flight portion of my test.

I got myself established in straight and level flight and I closed my eyes. Thinking I was smart, I figured I would listen to the sound of the engine as my main clue as to whether the airplane was climbing or descending. I knew through training that I wouldn't be able to rely on my senses, because they would be compromised without a visual reference.

At first, I did pretty good. My examiner even commented on how well I was holding my attitude. But then something odd happened: the engine sounded as if it were speeding up, but I knew that couldn't be possible because I was still flying straight and level. After about 30 seconds, the sound of the engine was making it quite clear to me that something was wrong. At about 45 seconds, my examiner asked me to open my eyes and recover. I was past a 40-degree bank angle and *climbing*! I was about 5 knots above my stall speed.

So much for relying on the sound of the engine.

Some attitude indicators will get confused if they reach excessive bank or pitch angles of 90 degrees or more. This is called *tumbling* because the gyro will simply lose its sense of horizon and tumble freely. Many modern attitude indicators are immune to this. But even if yours is old, you'll probably never have to worry about it. A 90-degree *pitch* angle is either straight up or straight down. A 90-degree *bank* angle is when the airplane is flying sideways with wings pointing straight up and down. Serious stuff. If you ever find yourself in excess of this degree, pray that an aerobatics instructor is in the right seat.

THE HEADING INDICATOR (DIRECTIONAL GYRO)

The *heading indicator* (also called *directional gyro*, *DG* or *HI*) is the cockpit instrument pilots use to determine and maintain their direction of flight. The display of the DG is based on the same headings used on magnetic compasses: north is heading 360, east is heading 090, south is heading 180, west is heading 270. Headings are usually spoken as individual numbers. So 360 is spoken three-six-zero. The heading 090 is spoken zero-nine-zero, or zero-niner-zero. I don't hear people say "niner" as much when talking headings.

The remaining headings are somewhere between 001 and 360. One degree south of east, for example, would be 091. 000 and 360 are the same direction, but typically you'll hear references to heading 360 or "north" instead of a heading of zero-zero-zero. There are no decimal headings, such as 340.3. It's either 340 or 341.

The DG is a secondary instrument for direction finding because airplanes are also equipped with traditional magnetic compasses, which are required by FAA regulations. But a compass is less easy to navigate by for reasons that I'll let your CFI cover. To make things easier on pilots, the heading indicator was developed.

The DG, like the attitude indicator, is based on a gyro. But unlike the attitude indicator, the DG isn't a set-it-and-forget-it instrument. The DG has to be reset every now and then during flight because it drifts somewhat. This drift is called *gyroscopic precession*. Your CFI will explain more about this infuriating phenomenon. You don't really need to know why gyros precess; there's

VACUUM
HEADING INDICATOR

FAA REGULATIONS

Heading indicators (also called "directional gyros") are not required by the FARs for VFR flights. A magnetic compass is the direction-finding equipment required by the FARs.

ERRORS

- DGs are prone to gyroscopic precession and must be manually reset to the magnetic compass heading every 15 or so minutes.

- Some heading indicators will precess after steep turns or after 180 degree turns at any bank.

As the airplane turns, so turns the dial on the DG, which indicates the airplane's heading. The knob enables pilots to set the DG heading to match the magnetic compass. The DG is prone to gyroscopic precession, so pilots must regularly check its alignment. The ticks around the dial give the pilot a visual aid to determine headings at 45 degree intervals. A heading of 110 (one-one-zero) is shown below.

not much you can do as a pilot to reduce the error. But you do need to know that it happens and remember to make adjustments periodically, as needed. (The attitude indicator has a built-in mechanism for automatically correcting its own gyroscopic precession.)

The magnetic compass is where you'll look for DG adjustments. A compass might be tough to use as a means of navigation, but it's plenty easy to use just to read a heading. When you're flying straight and level you can read your actual magnetic heading from your compass. You then align your DG to that heading and you're set.

You can't set your DG to your compass while you're turning, for obvious reasons. You can, however, set it once you're stabilized in a climb, descent or level flight. The idea is that you must be *stabilized* and flying straight ahead whenever you set it. This way the compass reading will remain steady. Compasses like to drift back and forth and will do so during and after turns.

Usually the DG's drift is gradual and undetectable, which is why you must keep on top of it. If you're following a heading and your DG is drifting 10 degrees or more per hour, you'll find yourself nowhere near your destination after a while.

A fairly standard time interval for setting the DG is every 15 minutes. If you know your DG is prone to drifting, however, you should check yours more regularly. If you *don't know* if your DG is prone to drifting, such as when you rent an unfamiliar airplane, check it more regularly until you can estimate its drift.

You should also confirm DG alignment after turns of 180 degrees or more. Some DGs drift considerably during significant turns like this. Also check its alignment after performing any steep-bank turns.

There's nothing worse than nailing your heading for thirty minutes or more only to realize that your heading has been drifting the entire time. If

> **[NEED TO KNOW]** VACUUM SYSTEM
>
> - Which instruments are vacuum driven?
> - What is the acceptable range of suction for your airplane?
> - How prone to precession is your DG?

you find yourself with nothing to do in the cockpit, check your DG, it could probably use an adjustment. (And then check your oil pressure and fuel gauges while you're at it!)

HEADING GAMES

Determining correct headings to fly can be confusing. Even when you know which heading you want, it's not uncommon for pilots to inadvertently turn to the wrong heading. There are a few tricks that can help you reach the heading you're after.

COMMON TURNING ANGLES

Certain turning angles are very common when flying an airplane. You'll often find yourself turning at angles of 45-, 90-, 135- and 180-degrees. In a car such turns are easy because there are plenty of ground objects to reference. But in the sky, something as simple as a 90-degree angle can be difficult to gauge.

If math is your forté, feel free to add the turning angle to your current heading and turn away. But for the rest of us, the DG manufacturers have provided a shortcut. There are small ticks located around the circumference of the DG dial that indicate these common turning angles. (Figure 67)

So if you need to turn 90 degrees from your current heading, you just look at the heading shown by the 90-degree tick mark. The DG in figure 67 is on a heading of 060. If that pilot needed to turn 90-degrees to the right, she would turn to heading 150, as shown in the image. A 90-

Figure 67: *TICK MARKS THE SPOT* All around the outer edge of the dials of most DG are tick marks that represent 45-degree angles from the airplane's current heading.

degree turn to the left would put her on heading 330. If she needed to turn 135-degrees to the right, she'd turn to heading 195.

It's important to choose the new heading *before* you start your turn because those numbers move with the dial.

If you need to turn around and head back to the direction from which you came—such as when you've mistakenly flown into a cloud, as discussed above—look to the bottom of the dial.

One trick to remember before you turn to any new heading is to verbally say the new heading before you start the turn. You'd be amazed at how easy it is to forget what heading you're supposed to roll out on when you're eyeball-deep in a turn. Saying it aloud beforehand can make it easier to remember.

If you think the likelihood of forgetting a new heading is slim, keep in mind that a standard-rate turn of 180 degrees—such as the one you'd

take to escape from a cloud—takes a full minute. A minute is a long time to wait when you can't see the horizon.

But even under less stressful turning conditions a new heading is easy to forget. During a turn you will be maintaining altitude, maintaining bank angle, watching your airspeed, watching for traffic, and perhaps even talking on the radio. To get a better sense of what a minute feels like in an airplane, practice standard-rate turns. Hell, I could forget my name in such time, let alone my roll-out heading!

DETERMINING RECIPROCAL HEADINGS

By looking at the opposite side of your heading on the dial, you can quickly determine your reciprocal heading without doing any math. For example, say you're heading 045 (northeast) and you need to turn around. The easiest way to know your reciprocal heading is to look at the bottom of the dial, which will read 225.

The last digit on reciprocal headings is always the same as the last digit of the original heading, so don't sweat it if you can't quickly determine the last digit clearly when glancing at the opposite side of the DG.

I'd like to offer you the perfect trick for determining the reciprocal of any heading without doing any math in your head. But I can't because I don't know of one. There are a few ways of considering the problem that can make it easier, depending on your ability to crunch numbers mentally. None are perfect for me because mental number-crunching is just above levitation on the list of things I don't do well.

First there's the most obvious: adding or subtracting 180. The reciprocal of any heading is that heading plus or minus 180 degrees. If you add 180 degrees to a heading and it equals more than 360, you must subtract 180 degrees instead. The opposite holds true if you subtract and end up with less than zero. So if your heading is 045, you can add 180 to that to get 225. (If you subtracted 180 you would have ended up with minus 135, which isn't a legitimate heading.)

For those that find adding or subtracting "180" to be less than simple, there's the option of adding or subtracting 200. This involves a second step, however, of adding or subtracting 20. So if your heading is 045 you can add 200 to that, which is 245. Then subtract 20, which leaves you with 225. The problem with this method is that you might forget that last step of adding or subtracting 20.

In either case, remember you only need to consider the first two digits. The last digit on the reciprocal headings is always the same.

The third option is the sexiest when it works, but it doesn't always work. If the first digit of the heading is 3, subtract 2 from the first digit and add 2 to the second digit. For example:

- Heading 314
  3-2 = 1
  1 + 2 = 3
  4 remains the same
  New heading = 134

- Heading 300
  3-2 = 1
  0 + 2 = 2
  0 remains the same
  New heading = 120

- Heading 350
  3-2 = 1
  5 + 2 = 7
  0 remains the same
  New heading = 170

Pretty hip, huh? It's not as easy for the headings that don't start with 3, however. The table below shows the formula for each heading. You can see that there is a pattern of sorts, but it's not easy to recognize and remember.

Perhaps the best way to remember this is that if the first two numbers are 00, 01, 10, 11, 18, 19, 28 or 29, you need a different formula. That's too much for my brain, however.

Hdng.	Form.	Recip.	Hdng.	Form.	Recip.
007	+1 -2	187	187	-1 +2	007
017	+1 -2	197	197	-1 +2	017
027	+2 -2	207	207	-2 +2	027
037	+2 -2	217	217	-2 +2	037
047	+2 -2	227	227	-2 +2	047
057	+2 -2	237	237	-2 +2	057
067	+2 -2	247	247	-2 +2	067
077	+2 -2	257	257	-2 +2	077
087	+2 -2	267	267	-2 +2	087
097	+2 -2	277	277	-2 +2	097
107	+1 -2	287	287	-1 +2	107
117	+1 -2	297	297	-1 +2	117
127	+2 -2	307	307	-2 +2	127
137	+2 -2	317	317	-2 +2	137
147	+2 -2	327	327	-2 +2	147
157	+2 -2	337	337	-2 +2	157
167	+2 -2	347	347	-2 +2	167
177	+2 -2	357	357	-2 +2	177

CROSS-CHECKING COCKPIT INSTRUMENTS

Three things are primary to keeping an airplane airborne:

- Bank angle

- Pitch angle

- Airspeed

If any one of these gets out of hand, you could lose control of the airplane. Not surprisingly, the "six pack" of flight instruments found on every trainer airplane is designed to help you monitor these conditions and make adjustments as necessary.

The focus of your private pilot training is to ensure that you are able to fly your airplane *without* relying on any instruments. Instrument cross-checking is generally reserved for IFR training because the accuracy of instrument indications under IFR is critical. I include it here because I think the skill not only helps you understand the purpose of each instrument better, but it gives you a head start on one of the most important aspects of instrument training.

If you had two of every flight instrument and every system in your airplane, it would be pretty easy to recognize a problem. Larger aircraft do often have duplicate instruments and systems, but our little trainers are not so well equipped. Even with the basic set of gauges we have, though, it's still possible to identify problems.

We're not comparing apples to apples, as we would be doing if we had duplicate instruments, so we need to think more in terms of *information* rather than hardware. For example, when cross-checking the altimeter, we don't simply look for another instrument that shows altitude. There isn't one. We look for another instrument that shows the same *core information* the altimeter offers. To do this you need to think beyond the instrument's face plate and consider what it's really telling you.

Consider, for example, a car's speedometer. We keep an eye on it every time we drive a car. But what does it *really* tell us? If your answer is "speed," then you're not thinking deeply enough. A simple speedometer tells a fairly detailed story:

- The engine is on.

- The car is moving.

- The car is accelerating or decelerating.

- The gas tanks are not empty.

- Gas is flowing to the engine.

- At least *some* spark plugs are firing.

- The car is in gear.

- The wheels are turning.

- The odometer is advancing.

Lots of information comes from that simple gauge. Most of that information is overkill to drivers, but pilots need all the information they can get.

This is how we want to think of our flight instruments. Primary information aside, what secondary information does a given gauge offer? For example, your DG *primarily* indicates the heading you're flying, and your turn coordinator *primarily* indicates when you're in a turn. But if the DG's dial is spinning, wouldn't that also indicate a turn? Conversely, a bank indication on the turn coordinator suggests that your DG dial should be spinning. If you see a bank indication on the turn coordinator and the DG dial isn't spinning, something is wrong.

You can be even more creative with cross-checking too. For example, if you want to verify that your electric system is active, tilt the wings and glance at your turn coordinator. Did the little airplane's wings tilt? If so, you have electrical power.

Think about this stuff during your flights. Consider which instruments "say" the same things. During VFR flights is the time to really learn this stuff. Later, during IFR flights, this knowledge can save your life.

Flight instruments can each be categorized as *pitch*, *bank* or *speed* indicators, with some fitting into more than one category. Once you understand which instrument fits where, you're half way home. Then just keep in mind that pitch, bank and airspeed is what you're trying to determine each time you look at the gauges. So if one gauge is dead, you won't panic. You'll just look for the information it supplies elsewhere.

No gauge in a training airplane is so special or unique that without it you'd be lost. There's a back up for everything. You just need to know where to look.

BANK INSTRUMENTS

To determine bank information, you look to gauges that do something when the airplane is turning. Forget specific indications for a moment, we're looking only for movement of some kind.

Does the altimeter do anything special just because the airplane is turning? Nope. It indicates changes in altitude only. Altitude can certainly change during a turn if that's the pilot's intention, or if she has not compensated for the partial loss of vertical lift, but turns themselves do not necessitate changes in altitude. So the altimeter cannot be considered a bank instrument.

Likewise, the VSI, airspeed indicator and tachometer show no direct or indirect indications of airplane bank angle.

Instruments that *do* offer bank information are the attitude indicator and turn coordinator, which tilt during turns, and the DG and magnetic compass, which rotate during turns. So are you turning or not? You have four different instruments that can tell you. Two are vacuum powered, one is electrically powered and one requires no power. So if you lose your vacuum system *and* lose your electrical system *and* the Earth loses its magnetic polarity, you will have no means of determining whether or not you are in a turn. Unless, of course, you look outside the cockpit window.

Talk about systems redundancy.

PITCH INSTRUMENTS

You have a similar wealth of information resources in the pitch-determining department. The altimeter and VSI are both all about changes in pitch. The attitude indicator also shows pitch changes by tilting forward and back. Even the airspeed indicator can help here because changes in pitch will affect airspeed unless the pilot makes intentional and precise power adjustments to compensate.

The turn coordinator and DG offer no pitch information. The magnetic compass is an odd duck. In theory it offers no pitch information, but changes in airspeed, which accompany changes in pitch, can make the compass move. But you cannot rely on it for pitch information.

So we have the airspeed indicator, altimeter and VSI all powered by the pitot-static system. And we have the attitude indicator powered by the vacuum system. Again, quite a bit of redundancy. There are no electrically powered instruments in most trainers that indicate pitch. Some airplanes do have back-up attitude indicators that are electrically powered, but these are usually found on more deluxe aircraft that are commonly used for IFR flights.

Another instrument of pitch determination is you. Again, look outside the window. That's what your VFR training is all about. (Figure 68)

AIRSPEED INSTRUMENTS

Of all the flight instruments, only the airspeed indicator itself can directly indicate changes in airspeed. The attitude indicator, altimeter, turn coordinator, DG and VSI are useless in this regard. The magnetic compass can rotate somewhat when airspeed changes, as mentioned, but that instrument rotates unnecessarily for so many different reasons that it's not a reliable indicator of airspeed.

Figure 68: *SIGHT PICTURE* These images show the view from the cockpit windscreen for a climb (top), level flight (middle) and a descent (bottom). The large attitude indicator images show how an attitude indicator in a cockpit might appear for each of these attitudes. The airplane profiles show how the airplane would appear from the side. Depending on how high you sit in your cockpit, your sight picture might differ. The trick is to get used to the way you see the horizon so you can set and judge your airplane's attitude by just looking out the windscreen rather than having to rely on instruments.

Airspeed determinations are difficult to make without a functional airspeed indicator. But even if yours stops working, you can still get your airplane safely on the ground using a back-up system. In this case, the back-up system is you.

Pilots determine power settings by looking at the tachometer. Unlike while driving a car, when flying an airplane you are not accelerating and slowing all the time. You set the power and you fly at that same power setting for what might be many hours before you adjust it again. And the power settings we choose are based on the airspeeds that we're after.

For example, when we enter an airport area in preparation for landing, we might want to be flying at, say, 85 knots. Instead of pushing and pulling on the throttle until the airspeed indicator reads 85 knots, a good pilot will set the power to a certain RPM knowing that the airplane will settle at the chosen airspeed. You need to learn these power settings for your airplane so if you ever lose your airspeed indicator, you'll know that by setting the engine power to a certain RPM, your airplane will slow or speed up to the airspeed you want.

The following chart depicts the systems redundancy found in most trainer airplanes. Instruments shown are grouped by system. To find an adequate back-up for a gauge, find a gauge driven by another system that provides the same or similar information. In the event of an instrument failure and not a complete system failure, other gauges with the same system might be used as a back up. The only way of being sure that a given system is functional, however, is to crosscheck its gauges' indications with another system.

We know this cross-checking business is most important for IFR flying in IMC. And we know that the chances of you, as a VFR pilot, flying into IMC are slim because you check weather all the friggin' time. So you might be wondering what the

	Bank	Pitch	Airspeed
Vacuum System Instruments			
Attitude Indicator			
	Tilts left or right to indicate change of bank angle.	Tilts up and down to indicate change of pitch angle.	If the attitude indicator shows you climbing or descending, assume a change in airspeed.
Heading Indicator / Directional Gyro (DG)			
	Rotates left or right to indicate a change in bank angle.		
Electrical System Instruments			
Turn Coordinator			
	Tilts left or right to indicate change of bank angle.		
Pitot Static System Instruments			
Altimeter			
		Altimeter hands move to indicate a change in pitch angle.	If the altimeter hands are moving, you are climbing or descending and should expect a change in airspeed.

	Bank	Pitch	Airspeed
Airspeed Indicator			
		Airspeed changes might indicate a change in pitch angle.	The airspeed indicator is the primary instrument for measuring airspeed.
Vertical Speed Indicator (VSI)			
		The VSI needle indicates a change in pitch angle when it's not at zero.	If the VSI needle is not on zero, you are climbing or descending and should expect a change in airspeed.
Misc. Instruments			
Magnetic Compass			
	Rotates left or right to indicate a change in bank angle. (The compass continues to rotate back and forth a bit after a turn until it has settled.)	The compass is sensitive to all aircraft attitude changes, and can therefore move when an airplane's pitch angle changes, but it is not a reliable pitch indicator.	The compass is sensitive to all aircraft attitude changes, and can therefore move when an airplane's airspeed changes, but it is not a reliable indicator of airspeed changes.
Tachometer			
		Changes in power settings can yield changes in pitch, but the tachometer is not a reliable option for verifying pitch angle.	If a pilot knows his power settings well, the tachometer can be used to determine airspeed.

chances are of you flying into IMC and then losing your vacuum system, pitot-static system, electrical system or all three.

The chances are pretty small, to be honest, but they are greater than zero.

I once heard a student pilot ask an instructor: "What happens if I fly into IMC and then lose my vacuum system *and* pitot-static system?"

Without missing a beat, the instructor replied, "If, as a VFR pilot, you inadvertently fly into a cloud and then lose both your vacuum and pitot-static systems, someone is calling you home."

The FAA will not expect you to know all of this systems redundancy stuff so intimately for your private pilot checkride. I'm asking you to learn it because it's good to know. If that reason doesn't work for you, try this one: If you lose your airspeed indicator in flight—which is possible in any kind of weather—you will become distracted. If you don't know that you can rely on specific engine power settings and pitch angles to yield certain airspeeds, you will be even more distracted. If you're on final approach with all that distraction and you get a sudden burst of 20-knot tailwind when you're coming in at only 5 knots above stall speed because you have no idea how fast you're really flying, you'll suddenly regain focus...but only for a moment.

For the record, this scenario is far more likely than losing both your pitot-static and vacuum systems inside a cloud.

The moral to this story is: I don't know when you'll need this knowledge and neither do you.

A first line of defense in recognizing any system failure is to check the *squawk sheets* kept by the place that rents you your airplane (called an *FBO*, or fixed based operator). Squawk sheets are lists of problems for a given airplane that have been found by other pilots. If someone else has reported that the DG and attitude indicator in your airplane are behaving oddly, then you know the airplane is suspect for a vacuum system failure.

Don't be shy about asking your FBO about airplane maintenance. If you feel unsure about something, skip the flight. Any FBO that charges you for

canceling a flight due to maintenance concerns that you have should be the FBO you *used to use*. Several times I have canceled flights because I was concerned about the airplane. Sometimes I was accused of being paranoid. But you know what? I'm in this for the fun of it. How fun would a long road trip in your car through the desert be if you knew that a water hose was leaking?

PERFORMANCE

This section of the book covers a topic that might account for more aviation-related deaths than you would think. Unlike automobiles, airplanes don't simply bog down when used beyond their capabilities. Airplanes have limitations that must be respected by pilots, or people die.

It happens all the time.

HOW HIGH? HOW FAST? HOW FAR?

If you were to evaluate an airplane's performance as you do the performance of a car, you'd ask how high it can climb, how fast it can go and how far it can travel on a tank of gas. Answering these questions accurately for airplanes, however, is impossible unless atmospheric conditions are taken into account. Atmospheric density greatly affects how high an airplane can fly, and wind greatly affects how fast and far.

Nonetheless, these questions are common yardsticks by which airplanes are judged. Airplane manufacturers offer performance charts that address these concerns. The figures in these charts are usually based on standard atmospheric conditions, so you must consider these conditions when reading the charts. If you're reading a chart that offers differing figures for temperatures beyond or below standard temperature, make sure you know the difference between the current temperature and standard temperature before you consider the performance predicted.

We'll talk more about standard and nonstandard atmospheric conditions later.

HOW HIGH?

We've already touched on the topic of service ceilings, or the airplane's maximum cruise altitude. You also know how density altitude can adversely affect an airplane's ability to climb. This is a huge concern at higher elevation airports, especially if higher terrain exists near the airport.

Your airplane's POH will have charts that show expected climb performance at various pressure altitudes. The charts will show performance variances for temperatures below and beyond standard temperature. This should ring a bell. What do we call pressure altitude adjusted for nonstandard temperature? *Density altitude.*

For example, the POH for the 1979 Cessna 172N says that the airplane should get a 770 foot-per-minute rate of climb at sea level on a standard-temperature day.

Quiz: What do airplane POH's, *Gone With The Wind* and *Winnie the Pooh* have in common?

Answer: They're all great works of fiction.

Can a 1979 Cessna 172N obtain a climb rate of 770 feet per minute today? The day you see pigs fly, you can rest assured that gravity on Earth has declined sufficiently to enable a 1979 Cessna 172N to obtain a sustained climb rate of 770 feet per minute today.

The 1979 172 I fly most often has a new 180 HP engine and a prop designed for improved climb performance. On a nice cool day I'm lucky to get climb performance like that when I'm flying alone. Add a passenger or two to the mix and you can forget it.

My point here is that POH performance charts *predict* and *estimate*, but they don't *guarantee*. Don't assume you'll get the numbers shown in these charts until you have actually flown the airplane

and verified the accuracy of the figures. Be conservative in your assumptions about airplane performance and you'll occasionally be pleasantly surprised.

After a while you'll get a better sense of what kind of climb performance you can expect from a given airplane on a given day with a given load. In the meantime, keep two things in mind: airplanes perform worse in atmospheres of lower-pressure and/or higher temperatures. The combination of the two is the pits, performance-wise.

Your climb performance will diminish as your altitude increases for reasons that I hope by now make sense to you. As air density thins, so thins your airplane's climb performance. So if you lift off the runway with a 500 feet-per-minute rate of climb, and you plan to cruise at 10,500 (one zero thousand, five hundred) feet, don't expect 500 feet-per-minute climb performance the entire way up.

My 1979 Cessna POH says that by 10,000 feet I should expect less than 300 feet per minute on a standard temperature day. Boy, did I learn one day just how generous *that* figure was! On my second solo cross-country flight I planned to cruise at 9,500 feet. I wasn't going that far, but I like to fly high. It was a hot day, which should have been my first clue that the *current* atmosphere wasn't *standard* atmosphere. I asked ATC for flight following. The controller asked for my intended cruise altitude. I told him I would be climbing to 9,500 feet. He came back on and asked me to verify 9,500. I confirmed. He said, "Uh...okay...let me know when you get there." I finally got to 7,500 feet about 5 minutes before I had to call him back to let him know that I was starting my descent. He just said, "Roger." But I knew he was thinking, "Bonehead!"

Remember, I was alone in that airplane! Nowhere near maximum weight and the darn thing just didn't want to climb. The excessive heat that day really hit home with me. When I landed, I whipped out my POH and reconsidered the performance chart. I realized that if I had actually factored in the non-standard temperature, as I was supposed to, the estimated climb rate would have been closer to what I got, but it was still far from accurate.

So much for performance chart predictions.

If temperature is such an issue, shouldn't we get better climb performance on cooler nights than we do during warmer days? Yes. For this very reason, many pilots plan their high-altitude airport departures and arrivals for early morning or evening, when the temperature drops. (And when the views can be most breathtaking.) You can't change a field's elevation, but you can reduce density altitude by flying when it's cooler outside.

Just to make sure I haven't confused you, the term "high density altitude" refers to an altitude that the airplane "thinks" is high due to *lower* air density. Conversely, the higher the air density, the lower the density altitude and the happier the airplane. Higher air temperatures also increase density altitude. It's a bit confusing at first, but then the Earth's atmosphere wasn't designed with airplane performance in mind.

If you need some help cutting through the confusion, keep this in mind:

High or hot is a hazard.

HOW FAST?

When someone asks how fast an airplane is, they are most concerned with how long it would take to get from point A to point B. It's assumed that the faster the airplane, the shorter the trip.

While this is true, it doesn't tell the whole story. Airspeed, which is the measurement we use of an airplane's performance, is an indication of how fast the airplane is flying through the surrounding air. But, thanks to wind, air moves. What really matters with regard to flight time is *groundspeed*, or how fast the airplane is traveling across the ground below.

I once made plans to fly some friends from San Carlos to Grass Valley, both in Northern California. My friends asked how long it would take. I told them 90 minutes or so, but I'd let them know for sure on the morning of the flight.

"Why?" one mused. "Are you expecting Grass Valley to move between now and then?"

"It could," I told him, offering fault-ridden California as the reason.

But the real reason I couldn't predict exactly how long the flight would take was because I had no idea what the winds would be like that day. On the morning of our flight I told them we would be airborne for 1 hour and 32 minutes. We touched down 45 seconds late.

I once prepared a practice flight plan for a flight between San Carlos and Lake Tahoe. This is typically about a 2-hour flight, but on that day it would have taken only 40 minutes! This is because the winds would have been right on my tail most of the way and they were absolutely howling. Granted, this would have been one very turbulent ride, but it does illustrate how dramatically wind can affect flight time.

So when you compare the performance specs of two airplanes and learn that one will do 110 knots per hour while the other can do 130 knots per hour, keep in mind that the winds on the day you travel will have more to do with the total flight time than the airplane you choose. (Though the 130 knot-per-hour airplane will always get there faster.)

HOW FAR?

The distance an airplane can fly without refueling, or its *range* as it's called in airplane circles, is another hard thing to determine that everyone wants to know. An airplane's range is basically the distance the airplane can travel with full tanks on a day without any wind. If the wind is coming from behind (a tailwind), the range is extended. If a headwind exists, range is decreased.

An airplane's performance specs might say that it has a 700 nautical mile range. But this really means very little. What's more relevant is the *amount of time* the engine can run with full tanks. This figure is called the airplane's *endurance*.

Knowing the rate at which an airplane burns fuel, and knowing how much fuel it can hold, it's easy to determine its endurance. If your airplane has 40-gallon tanks and burns 10 gallons per hour, your endurance is 4 hours.

How far the airplane can actually travel in that 4 hours depends on the winds. If your airspeed is 100 knots and you're fighting a 50-knot headwind the entire trip, your endurance (time aloft) will still be 4 hours, but your distance traveled will be half the airplane's published range. If you had a 50-knot tailwind, you'd be able to travel twice the published range in that same 4 hours.

In summary: an airplane's *range* (distance on full tanks) depends on the wind. And airplane's *endurance* (time aloft on full tanks) never changes.

FOUR SEATS FOR FOUR PEOPLE?

"I can't be over-drawn, I still have checks left!"

The two rear seats in Cessna 172s and Piper Warriors have lead to many misunderstandings. Inviting as they might seem to a very small person, they don't promise a trip for four.

Every airplane, no matter how large or small, has a maximum weight that it can hold. Additionally, each airplane has a certain range in which its center of gravity must fall. Disregard for these two very important performance limitations have killed many pilots and many passengers.

MAXIMUM GROSS WEIGHT (MGW)

Maximum gross weight (MGW) describes the absolute maximum an airplane can weigh at take off. It might well be the one performance limitation that pilots disregard most. After all, when you overload your car, it rides a bit low and

looks funny, but it still works. Airplanes still work when they're overloaded too, but not as intended. They might climb as well as you think they will, or they might not climb at all. They might require more runway to get off the ground than normal, or they might take more runway than you have.

The performance charts found in an aircraft's POH are useless if you overload the airplane. You can't rely on any of the performance estimates if your airplane is overloaded. CFIs like to warn students that they become test pilots when flying overloaded airplanes.

It's rare that you'll get four adults into a four-seat airplane. Think of those back seats as storage for the kids or your 90-pound supermodel friends. If you absolutely must get four into your 172, you'll have to leave some fuel behind. Fuel weighs 6 lbs. per gallon, so by decreasing your fuel supply, you reduce your gross weight and, of course, your airplane's endurance and range too. If your loaded airplane is 100 lbs over maximum gross weight, you'll need to leave about 16 gallons of fuel behind. This might not be a big deal for a shorter trip, but it might require an extra fuel stop on a longer journey.

CENTER OF GRAVITY (CG)

A sister component to MGW is *center of gravity* (CG). An airplane can be well within weight limits and still be dangerous to fly because its CG is outside the safe range defined in the POH. CG is determined by the forward and backward distribution of weight in the airplane. For example, if you have two 120-pound people in the front seats and 400 pounds of luggage in the rear luggage compartment, your CG will be more rearward and probably out of range.

CG affects the way an airplane handles. A rearward CG means that more forward pressure will be required on the yoke to keep the airplane level because the tail will want to drop, thereby raising the nose. This might be possible to accommodate in flight, but when you take off and land you want your airplane to be as neutrally balanced as possible. A rearward CG also reduces your changes of the airplane recovering from a stall. Think about it: when the load is properly distributed, all you have to do is let the nose drop to recover from a stall. But if you have to fight to keep the nose down, a stall might be easier to enter into and impossible to recover from.

A forward CG might seem desirable from a stall-recovery perspective, but it presents problems of its own. Part of the technique used in landing an airplane requires the pilot to keep the nose wheel off the runway for as long as possible. But if the nose is too heavy, the wheel will plop down long before it should, which can lead to a loss of control of the airplane.

A CG that is out of balance is also inefficient. If your nose wants to drop because of a CG that's too far forward, you have to apply constant back pressure on the yoke to keep the airplane level. This means that the elevator is constantly deflected into the relative wind, thereby increasing drag. The same applies if your CG is too far aft and you have to apply forward yoke pressure to remain balanced.

An easy way to imagine the effects of CG on flight is to consider a paper airplane with a paperclip "payload" attached to it. There will be a magical range where the airplane will fly well with the paper clip attached, even though the paperclip adds additional weight. But if you place the paperclip too far forward or too far aft, you'll have a very unhappy paper airplane that won't fly well. (Figure 69)

Every airplane's POH has a section on weight and balance. Included will be charts that depict the acceptable CG range for various gross weights. (Yes, the CG range can change depending on the airplane's payload.) You'll want to make sure you've loaded your airplane properly for each flight. The good news is that calculating *weight and balance,* as we call it, is not difficult to do. (Figure 70)

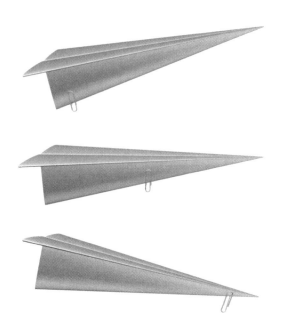

Figure 69: *CENTER OF GRAVITY (CG)* When an airplane's center of gravity is too far aft (top), or too far forward (bottom), the airplane is harder to control. Ensure that your airplane's load is always within the CG range specified in the POH. An airplane with a properly balanced load (center) is especially important during takeoffs and landings when the airplane's controllability is most vital and mistakes are most dangerous.

I CAN'T BE STALLED! I STILL HAVE GAS IN THE TANKS!

One of the performance figures you'll see published for an airplane is its stall speed. But, as we've already discussed, an airplane can theoretically stall at any speed. So what's up with this static stall-speed figure?

Recall from earlier discussions that an airplane stalls when its angle of attack becomes so great that the airflow over the wings is disrupted and the wing no longer generates lift. As mentioned, this is called the airplane's critical angle of attack. This *can* happen at any airspeed. But it *always* happens at the airplane's stall speed. Here's why:

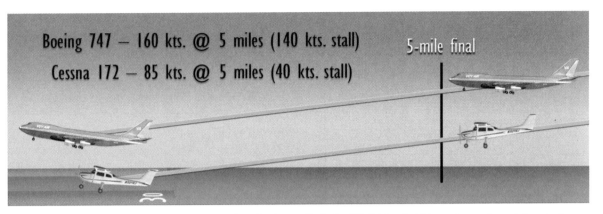

Boeing 747 — 160 kts. @ 5 miles (140 kts. stall)   5-mile final

Cessna 172 — 85 kts. @ 5 miles (40 kts. stall)

Figure 71: *APPROACH ATTITUDES* At five miles from the airport, this Boeing 747-400 is only 20 knots above stall speed. To maintain enough lift to fly, the pilot must keep the airplane in a nose-high attitude, which puts the airplane nearer its critical angle of attack. The Cessna 172 is flying at 85 knots on the same five-mile final approach. This airplane is in a nose-low attitude because the airplane is still flying at a whopping 45 knots above its stall speed. There is plenty of lift being generated, so the pilot doesn't need to increase the airplane's angle of attack. If he did, the 172 would climb. Just before touchdown, both airplanes have slowed to near their stall speeds and critical angles of attack. All airplanes transition from nose-low attitudes to nose-high attitudes at some point during the approach because all airplanes land somewhat near their stalls speeds. And for an airplane to remain airborne while near its stall speed, it must be in a high angle of attack. (Speeds listed are approximations; stall and approach speeds for big jets vary considerably with the aircraft's landing weight.)

As an airplane slows, less air flows over the wings and therefore less lift is generated. To maintain altitude, a pilot must increase the airplane's angle of attack by pulling back on the yoke. This is normal: a slow-flying airplane will always be at a steeper angle of attack than it is when it flies at full speed. But as the airplanes continues to slow, the pilot must continue to pull back on the yoke to remain airborne. At some point, the wing's angle of attack reaches the airplane's critical angle of attack and the wing stalls. The speed at which this happens is (approximately) the airplane's published stall speed.

This holds true for every airplane. The closer an airplane flies to its stall speed, the higher the pilot must keep the airplane's angle of attack to compensate for the loss of lift.

To see this phenomenon in action, pay attention one day to the stream of airplanes landing at a major airport near you. Moments before touchdown, every single one of those airplanes is in a nose-high attitude. Pilots don't land in nose-high attitudes just to prevent hitting the runway with the nose wheel. Nose-high attitudes are the result of the airplane flying near its stall speed.

Take another look at the airplanes while they're still several miles out on final approach. Behemoths, like the 747 and 777, are already in nose-high attitudes while still many miles away from the airport. Small prop planes, on the other hand, are still descending nose-low at that point. The reason is that the big jets are nearer their stall speeds at that point than are the little planes. (Figure 71)

Big jets stall at much higher speeds than do small prop airplanes. They also take longer to slow down and require more runway to stop rolling. So they must reduce their airspeeds pretty far out in order to stabilize themselves for the approach and landing. This gets them closer to their stall speeds pretty far from the airport, thus the nose-high attitude.

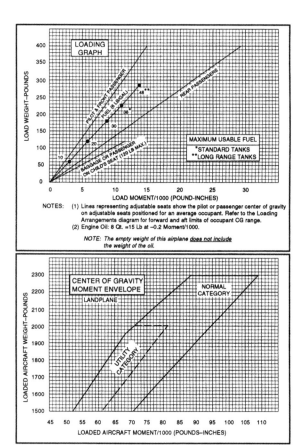

NOTES: (1) Lines representing adjustable seats show the pilot or passenger center of gravity on adjustable seats positioned for an average occupant. Refer to the Loading Arrangements diagram for forward and aft limits of occupant CG range.
(2) Engine Oil: 8 Qt. =15 Lb at −0.2 Moment/1000.

NOTE: *The empty weight of this airplane does not include the weight of the oil.*

Figure 70: *WEIGHT WATCHER* These charts are typical of those you might find in your airplane's POH. The chart on top enables pilots to quickly determine the "moment" of a given load. For example, follow the "Pilot & Front Passenger" line outward until you reach your weight, as shown in the left column. Look directly down to get the moment of your weight in the front seat of the airplane. Do this for the rest of the airplane's load and add up the moment values. Calculate the total weight of your airplane's load and find it in the left column of the lower graph. Follow that line rightward until you reach the sum of your moments. If the point of intersection falls within the dark line, you're set. If not, then you need to rethink your load. Your CFI will cover this process in detail with you.

Say a 747-400 stalls at 140 knots. The published approach speed for this airplane (the speed at which it comes in for a landing) is 160 knots, only 20 knots above stall speed. Meanwhile, a King Air, which is a twin-engine prop plane stalls at 81 knots. But in order to share the same approach path as the 747, the King Air would have to maintain a much higher airspeed during much of its approach.

So if you look a few miles away from the airport you'll see 747s flying at 20 or so knots above stall speed and King Airs perhaps flying at twice their stall speed just to stay out of the 747's engine intakes. The 747 will be flying nose high because it's so close to stall speed. The King Air will be flying nose-low because it's nowhere near its stall speed. But just before touchdown, you'll see even the King Air transition to a nose-high attitude as it slows toward its stall speed.

This explanation was one part over-simplification and one part exaggeration, because the magic of ATC sequences aircraft so that they don't interfere with one another's approach so dramatically. But it's not far from accuracy. I have landed a Cessna 172 at a major airport and found myself on final approach doing 90 knots. Normally I'd be down to 65 knots by the time I got anywhere near the runway.

So anytime you see an airplane descending in a nose-high attitude, you'll know that airplane is near its stall speed.

Several different stall speeds are usually listed for a given airplane. This is because the airplane stalls at different speeds depending on how its flaps and landing gear are set.

For example, one stall speed applies when the airplane is configured for landing. We also call this configuration *dirty*. An airplane is in the dirty configuration when its flaps and landing gear are down. A second stall speed applies to an airplane's "clean" configuration, which is when the flaps and landing gear (for airplanes with retractable landing gear) are up. Airplanes will stall at higher speeds when the flaps are up.

Airplanes are usually "clean" just after take off. The "dirty" configuration is how they are usually set up for landing.

The different stall speeds are part of the airplane's v-speeds, as mentioned earlier. The stall speed in the clean configuration is V_S (spoken: vee-ess). The stall speed in the dirty configuration is V_{SO} (spoken: vee-ess-oh).

So what does stall speed tell us about an airplane?

One of the most important things you determine by knowing an airplane's stall speed in the landing configuration (V_{SO}) is how slow you can be flying during final approach to landing. A Cessna 172 stalls at approximately 40 knots in the landing configuration. This tells us that a final approach speed of 60 knots leaves us with 20-knots of margin. If we maintain our airspeed and don't get blasted with a 20-knot tailwind, we should be fine. If the airplane's stall speed was 80 knots, then we'd have to come in at 100 knots to get the same safety margin. Right off the bat you know this will mean increased landing distance. But it also means you'd better have some good landing chops under your belt because landing at 100 knots is more difficult and more dangerous than landing at 60 knots.

Stall speed in the clean configuration (V_S) clues you into how fast you'd better be going down that runway before you pull back on the yoke to lift the airplane off the ground. V_S for the Cessna 172 is approximately 45 knots. Cessna recommends a rotation speed of 55 knots. (The moment you pull back on the yoke to lift the airplane off the ground is called *rotation* in airplaneland.) This leaves us with a safety margin of only 10 knots as opposed to the 20-knot margin we get while landing. But during takeoff, the airplane

continues to accelerate so this margin quickly increases. It's also pretty tough to keep the airplane on the runway at speeds much higher than 55 knots because it naturally wants to fly.

The important thing to remember about stall speeds is that they are estimates. Several factors affect the actual speed at which an airplane will stall. Published airplane stall speeds usually assume maximum gross weight. If your MGW is less, you can reduce the stall speed by a few knots. If you're flying above maximum gross weight, then smack yourself and remember that your airplane will stall at a higher speeds than published in the POH.

Bank angle also affects stall speed. Published stall v-speeds assume no bank angle. Airplanes stall at higher speeds while turning. For example, the 172 POH estimates a stall at 53 knots for V_S at a 45-degree bank angle.

Can you guess why increased bank angle increases stall speed? We know that vertical lift is reduced in a bank as some of the lift is diverted horizontally. Stalls are the result of loss of lift, so just by turning you're already on your way toward a stall.

CG is the final factor affecting stall speeds. Your airplane's POH should list stall speed differences depending on CG. A forward CG causes an airplane to stall at a higher speed because the airplane's critical angle of attack is reached at a more shallow angle of attack.

The bottom line here is not that you have to memorize every stall speed for every possible configuration and bank angle of your airplane. The point is to understand how different flight attitudes and configurations affect an airplane's ability to generate lift. By understanding this, you'll know instinctively that steep turns at slow speeds can be bad news. And you'll know that steep turns at slow speeds with flaps up are even worse.

Here are some basic points to remember:

- Flaps enable you to fly slower before stalling.

- Bank angles increase the speed at which you'll stall.

- A forward CG increases the speed at which you'll stall.

WHAT'S NEXT

This chapter has covered a lot of ground. Don't worry if you feel somewhat overwhelmed. There's a lot to know about an airplane before you fly it. The stuff you've just read is the very foundation upon which all of your know-how as a pilot will rest.

Next, we'll get into weather from the pilot's perspective. Take a good look out the window right now. You'll never see weather in the same way again.

6

Weather from a Pilot's Perspective

WEATHER MATTERS

During your ground instruction you'll cover weather in depth, but you won't learn enough. This is because groundschool instructors don't teach enough. And this, in turn, is because they don't know enough.

I'm not trying to insult anyone. It's just that weather is a tough subject to master. Think about it: how often are professional meteorologists completely accurate? If these experienced scientists can't know it all, then how could a 22-year old, can't-remember-life-before-MTV CFI that's just trying to build hours to fly for JetBlue?

Some 75% of weather-related general aviation accidents are fatal. Bad weather is not forgiving.

What's saddest about this statistic is that most weather related accidents could have been avoided if the pilot had just said "no" to flying that day. No one can predict weather with fail-safe precision, and bad weather can take down a 747. Keep this in mind each and every time you power up your aluminum "kite" beneath anything but clear skies.

FEAR THE REAPER

Unlike gravity and drag, weather is a force of nature that is largely unpredictable. We can *forecast* bad weather, but we can't say for sure when it will come, where it will go and when it will end.

The problem is that bad weather kills pilots.

Your airplane has control surfaces designed to help you turn, climb and descend, but it has nothing to help you negotiate the atomic-blast fury of a thunderstorm. If you ever find that you've flown too close to such a monster, yelling "Shields to maximum!" will do you no good. No airplane ever built can safely withstand the forces of a powerful thunderstorm. None. *Nada.*

But what about those pretty, puffy white clouds? How could they possibly be dangerous? And so what if a little ice shows up on the wings? What harm could ice do? Or, what about a gentle 10-knot crosswind during landing?

A staggering 76% of general aviation accidents that are weather-related identify "wind" as a causal factor, with crosswinds being the biggest culprit.

None of the pilots who contributed to that statistic took off assuming they'd crash on landing because of some bully crosswind.

In truth, much of what kills pilots with regard to weather is nothing more than bad judgement. If you can't handle a 10-knot crosswind, then you have no business flying when crosswinds anywhere near 10 knots are present, forecast or even likely. Moreover, if you fly your airplane into the core of a thunderstorm and come out on the other side a swirling mass of aluminum chunks, consider it a failure in judgement, not in structural integrity. Don't blame Cessna.

A big problem in aviation is that pilots tend to believe *only* the weather forecasts that serve our needs. If the forecast calls for good weather, which means that we can fly, we believe it. If it calls for bad weather, and we had our heart set on flying that day, we come up with all sorts of excuses why the forecast might not be accurate. Sometimes we even think we can outsmart Mother Nature: *"That storm won't be here for hours! We can make it!"*

One insidious ailment that strikes weary pilots returning from longer trips is called "get-home-itis." A common symptom of get-home-itis is the belief that there is no force in the Universe more powerful than a Piper Warrior. Many afflicted pilots also experience a complete loss of common sense and a nullification of the memory cells that stored everything they were ever taught in flight school.

Contributing to the problem of pilot stupidity is the fact that some weather reports *do* describe conditions that sound worse than they are or become. This is not because weather forecasting organizations are overly protective pessimists. It's because weather reports are based on specific reporting criteria and protocols, not just some observer's opinion. Sometimes those protocols result in reports that sound worse than they are. Sometimes not.

But rather than adopting an attitude, learn how weather forecasts and reports are prepared. It will help you understand when and why differences occur. You're all alone up there when you fly. Does it make sense to second guess the experience of weather scientists when your life might depend on it? Nature can be violent, and airplanes large and small are no match.

There's an old saying in aviation:

It's better to be down here wishing you were up there, than to be up there wishing you were down here.

Tired old sayings like this abound in aviation. I roll my eyes upon hearing them, but I find myself much chagrined when I'm in situations to which one applies.

GOOD LUCK FINDING ANSWERS

So where do you find all of that life-saving weather information that's missing from your flight training?

That's a very good question. A number of aviation weather books are in print today. I've read a few and found that while they answered some questions, they left me with many more.

You'll occasionally see classes on weather for pilots, but you probably won't find many ground breaking answers there: *"Bad weather should be avoided. Thunderstorms are the worst. Thank you for attending. Don't forget to have your parking tickets validated on your way out."*

One day I asked a meteorologist where I could learn about weather. He replied in the most theatrical whisper he could muster: "The very places you go to learn about life." I smiled nervously, certain he was about to pass me a joint, or worse.

After he let his dramatic moment pass, he explained that I could learn about weather everywhere I went and that everywhere I went, the weather would be different. He suggested I study weather by experiencing it and asking myself questions: "It's warm today. Why?" and "There are clouds in the sky today that weren't there yesterday. Why are they there now and what does it mean for tomorrow?"

His advice turned out to be good (and drug-free). It helped me consider the theories behind weather-related phenomenon. If I'm sitting in San Francisco on a hot summer day and there isn't a cloud in the sky, I can make some assumptions. One is that the winds will kick up in the afternoon (because they usually do) and it's likely that fog will come in from the ocean before evening. (Because it usually does.)

Is this a scientific assessment? Certainly not. It's an assessment based on personal experience. Maybe the winds won't kick up and maybe the fog won't come rolling in. But that would make for a nice balmy San Francisco Summer evening, and San Francisco is not known for its nice balmy Summer evenings. Hence my theory.

My meteorological guru's advice doesn't help me forecast weather, but it does help me maintain a certain sense of the way things are *supposed* to be. I can couple this with an official aviation forecast and either feel at ease knowing that everything is as it should be, or keep myself on guard knowing that something doesn't seem right.

Experiencing and considering the weather helps keep you more aware of the weather.

For more in-depth training, there's always the option of enrolling in a university for meteorology, but this isn't practical for most of us. And I know of no meteorology universities that offer crash courses for pilots, so to speak. Too bad.

Use your eyes to see weather and your brain to decide why that weather is happening at that moment. Ask experienced local pilots for their "gut" feelings about the weather, especially if you're flying in unfamiliar areas.

And under no circumstances should you ever fly without first consulting an official aviation forecast resource.

AVIATION WEATHER REPORTS (PAST & FUTURE)

There are two basic categories into which aviation weather information falls:

- Forecasts
- Observations

Forecasts predict weather to come (before the fact) and observations report on actual conditions as they occur (after the fact). Collectively, these reports help pilots get a truer sense of the weather.

Organizations that provide weather information like to refer to individual report types as *products*. I'll call them reports herein because if I asked you to consult as many "weather products" as you can, you'd think I was nuts.

Each report has a two-letter code that is used to identify it. It's not necessary to memorize each report code to use them, but it helps. From time to time you'll come across aviation texts that refer to the "FD," for example. Without knowing that the FD is the forecast of winds above ground level, you'll be confused.

The codes are listed below within the description of each report.

ENCODED REPORTS

You'll (quickly) notice that aviation weather reports are not printed in plain English. They're encoded using a flurry of contractions and abbreviations. For example, rain becomes RA, thunderstorms become TS, and a broken cloud layer is noted as BKN. A list of common contractions is available online. *(Visit **http://AirDiamond.com/sa** for a link.)*

Each geographic region has a set of contractions that are common to that area, so it won't take much time to get used to the ones that apply to your flights. For example, the contraction for volcanic ash (VA) won't be seen too much in areas no where near a volcano. Likewise, Florida-based pilots needn't memorize SN, for snow.

Once upon a time there was good reason for report encoding: the reports were distributed over phone lines at very slow speeds. The more verbose the report, the longer the distribution would take. Today we have communications options that offer much greater speed, but weather-reporting organizations claim there are still regions of the world using yesteryear's technology. They also claim that the process of converting to plain language reports is complicated because it requires the cooperation of the National Weather Service, the FAA and the International Civil Aviation Organization (ICAO).

Now *there's* your valid reason. If we need to get all of those children playing in the same sandbox, we might sooner learn to *control* the weather than report it in plain English.

There are advantages to the encoded reports, however. Once you get used to the format, you can scan and read them quite quickly. Plain language reports require much more hunting and pecking through the "fat" of common language to get to the goodies. Let's take a look at a snippet from a winds aloft forecast and compare:

Encoded:

SFO 122309

Decoded:

Winds in the San Francisco area will be blowing from 120 degrees at an intensity of 23 knots. The temperature will be 9 degrees Celsius.

You can immediately see the advantage encoding offers. I have received weather briefings that printed as 6 pages when they were encoded and over 20 pages in plain English!

Some weather information sources can automatically decode reports into plain English, but don't get used to this. Not every source does it and you won't fear the encoded formats forever.

Another big advantage to encoded reports is that not everyone can read them. Your friends will think you're cool because you can.

AVIATION TIME REFERENCES

Aviation weather reports reference time in what's called *Zulu time*. Zulu time is the same as Greenwich Mean Time—unless you're counting seconds—and is based on a 24-hour clock, like military time. So 1:00 p.m. GMT is referred to as "1300 Zulu," spoken as "thirteen-hundred Zulu."

Aviation resources reference Zulu time because it's the same all over the world at any given moment, so time zones references—and the confusion they cause—are irrelevant. If a storm is expected to pound western Montana by 1500 Zulu, you know exactly when it's expected without having to consider the local time zone for western Montana.

Depending on your local time zone, and whether or not Daylight Savings Time (DST) is in effect, you will have to add or subtract a certain number of hours from Zulu time to determine your local time. (You'll always be subtracting in the United States.) This could not be less fun for me because math is ranked just above dental procedures on my list of fun things to do. Add to that trying to remember if DST is in effect or not? I don't think so. So one day I sat down and came up with a little chart I could print out, laminate and keep with me. (Figure 72)

U.S. TIME ZONES (P.M. hours shown over black.)

PACIFIC	MOUNT.	CENTRAL	EASTERN	UTC	UTC/DST†
12:00	01:00	02:00	03:00	08:00	07:00
01:00	02:00	03:00	04:00	09:00	08:00
02:00	03:00	04:00	05:00	10:00	09:00
03:00	04:00	05:00	06:00	11:00	10:00
04:00	05:00	06:00	07:00	12:00	11:00
05:00	06:00	07:00	08:00	13:00	12:00
06:00	07:00	08:00	09:00	14:00	13:00
07:00	08:00	09:00	10:00	15:00	14:00
08:00	09:00	10:00	11:00	16:00	15:00
09:00	10:00	11:00	12:00	17:00	16:00
10:00	11:00	12:00	01:00	18:00	17:00
11:00	12:00	01:00	02:00	19:00	18:00
12:00	01:00	02:00	03:00	20:00	19:00
01:00	02:00	03:00	04:00	21:00	20:00
02:00	03:00	04:00	05:00	22:00	21:00
03:00	04:00	05:00	06:00	23:00	22:00
04:00	05:00	06:00	07:00	00:00	23:00
05:00	06:00	07:00	08:00	01:00	00:00
06:00	07:00	08:00	09:00	02:00	01:00
07:00	08:00	09:00	10:00	03:00	02:00
08:00	09:00	10:00	11:00	04:00	03:00
09:00	10:00	11:00	12:00	05:00	04:00
10:00	11:00	12:00	01:00	06:00	05:00
11:00	12:00	01:00	02:00	07:00	06:00

Figure 72: *TIME ZONED* Daylight Savings Time is in effect from the first Sunday of April, through the last Sunday of October. († UTC during Daylight Savings Time.)

To use it, I find the local time in the left columns and look across to the right columns to find Zulu time, which is abbreviated as UTC. (It's French; don't ask.) If DST is in effect, I take the number from the far right column. I made a note at the bottom of the chart to remind myself when DST is in effect. It works great for me. If a forecast calls for clear skies by 0200 Zulu, I can quickly look across the chart to the left and see that the local time will be 6:00 p.m. PST. Love that chart!

Some Internet-based weather forecast sources can convert Zulu time into local time for you. Just make sure you're aware of which time system is used on the reports you read.

You won't ever get away from Zulu time references entirely, so get used to them now.

FORECASTING WEATHER

Several different methods are used for weather forecasting. The simplest method is called *persistence*. The persistence method of forecasting relies on the likelihood that current weather conditions will remain as they are. For example, if the temperature at 1:00 p.m. is 86 degrees, one could forecast the temperature at 1:05 p.m. to be 86 degrees with some impressive accuracy. If your flight consists of only a few laps around the airport traffic pattern, persistence forecasting is for you. But if you plan to fly for more than a few minutes, you need to consider more sophisticated forecasting methods.

For example, let's say it's noon and you need to forecast the temperature for 10:00 p.m. that night. The persistence method of forecasting isn't going to help too much because by that hour the sun will have set and the temperature will have dropped. You could take a wild guess, or you could consider *trend*. Trend forecasting is not only used by professional meteorologists, it will be (or *should be*) used by you every time you plan a flight.

Trend forecasting relies on the probability that weather systems will continue to move and evolve with some consistency. If a weather system moves 400 miles in 24 hours, we assume it will move 800 miles in 48 hours. If that same system is half as strong today as it was yesterday, we expect that it will be gone sometime tomorrow.

But trend can also apply to developing conditions at a given location. Once the temperature starts dropping in the afternoon, we assume the trend will be a continued temperature drop on into the evening. Trend is a very valuable way to judge the accuracy of a forecast.

To be even more accurate about your 10:00 p.m. temperature forecast, you'd have to consider historical data. How cold does it *usually* get at night this time of the year in this part of the country? Better yet, do we have a computer model that can show what the temperature was at 10:00 p.m. the last five times we had a weather system like the one we have today?

This combined information would help you make your evening forecast. But even with all that data, the likelihood of accuracy would be less than it was for your 5-minute persistence forecast.

Now consider making forecasts days, weeks, months or even years in advance. It's possible, using historical data and computer weather models, but the likelihood of forecast accuracy decreases as the forecast time period increases.

Let me say that again: *The likelihood of forecast accuracy decreases as the forecast time period increases.* Promise me you'll never forget this.

So does this mean you should ignore long-range forecasts? Not at all. It just means you need to keep on top of changing conditions throughout your flight by consulting more current forecasts and reports. In other words, don't take off just because last night's forecast said it would be nice today. Use last night's forecast during last night's flight planning session; check today's forecast and trend before you depart.

If a 12-hour forecast says clear skies are likely to continue throughout the day and night, and there isn't a cloud in the sky for hundreds of miles in any direction, clear skies *are* likely. (But not guaranteed!) But if a 12-hour forecast calls for clearing skies after a period of heavy clouds and rain, watch that situation carefully. No one knows for sure when conditions will actually improve.

Pilots often complain about forecast reliability: *"What's the point of checking weather when the forecast is usually wrong?"* This is a common sentiment. To these pilots I ask: What's the point of checking the oil when the oil's usually full?

I admit I have seen forecasts that seemed somewhat fictional, but far more often, the forecast has helped me make intelligent "go/no-go" decisions.

Forecasts are weather predictions based on likelihood; they are not guarantees. Forecasts should never be considered a green light to fly.

FORECASTS OVER TIME

Forecasts are only good for given time periods, so be aware of the time period a forecast covers as you read it. If a forecast calls for clear skies, make sure you know when those clear skies are expected. It might not be for many hours.

Longer flights might extend through several forecast periods. Remember: longer range forecasts are less reliable, so get updates enroute. We'll talk about how you can do that later.

FORECASTS OVER DISTANCE

Also be aware of the region a forecast covers. A forecast that calls for clear skies at your departure airport by 0200 Zulu does you little good if by 0200 Zulu you've flown 400 miles east. You must also consider weather conditions along your route. Just because your departure and destination airports are both forecast to be clear doesn't mean the skies between the two will also be clear. The greater the distance between the two airports, the bigger a concern this becomes.

If a forecast for a particular area isn't available, it's tempting to just "average" forecasts for nearby areas. Some aviation texts even recommend this practice. Sometimes forecast averaging works, but sometimes it doesn't. The San Francisco Bay Area is a great example of a place where this practice can be misleading. The region's two largest airports, San Francisco International and Oakland International, each forecast weather for the local area. So if a pilot saw that both airports were forecasting (or even reporting) clear skies, he might reckon that a flight over The City on out to the Golden Gate Bridge would be a great idea. But it's not uncommon for both of these airports to report clear skies while the city of San Francisco itself lies beneath a blanket of the fog for which it's famous.

When in doubt, consult experienced local pilots for any areas of concern, or call a flight service station, which we'll talk more about later. At the very least, always have an escape route when you're flying into areas for which the current weather isn't known. Decide in advance where you'll go if the weather starts to turn on you. If there's no good escape route and the weather is questionable, then you'd call that a "no-go."

WEATHER RESOURCES

Weather sources abound for pilots, which is ironic considering how few pilots take weather seriously enough. The fact is, you can never use "lack of source" as a reason to fly without a weather briefing. It's just too easy to get reliable weather information that's free and (mostly) accurate.

YOUR EYES & COMMON SENSE

Here we have the two most accessible, and possibly most ignored weather resources available to pilots. While it's true your eyes cannot predict weather, your eyes can help you analyze current conditions. If the skies are forecast to be clear and they are not, then something's wrong with the forecast.

This is when you must rely on your inner nag factor—*common sense*—to determine your next step. All pilots have been tempted to fly based on a forecast for a nice day, even when the "real"

weather looks suspicious. I call this *selective weather analysis*: Pilots consider only those parts of the forecast that appeal to them.

Several times during my training I was tempted to fly in situations like this. It was usually a wind forecast that was in question. Winds were forecast to be 10 knots, increasing in the afternoon, but they were already 12 or so knots by the time I was ready to fly at lunchtime. Completely disregarding trend, I figured that I could fly because the winds were *forecast* to be okay.

Stupid, stupid, stupid.

Here's a rule of thumb: If your eyes and brain tell you the forecast isn't accurate and things are bad, forget the forecast and forget the flight. Even if your instincts turn out to be wrong, you'd make the flight with a sense of doubt, which is never a good thing.

MUST-SEE-TV

Believe it or not, those television weather reports are useful to pilots, at least for advance flight-planning purposes. Most of the information given in a broadcast is ground-focused, but you can see where and when weather systems are expected to move into the area.

By no means should you ever consider a TV broadcast a sufficient pre-flight briefing, but it can tell you the basics: Is it windy? Is it raining? Is bad weather expected for the weekend?

For the sake of pilot coolness, however, do not ever let anyone know that you're actually listening. Let them go on thinking we pilots have a magic link to the *real* weather information.

FLIGHT SERVICE STATIONS

As a student pilot, you should fly *nowhere* without first checking weather with a flight service station (FSS). The difference between getting weather briefings from an FSS and getting them elsewhere is that FSS "briefers" are experienced pros that not only read weather data to you, but also help you interpret it. Most understand weather and student pilots pretty well.

FSS services are provided free of charge and they're only a toll-free call away at 1-800-WX-BRIEF.

And talk about nice! I've yet to run into anyone in an FSS that was anything but professional, helpful and courteous. When I called as a student pilot, I often felt as though I was getting a briefing from my mother or father. If the weather was anything but perfect, I would be encouraged to consider my flight plans carefully.

Here's the (legal) catch: FSS briefers have no authority over your flight plans. They are not allowed to tell you what to do. It's up to you to decide if you should go. The funny thing about most briefers, however, is that they have a certain *style* of telling student pilots about bad weather:

"Uh, are you going to be flying with an instructor today?" or *"So, uh, does this flight have to happen today? Tomorrow looks like a great day for flying."*

FSS briefers do have one discouraging official term that they can use when conditions dictate: *"VFR flight not recommended."* This doesn't mean that *flight* itself isn't recommended, only that pilots should consider flying IFR, which of course requires an instrument rating. When you hear this phrase, take it seriously.

One time I heard a briefer jest about how pilots would sometimes ask, "Is VFR flight recommended today?" Some assume that if the FSS *doesn't* recommend VFR flight on bad weather days, it must surely recommend VFR flight on good weather days. But this briefer made it clear: The FSS *recommends* nothing. The FSS *suggests* nothing. The FSS *forbids* nothing. They simply provide information that we, as pilots-in-command, can use to make our decisions. Don't expect a briefer to make your go/no-go decisions for you.

You can call 1-800-WX-BRIEF from anywhere in the United States to reach a flight service station. Upon reaching a briefer, announce your request:

PILOT: *I'm a student pilot calling for a standard briefing. I'm flying Cessna 1186U from San Carlos to Columbia, leaving at 2:00 p.m. local, enroute for 1 hour. I'd like winds at 3,000 and 6,000.*

In the first sentence you alert the briefer that she should take a little extra time with you because you're a student, and you tell her why you're calling. Knowing what type of information the caller wants enables briefers to quickly load the appropriate screen on their computers. A *standard briefing* is a type of weather briefing. Your CFI will cover the various types of weather briefings with you.

The next part of the briefing request clues the briefer into the actual information you need. It defines your route of flight and the time you'll spend enroute. By saying "local" you let the briefer know that you want time references read back in local time as opposed to Zulu time. If you prefer to hear Zulu time references, then use Zulu time references in your request.

Briefers want to know the tail number of your airplane because they keep a temporary record of the briefings they give and use airplane tail numbers in those records. Those records are helpful in the event of an accident. Did the pilot obtain a weather briefing? Was it accurate? This helps on both sides of the argument: The FSS can prove they told the pilot what was going on. And the pilot can prove that she obtained a forecast for clear weather in case the FAA wonders why she flew directly into that nighttime cloud layer.

It's not really important which airplane you'll actually be flying. If you get your weather briefing using one airplane's tail number and end up flying another airplane, don't worry about it. When you call an FSS to file a flight plan, it *is* important that you give an accurate tail number. Your CFI will cover flight plan details with you.

You ask for winds aloft at altitudes near your intended cruise altitude. I usually fly at 5,500 when I'm going to Columbia from San Carlos. You don't need to know what the winds are doing at altitudes higher than those you intend to reach.

Wind forecasts are offered for a few specific altitudes only, including 3,000 and 6,000. If my intended altitude was only 3,000 feet, then I would not have asked for the winds at 6,000.

Have a pencil and a piece of paper ready. The briefer might ask some additional questions or she might just start spewing information. It can be tough at first to get a handle on all the information you hear, but practice will get you up to speed.

Call the FSS everyday and get briefings for imaginary flights. In fact, put this book down right now and call them. Ask for the San Carlos-to-Columbia briefing above. Ask the briefer to repeat or explain anything that doesn't make sense to you. They're happy to do it. Remember: 1-800-WX-BRIEF

You can also contact an FSS while airborne. The proper radio frequency depends upon the area in which you're flying at the time. You can see various FSS frequencies on navigational charts, which we'll cover later. A standard FSS radio frequency available in most locations is 122.2.

You can also contact Flight Watch on 122.0, which is a branch of the FSS dedicated to delivering enroute weather information and collecting PIREPs. The Flight Watch frequency (122.0) is the same everywhere.

Don't use the FSS as a replacement for your own hunting and gathering of weather reports. Use them as a back up. At first you'll rely on them completely, but eventually you'll start to get your own sense of the weather. But always consult them before longer flights or flights into unfamiliar areas. I do all it the time. It makes me feel more confident about my flight plans if I know someone more weather-savvy than me agrees with my weather assessments.

Another great thing about FSS briefers is that they can (and are happy to) answer general questions about aviation weather reports. For example, if you see an abbreviation in a weather briefing or on a chart that you don't understand, call the FSS and ask. Pilot assistance is the reason these folks get up in the morning. They really *do* want to hear from you!

ADDITIONAL WEATHER RESOURCES

Weather information is available at an ever-increasing number of websites, which is really handy during flight planning. In-flight weather updates, in addition to those provided by the FSS, are also available from a number of automated sources over your airplane's radio. Your CFI will explain more.

WEATHER WRAP UP

Most aviation training programs teach students to fly before they teach them anything about weather. Even then, many teach only the absolute minimum required by the FAA.

I put this chapter before the chapter on flying an airplane because that makes sense to me. There's no point in flying an airplane if you don't first have a basic understanding of the weather.

The next chapter is entitled, "Flying an Airplane is Easy" for a good reason: Flying an airplane *is* easy. Understanding weather is *not* easy. And flying an airplane through bad weather can be life threatening.

Check weather before each and every flight you make. Until you become an expert, make no assumptions.

If being weather-wise isn't good enough reason for you, keep in mind that only by checking weather will you learn of any flight restrictions along your route of flight.

It might be the most beautiful day of the year, with the sun shining, winds light and not a cloud in the sky. Visibility is unlimited and you can't believe how lucky you are to be a pilot. You pack a picnic lunch, gather up your best buddies and off you fly to your favorite remote spot.

Life couldn't be any better until all of a sudden an F-16 appears out of nowhere and blasts your sorry ass—sandwiches, corn chips and all—right out of the sky because you were on an intercept course toward Air Force One.

You should have checked the weather.

7

Flying an Airplane is Easy

So here we are, almost two hundred pages into this book and now, for the first time, we'll talk a bit about actually flying an airplane. The funny thing about flight training is that most of it won't focus on how to actually fly an airplane. In fact, controlling an airplane is so easy that your CFI will let you take the controls during your first lesson.

Landing an airplane, however, is a different story. Any confidence you build during training flights will often be browbeaten at touch-down time. Eventually you'll get the hang of it, and a "greased" landing will be a thrill that will plaster a smile on your face.

Even though I can't explain within these pages how to actually fly an airplane, there are some things we can cover that will make your cockpit training more enjoyable and effective.

FLYING AN AIRPLANE: 101

There are a handful of flight exercises and maneuvers you will practice with your instructor over and over again. I'll mention them each here, but we won't go into much detail. I just want to familiarize you with the terms and what they mean.

PREFLIGHTING

Hi David. This is the HAL 172. I wanted to alert you that I'm leaking oil and my nose gear tire has a small nail embedded in its left side. Other than that, I am fully functional and airworthy. Shall I start the engine or schedule maintenance?

If *only* it was this easy.

There are so many things that can go wrong with an airplane. Most problems are nothing more than inconveniences, but some can be deadly. In the example above, the airplane has a nail in one of the tires. This is a no-brainer. Most of a flight is spent in the air, but eventually we must land. And when we touch down those poor tires get a pretty good beating, as they squeal from 0 to 60 knots or more in an instant.

But the mythical HAL 172 also has reported an oil leak. How many flights do you think an airplane can safely make with an oil leak? One? Five? Fifty?

The correct answer is zero. Sure, the airplane might takeoff, fly and land without incident, but any oil leak that is not part of the aircraft's design, is a sign that trouble's brewing. And I know of no oil leaks that are part of an aircraft's design. (Overflow systems aside! Ask your CFI.)

Besides safety, which is always our number-one priority, we also must conduct each and every flight we make in adherence to Federal Aviation Regulations. Now, you're not going to find a regulation that governs an "acceptable" amount of leaking oil, but you will find an entire section of the regulations that governs aircraft manufacture. Student pilots aren't normally introduced to this section because most CFIs figure that we're not about to start manufacturing airplanes during our primary training.

But the importance of this section to us as pilots is to understand and appreciate that airplane models are certified airworthy by the FAA in a certain condition: *pristine*. What I mean is when the FAA gave Cessna their blessings to manufacture the 172, they didn't say, "Gee, nice airplane! We can't wait to see how it flies when you add a bigger engine!" They said, "Okay, we certify the 172 that stands before us as airworthy. Any substantial changes made to this aircraft made by anyone, manufacturer or owner, will invalidate this airworthiness certification."

It's an approval to manufacture, not to experiment. A beefed up engine is an experiment. An oil leak is an experiment too. A company that wants to stick beefed up engines in 172s can get certification from the FAA to do so, but you cannot just stick a new engine in your airplane like you were adding shiny new rims to your car. You'll hear aviators talk about STCs, or *supplemental type certificates*. An STC is basically the FAA's blessing of a specific airplane modification that has been tested and approved. You'll see STCs for higher-power engines, but not for oil leaks.

There's an FAA test question that asks who is responsible for ensuring an aircraft is airworthy before ever flight. They offer three choices. I won't mention the two wrong answers because I want you to hear the correct one first. The correct answer is *you*, the pilot-in-command. You confirm an aircraft is airworthy to protect you, your passengers, folks on the ground, the personal property of others, and your pilot certificate.

Preflights are not just a good idea, they are required by law for *all* pilots before *every* flight.

You'll perform them and you'll see the pilots of big jets perform them too. Ever notice the pilot of one of your commercial flights discreetly walking down the jet way staircase as the passengers are strategizing, clawing, fighting and trying to fool the laws of physics by stuffing Subaru-sized bags into the overhead compartments? The pilot is performing what is called the *walk-around visual inspection*. It involves exactly what its name implies: the pilot walks around the airplane and visually confirms everything is in working order.

In some respects, our visual inspections are even more intensive than those performed on the jumbos. We'll be tugging and pulling on wing struts, moving ailerons up and down and manually deflecting elevators and rudders to ensure there are no obstructions in the linkages. You just won't see a 777 captain hanging on one of her ailerons to ensure the aileron on the other wing moves opposite and freely. Those captains rely on maintenance crews and electronic systems to tell those tales. We do it the touchy-feely way.

Pilots do more than just the visual inspection during a preflight. We use checklists, which I'll talk about later, to ensure that we check everything and miss nothing. We check electronic systems, the engine compartment and more. The basic idea behind the preflight is to ensure that when you turn the ignition key and fire up the engine, you're safe and you're legal. (The preflight doesn't end there either. Additional system checks are conducted all the way until you take off.)

TAXIING

Taxiing an airplane refers to "driving" it on the ground, usually to or from a runway.

From the first moment you realize that turning the airplane's yoke (steering wheel) doesn't turn the airplane on the ground, you'll appreciate why taxiing is a skill that takes some practice.

Foot pedals are actually used to turn airplanes on the ground. Recalling our discussion on control surfaces, foot pedals actually move the rudder. When the rudder is deflected, the airplane turns because the prop's backward airflow hits the deflected rudder and forces the airplane's backside either left or right. On some airplanes, like the Cessna 172, the nose wheel is connected to the foot pedals and turns as the pedals are manipulated. This makes turning a bit more efficient.

To make use of the foot pedals even more confusing (at first), to activate the airplane's wheel brakes, you push forward on the top of the pedals with your toes. Each wheel has its own brake, so you must apply pressure evenly if you want to stop without pivoting the airplane on one wheel. Sometimes, however, this is exactly what you want to do. If you ever need to turn in a very tight radius, you'll use *differential braking*, which is a fancy term for applying more pressure to one brake and pivoting the airplane around the brake-locked wheel.

Once you have the basics, you can move an airplane around on the ground well enough to get it to and from the runway. But there are considerations to keep in mind while you're "driving" along those taxiways.

TAXI CLEARANCES
Before you can taxi anywhere at an airport with a control tower, you need to get clearance to do so:

PILOT: *San Carlos tower, Skyhawk 1186U, wash rack, taxi active, Charlie.*

This pilot has announced that Skyhawk 1186U is at the wash rack (where planes are washed) and wants to taxi to the runway in use. ATIS information *Charlie* has been heard and understood. ATIS is a cockpit radio frequency on which pilots

can hear pre-recorded messages of pertinent airport data, such as current winds and runway in use.

The tower responds:

TOWER: *86U, taxi three-zero via taxiway Juliet One. Give way to the Bonanza exiting the runway at Delta.*

The tower grants the taxi clearance, but instructs the pilot to use taxiway Juliet One and yield to the Bonanza that's getting off the runway at the Delta runway "off-ramp." The pilot confirms:

PILOT: *86U, taxi three-zero via Juliet One, will yield to the Bonanza.*

At airports without control towers, you need to announce your taxi intentions over the airplane's radio so that other pilots will know what you're up to. Each nontowered airport has a special radio frequency, called the *common traffic advisory frequency* or CTAF (spoken see-taf), that pilots use to talk with one another. The pilot below announces that she intends to depart the transient parking area (where visiting airplanes are tied-down) and head for runway 12:

PILOT: *Half Moon Bay traffic, Skyhawk 1186U, transient, taxiing one-two.*

There is usually no response from the other pilots unless someone sees a problem with the announced action, or has a question. For example:

PILOT: *Half Moon Bay traffic, Skyhawk 1186U, transient, taxiing one-two.*

PILOT 2: *1186U, Half Moon Bay is currently using runway three-zero.*

PILOT: *Roger that. 1186U will taxi three-zero.*

TAXIWAY ROAD MAPS
Here's one of the biggest tricks to safely taxiing at any airport: You must know the airport layout! Pilots are forever finding themselves lost and confused at unfamiliar airfields. The FAA likes to

Figure 73:   *THE LAY OF THE LAND* This airport diagram of the Palm Springs International Airport is from the Pilot's Guide directory. Taxiways are labeled as letters and runways are numbered. This airport has many examples of taxiways crossing runways. Familiarize yourself with your destination airport's layout before your flight. Airport layouts are far more confusing from the cockpit than they might otherwise seem.

believe that airports have adequate signage to direct pilots anywhere they need to go. Sometimes this is true, but don't count on it. Get a copy of the airport layout for every airport you visit. Become familiar with the taxiways, know where the transient parking area is located, and know where areas of danger exist. (Figure 73)

When you're at an airport unfamiliar to you, and you're not absolutely certain where to taxi, ask the ground controller for a *progressive taxi*. This alerts the controller that you're not familiar with the field. He will offer you turn-by-turn directions

throughout your taxi. It's very easy to get confused on the taxiways of complex airports. And it's very dangerous to taxi aimlessly. If you don't know exactly where you are and exactly where you need to go, ask for the progressive taxi.

Taxiways often cross active runways. Be extra alert at these intersections. Major aviation disasters have been the result of pilots either being in the wrong place on the airport, or misunderstanding a taxi or takeoff clearance.

One of the most seemingly frightening FAA regulations that has always bothered me says that once a tower controller clears you to taxi to a given runway, you are *not* supposed to stop at any taxi/runway intersections. You are, in fact, expected to proceed directly across that runway, active or not, and proceed to your assigned runway.

Keep in mind this is the same FAA that says the one responsible for an airplane's safety is the pilot, not the controller. Prior to crossing a runway, some pilots will confirm over the radio that they are cleared to do so:

PILOT: *Oakland tower, confirm 1186U is cleared to cross two-seven left.*

TOWER: *1186U, affirmative, cross two-seven left and hold short two-seven right.*

PILOT: *Roger. 1186U crossing two-seven left, will hold short at two-seven right.*

The controller at that point might be rolling her eyes at your extreme safety concerns. But rest assured, if she was, instead, filling out an accident report, she wouldn't be accepting any of the blame.

Just before crossing any runway, turn your airplane slightly, as necessary, so you can see both ends of the runway. This enables you to confirm that no one is landing or taking off.

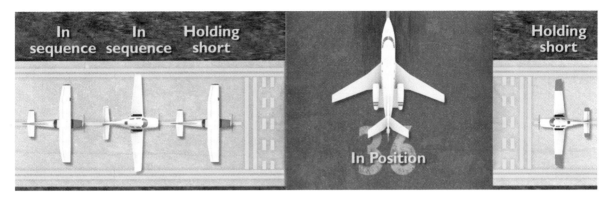

Figure 74: *TAKEOFF TURNS* The two airplanes on either side of the runway are "holding short," meaning they have reached the runway but have not rolled onto the runway. The sets of solid and dashed lines painted across the taxiway near the runway's edge define where pilots should stop when told by ATC to "hold short" of the runway. On the left are two airplanes "in sequence" for take off. Pilots "in sequence" aren't required to know their actual sequence position; controllers determine who goes when. There might be airplanes on the other side of the runway also "in-sequence" and "holding-short," so you can't assume your sequence just by looking at the airplanes directly ahead of you. The jet on the runway is "in position," meaning it is ready for takeoff. Only one airplane at a time can be in position on the runway.

TAXI TALK

The next trick to happy taxiing is to understand the terms used. A few key terms are used to ensure that everyone understands common instructions (Figure 74):

- **Hold short** – This means taxi up to a specified point but do not taxi onto or beyond that point. So "hold short of taxiway Bravo" means taxi up to the edge of taxiway Bravo, but don't taxi onto it. Runway edges at controlled fields have lines painted on the ground that define exactly where an airplane instructed to hold-short should stop:

  TOWER: *1186U, hold short three-six.*

  PILOT: *86U holding short three-six.*

- **In sequence** – When two or more airplanes are lined up to take off, they are said to be *in-sequence*. For example, say you were taxiing toward runway 30 and were ready to take off, but there was another airplane in front of you. You'd tell the tower:

  PILOT: *San Carlos tower, Cirrus 423MG, in sequence, three-six.*

- **In (into) position** – An airplane sitting on the runway ready to take off is *in-position*:

  TOWER: *1186U taxi into position.*

  PILOT: *Into position, 86U.*

OTHER TAXI CONSIDERATIONS

Wind must be considered whenever you're taxiing. Here's where your yoke becomes useful on the ground. The idea is to keep the upwind wing from popping up and flipping the airplane over. Light planes can be upturned due to high surface winds. This is much better left to your CFI to show you in the cockpit, so I won't go into it here. Keep it in mind and ask your CFI to demonstrate the best way to deal with surface winds on the taxiway.

Finally, we have what are called *runway incursions*. Extending beyond the scope of the runway itself, this term is used to classify airplane fender-benders that take place anywhere on the airport grounds. With all those airplane "parts" sticking out everywhere, it's no surprise that occasionally one airplane bumps into another while taxiing or parking. The key to avoiding such a mess is to keep your eyes open, remain alert and taxi slowly. Be especially aware of high-wing, low-wing considerations.

Aviation texts like to say that standard taxi speed is a "fast walk," but my experience has been that it depends on the circumstances. If you have a mile to taxi, in a straight line, and there are no other airplanes around, a "fast walk" will sure seem like a slow pace. Your CFI will help you determine an appropriate speed for various conditions.

The FAA has published a number of brochures they'd like you to read on the topic of runway incursions. Your CFI will have more to say about it too.

So what comes after you taxi your airplane from the parking area and are *in position?*

TAKEOFFS

Taking off in a training airplane is pretty easy stuff. Basically you push the airplane's throttle control all the way forward to apply full power, steer with your foot pedals to keep the airplane rolling straight down the runway (that can be a bit tricky at first), and once you reach a certain airspeed, you gently pull back on the yoke. Aerodynamics does the rest. As long as you maintain power and don't pull back on the yoke too much, you'll continue to climb.

Here's a safety quiz you can use to stump your CFI:

What's the very first action you take before starting the takeoff roll?

a. Apply full power.

b. Monitor the gauges for appropriate readings.

c. Use the foot pedals to keep the airplane's nose aligned straight down the runway.

d. None of the above.

The correct answer is "D." All of the answers are important, and must be considered during your takeoffs, but the very first thing that you must do is to *acknowledge your takeoff clearance!* If you never forget this, you'll never take off without a clearance to do so.

TOWER: *1186U cleared for takeoff.*

PILOT: *Cleared for takeoff, 86U.*

If you're at a nontowered airport, the very first thing you do is announce your takeoff intentions:

PILOT: *Skyhawk 1186U, departing three-zero.*

You'll have a pre-takeoff checklist that will ensure you've set up everything properly and that everyone's seat belts are fastened before you depart. Take this list seriously. Many aviation accidents can be traced back to items ignored on checklists. We'll talk more about them later.

Of course there's significant behind-the-scenes action involved in takeoffs too. Your passengers will think it's a piece of cake, but they won't see you monitoring your instruments for adequate readings, applying crosswind correction (as needed), keeping your eyes peeled for runway obstacles and birds, and all the while remembering your predetermined course of action if engine failure occurs on the runway, just after lift off, at pattern altitude, on the crosswind leg, or later.

AIRPORT TRAFFIC PATTERNS

Each airport has what's called a *traffic pattern,* which is like an imaginary roadway that airplanes use when entering or departing the airport area, and when taking off and landing.

The purpose of a traffic pattern is two fold:

* Airborne airplanes cannot stop to wait for other airplanes in their path, so some process of traffic flow is necessary. Traffic pattern

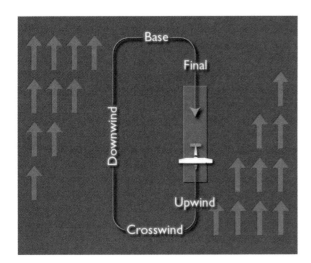

Figure 75: *PATTERN LEGS* The standard rectangular pattern includes the legs listed in this image. Later we'll see how airplanes actually fly these legs. (Wind direction is represented by arrows.)

flow is standardized, so everyone knows (in theory) where everyone else is likely to go next. This is very important because of the close proximity that airplanes fly to one another when near airports.

- Traffic patterns are determined with local obstacles and noise considerations (called *noise-abatement procedures*) in mind. A pattern's chosen route and altitude ensures airplanes remain clear of nearby terrain, towers and buildings, and, when possible and safe, will keep air traffic clear of noise-sensitive areas.

Think of a traffic circle at a busy city intersection to get the basic idea behind the airport traffic pattern.

Traffic patterns are rectangularly shaped, with the airport's runway making up most of one of the long legs of the rectangle. (Figure 75)

In "left-traffic" patterns, all turns are made to the pilot's left. "Right-traffic" patterns use right-hand turns. Left traffic patterns are standard because

pilot visibility to the left is better. (Pilots sit in the left seat.) If you're looking at a chart or other publication and no mention of the traffic pattern direction is made, it is a left pattern. Right patterns are specifically noted.

There are five sections of the pattern, each called a *leg*: upwind, crosswind, downwind, base and final. Upwind and final are centered on the runway.

Departing airplanes are said to be "upwind" as they roll down the runway and take off. Recall from earlier discussions that airplanes like to take off into the wind.

The upwind, crosswind and downwind legs are named for the airplane's presumed orientation to the prevailing wind direction, though these leg names don't change when the wind shifts. (If the wind starts blowing from the opposite direction, the opposing runway is used.)

After you depart and make your first turn in the pattern, you are "crosswind," implying that the wind is now crossing you from the side. You turn again and fly "downwind," with the wind now blowing from behind. The turn from downwind is called "base." (Don't ask me why.)

Once an arriving airplane aligns itself with the runway, it is said to be "on final," "on final approach," or, when the airplane is moments away from touchdown, on "short final."

Keep in mind that each physical runway surface is actually two opposing runways (18 and 36, for example, as shown in figure 76), and each runway has its own traffic pattern. If both runways use a "standard" left-traffic pattern, then the pattern for each runway will be on opposites sides of the fields (also figure 76).

When one side of an airport isn't suitable for a traffic pattern (noise concerns, or terrain), one runway will use a left traffic pattern while the opposite runway uses a right pattern. In these

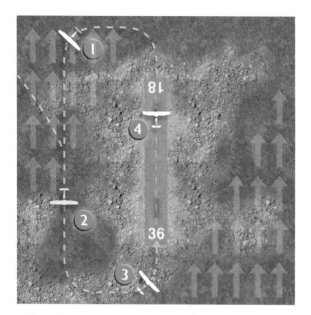 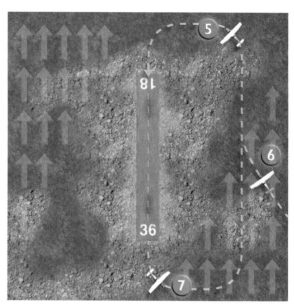

Figure 76: *FLYING PATTERNS* Scenic (but imaginary) Island Airport uses standard left-traffic patterns for both runways (18 and 36). Airplane number one is turning downwind for runway 36. Number two is flying downwind for runway 36. Number three is turning final for runway 36. Number four is upwind. Airplane number five is turning base for runway 18. Number six is entering the downwind for runway 18, while number seven is turning crosswind for runway 18. There are specific ways for pilots to announce their positions in patterns, which is explained shortly.

cases the traffic patterns cover the same physical area, but reverses direction depending on the runway in use.

The full pattern is used by pilots practicing take-offs and landings—we call this *flying the pattern*. You'll do this a lot during your early training.

But traffic pattern flow is also observed by pilots entering and leaving the airport area. Using pattern legs as reference, pilots can announce to others how they plan to leave or enter the pattern:

PILOT: *Island Airport traffic: Skyhawk 1186U, on a forty-five to enter downwind, left traffic, 18. Island Airport.*

This pilot intends to enter the downwind leg of runway 18's traffic pattern at a 45 degree angle. This is the preferred method of entering the pattern at a nontowered field. (See airplane number 6 in figure 76.)

For reference, notice how the 45° entry for the downwind leg of runway 36 (left image in figure 76) is totally opposite of the 45° entry for runway 18.

ENTERING THE PATTERN

At towered airports you might be offered all sorts of different pattern entry options. If your direction of flight has you somewhat aligned with the runway, you might get what's called a *straight-in approach*, meaning that you don't need to make any pattern turns at all. You can just fly straight onto the runway. Another option the tower might offer you is to enter the pattern on base leg, which

Figure 77: *HOLA AEROPUERTO!*
At towered airports, air traffic controllers ask pilots to enter the pattern all sorts of different ways, depending on the direction the airplane is flying. A straight-in approach (left) is the most convenient. Entry on the base leg of the pattern (middle) can sometimes be the most difficult method of entry because it can be harder to see the runway from that angle. A downwind pattern entry is an another common entry at towered airports when the airplane is approaching opposite the runway in use.

means you're only one turn away from final approach. Entering the pattern on downwind is a third option. (Figure 77)

If there are no traffic conflicts, a tower controller might clear you for a *short approach*, which authorizes you to make a beeline, sweeping turn toward the runway, bypassing any standard traffic pattern legs. You have to request this approach, however, controllers don't automatically offer it.

These short-cut pattern-entry options are suitable only when you're flying at towered airports. At nontowered fields, however, pilots should remain less creative. There's enough potential confusion at nontowered airports without adding to the mix by entering the pattern in ways that might confuse other pilots. No mid-air collision was ever expected. Anything you can do to keep your actions predicable reduces your likelihood of a mid-air collision with another airplane.

A 45° entry to the downwind leg is considered standard for nontowered airports, but the best way to get onto that 45° angle might seem a bit odd at first. Have a look at figure 78. This airplane is overflying the field before entering the downwind

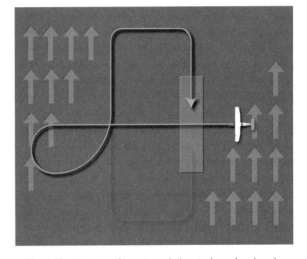

Figure 78: *OVERFLY* At nontowered airports the preferred method of pattern entry is to overfly the airport (so you can see the windsock, determine the best runway to use, and ensure there are no obstacles on the runway), and then enter the downwind leg at a 45 degree angle. This "eases" you into the pattern, offering other airplanes a better chance to see you.

leg. I figured this was the most convoluted thing I had even seen when I was a student pilot. Who came up with this mess?

I'll show you now why it's actually a very clever procedure. Many times that you land at a nontowered field, you'll be the only pilot around. So you'll have no idea which runway is best, based on the current winds, and you'll have no idea if the runway surface is clear or if a family of cattle have made it "home." Flying over the field before you land is the only way you have of determining which runway is best and if the runway is suitable for landing.

Even when there is another airplane in the pattern a fly-over is a good idea. Can you trust the other pilot's assessment of the proper runway to use? One day I did. I entered the airspace for a nontowered airport and heard a pilot announce over the radio that he was on final for a certain runway. I figured that I didn't need to do a fly-over because that other pilot must be using the best runway.

As it turned out, that pilot was practicing crosswind landings. He intentionally chose a runway that crossed the winds to make his landing as challenging as possible.

I wasn't looking for a challenge at that point. I aborted the approach and had to go out and start all over again.

If there are two or more airplanes using a given runway, you really have no choice. You certainly don't want to land on a runway that opposes other traffic at the airport. If everyone is practicing crosswind landings and you're not up for it, land somewhere else.

LEAVING THE PATTERN

Leaving a traffic pattern also requires some consideration, especially at nontowered airports. Reporting your departure intentions at nontowered fields involves determining what direction you want to fly after takeoff and announcing it:

PILOT: *Island Airport traffic: Skyhawk 1186U, taking-off 36, crosswind departure. Island Airport.*

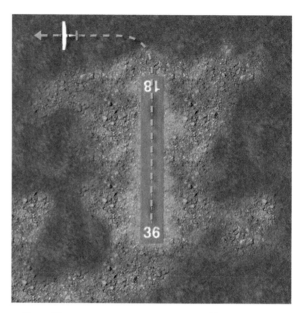

Figure 79: *CROSSWIND DEPARTURE* This pilot is leaving the airport area on the crosswind leg of the runway 36 traffic pattern.

This pilot has announced that after takeoff on runway 36, she will fly upwind, turn left to fly crosswind, but she will leave the area before turning onto the downwind leg. This gives other pilots a good sense of what she'll be doing after she takes off. (Figure 79)

Pilots also depart on the upwind leg, which is commonly called a *straight-out* departure. Pilots don't usually depart on the base leg because it makes no sense and can be dangerous. A base leg departure flies the airplane right across the final approach corridor. Figure 80 illustrates several departure options.

If a pilot needs to turn opposite the crosswind leg after takeoff, he does so by announcing his intended direction of travel:

PILOT: *Island Airport traffic, Skyhawk 1186U, taking off, 36, departing to the east. Island Airport.*

Figure 80: *ADIOS AEROPUERTO!* Leaving an airport traffic pattern area is easy, but following the rules of the pattern makes it safer. Once you're clear of the pattern, you can turn any direction you want. This image shows an upwind departure (left), a crosswind departure (middle) and a downwind departure (right). Upwind departures are also called straight-out departures.

As this pilot starts his takeoff roll down runway 36, he will be flying north. (More on that later.) By announcing that he plans to turn to the east, other pilots know he will be making a right turn after departure and not be turning left onto the crosswind leg. (Look back at figure 76 to better visualize this departure.)

All departures fly the full upwind leg because it gives the airplane time to gain some altitude before any turns are made. Turning too soon might be dangerous if terrain or radio towers are nearby.

At towered fields there might be defined departure routes. In this case, you'll tell the tower which you plan to use:

PILOT: *San Carlos tower, Skyhawk 1186U, holding short 30, Bay Meadows departure.*

This means that 86U is sitting just off runway 30 and ready to go. After departure, the airplane will follow the defined departure route named "Bay Meadows." The names of departure routes will differ at each airport. They are typically named for prominent landmarks airplanes fly over during the departure. The benefit to a departure like this

is that the tower will know where you plan to go, which will help them keep other airplanes out of your way.

The standard straight-out, crosswind and downwind departures are also used at towered airports.

TRAFFIC PATTERN ALTITUDE

Each traffic pattern has a specific altitude airplanes should be at when entering and flying the pattern. This altitude is called the *traffic pattern altitude* (TPA). The TPA helps keep airplanes clear of obstacles below, airspace boundaries above (if any exist), and each other. It's difficult to see airplanes directly below or above you. If everyone flies at the same altitude, landing on top of one another is less likely.

The standard TPA is 1,000 feet above ground level (AGL) for light aircraft like the ones we fly. Sometimes a smaller airport's TPA will be lower than standard because a larger airport "owns" the airspace overhead.

At some point while flying the pattern, the airplane must start a descent for landing. The actual location to start the descent depends on several factors that are better left for you and your

CFI to discuss. Sometimes you'll start your descent on downwind and other times you might not start it until you're on final approach.

As mentioned, all departing aircraft fly the entire upwind leg because it ensures that the airplane has reached the TPA before any turns are made.

CALLING YOUR POSITION

Using pattern leg names, pilots and controllers can report airplane positions in terms that everyone can immediately recognize.

At nontowered fields it's *imperative* that you announce your positions over the airport's CTAF (common traffic advisory frequency). Doing so alerts other pilots to your whereabouts and intentions.

Sometimes smaller airports share the same CTAF. It's not uncommon to be at one airport and hear pilots at another. By naming the airport in your announcement, you eliminate potential confusion. Repeat the name at the end of each transmission in case anyone missed it the first time:

PILOT: *Half Moon Bay traffic, Skyhawk 1186U turning right, crosswind, 30. Half Moon Bay.*

It's best to announce your position just before or during turns because your airplane will be angled in the turn (*wings up*, as we call it), which makes it easier to spot. Mentioning the direction of the turn and the runway in use serves as a notice to pilots that might be inbound to the airport as to which way the traffic is going.

Announce traffic pattern position even when you're planning to leave the area. Just let everyone know your intentions:

PILOT: *Half Moon Bay traffic, Skyhawk 1186U turning right, crosswind, 30. Departing on downwind. Half Moon Bay.*

Using the word *traffic* in your announcement says that you are addressing other pilots in the area, as opposed to a tower controller. When flying in the traffic pattern of a controlled airport, you talk to the tower, not to other pilots. In these cases you'd start calls with, "Anytown Airport *tower...*" not "Anytown Airport *traffic.*"

Airplanes in the pattern at towered airports don't announce pattern positions because the tower controller is already aware of everyone's position. If things get busy, however, a controller might ask you to report a specific turn as a reminder:

TOWER: *Skyhawk 1186U, report turning base.*

PILOT: *Wilco. 86U will report turning base.*

Here the tower has asked the pilot to announce when he starts his turn to the base leg. The pilot has responded *wilco*, which means he will comply. When the time comes to turn onto the base leg of the traffic pattern, the pilot would say:

PILOT: *86U turning base.*

The tower might also want to determine when you make your next turn. For traffic separation reasons, the controller might need you to extend the leg you're currently flying:

TOWER: *86U, proceed downwind, I'll call your base.*

PILOT: *Roger. You'll call my base. 86U.*

Here the controller has asked the pilot to keep flying straight ahead along the downwind leg until told to turn onto the base leg. The pilot's response, *roger*, means he has heard and understands the communication. Contrast this with *wilco*, mentioned above. Wilco means the pilot has heard the controller's instructions *and* he will comply with the instructions. In this situation, the pilot wasn't asked to do anything. The controller is the one who will be doing something (telling the pilot when it's time to turn base). The pilot just needs to confirm that he has heard the controller's intentions. Roger does the trick.

As a side note, a third option to a controller's instructions is *unable*. Reserve this for those times when the controller asks you to do something that you cannot do or choose not to do because of safety:

TOWER: *Skyhawk 1186U, turn left 20 degrees.*

PILOT: *Skyhawk 1186U unable to maintain VFR at that heading.*

Here, the controller would like the pilot to turn left 20 degrees, likely for traffic separation. But, by the pilot's estimation, doing so would put him in the clouds, where he would no longer be able to fly VFR, or by visual references. The controller would then have to come up with a different plan.

Back now to the controller who's about to call the pilot's base leg.

Controllers often tell pilots when to turn onto certain pattern legs when the controller needs some time. Perhaps there are many airplanes in the pattern and the controller is trying to increase the space between them, or the controller is trying to get an airplane off the ground between landings.

One option you have in situations like this is to simply slow down your airplane. Many students forget that these airplanes have speed controls! After all, why fly halfway down the county waiting to hear that it's okay to turn base when you can alternatively slow the airplane down and turn base much closer to the airport? Remember, once you fly outside the airport traffic pattern area, you might no longer be clear of terrain or other objects. Slowing down, however, is a much better option if there are not faster airplanes behind you.

The most important consideration for a pilot to remember when a controller wants to call a turn is that the pilot is responsible for the aircraft's safety. Don't assume that the controller knows best. If you're not comfortable with your position in the pattern, speak up.

What's more, controllers do forget things from time to time. If a controller has said she'd call your next turn and you're getting ridiculously far from the traffic pattern, a gentle reminder is in order.

LANDINGS

Every flight results in a landing of some sort. And every landing is a little bit (or a lot) different.

Landing is one part process and one part feeling. The *process* part is easy: Every airplane has a prelanding checklist that pilots are to perform and every landing involves the same basic steps. It's the *feeling* part of landing that earns it the well-deserved reputation as the hardest part of flying an airplane.

Do you ever stop to think about your car-parking skills? Sometimes you pull into a spot with minimal effort or thought, and other times you find yourself shifting gears back and forth endlessly while you try to squeeze in. You park a car by *feel*, not by process. You don't get out and start making measurements to ensure you enter the spot at just the right speed and angle. Sometimes you feel it properly and other times you don't. But you have to admit: most of the times you get it wrong are due to not paying attention.

Landing an airplane is similar. You eventually get a feel for what aileron, rudder, flap and power adjustments you need to make to touch down smoothly on a chosen spot. Don't fret if this part of your training repeatedly zaps the confidence you build as a master of the takeoff. After all, backing up a few times to get into a parking spot doesn't make you want to give up driving. Hell, you probably forget all about bad parking jobs by the time you've locked your car door.

Allow yourself some bad landings, but keep in mind they were likely the result of not paying close enough attention to the process.

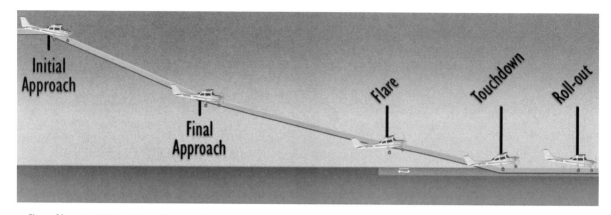

Figure 81: *LANDING PHASES* Starting with the initial approach, an airplane continues to descend until the final approach begins, which is the moment the runway comes into sight and the only thing the pilot has left to do is fly and land the airplane. The flare slows the airplane's descent rate so that the touchdown will be smoother. After touchdown, the pilot slows and eventually stops the airplane during the roll-out phase.

A landing is made up of several different phases: (Figure 81)

- Initial approach – This is when you begin your descent from your cruise altitude in preparation for landing.

- Final approach – When you have the runway in sight and all you have left to do is fly the airplane down, you're on final approach.

- Flare – Just moments before touchdown, the pilot reduces power and pulls slightly back on the yoke to prevent the airplane from slamming into the ground. The airplane's speed decreases and the airplane continues to drop, but at a much more gentle rate. This is the flare and is often the most difficult part of landing for new pilots.

- Touchdown – When the wheels hit the runway, you've touched down.

- Roll-out – Immediately after touchdown the pilot starts to slow the airplane by cutting power completely and applying brakes. The amount of distance this requires is called the roll-out. A 172 requires far less roll-out than a 747. And a 172 in a 20-knot headwind requires far less roll-out than a 172 landing in no wind.

STARTING WHAT WHEN

There are no hard and fast rules as to when you start one phase or transition to the next. A 777 pilot flying at 36,000 feet might start her initial approach some 40 minutes before touchdown. A 172 pilot's flight might be less than 40 minutes in its entirety.

But there is one reality about landings that you just can't escape: The better you execute one phase, the easier subsequent phases will be. It's very difficult to perform a great touchdown when you've just performed a shabby flare. And a good flare is tough when you've screwed up your final approach. You need to allow adequate time for everything.

The best way to determine when to start each phase is to work backward from the point that you want your airplane to stop on the runway.

How much runway do you need for the roll out to reach that spot?

Many factors affect roll-out distance requirements, including the type of airplane, the current atmospheric conditions, the airport's elevation and your airspeed (and groundspeed) at touchdown. Determining this stuff for your flights is best left for your CFI to cover with you.

If the length of the runway is longer than any roll-out distance your airplane could ever require, you don't have to concern yourself with this too much. For example, if your airplane's POH (pilot's operating handbook) says the most runway surface you'd ever need is 2,000 feet, and the runway up ahead is 6,500 feet, then you can rest assured you won't have any roll-out problems.

Runway length is far more a concern for those flying larger, faster aircraft. Many of the runways you land on in your Cessna 172 or Piper Warrior won't even be suitable for smaller multi-engine prop planes, let alone small or large jets.

For this reason, many pilots of smaller aircraft tend to disregard any concern for runway length. Let me tell you why you shouldn't be one of those pilots: the most significant landing of your life will be made with a dead engine on some corn field, some stretch of beach or some highway. When the surface you intend to land on is not a runway, you'd better be damned familiar with how much surface you'll need because you'll get only once chance.

Once you know how much roll-out distance you need, you'll know where you need to touchdown on the runway to stop in time. Again, if it's a long runway, this won't matter too much. But on shorter runways (we call these *short fields*), you might need to touchdown right at the start of the pavement in order to have enough runway surface for your roll-out.

Once you know where you need to touchdown, you'll know where to begin your flare. Your CFI will go over (and over) the flare process with you.

Knowing where to start the flare clues you into where you want to be at the end of your final approach. During final approach you should be in a steady descent at a steady airspeed. If you're flying in an airport's traffic pattern, your final approach will begin as you turn from the base leg to the final leg. If at this point you're too high, you might overshoot the runway. If you're too low, you might need to apply additional power so that you don't land short of the runway.

So what about the initial approach? Here's where you have some leeway. A properly timed initial approach gets you from your cruise altitude to a lower target altitude by the time you need to be at that altitude. Usually, the target altitude will be your destination airport's traffic pattern altitude, but you might have another altitude in mind.

To determine the start of your initial descent, you need to know four things:

- Your preferred rate of descent

- Your starting altitude

- Your target altitude

- Your groundspeed

Let's say we want a 500 foot-per-minute rate of descent. We're cruising at 5,500 feet and we want to get down to 1,000 feet. Our groundspeed during the descent will be 100 knots.

It works like this:

STEP 1. How much altitude do we need to lose? (5,500 minus 1,000 is 4,500 feet)

STEP 2. How many minutes will that take, given our preferred rate of descent? (4,500 divided by 500 is 9 minutes)

STEP 3. Given our current groundspeed, how do we know when we're 9 minutes away from the airport area?

This last step is a basic math problem, but we don't want to do even basic math in a cockpit if we can help it. Instead, we'll use a rule of thumb that offers a pretty good estimate.

The following rule of thumb should be used *only* for local flights for which you haven't made a complete flight plan. A good flight plan will include exactly where to start your initial approach.

Here's the quick way for now:

Drop that last two digits from the altitude to lose and divide that number by 3 to find out how many miles away from the airport you should start the decent.

We need to lose 4,500 feet.

- 45 divided by 3 is 15 miles out.

What about 10,000 feet?

- 100 divided by 3 is 33 miles out.

Keep in mind that winds and groundspeed do matter here. If you're facing a strong headwind, this formula will get you down long before you need. A strong tail wind (faster groundspeed) will require that you start your descent farther out. This is where good flight planning comes into play.

You also have the option of increasing or decreasing your rate of descent to get where you want when you want, but keep in mind that if sloppy initial-approach planning has you adjusting and readjusting your rate of descent, that sloppiness is likely to follow you all the way to touchdown.

Greased landings rarely happen in spite of a pilot's sloppy performance. Airplanes don't like to land; they like to fly. Making a smooth transition from airborne to "groundborne" isn't the easiest thing you'll ever do. You really have to learn to "feel" it.

I know that sounds ridiculous now, but one day things will click and you'll feel it for the first time. Your confidence will soar until the very next time you land, which will stink all over again.

It happens to all of us.

STALLS AND MANEUVERS

During your checkride you'll be asked to perform a series of flight maneuvers that are intended to demonstrate your proficiency behind the yoke. We're not talking aerobatics here. These maneuvers are nothing more than examples of the types of maneuvers that are often required during regular flight.

There is a standard set of parameters that examiners use to determine your success with a maneuver. For example, some require that you maintain airspeed and altitude within a certain range all throughout the maneuver. Your CFI will cover those parameters with you. You can also read about the various require-ments in the Practical test Standards book discussed back on page 67.

Below is an overview of each maneuver and an explanation of its purpose.

SLOW FLIGHT

This has got to be the dullest of all flight maneuvers, but it does come with its challenges. The name *slow flight* describes the maneuver accurately: flying your airplane slowly.

One of the challenges of slow flight is that the airplane's performance is compromised. If you think back to our discussion on lift, you'll recall that as the airplane's airspeed decreases, so decreases its ability to generate lift. At low airspeeds, the airplane controls feel sluggish, requiring exaggerated yoke motions in order to turn the airplane; the airplane climbs poorly, if at all; and, perhaps most importantly, this all happens quite close to the airplane's stall speed.

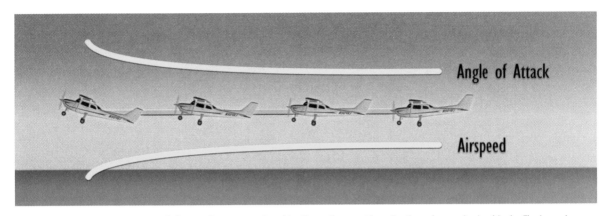

Figure 82: *POWER-OFF STALL* A decrease in power requires this pilot to increase his angle of attack to maintain altitude. The increasing angle of attack reduces his airspeed, which requires him to pull back on the yoke even further. This cycle eventually gets the airplane to its stall speed in the "dirty" configuration (flaps down, landing gear extended), and to its critical angle of attack.

The object of slow flight is to master the use of engine power and yoke control to maintain a slow speed while still being able to maneuver the airplane safely. This is exactly what you need to do each time you set your airplane up for a landing.

STALLS

An airplane is said to be stalled when the airflow over a wing is reduced or disrupted to the point where the wing can no longer produce lift. We talked about the theory behind stalls back in the "About Your Airplane" section, so we won't cover it again here.

There are two basic types of stalls:

- Power off

- Power on

The *power-off* stall involves getting your airplane into slow flight, dropping power to idle and then gently pulling back on the yoke until your airspeed drops below stall speed and the airplane stalls. (Figure 82)

A stall is indicated by a couple of things:

- A stall warning horn will go off in the cockpit.

- You might notice the airplane shaking a bit.

- The airplane's nose will drop.

As you enter a stall, you'll notice that your ailerons and rudder have seemed to stop working! In fact, they have. When an airplane is stalled, there is not enough airflow over the wings to generate lift. But there is also insufficient airflow to enable the various control surfaces (ailerons and rudder) to deflect enough air to affect the airplane's attitude.

The power-off stall is meant to simulate stalls likely during approach and landing, when your flaps are extended and your airspeed is slow.

The *power-on* stall simulates stalls more likely on takeoff, when you're at full power, flaps are retracted and your nose is high.

To perform a power-on stall, you first slow the airplane to the speed you're at when you lift off the runway (called *rotation* speed). Then you apply full power and pull back as if you were taking off too steeply. During the steep climb

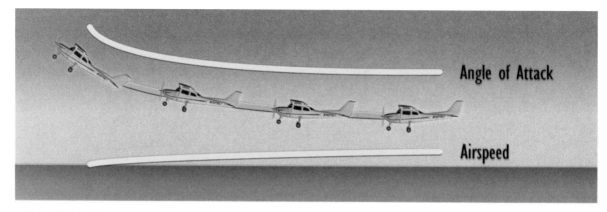

Figure 83: POWER-ON STALL This pilot is using full power, but climbing at such a high angle of attack that her airplane cannot maintain enough airspeed to avoid a stall. The airspeed continues to drop as the angle of attack increases. Eventually the airplane reaches its stall speed for the "clean" configuration (flaps and gear are retracted), and its critical angle of attack.

your airspeed drops and eventually reaches the airplane's stall speed for the "clean" configuration. (Figure 83)

The first step toward recovery of either type of stall is to lower the airplane's nose to regain airspeed. This is because all stalls—power on and power off—are all about loss of airspeed. Get that airspeed back, and you're fine.

It's important to note that although these stalls simulate conditions close to the ground, you will always practice them up at an altitude that allows at least 1,500 feet for recovery.

STEEP TURNS

A *steep turn* is a maneuver in which the airplane flies in a 360-degree circle all the while maintaining a bank angle of 45 degrees and a constant altitude. You'll use visual references to the horizon to determine your bank angle. (Figure 84)

To enter a steep turn you simultaneously apply power, turn and pull back on the yoke, and apply rudder pressure as needed to keep the turn coordinator's ball centered. Lots to do, but it becomes second nature the more you do it.

During the turn you are expected to maintain your bank angle, airspeed and altitude within certain ranges that your CFI will cover with you.

Your steep-turn know-how comes handy anytime you need to turn your airplane around in a tight space, such as when sight-seeing or when you've flown yourself into a tight spot that you need to get out of in a hurry.

TURNS AROUND A POINT

Imagine your airplane connected to an object on the ground by a (really strong) string. As you flew, you'd be rotating around the object to which you were tied in a perfect circle. We simulate this situation in a maneuver called *turns around a point*. (Figure 85)

At first, this maneuver seems much like the steep turn, but there are important differences between the objectives of the two maneuvers. Turns around a point is about maintaining a *static distance* from the object. Wind differences throughout the turn require that you adjust bank angle as necessary so that you don't drift away from (or toward) the ground reference point.

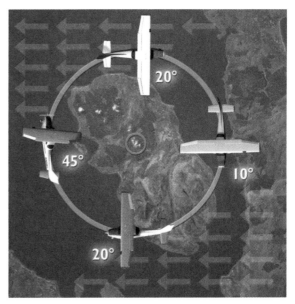

Figure 85: *TURNS AROUND A POINT* This maneuver tests the pilot's ability to compensate for wind drift by adjusting his bank angle during the turn. Equal bank angles are used when the airplane is flying with a direct head- or tail-wind. The highest bank angle is required when the airplane is flying through the left "crosswind" portion of the circle, to keep it from drifting. (Arrows indicate wind direction.)

Figure 84: *STEEP TURNING* The steep turn maneuver requires pilots to maintain a 45° bank angle while also maintaining a steady altitude and airspeed. The horizon is considered the pilot's primary tool for determining his exact bank angle, though a quick glance at the attitude indicator can verify your accuracy.

Easier said than done, believe me.

The steep turn, on then other hand, is about maintaining a certain bank angle regardless of the effects of the wind. Other objectives, like maintaining altitude and airspeed, are shared by the two maneuvers.

You'll use turns around a point in everyday flying more often than you might think. Your ground reference point might be a wind sock you're trying to see, or it might be a magnificent gray whale breaching off the coast of California. In either case, you want to remain centered on your object. Your passengers will think you're simply turning the airplane. You'll know differently.

S-TURNS

S-turns are easy to visualize based on their name. (Figure 86) The ground reference point used for this maneuver is a straight line, like a highway, coast line or train tracks. The objective is to perform a series of alternating 180-degree turns across the reference line (at a 90° angle to the line) while remaining at an equal distance from the line on both sides.

So when would you use S-turns in everyday flying? I haven't ever used them. Not that there wouldn't be a purpose, but I never felt that they were safe enough to do just for fun. Others might disagree on this point, but here's the way I see it: You're flying in a manner that would

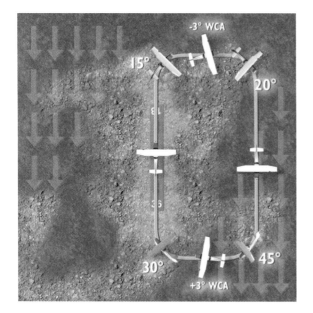 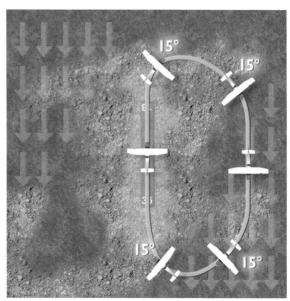

Figure 87: *A RECTANGLE IS A RECTANGLE* The image on the left shows proper bank and wind correction (crab) angles for flying a rectangular course, like an airport traffic pattern. (Actual angles depend on the strength and direction of the wind.) The turn from upwind to crosswind requires the least bank angle because the wind direction, combined with the airplane's relatively slow groundspeed, automatically makes for a tighter turning angle. A slight crab angle is used on the crosswind leg to keep the airplane tracking forward. A slightly steeper bank angle gets the airplane onto the downwind leg as its groundspeed increases. No crab angle is required when flying directly into or away from the wind. The steepest angle in the course is required to get the airplane cleanly onto the base leg because groundspeed is highest and the effects of the wind want to blow the airplane away from the course. The bank angle is lessened to get the airplane onto the upwind leg, which in a traffic pattern is called final approach. This is where you have to keep stall speed in mind. You're using a steep bank angle combined with a slow airspeed. Without compensating for the wind, the airplane on the right drifts freely in the direction the wind is blowing.

seem somewhat random to another airborne pilot watching you. Only after seeing you complete several iterations of the maneuver would the other pilot be able to anticipate your next move. But a complete S-turn can take a minute or more to complete. Throughout all that time the other aircraft is wondering what the heck you're doing. And chances are you haven't see the other aircraft coming because you're preoccupied with flip-flopping for fun.

RECTANGULAR COURSE

Last on the list of the wind-watching maneuvers is the rectangular course. Few CFIs make students practice this maneuver much because

it's basically the same as flying the airport traffic pattern. Your rectangular course practice comes each time you land.

The challenge behind the rectangular course, like the airport's traffic pattern itself, is that you have to compensate for the effects of wind to fly a solid rectangle. If you don't, and the wind is strong, you'll fly something more like a parallelogram. (Figure 87)

And there you have an introduction the private pilot flight maneuvers. Keep in mind what you're supposed to be learning from each maneuver and you'll get much more out of them.

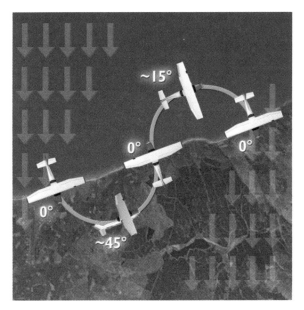

Figure 86: *NOW IT'S YOUR S-TURN* This maneuver requires a pilot to consider the effects of wind in alternating directions in order to maintain a clean 's' pattern. This pilot has chosen the coastline as a reference line. The initial turn from downwind (left) requires the steepest bank angle because the wind wants to blow the airplane away from the reference line. In the turn from upwind (right), a shallower bank angle is used to offset the wind's tendency to blow the airplane too close to the reference line. As with all maneuvers, the actual bank angles used depends on the size of the turns and the force and direction of the wind. In a no-wind situation, the bank angles for each turn would be the same.

NAVIGATION

Once you decide to venture outside the airport's traffic pattern, it's time to start navigating. Even when you know the local area, you'll find it's quite easy to get lost in an airplane if you don't properly prepare yourself for each flight.

The navigation resources we use as private pilots range from our eyes and common sense, to printed maps called *charts*, and electronic options you'll explore with your CFI once you start your training.

Figure 88: *CHART CHUNK* This small portion of a sectional chart shows many airports (the small magenta circles), lots of water bodies (blue patches) and the range of elevation charts show: green to show sea level areas and darker browns to show mountains. You can also see some highways and even power lines (look for the little power towers along dark lines). The large magenta circles are airspace designations that you'll cover with your instructor. Like all aviation charts, this chart chunk is oriented with north being straight up.

The two most common means of navigation for private pilots are:

* Pilotage

* Dead Reckoning

PILOTAGE

Reading a chart and determining your position by comparing what you see on the chart to what you see outside your airplane is called *pilotage.* (Spoken: *pilot-idge*) This is pretty much how you'd use a map in a car.

While pilotage is considered the most basic method of airplane navigation, and therefore should be considered the easiest, it's not foolproof. The trick is that things look very different from the air. Street signs are not visible, roads tend to look the same, and objects that appear on charts are often obscured by terrain, buildings or other obstructions when viewed from the pilot's line-of-sight airborne perspective.

The result of these concerns is that pilots can find themselves unable to pinpoint exactly where they are, even on the clearest of days. The best way around this is to maintain an awareness of your location throughout your flight. Track your progress on the chart from the very beginning and you'll find it much easier to determine your whereabouts.

Ride along with other pilots as often as you can. Sitting in the right seat (where your CFI will be sitting during your lessons) is a great time to practice chart reading. You'll help yourself and, chances are, the pilot in the left seat could use the practice, too.

DEAD RECKONING

Taking pilotage a step further, *dead reckoning* is a method of navigation that enables you to estimate your position along your route and track your progress in flight.

The advantages to dead reckoning over pilotage alone are significant. You can:

- Estimate flight time

- Estimate fuel requirements

- Ensure navigation accuracy

The advantages of those first two items are pretty obvious, but the third requires some explanation.

Dead reckoning is usually based on two or more visual checkpoints that lie between your origin and destination. For example, say there is a giant water tower that lies along your route of flight right between the two airports. The first segment of your trip would be a calculation of distance and time enroute to the water tower. The second segment would be a calculation of distance and time enroute from the water tower to your destination airport.

So, if you took off and headed in the wrong direction, you'd know you were lost halfway through your flight because you'd be expecting to see a water tower that wasn't there. Better to know that something's wrong halfway through the flight than when you're looking for your destination airport and all you see is swampland.

The other advantage that dead reckoning offers to navigation is flight progress. You might be headed in the right direction, but the winds might be different than you had planned. If the water tower was supposed to appear 15 minutes into your flight and there it was, only 10 minutes after departure, you'd know that the winds were working with you. If, on the other hand, the water tower wasn't there at 15 minutes, but you absolutely knew you weren't lost because you had been carefully tracking your progress throughout the flight, then you'd know you were up against a strong headwind and you'd be burning more fuel on than flight than you estimated.

On a short 30-minute flight this might not be such a big deal. But if your flight was several hours long, dead reckoning can help you realize that you need to make a fuel stop before the sound of a sputtering engine makes the suggestion for you.

CUMBERSOME COCKPITS

The very first thing you're likely to notice about the cabin of the airplane you train in is how small it is. The likelihood that you and your CFI will both fit without fighting for elbow room is slight. But you get used to it. After a while, you won't even think about its size until you take a first-time passenger along and hear: "Oh my God! It's so small! I'm not getting on that thing!"

Female pilots just laugh at reactions like this. Male pilots, however, defend the cockpit's design and offer all sorts of reasons why its size is actually appropriate.

But small it is, and it's up to you, as pilot-in-command, to keep your cockpit organized and comfortable so you can perform all of your duties safely and properly. The trick to maximizing cockpit space is to minimize cockpit clutter.

TAKE ONLY WHAT YOU NEED (DAY AND NIGHT)

FARS GOVERNING AIRCRAFT EQUIPMENT

The FARs have something to say about equipment requirements aboard all aircraft. The following sections are not meant in any way to circumvent those regulations. The FARs do not, however, govern personal equipment that pilots might need, such as pens, paper or flashlights. FAR equipment requirements govern aircraft components only, such as navigation lights, cockpit instruments, etc.

Thinking in advance about what you're likely to need on a flight serves two important purposes. First, it enables you to make the most efficient use of the space available. Secondly, it forces you to imagine all of the possibilities that you might encounter enroute. This skill is honed with experience, but you can never start exercising it too early.

The most basic consideration that even the most novice student pilot can consider is the time of the flight: day or night? Most early training flights will be during the day, so let's start there.

DAYTIME EQUIPMENT

The actual personal equipment that you will need for each flight will vary from flight to flight. For example, if your CFI plans to test you on the use of an E6B flight calculator (explained later), then you'd certainly need to take one with you.

Additionally, if a cross-country flight takes you into an area not covered by your regular charts, you'll need to buy another chart.

But don't take more than you'll need. When I first started flying, I took everything with me on every flight. "Better safe than sorry," I reasoned. What a mess I was. Though better safe than sorry is a philosophy that's hard to argue, "better organized than overwhelmed" gives it a good run for its money. If you're flying around your airport's traffic pattern practicing takeoffs and landings, you probably won't need ready access to your entire collection of charts, your flight computer, your copy of the federal regulations or your hand-held GPS unit.

Keep your cockpit clean and organized. If you think your flights through ahead of time, you'll have a good sense of what you'll need. This becomes easier with experience.

Eventually, even I started thinking my flights through before I loaded up my lap. Would I need flashlights at 11:00 a.m.? Or what about my encyclopedia-sized flight training manual? Was I actually prepared to break it out mid-flight and read up on something that I didn't understand? It got me thinking: What is really necessary to safely and legally fly an airplane? I made a list:

- **Student pilot certificate/medical certificate** – The FARs require students to have valid medical certificates in order to fly solo. Your medical certificate is also your student pilot's license; they are printed on opposite sides of the same piece of paper. Get it as soon as you can, and get into the habit of keeping it with you, even when you fly with your CFI. I taped an envelope to the inside front cover of my logbook and kept mine in there.

- **Logbook** – The regulations also require students to carry their logbooks with them during solo flights. This is why your logbook is a great place to keep your medical certificate. Once you're licensed, however, the decision to keep your logbook with you on flights is yours to make, but you must *always* have your pilot certificate, photo identification and medical certificate with you on every flight.

- **Checklists** – Each airplane has official checklists printed in its POH, but I made up my own. I explain why in a moment. Always have a checklist with you. Many aviation accidents are the result of pilots forgetting to do something—like switching fuel tanks—that they would have remembered to do if they'd consulted a checklist.

- **Relevant charts** – In some geographic areas you might find that you need several charts to cover all the places you'll fly. Areas within the vicinity of major airports usually have special charts that are "magnified" versions of the regular chart. They show higher levels of detail for a smaller area.

- **Note pad and pens** – There's always something to write down. Whether it's your time of departure, ATIS information, or any number of other things, you should always have a pad and pen handy. Keep several pens around for when you drop one or one runs out of ink. Pencils work fine too; it's most important to pick the implement that enables you to write as clearly as possible. You decide which you prefer.

So far, all we have with us is paper and a few pens. This is a good thing. These items don't take up much room, they're cheap, and they're really all that you *absolutely* need. But my list continues below. Some of the additional items are optional and some are not, depending on your flight and your personal requirements. Your CFI might determine some of this for you.

- **Headsets** – As cumbersome as it is to carry your own headsets with you, the quality of the headsets offered with rental aircraft make the hassle well worth it. Once upon a time, it was considered acceptable for pilots to use the airplane's built-in speaker and microphone when talking over the radio. Once upon a time it was also considered acceptable to rise up from your sofa to change the television channel. Times change. It's difficult to hear well enough over the roar of the engine when using the airplane's speaker. Further, studies have shown evidence of hearing loss in long-term "speaker" pilots. Help in understanding various headset options can be found in "Headsets" on page 252.

- **E6B flight calculator** – I was so excited when I first heard this device mentioned. I was imagining a high-tech gadget that would surely make for hours of in-flight fun. Here's the deal: it's a slide rule. You're required to know how to use one for your flight tests, so you'll need to get some practice with it.

- **Navigation tools** – The tools I'm talking about here are the plotter tools you'll use with charts to determine your location and course.

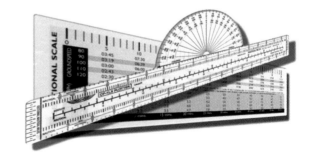

- **Water** – In-flight beverage service on training flights is rare. If you're the type to require water, take it along. But remember that in-flight "facilities" on training flights are even rarer than beverage service. The two often go hand in hand, so to speak.

- **Lap board (organizer)** – Here you have the hub of your airborne world. A lap board can be like a personal organizer that you strap to one of your thighs. You need your hands free, yet you need your charts, note pad and checklists at the ready. Your lap is the most accessible flat surface you have in a cockpit. The trick to selecting the best lap board is to make sure it can carry all you need, but also that it's not too big. I'll tell you how I solve this issue in "Lap Boards and Organizers" on page 256.

And there you have it, several items, but all fairly small.

Another important item that needs to be on board is the POH for the airplane that contains the airplane's operating limitations. [FAR 91.9] While a POH isn't something you would consider a personal item, if a copy of the airplane's operating limitations isn't on-board, you can't legally fly the airplane. For this reason, I also kept a copy of a Cessna 172 POH in my flight bag. During flight planning you'll need a copy of the POH for the airplane that you'll fly, so you might as well keep one in the flight bag.

There are several other "toys" in my flight bag, I must admit. But none are required. We'll talk more about such toys in "Gizmo Stockpiling" on page 251.

NIGHTTIME EQUIPMENT

Let me start this section by saying something obvious: the only difference between daytime and nighttime flying is that it's dark at night. That's it. Your airplane has no idea what time of day it is, nor does it care. Equally ambivalent about time of day are radio towers, hillsides and other ground obstacles.

That in mind, we simply need to take our daytime arsenal and supplement it with whatever we need to deal with darkness. And that would be artificial light.

In theory, all airplanes should be equipped with adequate cockpit lighting so pilots can read charts and see instrument gauges. But, as they say, that'll be the day. You're better off just assuming that the airplane's interior lights will be dreadful. Have your own collection of small flashlights and other light-emitting gadgets so you'll always be ready for anything. ("Flashlights" on page 255 describes different types suitable for the cockpit.)

There's nothing you can do about the airplane's exterior lighting. It's either there or not. And if it's not, you can't fly at night. The regulations require certain external lighting, which we'll talk about later. The problem with inoperative airplane lighting is that you usually don't discover it until you're preflighting for a night flight. To circumvent this frustration, check the airplane's external lights during your daytime preflights too. That way you're more likely to discover a burnt-out bulb during the day, when it's less likely to cancel your flight plans.

It might take you many flights before you determine what you like to have along. Give it time, but keep in mind that less means more, by way of cockpit room.

CHECKLISTS THAT MAKE SENSE TO YOU

As mentioned, some aviation disasters could have been avoided if pilots had properly followed checklists. The concept is simple: The airplane needs certain things done at certain times. Given the anything-could-happen environment of an airborne cockpit, a checklist is the safest way to ensure all of those things are done when they need to be done. Lowering the landing gear is a great example of something that should be done before every touchdown, yet you'd be amazed at how many pilots forget to do so, some more than once.

CHECKLIST OVERKILL

The more complex your airplane, the more necessary checklists become. I used to argue with my CFI that getting out a checklist to ensure that I'd performed the same handful of tasks before each landing—that I'd done hundreds of times before—was actually a safety risk, not a benefit. After all, there I am in the traffic pattern with all those other airplanes nearby. Shouldn't I be paying attention to flying the plane?

It's hard to appreciate the value of checklist observation when you're flying a simple Piper Warrior or a Cessna 172. And to be honest, I'm more likely to perform tasks from memory enroute than I am to pull out the same checklist every 15 or so minutes. But it's important to remember that your flight training is preparing you to fly *any* airplane, not just a trainer. Getting into the checklist habit now will make it easier for you to transition to more complex aircraft later.

Figure 89 offers a comparison between pre-landing checklists for a Cessna 172, King Air (a twin-engine turbo-prop), and a Boeing jet.

Let's take a deeper look at the Cessna list:

- Fasten our seat belts? Well, chances are that they're already fastened. But this is an FAA regulation, so it's good that they put it in. Forgetting this step on your checkride is cause for failure.

- Next we need to make sure that our fuel selector switch is set to both tanks, as opposed to one tank or the other. There's really no reason that it wouldn't already be set that way. Unlike some other trainers, you don't need to switch fuel tanks in a 172 because of this wonderful "both" position, so

I can't think of any reason to just not leave it set there all the time.

- Setting the mixture to the full-rich setting is a good idea, but we've probably already done that earlier in the flight during our descent. If we've been flying at less than 3,000 feet mean sea level (MSL), we would have already been at full-rich.

- Next we're reminded to turn the carb heat on. But in reality, we turn the carb heat on when we drop the engine power setting below 2000 RPM, so that's probably already done too.

- And turn off the auto-pilot and air-conditioning? Yeah, I'll get right on that one. (The likelihood that you're going to be training in an airplane equipped with auto-pilot and air-conditioning is pretty small.)

You could forget all of these things and still land the airplane safely *most* of the time. Some of the items listed are important only if you need to execute a go-around. The others are tasks that you probably already performed using earlier checklists.

So there we have a pre-landing checklist that would leave many Cessna pilots thinking, "Duh!"

The King Air's checklist is a different story, however. This thing is so packed full of stuff to do that they don't even bother reminding the pilot about the seatbelt. After all, there's landing gear that must be extended! Notice how they have the pilot check it twice.

The Boeing checklist further drives home the importance of a checklist. Not only are there many things to be done, but once you're in a complex airplane like that, time becomes more precious. The jet is flying fast and things are happening very quickly. You have plenty of time before touchdown to verify that everything has been set properly in a 172. But when checklists

CESSNA 172
BEFORE LANDING
Seats, Belts Harnesses . . . . .SECURE
Fuel Selector Valve . . . . .BOTH
Mixture . . . . .RICH
Carburetor Heat . . . . .ON
Autopilot (if installed) . . . . .OFF
Air Conditioning (if installed) . . . . .OFF

BEECH KING AIR B200
APPROACH
Pressurization . . . . .CHECKED
Altimeters . . . . SET
Cabin Sign . . . . FSB
Autofeather . . . . ARMED
Flaps . . . . APPROACH

BEFORE LANDING
Gear . . . . .DOWN
Lights . . . . .AS REQUIRED
Cabin Sign . . . . .BOTH
Radar . . . . .AS REQUIRED
Prop Sync (Type I) . . . . .OFF
Brake De-Ice . . . . .AS REQUIRED

LANDING ASSURED
Gear . . . . .RECHECK DOWN
Flaps . . . . .DOWN 100%
Yaw Damp . . . . .OFF

BOEING JET
INITIAL DESCENT
Seatbelt light . . . . .ON
Main Air Valves . . . . .ON
Descent Pitch . . . . ESTABLISHED
Descent Power . . . . SET
Pressurization . . . . .SET AND CHECK
Icing Systems . . . . .AS REQUIRED
Altimeter . . . . .SET BELOW 18,000ft

APPROACH TO LANDING (10,000ft)
Airspeed . . . . .250 KIAS MAXIMUM
Flaps . . . . .AS REQUIRED
Fuel Pumps . . . . .ON

Landing Lights . . . . ON
Cabin/Lav lights . . . . .AS REQUIRED
Icing Systems . . . . .AS REQUIRED
Altimeter . . . . .SET FOR LANDING
Instruments . . . . .SET FOR LANDING
Nav/Com . . . . .SET FOR LANDING
Pressurization . . . . .SET FOR LANDING

FINAL LANDING APPROACH (10 miles inbound or Outer Marker)
Flight Attendants . . . . SEATED
Runway Alignment . . . . .ESTABLISHED
Glide Path . . . . .ESTABLISHED
Approach Speed . . . . .ESTABLISHED
Vertical Rate . . . . ESTABLISHED FOR FINAL APPROACH
Gear . . . . DOWN
Pressurization . . . . ZERO
Icing Systems . . . . .AS REQUIRED
Flaps . . . . AS REQUIRED FOR LANDING
Gear . . . . .VERIFY DOWN AND LOCKED

TOUCHDOWN
Spoilers . . . . .DEPLOY
Thrust Reversers . . . . .DEPLOY
Thrust Levers . . . . .FULL POWER
Wheel Brakes . . . . .AS REQUIRED
Thrust Levers . .IDLE BEFORE SLOWING TO 70 KNOTS
Thrust Reversers . . . . RETRACT

Figure 89: *CHECKLIST COMPARISON* These three checklists demonstrate the dramatic differences between preparing to land a Cessna 172, a Beech King Air B200 and a Boeing jet. Seeing what's expected of a Boeing captain can help you appreciate why you should get into the habit of using checklists now. Oddly, it can be harder to make use of the short checklists in trainer airplanes because pilots can feel silly using them. If it helps you take your Cessna lists more seriously, consider it a subset of this Boeing checklist. Better yet, add "deploy thrust reversers" as the final item on your 172's after-landing checklist.

become long and complex, as with a Boeing jet, you often don't get a second chance; there simply isn't time.

Read through the Boeing checklist and then, whenever you hear the voice in the cockpit say, "Flight attendants please be seated," an image of this page will pop into your mind. You'll know you're on final approach, someone is reading from a checklist, and that you're a few moments away from hearing the landing gear come down.

Every 747 has a 172 inside of it; they're all the same. You're learning to fly them all.

CHECKLISTS A LA ME

Cessna tells me that certain things need to be done when I fly a 172. But they have no idea what I do and don't understand and, even worse, their checklists are ugly, lacking any design sense whatsoever.

Checking magnetos might be neat-o, but the checklist phrase, "Magnetos - Check" might mean nothing to a student pilot. The point to checklists is to communicate information to you. If you don't understand what you're reading, then they do you little good. This was the case for me when I first started to fly:

"Flight Controls - Free and Correct"

Free them from what? And shouldn't a mechanic be making corrections? Further, why would the checklist presume they needed correction at all?

I took the Cessna lists, learned what they were *trying* to say, and I reworded everything into my own language. (Not to mention my own *flawless* design-savvy layout.) The result was a longer list, but one that made sense to me, and impressed my CFI from a design perspective. I reworked my lists from time to time. As I gained experience I was able to shorten explanations and eventually came up with lists that are even shorter than Cessna's, yet include all the same information. (And still look much nicer.)

Another benefit to working up your own checklists is that it forces you to really understand what it is you're reading and supposed to be doing. It's a good exercise for you and your CFI to work on together. Don't ever rely on a home-brew checklist that your CFI hasn't blessed.

After you become familiar with the checklists for your primary training airplane, ask your CFI to introduce you to some checklists from other types of airplanes. It will help you see how, despite some feature differences, all airplanes—collectively governed by the same laws of physics—are basically the same beasts.

I'm happy to say that now before each flight I ensure that the movement of my flight control surfaces is *unobstructed* and *proper*.

FLIGHT THEORY IN FLIGHT (IN THEORY)

One hundred and twenty days is the correct answer. The question is—in case you wondered—within how many days must a parachute be packed by an licensed parachute rigger? This is an FAA test question that I never forgot, probably because I was so dumbfounded at the absurdity of having to memorize it.

By the time you finish groundschool, your head will be so stuffed full of FAA-mandated aviation info and theories that you'll immediately become a bore at parties and a person for whom second dates become increasingly hard to secure. (Until you get your license.)

But right after you finish groundschool and pass your written test is the best time to actually start applying the more useful theories you've learned. Instead of pushing and pulling on the throttle like you were milking some tin cow, you can choose power settings and control surface positions and let the airplane catch up to you. Instead of being a hopeful and optimistic pilot, you can be a calculating and deliberate pilot. You can fly, as we say, *in front of the airplane.* A pilot that is in front of the airplane makes decisions based on his understanding of the airplane and flight theory. He knows what he needs to do to get the airplane to perform a certain way. He does not react to the airplane; the airplane reacts to him.

This sort of piloting—usually considered within the realm of commercial flight training—requires some real understanding of how it all works. But if you've gotten this far into this book then I'm guessing you're all about becoming the best pilot you can be.

PRIORITIZE THE GROUNDSCHOOL BRAIN SATURATION

The FAA won't prioritize your flight training for you. It's all equally important to them. But I'm here to tell you that the number "120" as it applies to parachute rigging requirements isn't nearly as important as the number "41" as it applies to stall speed. If you can remember only one of those numbers, choose wisely.

Triage your groundschool instruction. Try to separate the practical flight information from the regulations. Don't get me wrong, the regulations are very important, but they won't land an engine-dead airplane or help you recover from a stall.

Don't be shy in groundschool; ask your instructor what practical purpose a given lesson or regulation offers. You might be surprised at how something that seems ridiculous actually makes sense.

VISUALIZE THE FORCES ACTING UPON YOUR AIRPLANE

One day, while visualizing whirled peas, also visualize the forces of nature that act upon your airplane. Think about climbing and ask yourself why it's possible. (Lift is overcoming gravity, but why?) Do the same for straight and level flight and also for when you descend.

Here's an exercise that might seem a bit esoteric: Think of the controls in your airplane as "force" manipulators. Don't think of turning the yoke as means for controlling the ailerons, think of it as a way to redirect the downward lift generated by your airfoiled wings to one side or the other. Remember that if you don't pull back on the yoke as you redirect the lift, the airplane loses altitude.

But why? Let's briefly revisit this again:

By redirecting some of the vertical lift sideways, you force (turn) the airplane left or right. But an airfoil can generate only so much lift. So if you borrow some to move the airplane sideways, you lose some force that was keeping the airplane at altitude. To replace that missing lift, you need to pull back on the yoke, forcing the tail of the airplane down, to increase the angle of attack of the wings. This increases lift, but, as we learned, also increases drag. You maintain altitude but lose airspeed. To maintain airspeed you have to increase power.

Now let's translate that knowledge into pure force manipulation. We start out with a given amount of lift that keeps us at a given altitude. We subtract some of that lift to move the airplane sideways. The airplane moves sideways, but starts losing altitude because we've borrowed some of the vertical lift to move us sideways. We add more lift. We maintain altitude, but we also start losing airspeed because anytime you increase lift, you increase drag. We increase thrust to overcome the increased drag.

I know this might be hard to follow and might not even seem like it's worth following, but there is a real lesson to be learned here. If you can see your flight controls as ways to manipulate the forces of nature, you'll know what control to reach for when you need it. In some cases there are several options that yield the same result. But usually one option is the best, and sometimes there might be only one option.

For example, say you need to increase airspeed. You could add power, but if you're already at full power, this isn't an option. The trick is to think in terms of force manipulation: What are you actually trying to do? You're trying to increase thrust, but your engine is already maxed out. So what offers the same net effect as an increase in thrust? A *decrease* in drag. We know that pulling back on the yoke increases drag (as it increases lift), so pushing forward on the yoke, must yield the opposite effect.

So, you need to increase airspeed when you're already at full power? Push forward on the yoke and reduce some drag. There's that same lesson on controlling the airplane during slow flight told from another angle.

There's a yin and yang to every force acting upon your airplane. Gravity is a constant force over which you have no control, so you must think in terms of how you can manipulate the other three forces to fly your airplane.

Let's consider some other situations:

LOSING ALTITUDE

- **Cause** – Inadequate lift. (Not an increase in gravity, because gravity is constant.)

- **Corrective theory** – Increase lift-to-gravity ratio.

- **Corrective actions**:
  1. Pull back on yoke to increase lift.
  2. Add power to increase airflow over the wings, which, in turn, increases lift.
  3. If turning, decrease turning radius, which redirects horizontal lift back to vertical lift.

GAINING ALTITUDE

- **Cause** – Excess lift.

- **Corrective theory** – Decrease lift-to-gravity ratio.

- **Corrective actions**:
  1. Push forward on yoke to decrease lift.
  2. Reduce power to reduce the airflow over the wings, thereby decreasing the lift generated.

LOSING AIRSPEED

- **Cause** – Inadequate thrust.

- **Corrective theory** – Increase thrust-to-drag ratio.

- **Corrective actions**:
  1. Add power.
  2. Push forward on yoke to reduce drag.

GAINING AIRSPEED

- **Cause** – Excess thrust.

- **Corrective theory** – Decrease thrust-to-drag ratio.

- **Corrective actions**:
  1. Reduce power.
  2. Pull back on yoke to increase drag.
  3. Drop anchor.

If you're as clever as I like to pretend I am, you might have noticed that each of those four situations require manipulations of *three* of the four forces of nature: lift, drag and thrust. Gravity is constant and therefore outside of our control.

Looking deeper, you can see that none of those forces can be manipulated without affecting the others. For example, you can't increase thrust (airspeed) without increasing lift, which, in turn, increases drag, thereby resisting the added thrust. And you can't increase lift without increasing drag, which reduces thrust and therefore hinders the development of added lift. And you can't reduce drag without decreasing lift, which increases thrust and—you guessed it—increases drag.

So every force you add to the mix eventually resists itself. Remember how perpetual motion isn't possible in an atmosphere like ours? That's why.

Let's look closer at the effects of some of the corrective actions listed above:

- **Pull back on yoke** – When you pull back on the yoke you increase lift, which increases drag, which reduces airspeed. As airspeed is reduced, lift is reduced and drag is reduced. To compensate for the loss of airspeed, you must add power or the airplane will eventually stall.

- **Push forward on yoke** – When you push forward on the yoke you decrease lift, reduce drag and increase airspeed. As airspeed increases, so increases lift and drag. To compensate for the increase of lift, you must push forward harder on the yoke to maintain your descent angle. But this also increases airspeed, so a reduction in power is required.

- **Add power** – When you add power you increase thrust, thereby increasing the airflow over the wings, which increases lift and drag. To maintain the same altitude, you'd have to push forward on the yoke to overcome the additional lift the power increase creates.

- **Reduce power** – A reduction in power reduces thrust and, in turn, the airflow over the wings. Lift is reduced and so is drag. The decrease in lift causes the airplane to descend, which causes an increase in airspeed if the airplane is in a nose-down attitude. If the airplane's attitude is held level, airspeed is reduced until the airplane stalls.

And, finally, let's look at the combined use of various flight controls to achieve a desired effect:

- **Climb while maintaining airspeed** – Pull back on yoke and add power. The maximum amount that you can pull back on the yoke without losing airspeed (the angle of your climb) is determined by the available power. If you're already flying at full power, you cannot start a sustained climb without losing airspeed. Climbing without losing airspeed just isn't a practical objective in a training airplane.

- **Descend while maintaining airspeed** – Push forward on the yoke and reduce power. The amount of power to be reduced is determined by the angle of your descent. The steeper your descent, the more you'll need to reduce power.

- **Increase airspeed while maintaining altitude** – Add power and push forward on the yoke as airspeed increases. The higher the airspeed, the more you'll have to push because the increased airflow over the wings will generate additional lift. Don't worry about not having the strength to push forward due to excess airspeed. Pilots flying training aircraft simply aren't that lucky.

- **Decrease airspeed while maintaining altitude** – Reduce power and pull back on the yoke. The lower your airspeed drops, the more you'll have to pull back to maintain altitude.

Think about situations of your own. You'll find that you can't consider the forces of nature independently. The benefit of this understanding is that you'll also realize you can't consider the flight controls of your airplane that way either.

PREDICT THE OUTCOME OF WHAT YOU DO

Once you get the hang of thinking about flight controls and the forces they affect, you can move to the next level of flight understanding. This is where you manipulate flight controls to achieve a specific flight attitude.

This is tricky at first because it's counter to how we go through most of our daily routines. For example, when you reach for the wall

Figure 90: *PATTERN SET UP* By setting a Cessna 172's power to 2000 RPM and adjusting the yoke so the attitude indicator is one bar above the horizon, the airplane will slow to 85 knots and remain level, perfect for entering and flying the pattern. (Settings vary for different airplane models.)

dimmer, you adjust it until the room lighting is set the way you want. You don't look at the dimmer and imagine that a 32-degree clockwise turn is what's indicated to achieve a room ambience of 2800 Kelvins.

But this sort of calculated thinking is exactly what you want as a pilot. Let's say that you're entering the traffic pattern of an airport. For the first part of the pattern, say you want to maintain an altitude of 1,000 feet and an airspeed of 85 knots. You could yank the yoke and pull the power until you get the speed you want, but by that time you're probably ready to slow and descend further. Or, you could set the power to 2,000 RPM and adjust the yoke so the attitude indicator is set at one bar level above the horizon. (Figure 90) As you go about your pre-landing checklist, your airplane will dutifully slow to 85 knots and

maintain altitude. (These settings are different for different airplanes. Learn the settings work for your airplane.)

It's worth taking note of this stuff during a flight. Try different power settings and attitudes and come up with a chart of the airspeeds you get with each configuration. You'll see a pattern. Study that pattern and consider it before you reach for any control.

This is how real pilots fly. It might seem like overkill to you now, but once you start your IFR training, you'll be so glad that you don't have to chase needles and milk the tin cow.

ANALYZE SOME TURNS & DESCENTS

One day I heard an aviation old-timer remark that in-flight "inconveniences" (his term) like engine failures, are only dangerous because pilots don't expect them: "The very first thing I do when I apply power [to takeoff] is *expect* that engine to fail. And in forty years, I've never lost one. They never quit when you're expecting them too!"

He had a laugh that ranked somewhere between jolly and insane, and he exercised it liberally.

I thought his logic curious, but I suppose there's some truth to it. If you *were* expecting an engine failure, it might not give you any more influence over the powers of the universe, but at least you'd have a plan to deal with it. This is especially important on takeoff when you're flying close to the ground and your options are limited.

Conventional wisdom tells pilots that turning back to the airport after an engine failure on takeoff can be disastrous. The theory is that in a panic to get back to the airport, pilots might turn too tightly at their already relatively slow climb-out airspeeds and stall/spin the airplane. Instead, pilots are told to land straight ahead if the engine goes, regardless of what "straight ahead" might mean terrain-wise.

But at some point you *must* be high enough to turn back safely. Right? So how high is high enough? No one is going to tell you this magic altitude because it depends on an almost limitless set of variables. What's the wind doing? How fast were you going when the engine died? What *is* the terrain like ahead of you?

If you have nothing but flat land ahead of you, you'd be foolish to try to turn back. But if you're headed toward a view accented with rugged peaks and tree tops, then a turn-back becomes more tempting.

The idea is to make this decision *before* you take off. Times of stress are not conducive to making intelligent life or death maneuvering decisions. The number of pilots that have killed themselves because they spun their airplanes into the ground while trying to turn back supports this theory.

Before each takeoff you should ask yourself these three questions:

- What do I do if I lose power on the runway?

- What do I do if I lose power at an altitude of less than *x* feet?

- What do I do if I lose power at an altitude greater than *x* feet?

Fill in that x variable with your instructor. At my home airport the magic number is usually 500 feet or higher if the winds are strong.

The answer to the first situation is easy: pull power and apply brakes to stop the airplane. Even if it means that you'll roll off the end of the runway, you don't ever want to try to lift off if the engine is coughing and gagging.

The answer to the third question is usually to turn back to the airport and land on the most suitable runway, which might be the one opposite the one you just departed. For example, you took off from runway 30 and landed on runway 12: same surface, different direction.

The second question is the tough one. The correct answer will be determined by many variables, including wind and terrain. And it must be determined before *each* departure. It's also the primary reason for this subheading of the book.

After you've made your decisions, mentally remind yourself of those decisions during your takeoff. While I'm rolling on the runway, I keep my ears especially tuned to the sound of the engine and regularly glance at the readings on the engine gauges. If the engine so much as burps, I pull power and apply brakes. If not, I roll on.

After lift off I remind myself that if the engine goes, I will land straight ahead. I immediately look for the most suitable location. Once above *x* feet, I remind myself that I'm going to turn back and land at the airport.

The direction in which I'll make the turn back depends on the wind and if I was already inside a turn when the engine quit. If I'm flying straight out and the wind is coming from my right, for example, I'll turn to the left to take advantage of the extra momentum the tail wind offers. But if I've already begun a turn one way or the other, I'll continue that turn back to the airport.

If that old man is correct, I'll never have an engine failure on takeoff because it's just what I'm expecting. If you subscribe to the New Age philosophy that you must always think positively, feel free to assume that nothing will ever go wrong with your airplane. If something does go wrong, consider it karma.

Now, on with the meat of this section.

I'm betting that most of this section made sense to you, but you're still not comfortable with the idea of choosing an altitude at which a turn-back would be safe. This, after all, is the million dollar question. Get it right and you return safely to the airport with an exciting tale to tell. Get it wrong, and you become another example of why so many say that landing straight ahead after an engine failure on takeoff is the best thing to do.

But if you were armed with an intimate knowledge of your airplane's performance in turns, you'd be able to make a more informed decision. Certainly you've had occasion while driving your car to "eyeball" intersections where you could or could not pull off a u-turn. Sometimes you know you can make it and other times you'll know that your only turn-around option is a 3-point turn.

You have this sense because you are familiar with your car's performance. If you flew your airplane as often as you drive your car, you'd get a pretty good sense of its performance too. But it's unlikely you'll ever be so lucky to fly as much as you drive. What you can do is take some time during a few flights to perform some turns and take note of the results.

For the purposes of this discussion, we'll say that your airplane's "best glide" speed (V_G) is 65 knots. Best glide is a predetermined speed that produces the least drag for your airplane, and therefore extends its power-off glide range. Your CFI will cover the theory behind this with you. One of the first steps in most engine-failure emergency checklists is to get the airplane to its best glide speed.

The most important thing to keep in mind before executing any power-off turn-around is that you will lose altitude. Remember, a turn is the result of redirecting some of the airplane's vertical lift horizontally, regardless of whether or not the prop is spinning. But without a working engine, you will have no way of regaining that lift by adding more thrust, so you need to factor the loss of altitude into your estimations.

If your mind just wandered off into thoughts of pulling back on the yoke to maintain altitude, be aware that this is the cause of the stall/spins that are the sole reason this maneuver is so controversial. When you pull back on that yoke, you start eating airspeed. Loss of airspeed reduces lift, steep bank angles reduce lift, and before you know it, wham!, you've stalled in a steep turn.

You want to get your airplane to its best glide speed after an engine failure and keep it there as best you can. A secondary advantage to best-glide is that it keeps you above the stall speeds for *reasonably* steep banks. If you panic and turn back at a bank angle of 80-degrees, all bets are off.

Go up with your CFI and perform a series of engine-idle, 180-degree turns (simulating a turn-back) at 10, 20, 30 and 40 degree banks. Perform each turn several times and have your CFI jot down how many feet were lost during each one. Study the results after your flight. There will be a pattern. You'll see what turning radius is most efficient and you'll be much better at determining the value of x as it applies to minimum turn-back altitudes.

If you lose 400 feet, for example, in a 20-degree turn-back, you'll know that such an option at less than 500 feet would be extremely dangerous.

Get your airplane to its best glide speed A.S.A.P. after you drop engine power to idle. The best way to do this is to know ahead of time what approximate indication on your attitude indicator will yield best-glide speed at idle power. It could be one bar's width up, one and a half bar's width up, or something else entirely. (Figure 91)

This isn't a set-it-and-forget-it process, however. As soon as you start your turn you'll need to make yoke adjustments to maintain best-glide speed. But it does serve to get you to best-glide for the first few moments after the engine starts coughing, while you're making your decision to turn back or not. You might find, for example, that your engine is fine, but you have inadvertently done something to shut it down. In this case, you'd start it up again and keep flying forward rather than risk the turn-back.

Figure 91: *RAISING THE BAR* Depending on your airplane and its configuration at a given moment, your best-glide speed might be achieved by adjusting the yoke to get the attitude indicator at one or more bars above the instrument's artificial horizon. The attitude indicator on top is set at one bar. The one below is at one and one half bars. Even a slight difference like this will affect your airspeed.

Engine failures just after takeoff are by far the most dangerous. You need to react very quickly and make clear choices as to what you plan to do about the situation. This is why it's so important to answer many of these questions on the ground before you depart.

Engine failures at altitude, during the cruise portion of your flight, also require prompt pilot action, but there are more options from which to choose when the ground is several thousand feet below as opposed to a few hundred.

I bring this up here because we've just talked about how most emergency checklists instruct the pilot to get to best-glide speed as a first course of action after an engine failure. There's

a better "first" thing to do if you have an engine failure while you're cruising at higher altitudes and faster airspeeds.

In the previous section we talked about how all of the forces of nature affecting flight were interrelated: you can't adjust one without affecting the others. This can work to your advantage when you have an abundance of one of those forces, as you do when you're flying at cruise speed at high altitudes.

Let's flex our mental muscle and consider what we've learned about force manipulation. The one thing you need more than anything after an engine failure is *time*. You need time to react, time to find a suitable landing spot, and time to set yourself up for the landing. The one thing that buys a pilot time is altitude. If you lose an engine just after takeoff, you have only a few moments to react because that ground will be creeping up fast. But if you're at 10,500 feet when the prop poops, you've got a while before touchdown.

Altitude not only gives you time, but it gives you, obviously, *altitude*! Even an extra 50 feet or so can mean the difference between hitting an obstruction or not on final approach. Every little bit helps.

You want to increase altitude, if possible, and maintain it for as long as you can. Best-glide speed helps you maintain altitude, but *excess* airspeed is your only chance of gaining any after an engine failure. Here's where your understanding of force-manipulation comes into play.

If you're cruising along at 110 knots and your engine goes, your emergency checklist says to get to best-glide speed. Obediently, many pilots will set the attitude indicator to the proper indication for best-glide and sit patiently while all that excess airspeed drains into oblivion. This is nuts! Airspeed is thrust! Thrust is lift! Cash that airspeed in for additional altitude.

When that engine goes, you immediately pull back on that yoke and use your excess airspeed to *climb, climb, climb* until you reach best-glide speed. Then, lower the nose to maintain that speed and thank Mother Nature for the additional altitude. You might get only a hundred feet or so, but you might be loving that hundred feet later.

COMMON IN-FLIGHT TROUBLES

Experienced CFIs can usually predict what troubles student pilots will face. This is because so many of the problems students face are the same. We can't land smoothly, we can't maintain altitude reliably, we're confused by navigation equipment, etc.

In a perfect world, when many students have the same trouble with a given topic, the instructors devise up with better ways to explain it. But pilot training is not a perfect world, so I'll give you some hints here that I'm hoping will help.

COULD STRAIGHT-AND-LEVEL BE ANY HARDER?

When we say *straight and level* in aviation, we mean flying straight ahead without altitude or course deviation. Think it's easy to fly an airplane straight and level? I used to think so.

Unlike a car, an airplane has no solid surface on which it rides. The "surface" that keeps us airborne is the air around the airplane, which is in constant motion itself. For this reason, straight and level flight requires an ongoing series of adjustments. Most adjustments are minor, but in bumpy air the adjustments can be extreme.

A common problem that many new student pilots face is over-compensating for minor deviations. For example, the airplane starts to drift slightly to the right so the student turns excessively to the left. The same problem occurs with altitude adjustments. A slight unintentional gain of altitude is rectified by the student with a veritable

nose dive. The result is a zig-zagging flight path that approximates the intended flight path, but rarely aligns to it.

Let's break straight and level into its two components.

FLYING STRAIGHT

Thanks to careful flight planning, you'll know exactly which heading you should be flying at any given time during your flight.

But *knowing* the heading is only half the battle. *Flying* it is something else entirely. It's easy enough to say, "keep the DG centered on heading 110 to stay on course." But it's also easy to say, "You're the only one I'll ever love!" People drift. It's our nature. You might intend to fly 110 but end up flying anything and everything between 100 and 120, or worse.

The best way to remain faithful to your headings is to recognize the reasons you drift. Here are some common problems:

- **Arm fatigue** – If you've been gripping the yoke so tightly that your hand is numb from lack of circulation, chances are that your arm is getting tired too. When arms get tired they tend to droop, taking yokes with them. You might not even recognize that it's happening. If you find yourself regularly drifting one way or the other, take notice of the way you hold the yoke. Relax your grip.

- **Heading chasing** – Don't make sweeping yoke adjustments to compensate for minor drift. Make small corrections and allow the airplane to catch up. Large changes will have you flying back and forth across your intended flight track.

- **Rudder rigging** – Each airplane's rudder is "rigged" differently, meaning that the rudder is adjusted to rest in a position that best facilitates straight and level flight. In theory, you shouldn't have to keep either rudder pedal deflected during straight and level flight. But this isn't always the case. Some airplanes need constant rudder deflection on one side or the other in order to fly straight. Usually it's only a slight amount, but without it, the airplane will drift. This can and should be corrected in maintenance, but you have to deal with it in the meantime.

- **Rudder misuse** – Regardless of rudder rigging, you need to make sure your use of the rudder pedals is correct. Your airplane will turn if you have one of the pedals deflected. If you're tall, you might have a tendency to rest your feet on the pedals, which might cause an inadvertent deflection and drift. Use your airplane's turn coordinator to help you gauge proper rudder use. If the ball is centered, you're doing fine. If not, "step on the ball," as they say, which means to press on the rudder pedal that's on the same side as the ball. (Figure 92)

- **Pay attention!** – This one might seem too obvious to be considered, but it's not. If a pilot pays careful attention to his heading, he will maintain that heading no matter which of the other drift tendencies mentioned here might be at work.

FLYING LEVEL

Holding a specific altitude is another tough one for pilots. Recalling how the four forces of nature affect one another helps here. But there's a fifth force of nature we have to consider too— weather. Updrafts and downdrafts can bounce an airplane up and down to the point where maintaining a specific altitude is almost impossible. In these cases, the object is to average out the ups and downs rather than zeroing in on a specific altitude.

There are a few pilot-controllable factors at work too.

Figure 92: *STEP ON THE BALL* This turn coordinator indicates that the airplane is flying straight, but is yawed to the left. This is typical during a climb as the airplane's left-turning tendencies peak. Below, left, is the top view of this situation. The airplane is yawed, but still flying straight along the flight path (orange line). The airplane on the right shows how additional pressure on the right rudder pedal moves the airplane's tail back in line with the flight path. Drift due to yaw can be offset with the yoke (ailerons), but this reduces flight efficiency because an angled airplane increases drag.

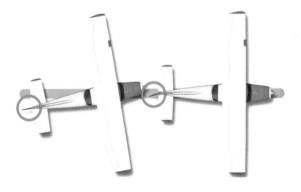

- **Arm fatigue** – If your arm is getting tired you're probably also playing yo-yo with the altitude as well as your heading. Lighten up on that grip!

- **Lift levels** – What happens when the amount of lift an airplane generates increases? It climbs. And what happens when that lift is decreased? That in mind, what happens when you add power? And reduce power? Keep in mind that each time you make a power adjustment without making a corresponding pitch adjustment, you will affect your altitude.

Most training airplanes have what's called an elevator *trim tab*, which is a small surface that extends back from the elevator and rotates slightly up or down. (Figure 93)

The intent of a trim tab is to reduce the yoke pressure the pilot feels while trying to hold the yoke in a given position. The cockpit will have a control for the trim tab. The Cessna 172 uses a large vertical wheel that's located on a pedestal beneath the instrument panel, like the one in figure 93.

A trim tab is not something you set and forget throughout your flight. Ideally, you can trim the airplane and it will stay in that configuration for a while, but weather, weight differences due to fuel burn, altitude changes, power adjustments and other factors will require you to retrim regularly.

For example, say that you're flying straight and level and you want to climb. You pull back on the yoke, which raises the elevator to initiate the climb, but you feel some resistance on the yoke because the on-coming airflow is trying to push the elevator back down. The trim control enables you to compensate for that pressure and "zero" the elevator out at its current position, which keeps the airplane climbing at the angle you chose and reduces the pressure you feel on the yoke.

An airplane is said to be "trimmed" when it flies at a specific pitch angle (level, climbing or descending) without the pilot having to hold the yoke.

Figure 93: *TRIM SYSTEM* Rolling the trim wheel (above) rotates the trim tab (below) up and down. Some airplanes have electronic trim control switches on or near the yoke instead of a wheel. Trim tabs are not controlled by the same mechanism that controls the elevator itself. So if your elevator's control mechanism ever fails, keep in mind that your trim tab might be able to offer some help.

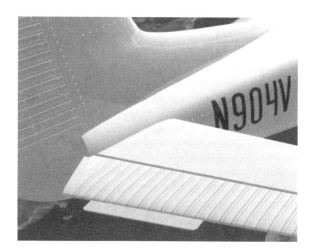

And therein lies the trick to the most effective means of straight and level flight: take your hands off the yoke! After you trim the airplane, let it do its thing without your bored little fingers pushing and pulling at the yoke every few seconds. Give your hands and arms a rest. You'll be amazed at just how well you can hold your heading and altitude by *not* flying the plane! Tap out rhythms on the top of the instrument panel. That's what I do. It keeps my hands off the yoke and keeps my eyes looking outside the cockpit.

The only problem is that it annoys my passengers.

MIXED UP ABOUT MIXTURE

Many airplanes have mixture controls that determine the ratio of fuel and air that is burned in the engine. A setting that allows the most fuel into the mixture is said to be "rich." A setting that reduces the amount of fuel in the mixture is said to be "leaned." (Figure 94)

A problem common to students is forgetting to adjust the mixture as needed. If you climb too high without leaning the mixture, the engine runs too rich, meaning that it's burning too much fuel and the spark plugs could become fouled. If you remember to lean the mixture as you climb, but forget to enrich it again as you descend, you run the risk of overheating the engine or stalling it completely. Mixture is always one of the first things to look at if your engine starts to cough in flight.

But when do we use what setting? The official answer is to consult the POH for your airplane and set the mixture as it recommends.

But don't think about mixture as a "rules" thing; think of it as a "theory" thing. Rules only work so long as there is one that applies to every situation. But there are no such hard and fast rules of setting mixture.

The basic mixture "rule" is that you run full-rich below a certain altitude and you increasingly lean above that altitude. With a Cessna 172, for example, you're supposed to run full-rich below 3,000 feet MSL.

The basic keep-in-mind theory behind mixture settings is that an engine runs cooler when the mixture's rich and hotter when the mixture's lean.

Figure 94: *IN THE MIX* With the mixture (red) knob all the way in (above), the mixture is fully rich. This is how it should be for takeoffs at or near sea-level. As the mixture knob is pulled backward, the mixture is leaned, meaning less fuel is sent to the engine. Pulled all the way back, the engine is starved of fuel and quits. This is, in fact, how we stop the engine after flight. The mixture knob is adjusted by first pressing the outer button (shown depressed, below) and then moving the knob back and forth. This button helps ensure that the knob is not inadvertently pushed in or out during flight.

So anytime you pull the mixture out, you are heating up the engine. We do this when we first start the airplane to help warm it up.

Pushing the mixture in to full-rich cools the engine. It might be a good idea to run full-rich during all climbs on hotter days, regardless of altitude. I have found that while climbing on hot days, the engine temperature might get too hot if I lean, even after I get above 3,000 feet. Airplanes fly slower during climbs so the engine has less airflow to keep it cool. Keeping the mixture rich helps.

This is a very important point to address with your CFI. Your airplane might differ from the ones I fly. What works for mine might not work for yours. Just make sure that you know when to lean and enrich the mixture, and find out if you can use a richer mixture to help with engine cooling when you need it.

COMMON LANDING TROUBLES & SUGGESTIONS

If you (now) think that flying straight and level seems complicated, you'd better sit down for this section. One of those tired old aviation sayings proclaims: "Flying is the second greatest thrill known to man. Landing is the first." Landing is an art and any pilot who can grease a landing every time is, in my book, an artist.

The truth is that each landing is different and it's not easy to execute them all perfectly. It's also been said in aviation that a *good* landing is one from which you can walk away. This assessment is generous, but it does underscore how permissible it is for pilots to make *good* landings every now and then in lieu of *greased* landings.

SHIFTING RUNWAYS (AIRPLANE NOT ALIGNED WITH THE RUNWAY CENTERLINE)

A basic objective when landing an airplane is to align the airplane with the runway's centerline. (The centerline is a row of broken lines that identifies the runway's center.) While this is a simple concept in theory, that damned centerline is a nasty little monster that seems to drift randomly from side to side.

The trick to taming this beast is to identify and correct what it is that makes you drift. Here are some common causes:

- Arm position – Rather than focus on a fatigued arm here, as we did with straight and level flight, we'll focus on the position of your arm. Just before touchdown you will be increasing backward pressure on the yoke during what's called the landing *flare*. (Described later.) You need to pay attention to what happens to the yoke as you pull back in the flare. For me, the problem was that I would pull slightly *down* as I was pulling back. This caused the airplane to drift to the left just before each touchdown. It took me a long time to realize what I was doing wrong. Even my CFI was baffled by my consistent drift. I liked to blame it on the crosswind, even when there was no crosswind.

- Crosswinds – These are covered in detail in a bit, but they can be a meaty opponent when trying to remain centered.

- Visual focus – Your airplane tends to follow your eyes. If you're looking in the wrong place, your airplane will likely land in the wrong place. CFIs will bark at you to "look down the runway" during your landings. This is good advice, but it makes no sense at first. Here's a trick that not only makes sense, but works. *Forget the runway centerline!* Don't focus on it. Instead, look at the outline shape of the entire runway surface as it appears to you when you're on final approach. Maneuver your airplane until that shape appears symmetrical. (Figure 95) I can't tell you how much this helped me. I nailed my very next landing after I heard this advice. My CFI was amazed. Centerline was never a problem again. This advice becomes even more valuable for night landings because most airports don't have centerline lighting. Your only option at night is to gauge the runway's center by "aligning" the side lighting.

RUBBER RUNWAYS (AIRPLANE BALLOONS UP THEN PLUNKS DOWN)

New student pilots are famous for their "buoyant" landings. If you watch landings at your local airport, you'll see this all the time: The airplane is on final approach...everything looks good...then

Figure 95: *SHAPELY RUNWAYS* When on final approach, look at the overall shape of the runway as it appears from your perspective. Does it appear symmetrical? If not, you're not going to land in the center of it. The image on the left shows what the runway will look like if you're too far to the left. The opposite is shown on the right. The image in the middle shows a nice symmetrical runway shape, which means the pilot is doing great. By keeping your eyes focused on the runway's shape, you will also keep your eyes focused farther down the runway, which will help you land more smoothly.

all of a sudden, just a few feet above the ground, the airplane balloons back up a few feet and then plops down hard, bounces a few times and then finally lands.

Students are usually so horrified by the experience that they completely forget everything that led up to it. CFIs later try to describe the student's actions, but what CFIs remember and what students remember often differ. Students are thinking there was something wrong with the airplane or the wind (or their pilot training).

CFIs recall it differently:

"You were doing fine and then just before you started your flare you began chanting in foreign tongues, you closed your eyes and thrashed your head wildly about. Then you jumped into the back seat and curled up into a ball."

"No I didn't," you'll say. Now you *know* it was bad training.

It's not that your CFI lies, but you'll be amazed at how different your perceptions of what happened can be.

The key is to have a clear sense of what each phase of a landing entails and to know what to do if something goes wrong at any point.

So before we go any further, we'll dissect a landing, starting with final approach (in reality, preparation for a good landing starts long before final approach):

LANDING PHASE 1: FINAL APPROACH
During final approach you should have your airplane stabilized (trimmed) in a descent that will put you down where you want to land. You should

Figure 96: *FINAL APPROACH* Final approach is all about decision making. Are you too high? Too low? Centered? Is the runway clear? Is your airspeed proper? This image shows a tiny red X just above the "30" runway numbers. That's our touchdown target. We'll cover this more in a moment.

Figure 97: *OVER THE FENCE* An airport doesn't require an actual fence in order for you to be "over it." The phrase simply refers to the moment that an airplane flies into the airport's physical boundary.

be at the airspeed and flap configuration recommended by your airplane's POH for an approach in the prevailing wind. You should be observing the shape of the runway to determine your alignment with centerline. (Figure 96)

If the approach doesn't feel right for any reason, abort the landing and do a go-around. Discuss go-arounds in depth with your CFI. Don't continue an approach that doesn't feel right. The closer you get to the ground, the fewer options you have.

LANDING PHASE 2: "OVER THE FENCE"

Just as you enter the airfield's boundaries and the runway edge is only moments away, you can reduce power to idle. You continue your gliding descent while allowing your airspeed to drop. Your CFI can help you fine tune the appropriate moment for this, depending on your airport. (Figure 97)

A go-around is still an option at this point, though it's more dangerous because of your decreasing airspeed and closer proximity to the ground. (If you pull back on the yoke too much, you will stall the airplane.)

LANDING PHASE 3: THE FLARE

Here's where many student pilots lose it. Flaring is the process of slowly increasing back pressure on the yoke to keep the airplane flying as airspeed continues to drop.

I don't want to gloss over that point: *The purpose of the flare is to allow your airplane time to lose airspeed.*

When you start your flares, I want you to be conscious of the fact that you are doing so to reduce airspeed. That way you might think to glance down at your airspeed indicator to see just how much airspeed you need to lose. After all, if you need to lose 20 knots, you'll need to flare for much longer than you will if you're already just a few knots above stall speed.

There are three airspeeds to keep in mind during the flare:

- **Final approach speed** – What speed were you at when you started the flare? That clues you in to how much you have to lose.

- **Rotation speed** – Why would you be thinking of your takeoff speed during landing? Because it's silly to think that your airplane will want to land at speeds much higher than the speed it's at when you take off. Right?

- **Stall speed** – How far are you from your airplane's stall speed in the landing (dirty) configuration (V_{so})? Somewhere between stall speed and rotation speed would be a great airspeed to be at when you touchdown. But you certainly don't want to reach stall speed when you're more than a foot or so above the ground.

As you gradually increase back-pressure on the yoke, your airspeed and your altitude will drop. Airspeed drops because you're increasing drag by raising the elevator. (And because you're running on idle power.) Altitude drops because the drop in airspeed is causing a reduction in lift. The idea is to allow both to happen smoothly and to be only a few inches above the runway surface by the time the airplane is just a few knots above its stall speed. That way you can set it down gently in one of those "greased" landings. (Figure 98)

The most common problem students have in the flare is pulling too far back on the yoke while they still have too much airspeed. This causes the airplane to "balloon" back up because an airplane with enough airspeed wants to fly. This gets the airplane in a nose-high attitude at which airspeed drops rapidly and then, plop!, it drops back down to the runway.

Another common problem is allowing airspeed to drop too quickly before altitude drops. Here, too much back-pressure on the yoke is preventing the airplane from losing altitude as it loses airspeed. The airplane reaches its stall speed while it's still several feet in the air and plunks down on the runway.

Again, the goal is to gradually lose airspeed and altitude at the same time. If you lose one without losing the other, you'll either stall and plop, or hit the runway hard and bounce back up again.

LANDING PHASE 4: TOUCHDOWN

Once you're *below your rotation speed*, you can relax the yoke enough to set the airplane down. The airplane won't balloon back up again because there isn't enough lift to get it back in the air.

If you've flared properly, your main wheels will touchdown first. Hold the nose wheel off the ground, by pulling back on the yoke for as long as possible. Eventually even the most back-pressure you can apply won't be enough and the nose wheel will drop gently to the ground.

When all three wheels are on the ground, you'll apply brakes (and usually retract your flaps) to reduce speed, which ensures that you've eliminated as much lift as possible. (An unexpected gust of wind can toss a small airplane around, so you want to be firmly planted on the ground as soon as possible.)

Landing is really the process of safely reducing airspeed from cruise speed to zero. In other words, you can't safely or cleanly land an airplane without regard for airspeed control.

Along with takeoff, landing is the most dangerous time of a flight. Fortunately, landings happen in slow motion right up until the end. You have plenty of time during the approach to abort and do a go-around if needed. Good pilots do go-arounds; bad pilots don't. Often the reason for a go-around

1. The pilot reduces power as the airplane crosses the fence.

2. Slight back pressure on the yoke is applied as the airplane slows.

3. Additional back pressure "fights" the airplane's tendency to drop too fast.

3. Airspeed and altitude continue to drop as additional back pressure is applied.

4. The airplane's main wheels touch down gently.

5. The pilot gently relaxes yoke pressure until the nose wheel touches.

Figure 98: *DEVELOPING A FLARE FOR LANDING* During a flare, the airplane drifts down the runway as it gradually loses airspeed and altitude. If a pilot doesn't flare, the airplane will likely hit the runway hard and, if going fast enough, bounce back up in the air again. If the runway is short, a pilot might opt to intentionally reduce the airplane's approach airspeed and minimize the flare so the airplane touches down as soon as possible, albeit harder than usual. We call these "short field" landings.

has nothing to do with the pilot's skills or the quality of the approach. There might be a slow airplane on the runway, or you might have been tossed by a wind gust.

Once you pass the fence, don't flare as a mechanical reaction you think you're supposed to do just because you're about to land. The faster you come in, the longer your flare will take. And if you come in very slow (as we do during shortfield approaches), you might have little flare if any. Continue your flare as long as necessary to bleed off airspeed.

CROSSWINDS MAKING YOU CROSS

Let's get something straight right now about crosswinds. They are not evil, nor do they make landings impossible or even unsafe. (Assuming they are within the limits suggested by your airplane's manufacturer and, more importantly, within the limits of your abilities as a pilot.)

Crosswinds make landings *different*, that's all. A different technique is required during final approach, flare and touchdown. You should practice this technique with your CFI each chance you get. Do not allow yourself to take your checkride without being comfortable in crosswinds.

I'm not going to try to teach you how to land in a crosswind. But if we cover some of the theory behind these landings, you might feel less intimidated by them. There are two basic schools of thought on how to handle a crosswind landing. We've touched on this earlier in the book, but I want to cover it again here since it's in context with our current discussion.

- Crabbing – Crabbing an airplane means adjusting your heading to compensate for the effects of a sideways-blowing wind. If the wind is blowing from the left, you apply left aileron—which points the airplane's nose into the wind—to compensate. (Figure 99) The airplane starts to fly "yawed," somewhat sideways but tracking forward, hence the "crab" name. The crab angle cancels out the wind drift effect and allows the airplane to track straight ahead. If you added even more aileron, the airplane would start to turn. A crab is a "turn" that's just forceful enough to offset the effects of wind but not forceful enough to actually turn the airplane. It's important to remember to remove a crab angle just before touchdown. If not, you'll slam the wheels down at a sideways angle, potentially collapsing the landing gear.

- Forward slip – In a forward slip, you use the ailerons to keep the airplane from drifting downwind, just as you do with a crab, but you also use the rudder to straighten out the nose so the airplane's longitudinal axis is aligned with the runway centerline. This results in a "tilted" airplane that's tracking straight ahead. (Figure 99) Say the wind is blowing from the left. Turning the yoke to the left angles the airplane into the wind thereby cancelling out the wind's drift effect: a typical crab. But now your nose is no longer aligned with the runway. The next part of the forward slip is to use *opposite* rudder to align the airplane's longitudinal axis with the runway. So now you're flying straight ahead, but you're banked thanks to the ailerons trying to turn the airplane. This is what takes getting used to. My body just didn't like that it all. I wanted to be level. I fought and fought the urge to level the airplane. But leveling the airplane allows the wind to carry it off sideways. You keep the bank angle all the way through touchdown, meaning that the upwind wheel touches down first. It seems pretty strange, but it does work.

The crab and forward-slip methods for handling crosswinds are fairly easy to understand in concept, but they do require practice. And, as with every other piloting maneuver, you can't apply these methods mechanically. In other words, just because a crosswind is present doesn't mean that you can choose one method or the other, yank the yoke, push the rudder and land.

Wind is erratic, especially near the surface. You need to "ride" the crosswind during your approach. You might have to adjust your yoke and/or rudder deflection throughout your entire approach. If the wind is constant, you can sort out what yoke/rudder positions work and hold them.

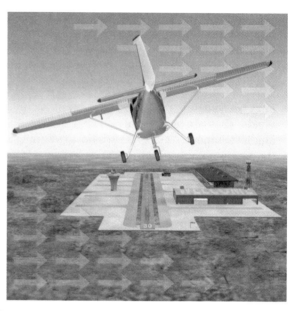

Figure 99: *CRAB AND SLIP* Crab (also called "sideslip") and forward slip techniques can be used to offset the effects of a crosswind on final approach. Only the forward slip technique (right) can be maintained all the way through to touchdown because of the wheel alignment. This usually makes the forward slip a better option.

But it's more likely that gusts will temporarily blow you off a bit. No problem, adjust as necessary and keep on flying.

PICK YOUR TOUCHDOWN SPOT FOR EVERY LANDING

During each approach, try to guess the spot on the runway at which you'll touchdown. Making this judgement is a requirement for the part of your practical test known as *short field* landings. But it's also a good idea for every landing.

Landing at a chosen spot is certainly not a safety requirement at airports with longer runways. But knowing exactly where your airplane will touchdown is vital during emergency landings, when the landing "strip" can be less than ideal and a go-around isn't an option.

The trick to picking the touchdown spot consists of two parts. The first part is determining the spot in your windscreen that appears to remain

stationary as you fly toward it. That is, the spot that isn't moving up, down or to the side. Sounds odd, I know, but it works. During this discussion, we'll call this spot the "target."

When you drive a car, you peer out the windshield and see objects all around you. As you drive, some objects pass to your side while others pass underneath or above the car.

For example, you see the word "STOP" painted on the road at an intersection up ahead. Above the intersection you see a street light. Both objects appear close to one another, when viewed from a distance. But as you approach, words painted on the ground pass beneath the car, while the street lights pass above. Other objects pass to the side. These objects pass the car because the car was never actually headed toward them, even though it appeared as such from a distance.

Your clue to knowing the side on which an object will pass your car lies in judging its apparent movement in the windshield. Objects, such as the traffic light, will appear to move upward, and objects like roadway markings will move down. Objects that don't appear to move at all, but just grow larger, are the ones you're headed toward. This is how the car ahead of you might appear.

It works the same way in an airplane. The spot you're headed toward grows larger, but doesn't move. (Figure 100)

Now that we have that concept down, let's throw the old wrench into the mix that we've come to expect from all things aviation. When we land an airplane, we don't actually touchdown at that target point at all. We reach that point but then start our flare to allow our airplane to bleed off enough airspeed to touchdown without bouncing. (Figure 101)

So how far do we flare?

This is where experience comes into play. The length of your flare depends on several factors, including the headwind, your approach airspeed and your airplane's design. If you're coming in fast or you have significant headwind, your airplane will float farther. If you come in slowly, or you're flying against a significant headwind, you might actually be able to touchdown at or near your target spot with little or no float. This is how we execute landings at short fields. By coming in at a reduced airspeed, we can touchdown much closer to our target.

Learn to take these factors into account and determine a point farther down the runway where you're likely to *actually* touchdown, and don't just guess! Determine your touchdown point by considering the factors at play during your approach.

Try some approaches with your CFI at different airspeeds and note the difference in flare distance. Coming in just 5 knots faster than normal can extend the flare considerably.

Make choosing your touchdown-target a game you play with yourself during every approach. Then, if you ever have to land with a dead engine, all that game playing will pay off.

THINGS TO NEVER NOT KNOW

Many important factors change regularly throughout the course of a flight. Pilots need to constantly keep themselves aware of current situations so the answers to the following questions are always known. This is part of what's called *situational awareness*. Sometimes pilots assume this term refers only to knowing where you are at any given moment. But knowing *how* you are at any given moment is just as important.

HOW MUCH OIL IS IN MY AIRPLANE?

You'll be taught to check your oil level before every flight. If your CFI doesn't get you into this habit, find another CFI. An airplane without oil flies like a donkey sings.

But do you know the rate at which your airplane burns oil? If your POH says that you need to have between 4 and 6 quarts of oil in order to fly, and you have 4 quarts, then, in theory, you're set. But how long can you fly before you have only 3 quarts?

It's difficult to know this sort of information about every rental airplane you fly. Some FBOs (airplane rental places) keep logs of oil usage for each airplane. This is such a fantastic idea that it's a wonder not every FBO does it. An airplane that starts burning too much oil is an airplane in need of maintenance.

1. We see the touchdown spot in the center of our windscreen.

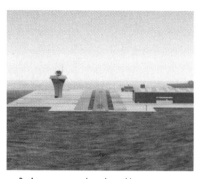

2. As we approach, other objects appear to move out of frame.

3. The horizon is moving up, the control tower is moving left...

4. ...the buildings are moving right and the runway numbers are moving down.

5. Our touchdown spot remains stationary in the middle of our windscreen.

6. You'll pass over downward-moving objects, such as the runway numbers.

7. Objects moving up in the windscreen are beyond the touchdown spot.

8. Objects appear to move faster out of frame as you approach...

9. ...but the touchdown spot remains centered all the way.

Figure 100: *X SPOT* The landing spot you're headed toward will not appear to move up, down or sideways, no matter how close you get. This trick works equally well for determining if you'll clear a mountain top, cloud clusters, or even another airplane that appears to be coming directly toward you.

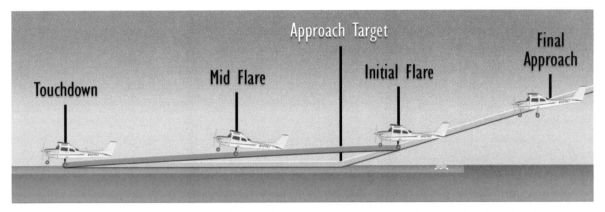

Figure 101: *FLOATING FUN* During your approach you'll pick a spot on the runway as a target, but you won't likely reach it. As you start your flare, the airplane's descent rate will lessen, causing the airplane to float down the runway. At short airfields, when you want to get on the ground as close to the start of the runway as possible, you're reduced approach speed will require less flare, which enables you to touchdown sooner, but you usually hit the runway a bit harder than normal.

If there is no reliable record of a given airplane's oil-burn rate, there's an easy solution: don't fly without a full load of oil.

That's how I deal with it.

HOW MUCH FUEL IS LEFT?

Your airplane will burn fuel at a much faster rate than it burns oil, so you *absolutely must* know your airplane's fuel-burn rate before you fly.

An airplane's POH will offer fuel burn estimates for different flight circumstances, but unless your airplane is brand new, you should consider these numbers as *minimum* fuel-burn rates. I usually tack on a few gallons per hour to whatever the POH says until I know for certain what the airplane burns.

For example, if a POH says to expect to burn 8 gallons per hour, I plan to burn 10. Once I get to know the airplane's actually burn rate for myself, I might be less conservative. As soon as I get to my destination, I recheck my fuel levels. That way I know for certain what the airplane is

burning that day. This is handy information when deciding if a top-off is necessary to get back home again.

If math isn't your forté, make yourself some notes about how much fuel should be left at various points of your flight. You can make these notes on your flight plan.

With regard to airplanes, fuel requirements are based on time rather than capacity. In other words, we don't care that there are 20 gallons left, we care that we have 2 hours flight time left. If you ever have to divert from your original flight plan, you want to make sure that you have enough fuel to get to your new destination airport.

The actual amount of ground you fly over in a given amount of time depends largely on the winds, but you can make your fuel estimates for a diversion assuming no wind and then add or subtract, as necessary. This is one reason that pilots always need to know what the winds are doing, which is covered in a bit.

One trick to knowing how far you can travel at any point is to visualize circles on your aviation charts (maps) that reflect how far you could travel

Figure 102: *FUEL CIRCLE* This red circle visually indicates to the pilot how far she can travel on her fuel reserve once she reaches her destination (top of orange route line). A reminder like this would be a good idea if weather or other considerations might prevent you from actually reaching your destination airport. This circle doesn't take into account the effects of wind.

from that point on your available fuel. As you progress along your route of flight, those fuel circles would diminish in size. Factor in the prevailing winds to make those circles more oval. You'll travel farther with a tail wind. (Figure 102)

IF MY ENGINE QUIT, WHERE WOULD I GO?

Though technically correct, "down" is not the answer we're looking for here.

During your training, your CFI will ask you to pick emergency landing spots from time to time. This is a required step prior to performing any flight maneuver. It's not that your chances of needing to make a forced landing after a maneuver are so intense that you need to have one picked out. It's more about getting you into the habit of analyzing the terrain below you. I used to think, "Damn, if I need to be picking emergency landing spots before all of these maneuvers, maybe I shouldn't be doing them!" (To this day I turn an airplane *only* if it's absolutely necessary.)

Picking the most suitable emergency landing spot is a skill for which there is no evaluation for competency until after the fact. In other words, you can pick all the emergency landing spots you want, but until you need to actually use one, you won't know how good a picker you are. This is one reason that picking your touchdown spot for every landing comes is so important. At least you can hone your estimating skills there and know how well you're doing.

But a suitable emergency landing spot has more than "runway" length going for it. A half mile of flat land does you little good if it's saturated with cattle. (I'm not a cattle-behavior specialist, but I'm guessing that an oncoming Cessna might prompt cattle to observe, but not move.)

Another landing-spot gotcha is difficult-to-see electrical wires. Wires are an obvious but often invisible trap. Don't look for wires so much as you look for wire towers. Wires have to be suspended by something. Even if you can't see the wires themselves, tower locations can give you an idea of where they lie. Wires are also likely to be where they can be easily serviced, such as along roadways.

Surface condition is another important factor. A mile stretch of swamp land is less desirable than a quarter mile of dry grass. Try to imagine what your wheels will do when they come in contact with the surface. Are they going to roll along or dig in?

That said, a mile's worth of swamp is preferable to a forest packed with evergreens.

WATER LANDINGS: FACT AND FRICTION

We hear so much about water landings that many students assume that if the engine goes, they should head for the sea. There are a few popular aviation theories that apply more to large commercial aircraft than they do general aviation. This is one of them. Another is that "flying is the safest way to travel." Sorry, but this popular pilot's mantra considers commercial flight statistics only.

A water landing is a great idea if your airplane is a seaplane. Otherwise, ground is usually preferable.

But, if you were flying a 747 and needed to make an emergency landing, where would you go? The goal to an emergency landing is to keep the airplane intact so passengers can survive. But where could you put down such a huge airborne beast to even stand a chance of keeping it in one piece? A freeway? A swap-meet? A park? There just aren't many ground locales that are suitable for landing large commercial aircraft. Water isn't ideal, but at least the wings won't be clipping cars and trucks, bargain shoppers, buildings (or cattle). Water landings reduce the likelihood of human casualty simply because there probably aren't any people out there in the water.

Even still, water landings tend to tear large airplanes apart. Water is a lot like concrete when you hit it with any considerable velocity. You know this if you've ever belly-flopped from a high-dive or watched the news coverage of the JFK Jr. crash. The force of the impact tends to rip the airplane apart, unless the airplane was flying slowly and touched down at a very shallow angle with its landing gear retracted. An airplane with no extended landing gear tends to be more boat-like when it hits the water. The fixed gear on most trainers increases the likelihood that the airplane will flip over or rip apart as it hits the water's surface.

Water also tends to mask a crash site. It's easier for rescuers to find an airplane, and therefore any survivors, on the ground than it is in water. Further, it's possible to be knocked out during an emergency landing but still be alive. A lot of good this "fortune" does you, however, if you're unconscious in a sinking airplane. Further, unless the water is warm, you won't be loving the swim to shore.

But water isn't *all* bad. After all, next to many water bodies is a beach. This is not to say that after a successful water landing you can soak up some rays. The beach itself can be a great landing spot. Loose sand isn't an ideal landing surface, but closer to the water's edge the sand might be more tightly packed. And the nature of the wet sand will ensure that you won't need much distance to stop the airplane. So even if the beach is a small one, you might be able to make it work. But you will still need to accurately gauge your touchdown point because a go-around isn't an option in most emergency landings.

Think this stuff through when you plan your flights. Consider the terrain you'll be flying over. Where are the best emergency landing spots along the route? Make a note of them. Ask yourself from time to time during the flight, "If I lost my engine right now, where would I go?" The best spot might be behind you. If there is no good spot, then you didn't plan your flight very well.

WHICH AIRPORT WOULD I CHOOSE IF I NEEDED TO DIVERT?

Just after something goes wrong is not the time to start choosing suitable airports. You need to know in advance where you should go.

Here's a checklist for choosing the best alternate airport:

- Where are the nearest suitable airports that I can reach?

- Which of those airports offer services such as fuel and maintenance?

That first point is paramount and considers three important factors: *nearest, suitable* and *reachable.*

"Nearest" doesn't necessarily mean the shortest linear distance. When deciding which airports are near, you must consider how accessible they are from your location. Are there mountains or restricted airspace in the way? The nearest field might be only 10 miles away, but if it's directly on the other side of the White House, a straight line of flight isn't an option. The restricted airspace above the White House is taken very seriously. By the time you circumnavigate that airspace, the "nearest" field would hardly be near at all.

"Suitable" is an important concept that only you can define. If your airplane requires 2,500 feet of runway to land, and the nearest airport offers only 1,500 feet of runway, then suitable it's not. If a nearby airport's runway has been torn up for resurfacing, then it's another field that's not suitable. Fortunately, you can usually determine suitable alternates during your flight planning. NOTAMs, as introduced back on page 80, alert you to airport and runway closures in effect before your flight. Now you have a really good reason to read them.

"I can reach" means you have enough fuel to actually get there. If the only suitable alternate airport is 1 hour away and you have only 30 minutes of fuel, your diversion just became an emergency. Contact ATC and declare it as such immediately.

For the record, the radio frequency 121.5 is reserved for emergency communications. ATC, the U.S. military and others monitor this frequency 24/7. But if you're already in communication with ATC on another frequency, announce on that frequency.

Never try to handle an emergency on your own. ATC can't reach up and pluck you safely from the sky, but they might have some suggestions that your panic-struck brain hasn't considered.

If you think you *might* be able to reach the destination airport on your remaining fuel, contact ATC, tell them you're diverting and that you're flying on "minimum fuel." Those magic words mean: "Don't mess with my flight, I need to land soon." They might even know of a closer airport for you to consider.

The second alternate-airport checklist item, regarding fuel and maintenance, is important if your diversion is due to mechanical failure. In this case, choosing an airport without maintenance services will do your failed system little good. Granted, if a no-services airport is your *only* option, and your diversion is an emergency, land there and kiss the runway. You can fly a mechanic in later. But if it's between an airport that's 5 miles away without services and one that's 15 miles away that has services, go for the services if you have the fuel and your situation is not an emergency.

If there are no suitable alternate airports near your destination, consider making a fuel stop enroute and top off the tanks. That way if you need to divert at the last minute, you'll have at least enough fuel to turn around and get back to the airport where you refueled.

Topping off the tanks enroute is especially important if your destination airport offers no fuel. You don't want to be left with 30 minute's worth of fuel on the ground at an obscure little airport that's an hour away from the nearest fuel pump.

You might have to divert to another airport at any moment during your flight. But choosing a suitable alternate enroute shouldn't be a big event. If you've determined, in advance, which airports will work, you simply choose the closest one and go. The cockpit isn't the place for research. Do your research on the ground and play "multiple choice" enroute.

Say, for example, that you're on frequency with ATC using the Flight Following service. They announce that your destination airport has just been closed and you're still two hours away. Knowing you have a minimum of two hour's worth of fuel, you can take some time deciding what to do. The controller, however, will likely ask for your intentions right away. If so, just tell her to stand by while you make your decision. Their advice is there for the asking, but ATC will *not* tell you what to do. As pilot-in-command, it's your job to determine the outcome of your flights.

If your airport closes while you're, say, turning final, things are quite different. (If you're wondering what could close an airport while you're already in the traffic pattern, ask yourself what happens when an airplane becomes disabled on an airport's only runway.)

Okay, so the airport just closed and you need to decide what to do. If the field has a tower, the controller will likely ask for your intentions. Ask for an estimate of when the field will be reopened before you make any choices. If the tower says "indefinitely" or estimates a time frame that would leave you dangerously low on fuel, you need to move on. Don't waste your remaining fuel circling the field while you decide where to go. You should know where the nearest suitable airport is and start flying in that direction.

Now let's take a moment and appeal to your common sense. If your airport has been closed because another 172 has sputtered out and is sitting lifeless on the runway, chances are you should circle around the pattern a few times. Just about anyone can drag a 172 off a runway. Ask the tower for an estimate of how long the airport will be closed and ask to stay in the pattern if you think that's the best idea.

If the field is nontowered, the airport wouldn't be closed because of a disabled aircraft because there would be no official present to declare it closed. If you see an airplane stranded on the runway at a nontowered field, ask what's up on the airport's common traffic advisory frequency (CTAF). Chances are there's someone who wants that airplane moved even more than you do.

If any airport is closed due to a crash or some other catastrophic event, you'd be wise to move on if you can. Rescue and investigation teams can take a very long time to do their thing. But if you think you can't make it to another airport for any reason, don't be shy! Tell the officials on the ground that you *absolutely* need to land and they *absolutely* need to move that airplane, or what's left of it. If they can't, they might agree to clear a taxiway for you.

If at anytime during your flight you have a mechanical failure that prevents you from flying safely, you need to consider emergency landing procedures, as discussed above. Most diversions aren't due to emergencies. Most are due to bad weather or even a pilot's decision to go somewhere else just for the heck of it. Diversions can, however, become emergencies if you're not prepared to handle them.

Diversions are part of your FAA practical test. One of the things the examiner will be looking for is that you have the sense to point your airplane in the general direction of where you'll be going before you fine tune your heading or make any time estimates. Don't guess. Know which way to go and go there.

But if you remember only one thing from this section, make it this: If you are *ever* in an urgent situation, don't be shy and don't be proud! Ask for help, soon as possible, from whomever can provide it.

So what's an urgent situation? Any moment that you feel that you are not in full control of your circumstances and you wish there was someone there to help. If you ever feel this way while flying, your situation is urgent. If you don't ask for help, your urgent situation could easily become an emergency.

WHERE IS THE NEAREST BAD WEATHER?

There are two important things to always know about the nearest bad weather:

- Where is it?

- Which direction is it moving?

Not that you'd ever plan to fly toward bad weather, but when flight diversions become necessary, you want to know which direction is *not* a good idea before you choose the best direction. Knowing where bad weather is enables you to avoid it. Knowing where bad weather is *going* enables you to pick a new heading that won't send you and that bad weather to the same place at the same time.

Keep weather in mind when making suitable alternate airport choices. Weather is the most common reason that an otherwise suitable airport might become a bad idea. If your flight takes you through any area that has other than clear blue skies, you need to consider weather patterns and alternate airports very seriously. (Figure 103)

WHERE AM I ON THIS CHART?

Track your flight progress using aviation charts. You need to know where you are on a chart as much as you need to know where you are in the sky. That might sound odd, but it's true. But if you

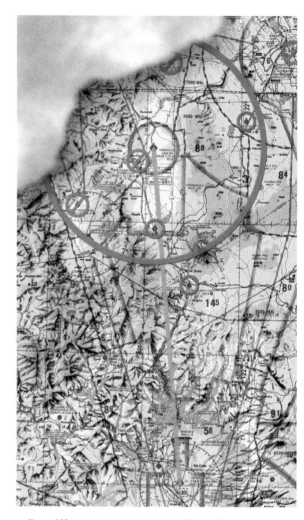

Figure 103: *SEE A SILVER LINING?* This weather system was moving slowly eastward at departure time, but it could pick up speed. Suitable alternate airports are circled in green. The airport south of the fuel circle is suitable only because we have the option of landing there before we go too far. The unsuitable airports are either outside the fuel circle or would likely be no safer from the clouds than our destination airport.

know where you are in the sky—meaning that you recognize landmarks outside the window—why is the chart so important?

Charts depict things that cannot be seen through the cockpit windows. You might know what heading will get you to your planned destination, but you might not know where airspace boundaries lie, how high that mountain ridge up ahead is, or what heading you'd take to reach the nearest suitable alternate airport.

Knowing where you are is the bare necessity of true situational awareness. It's tough to maintain situational awareness when you're not following your flight path on a chart.

If you're still not convinced, recall our discussion on the need for systems redundancy. Airplane designers install redundant systems so that if one system fails, there's a back up. You might be totally aware of your position by checking outside visual references, but if for any reason you lose track of where you are, you'll want a back-up "where am I?" system. Your chart serves this purpose nicely.

WHOSE AIRSPACE AM I IN?

Knowing the airspace you're flying through is one of the need-to-know items of situational awareness because there are different rules for each airspace type.

The foremost important rule is entry requirements. Never enter the airspace designated as Class Alpha, Class Bravo, Class Charlie or Class Delta without first talking with ATC. If while following along on your chart you realize you've entered one of those airspaces without permission, immediately contact ATC and identify yourself. You might get a good spanking from the FAA when you land, but better that than an airborne visit from an F-16.

These days, general aviation pilots must be extra careful to play by the rules and do nothing that might seem like a potentially hostile action to those on the ground. If you wander into, say, the airspace of Los Angeles International, the first thing ATC is going to try to determine is if your

intentions are hostile or if you just made a boo-boo. They might get it wrong. Call them and beg forgiveness. This is a great reason to monitor the radio frequencies of those in charge of a given airspace while you're nearby. If a stray aircraft wanders into an ATC-controlled airspace, the controller will likely alert other aircraft in the area or try to contact the aircraft directly. If you hear of such a fuss, it might dawn on you that you're the culprit.

Another important consideration for each airspace type is visibility. Each airspace class has its own set of requirements for visibility for VFR traffic. Only by knowing which airspace you're in can you be certain that you're in compliance with those regulations. And only by understanding aviation charts can you know where you are airspace wise.

WHERE ARE THE WINDS COMING FROM RIGHT NOW?

Winds affect the speed at which an airplane travels across the earth below (we call this: *groundspeed*). But wind also affects how far an airplane can glide without power. If you lose your engine, knowing which way the wind is blowing will help you determine which airports you are more likely to reach. You'll be able to travel farther with a tail wind than you will with a headwind. If the wind is strong, the difference in glide distance can be considerable.

If you're flying into a nontowered airport, you might need to choose the runway on which you'll land. Usually the airport's windsock will help you make this decision, but knowing in advance how the wind is blowing helps you plan your approach. There's no point planning for arrival on runway 13 when runway 31 is the better choice. Sometimes winds on the ground differ in direction from winds aloft, but the difference is seldom significant enough that you couldn't guess which runway was in use. For example, if the winds at 3,000 feet are blowing from the north at 12 knots and your destination airport has a runway that's aligned north and south, chances are good that you'll be landing toward the north.

Wind correction angle is another factor that you can only determine by knowing the current wind direction and velocity. If your course is 090 (heading east) and the wind is blowing from the north, you'll have to fly a heading less than 090 to track 090. For example, depending on the wind velocity you might have to fly 080 or 075 (north-easterly headings). Imagine driving a boat with a water current coming from the left. To go straight ahead, you'd have to turn slightly to the left (into the current) to compensate for the sideways push. Same thing with wind.

IS MY CURRENT SITUATION AN EMERGENCY IN THE MAKING?

We mentioned before that most aviation catastrophes are the result of a series of events gone wrong. That said, many of those disasters could have been averted if the pilot had recognized the early warning signs of impending doom. But recognizing those signs can sometimes require some great discipline and honesty. Let's "reverse engineer" some accidents and look for the early warning signs:

VFR PILOT LOSES CONTROL IN LOW VISIBILITY

- Situation – This flight took place over open water. Departure time was early evening. There was haze, but conditions were legally VFR.

- Considerations – First off, it's always harder to maintain a sense of the horizon at night. Early evening can be tough too because the increasing greyness of the sky tends to blend in with the increasing greyness of the horizon. This effect is intensified when the horizon is over water. Haze makes things worse.

- Warning signs – The first warning sign here was the time of the flight. When flying at night a pilot must be extra sensitive to factors that might impede visibility. Next comes the haze. Haze at any time of the day can severely reduce visibility. Haze in the early evening can all but remove any distinction between the sky and ground at the horizon. And, finally, a featureless ocean makes it all the harder to determine where the sky ends and the water begins.

- Pilot arguments justifying flight – "I've made this flight many times." "Legally, this is VFR." "I'm part way through my instrument training, so I'll be able to handle reduced visibility."

- Conclusion – This pilot's decision to fly out over the ocean, in haze, at dusk, was a disaster in the making. If any one of these three factors has been eliminated, this plane might not have crashed.

AIRPLANE RUNS OUT OF FUEL DURING DIVERSION TO ALTERNATE AIRPORT

- Situation – This daytime flight took off in good weather and was headed for an airport that was reporting a 70% chance of thunderstorms. The pilot checked weather and determined, based on the time the storms were forecast to arrive at her destination airport, she could arrive in time. If not, she would divert to an airport she had selected. The airplane had enough fuel on board to reach the destination airport and then make the diversion, if necessary.

- Considerations – It's hard here to find fault with the pilot's preparation. She considered the weather forecast and even determined a suitable alternate airport. She planned for the diversion and made sure she had the required fuel. What she did not consider was the movement of the storm system. As luck had it, the storm beat her to her destination. She diverted as planned, but soon realized enroute that her alternate had begun reporting storms too. She had to get away from the storm, but there was no suitable airport within range.

- **Warning signs** – Storms are so much more powerful than airplanes that it's stupid to plan to outrun one in anything but a jet. Even if you do beat the storm's rain fall, there are other factors to consider, such as turbulence and downdrafts, which can be severe. Flight into a forecast storm area was this pilot's first mistake. Her second blunder was not taking into consideration that the storm's path might also affect her alternate airport. If she had considered the storm's movement, she could have chosen an alternate airport out of the storm's path. Further, had she gotten an enroute weather update, she would have been able to choose and divert to a suitable airport sooner. Instead, she waited until she arrived at her stormed-sodden destination to make her decision. Don't *ever* plan a trip that will leave you with minimum fuel at *any* stage of your flight, even during a pre-planned diversion! The FAA regulations that require pilots to carry enough fuel to reach their destinations and fly for an additional 30 minutes during the day, or 45 minutes at night, are simply not adequate. [FAR 91.151] Choose your own minimums. If any of my flights would have me landing with anything less than an hour's worth of extra fuel, I'll make a fuel stop.

- **Pilot arguments justifying flight** – "I'll probably arrive before the storm hits." "I picked an alternate, so I should be okay." "I'll remember to get a weather update along the way."

- **Conclusion** – This pilot's failure to obtain an enroute weather update while flying into a forecast storm zone was an emergency in the making.

GENERAL AVIATION AIRPLANE COLLIDES WITH COMMERCIAL JET

- **Situation** – A pilot chooses to fly in the complex airspace of Southern California, unfamiliar with the area, and without ATC assistance. A commercial jet is inbound to LAX.

- **Considerations** – The Class Bravo airspace surrounding LAX is complicated to navigate. There are many seemingly random "chunks" of airspace that are difficult for pilots to determine because the airspace boundaries are not aligned with any obvious landmarks. Commercial jets fly very fast and it isn't easy for those pilots to see our small aircraft.

- **Warning signs** – This pilot was flying in unfamiliar airspace. This was factor number one. The complexity of this airspace is enough to account for factors two and three, believe me. Failure to communicate with ATC lead to his unauthorized (not to mention illegal and terribly unsafe) entry into LAX's Class Bravo airspace. The pilot was unaware of the approach paths used for jets flying into LAX, so imagine his (momentary) surprise when he became the hood ornament on a 727 at 6,000 feet.

- **Common pilot arguments in favor of flight** – "I'm not required to talk to ATC." "I'll keep track of my position on my chart." "Jets are easy to spot, so I can get out of the way if necessary."

- **Conclusion** – Flight into any unfamiliar area should always prompt a pilot to use every available resource to increase flight safety. ATC is one such resource. ATC will not steer you through your flight, but they will certainly let you know the moment you do something wrong with regard to airspace. Further, you can query them as to your exact position whenever you're in doubt. This pilot should have also made himself familiar with the approach paths of jets flying into LAX. That would have given him a better sense of which areas were most dangerous with regard to commercial traffic. If you fly near any commercial airport, contact the local controlling facility and ask for a chart that depicts their arrival and departure routes. 747s *do* fly at 3,000 feet, just like your Piper Warrior. Don't think of them as flying only at altitudes above those you can reach. They have to land and takeoff too. And airliner pilots are simply not expecting us to be in the way. Remember, those jets are on IFR flight plans and they're flying in airspace that has been reserved specifically to isolate IFR traffic from meandering VFR traffic. I'm not saying that commercial pilots don't ever look out their windows, but our tiny little airplanes are all but invisible to pilots flying at 250 knots. This pilot's failure to take advantage of ATC's help while flying in unfamiliar, complicated and heavily-trafficed airspace was an emergency in the making. The use of ATC's flight-following service might have saved many lives in this situation.

These are just a few of the many times that a series of unfortunate events has lead to news coverage. But this is not to say that every flight you ever take will be completely free of possible danger. You, as pilot-in-command, must determine for yourself if your flight can be conducted safely.

On a flight from Los Angeles to the San Francisco area, I had to face this decision. The "possible danger" factors affecting my flight were:

- **Weather** – There was a significant amount of cloud coverage all along the route. The San Francisco area was reporting low ceilings that might or might not burn off by the time I arrived. I would be flying with no less than a 30-knot headwind the entire time, increasing my flight time (and fuel requirements) considerably.

- **Airplane electrical system** – I had been warned of an electrical system problem in this particular rental airplane (a brand-spanking new Cessna 172) that resulted in a dead battery for no apparent reason. Mechanics were at a loss for why it happened. When I tried to start the airplane in Los Angeles, the battery was, in fact, dead. I needed a jump start to get it going. Once the airplane fired up, I saw that the battery was not taking a charge, meaning that if I stopped the engine I likely would not have gotten it going again without another jump. More importantly, however, this meant that if I lost my alternator (the thing that supplies electrical power during flight and charges the battery), I would have immediately lost all electrical power because my battery was already dead.

- **Time of day** – It was 3:00 p.m. when I was to depart, but with that headwind there was no way I could get into San Francisco before dark. I would definitely need electrical power once I got near the area.

Keeping those factors in mind, I considered whether or not I was an idiot to make the trip:

- **Weather** – The entire first part of the trip was fine weather-wise, aside from that terrible headwind. I would get weather updates enroute to see if things were improving to the north.

- **Airplane electrical system** – I knew that I'd be in bad shape if my alternator went, but my airplane *was* brand new, after all. I figured the likelihood of the alternator failing was less than it would be on an older airplane. After I started the airplane, I let it run idle for almost an hour to see how the system behaved. The battery was not taking a charge, but everything else was working fine. Even with all of the avionics (radios, nav gear, etc.) on, the system worked. I also had a fully charged hand-held GPS unit with me. If I did lose my electrical system, I'd at least have navigation to find the nearest suitable airport. I also had several flashlights with me that would enable me to see my instruments in the dark.

- **Time of day** – The lion's share of the trip would be during daylight. If I lost my electrical system I could find a suitable airport and land the airplane. By nightfall, I would already be in the San Francisco area, where I was familiar with the terrain and airport options.

I also planned a route that would have me near a suitable landing airport the entire time–well almost the entire time. I reasoned that if anything seemed odd I would land the airplane immediately. I was also aware, however, that each of these factors was an emergency in the making if more than one factor became a problem at the same time. Clouds are hard to see at night, especially when you're looking for a suitable landing spot because you just lost your electrical system.

I was making the flight with a friend that was a student pilot, far along in his training at the time. The fact that he could help with navigation and the search for a suitable landing spot increased my confidence in our chances.

During the flight, we planned for several diversions and gave ourselves "decision-making points" along the way: "If ceilings drop at San Jose by the time we reach Salinas, we land at Salinas." As we approached each possible diversion airport, we had all the information required that land at that airport ready to go. We used ATC flight following along the entire route so that if we did go down somewhere other than an airport, someone would miss us and call for help.

The flight required little more than dodging a few clouds here and there to remain within legal VFR cloud-clearance requirements. The alternator held up and we landed safely in San Carlos, though many hours after we departed, thanks to that headwind. (In fairness to that headwind, as a tailwind it sped us along at over 180 knots on the way down to Los Angeles!)

Keep yourself aware of the events that are transpiring before and during your flight. Ask yourself if any situation that you're in could lead to catastrophe and act accordingly. If you ever get the sense that something's not right, find a suitable airport and land your airplane. Do your serious thinking on the ground. Even if you later discover that there was nothing wrong, consider the precautionary landing extra practice.

You can never land too many times.

8

Gizmo Stockpiling

After my first flight lesson I asked a pilot friend if he had any advice for me.

"Do you have a credit card?" he asked.

"Yes," I replied.

"Give it to me now. I'll give it back when your training is over."

I was expecting to hear about landing tips or, at the very least, some clever way to relate to my 20-year old CFI who had mastered the application of the word "dude" to more diverse situations than I had ever thought possible.

But no, his advice was about the impending gizmo spending spree that claims most, if not all, student pilots. I figured that any product whose name included the words "aviator" or "pilot" absolutely *had* to be in my flight bag: sunglasses, wristwatches, electronic calculators, bomber jackets, you name it. Piloting was hard work, I reckoned, we pilots needed special things.

Nowadays my opinion on gizmos differs considerably: If it doesn't *clearly* make my life easier, or if it weighs more than a pound, I do without it.

Eventually you get to the point where you realize that the only aviation "gizmos" that make any difference have numbers and require far more purchasing muscle than a credit card.

APPAREL

Choosing clothing for flying is very complex: If it will be warm inside the cockpit, you need to wear clothing that will help you keep cool. If it will be cold, you need to wear warmer clothing. If you anticipate a change during your flight, you need to have a means for adjusting your outfit enroute.

Do you see what I mean? In what other activities are the apparel-selection requirements so utterly exhausting? It's no wonder piloting requires such advanced training and study.

That said, some things make more sense to wear while flying than others. You want to remain comfortable because you don't want anything to distract you from your job as pilot. Skirts, dresses and kilts are bad because the preflight alone would be comically disastrous. You also don't want to wear anything that you're afraid of getting a bit of oil or dirt on. It's hard to remain completely clean during a preflight inspection, or at least one that's done properly.

Turning morbid for a moment, some types of clothing have proven more or less safe during aviation accidents. The following applies for commercial travel too.

Denim is sturdy and fairly heat resistant. As was witnessed in New York City, back in September of 2001, jet fuel burns hot. NTSB accident reports have suggested that some women have died in commercial jet accidents not by the crash impact itself, but because the heat from the ensuing jet fuel fires melted their nylons to their legs, rendering them immobile and unable to escape the spreading flames. A horrible thought, but something to consider.

Though you certainly won't be training in anything that burns jet fuel, those reports illustrate the benefit that sturdy clothing offers.

Also consider the possibility of an emergency off-field landing. It might be hours before help arrives. A warm coat could make all the difference.

Generally speaking, layers work well. If it gets cold, you add. If it gets hot, you remove. There are no points for high fashion in a Cessna. Wear what feels good.

PILOT HERO CLOTHING

You'll see jumpsuits, bomber jackets and other pilot-targeted apparel in the catalogs of many pilots shops. Clothing like this is commonly worn by military aviators because of the potentially extreme flight conditions they face.

As a private pilot you're not going to face such extreme conditions. If you make an emergency landing in a field, chances are you won't have to hide from enemy fire or brave many days and nights in arctic temperatures. (If you do, then you didn't do a good flight plan!)

Further, if you show up for a flight lesson in a military-issue jumpsuit, your CFI is going to have a very hard time keeping a straight face: *"Oh my God, Dude, like what are you wearing?"*

Figure 104: *HEAD'S SET* A good quality headset makes all the difference, especially when you're learning the ropes with regard to using the radio.

HEADSETS

Here's where that credit card really comes in handy. Good quality headsets make all the difference in a noisy cockpit. Good quality headsets are expensive, so make sure that flying is for you before you invest. But the moment you do decide flying is for you, start shopping. (Figure 104)

It can be tough to decide on a headset because you'll get many different opinions as to which are best. The truth is that the perfect headset for you will depend on many factors that others cannot determine for you:

- Your head size

- Your sensitivity to noise

- Your airplane

- Your budget

Some CFIs have an extra set they loan to students. If yours does, try them out. Try as many as you can.

FEATURE FACTORS

The two biggest factors to consider when choosing headsets are noise reduction and comfort. Beyond those two core characteristics, however, different headsets offer additional features.

NOISE REDUCTION

My CFI let me borrow a headset that electronically reduced cockpit noise. Headsets like these are called *active noise reduction (ANR)*. Let me tell you how fast I fell in love with them. You push a little button and can actually hear the noise sucked out of your ears.

ANR headsets work by "listening" to the surrounding noise, determining the frequencies of any droning sounds—like engine noise—and then filtering those frequencies. Surprisingly, CFI chatter doesn't qualify as droning.

ANR headsets require batteries. If the batteries go dead during a flight, they become *passive noise reduction (PNR)* headsets. Some ANR headsets can optionally get their power from an outlet in the instrument panel, but I doubt you'll find such an outlet in a rental airplane.

PNR headsets rely on physical factors to reduce noise, such as the design of the ear pieces and the way in which they fit over your ears. They use no batteries.

Some argue that a set of good quality PNR headsets work just as well as ANR models. I've tried the best of both and I prefer the ANR models.

I purchased two ANR sets from a company called Lightspeed. I bought their high-end model at that time (25XL) for me, and a pair on the lower end of their product line (15XL) that I loan to passengers.

Despite a price difference of several hundred dollars, I can't say that the high-end model is that much better. Both, however, are fantastic.

A long-time leader in PNR headsets is a company called David Clark. What John Deere did for green in the tractor industry, David Clark has done in the world of headsets. David Clark headsets are visible everywhere. If you've ever noticed a pilot in a movie wearing light green headsets, they were likely David Clark's.

David Clark also offers an ANR model, which was the first headset I bought. I figured that if their passive models were so good, their ANR models might even make CFI chatter bearable. It didn't turn out that way. Fortunately for me, they offered a money-back guarantee, which turned out to be handy. I preferred the Lightspeeds and was able to almost pay for both Lightspeed headsets for the price of the one ANR David Clark headset.

These are the only two brands I have personally experienced for any length of time. Others might be good too. Money-back guarantees are great because you won't have any idea how well the headsets work until you're airborne.

CONSTRUCTION QUALITY

You are going to drop, sit on, close doors on, and otherwise abuse your headsets. Make sure that the brand you choose is durable. Is the cable thick enough to withstand getting kinked in the door? Will the cross bar (the part that connects the two ear pieces) bend or break if you sit on it?

Ask other pilots for their war stories with regard to beating their headsets. David Clark's are known for durability, but my Lightspeeds have never fallen apart on me either.

AUDIO QUALITY

The hardest part about judging the audio quality of headsets is that most of the time the poor audio quality that someone might blame on a headset is actually the fault of the airplane's radios. You'll pay $500 or so for a new set of mega-deluxe headsets, plug them into a rental airplane and cry because everything sounds so bad.

If you can test the headsets in a store and actually hear radio communications on them, that's great. If you don't have that option, going with a name brand like Lightspeed, David Clark or Bose, is pretty much a guarantee that you won't go wrong sound-wise.

Keep in mind that airplane radio frequencies come in on a very limited frequency range. Even the finest headsets in the world are not going to make the voice in the tower sound like Pavorati.

COMFORT

You're going to be wearing these things for hours, sometimes in some pretty miserable heat. If they're not comfortable, your focus will drift from flying the airplane to mentally shopping for a new model.

There are pluses and minuses to all models. ANR models tend to be bigger to accommodate their electronics. PNR models tend to fit tighter because they rely, in part, on a tight deal for their noise reduction. Some companies make dainty little feather-light models, but they're really intended for quieter airplanes than the dragon's that we fly. If a headset doesn't *look* like it can cancel out noise, it probably can't.

Having a pair of Lightspeeds on your head is a lot like wearing a Carmen Miranda head dress. If you have a little head, you might find yourself looking like one of those little dog statuettes with the bobbing heads. This is the price you pay for ANR. The electronic circuitry must go somewhere, therefore the ear cups are larger.

David Clark's headsets have earned the nickname "David Clamps" because of the way in which they effectively and relentlessly grasp your head. But that's where their effective passive noise reduction comes from. If the seal was loose, the

noise would come through. If the seal was surgical, the noise reduction would be fantastic. David Clark headsets are somewhere in between. They give me a headache after about an hour. But then, I have a pretty large head. One CFI of mine, with her petite little head, swears by them.

Another comfort consideration is eyeglasses. If you wear them, you want to make sure you can still get your headsets on comfortably. This goes for sunglasses too. Eyeglasses can also interfere with the noise reduction of both passive and active headsets. Both the David Clarks and the Lightspeeds worked fine for me when using them with my sunglasses.

STEREO

Some models offer stereo sound, meaning separate left and right audio channels. This is great for when you pop your favorite new CD into the in-dash CD player found aboard most rental aircraft. After reading several hundred pages of my sorry sense of humor, you probably know by now when I'm joking. Believe it or not, however, some aircraft *do* have CD players and some pilots do listen to music during flights. Advanced audio systems can even mute the CD player when someone's talking over the airplane's radio.

I'm not going to debate whether or not listening to music while you're flying an airplane is a good idea—you can guess my opinion on that one—but the point is that it's not something you'll be doing during your training. I've never once seen a training airplane that had a music system.

Some headsets are available with two channels only. This is fine so long as they have a "mono" button that will patch the single audio channel through both sides of the headset. If you plug a stereo headset without a mono option into a mono jack, like those found on most trainers, you'll hear audio through only one side. Stereo isn't something to avoid, so long as that mono option is there, but it's not something to pay extra for.

AUTOMATIC POWER-OFF (ANR ONLY)

If you buy an ANR headset, make sure it has an automatic power shut-off feature. This handy feature automatically shuts off the headsets after a period of inactivity. Without this feature, you'll drain your batteries each time you forget to switch the unit off after a flight. I forget to switch mine off about 90% of the time, so it's a good thing mine have this feature.

FUEL LEVEL CHECKER

This simple hollow glass wand enables you to determine how much fuel is physically in an airplane's tanks. Dip it into the tanks until it touches the bottom, hold a finger over the top hole to create some suction and remove the wand. The fuel inside the wand stays put until you release your finger. Numbers on the side of the wand indicate how many gallons are actually in the tank.

Simple ideas are always the best.

Unless an airplane's fuel tanks are full, it's very hard to see how much fuel they contain. It's dark in there and an eyeball estimate isn't a safe idea anyway. You know how many gallons of fuel your airplane burns in an hour, so if you know how many gallons you have, you'll be able to safely estimate fuel reserves.

This is the cheapest flight safety you'll ever buy. You might find one of these handy gadgets aboard the airplanes you rent, but you might not too. Buy and keep one in your flight bag just in case.

FLASHLIGHTS

Nighttime flights happen when you least expect them. Long day trips turn into nighttime returns, and rental aircraft delays often stretch daytime lessons into evening hours.

"Flashlights" is a broad category in a cockpit. It can mean just about every type of handheld light-emitting device imaginable, *except* the traditional flashlight that we all have in our homes. Household flashlights are too big and too bright to be of much use in an airplane.

This is the oddest place to bring up this topic, but an important aeromedical factor to consider for nighttime flying is called *night vision*. When all other light sources are gone and your eyes adjust to the darkness, this is your night vision. It can take upwards of 30 minutes for your eyes to optimally adjust to low light conditions. You don't want to blow it by switching on one of those mega-wonder, maxi-lights that can illuminate Maine from California.

Flashlights appropriate for cockpit use are relatively dim, small and usually emit some color other than white. Amber is good because it is close to white in the color spectrum, but doesn't adversely affect night vision in the same way. Red can work too, but I find amber to be more effective.

The thing to remember when using any colored light source on charts is that certain ink colors will not appear. An amber light pretty much washes out all terrain color coding. Orange route lines, which work great during the daylight, also vanish when viewed under amber light.

I have found the basic little pen-sized lights to be most useful in the cockpit. I take several of them just in case I drop one or the batteries die. You can keep a spare set of batteries on hand, but who wants to change batteries in the dark? (Figure 105)

You can use a larger flashlight for your preflight inspection of the airplane exterior, but you still don't want a super bright one. During the preflight is when your eyes will be adjusting to the dark. A bright flashlight won't help the process. Absolutely

Figure 105: *LOTSA LIGHTS* Penlights are small and emit enough light to be useful, yet not ruin your night vision. Some models offer interchangeable colored lenses. Having several flashlights on hand is a better option than having to change dead batteries enroute, or trying to find one that you've dropped on the cockpit floor.

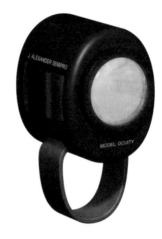

Figure 106: *BEAMING DIGITS* A fingerlight wraps around your finger and emits a small beam of light wherever you point.

make sure that your preflight light is durable because you're going to drop it on the ground more times than you'll be able to count.

GADGET LIGHTS

I was amazed to learn of all the clever ways in which manufacturers were able to package a light source. There are lights that attach to your headsets, lights that clip onto your fingers and even lights that you hold in your teeth.

I use an amber-colored finger light, but I don't love it. I find it to be a bit clunky wrapped around my finger. It comes in handy for reading charts though. I lay the chart in my lap and just point to the area I'm reading. It's also useful for illuminating dark gauges. (Figure 106)

Don't ever imagine that an airplane's panel will be lit as effectively as your car's dashboard. There's always at least one light that's burnt out or missing entirely.

Pilot supply shops sell all sorts of cockpit-appropriate lights. You'll probably waste some money trying out different types until you find the ones that you prefer.

LAP BOARDS AND ORGANIZERS

Cockpit organization might be the one thing that's even more challenging to master than landing. The cockpits in our trainer airplanes are small and offer no shelf space. As discussed, your lap is the only flat surface you have, so you want to make the best of it.

There are two basic options for turning your lap into a useful surface:

- Kneeboard

- Lap organizer

A kneeboard is basically a flat surface that attaches to your thigh by a nylon strap. It's simple, provides a hard surface suitable for writing things like ATIS reports and ATC instructions, and most have a slot or two for pencils. They are also pretty affordable, which is always welcome. (Figure 107)

A lap organizer also attaches to your thigh, but offers pockets to store things. (Figure 108)

As your flight experience increases, you'll find ways to condense your cockpit organization needs into smaller and smaller spaces. When I started flying, I figured that a large, triple-fold organizer would be best because it offered so

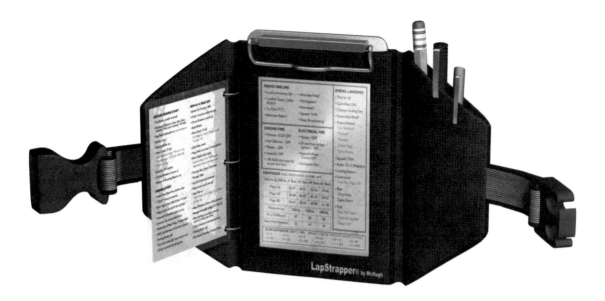

Figure 108: *IKEA TO GO!* My whole aviation world came together as soon as found this wonderful organizer. It's not too big, yet has the space I need to hold everything. I normally have a pad of paper under the clip, but I removed it so that you could see where I keep my emergency checklist. Not seen is my preflight checklist, which is on the reverse side of the emergency list. Chances are I'm only going to need one of those at a time. Right? My laminated enroute checklist is double sided and held in by three rings. I also like to stuff my diversion calculator (the big ruler thing that we used during our flight planning) and my compass rose behind the metal clipboard.

Figure 107: *A NEED BOARD* A kneeboard straps to your lap and can be used to hold pencils, checklists or note pads. Another advantage it offers is a hard writing surface for jotting down ATIS or other notes.

much storage space by comparison to other options. My first organizer had space for everything: charts, pens, flashlights and even my (full-sized) E6B. Fully loaded, it weighed about 400 lbs. What's more, it was so long (hip to knee wise) that it actually prevented me from fully deflecting the yoke in either direction. I felt like I was strapped to a desk.

So much for storage space.

I tried a few other options before I found the one that works best for me, which is what figure 108 illustrates. I still use it today. It has a double fold and binder-type rings that enable me to add checklists or Pilots Guide pages, as needed. It also has a clear pocket in which I hold my emergency checklist so it's always immediately available. The best thing about it, however, is that—like my thigh—it's short, so it doesn't get in the way of the yoke.

Pilot supply store catalogs are packed with organizer options. Be weary of the more elaborate models. The point to a laptop organizer is to offer ready access to the things you need most during flight, which are checklists, pens (pencils) and paper. These things don't take up much room. You needn't consult Martha Stewart on clever ways to organize your cockpit.

Charts, your airplane's POH and your E6B are also needed in flight, but an organizer pocket is not the best place for them. You need your chart out and ready, not hidden in some pocket. Your E6B and POH can be left in one of the airplane's built-in compartments, or your flight bag. You won't need them all the time.

You don't need ready access to absolutely everything. Prioritize the important stuff so you can keep your valuable lap space as uncluttered as possible.

CHART CLIPS

I give both my thighs something to do during flights. My right thigh holds my organizer while my left thigh gets to hold my chart clip, or garter belt as several passengers have called it. Also attached by a nylon strap, a chart clip securely holds your charts in place, obscures only a small portion of the chart at a time, and enables you to easily access the charts to refold as necessary. (Figure 109)

Several organizers have clear pockets intended to hold charts, but these pockets are usually so small that you'd be pulling the charts out to refold them every 20 minutes. (Unless your airplane is really, really slow.)

Figure 109: *GARTER BELT* While one leg is busy with a kneeboard, your other leg can hold your charts. Chart clips are handy because they hold charts securely and enable pilots to easily to flip them over when needed.

I like to fold my charts into squares and arrange them in the order in which I'll need them. As I fly "off" a chart, I either turn it over and stuff it back into the clip, or remove it and have the next chart ready to go underneath. (Figure 110)

The chart clip is made of a strong metal so you can stuff it full of charts and not worry about breaking it. They're inexpensive and just a wonderful, simple idea.

EASY JETTISON A MUST

There will be times that you'll need to be totally unencumbered for safety. No matter how small a lap organizer or chart clip might be, they can get in the way during landings. A strong crosswind might require full deflection of the yoke, which might be tough if your lap is full of stuff. Make sure that whatever you buy can be released quickly and easily using only one hand.

Figure 110: *AT THE READY* Fold your charts so that you can see as much of the chart surface as possible. I prefer to leave mine opened two panels wide. They still fit nicely into the chart clip, but I can see far more chart at a glance. You can see here how the route for our entire flight could be easily seen at once.

I remove my lap-mounted devices as the last part of my prelanding checklist. I like to clear my lap for landings because I just never know what fancy flight maneuvers might be required. Once all the checklist items are complete, the only thing left is to land the airplane. You won't need pens or charts to do that.

LEATHERMAN

Though the Village People's leatherman might be a fan of flying, he's not what I'm talking about here. A Leatherman is a swiss-army knife-like device perfect for pilots. It has cutting blades, screw drivers and all sorts of other useful gadgets.

This is one of those devices that pilots, in theory, should have no use for. What do we ever need to cut or tighten?

There will be times when, during your preflight, you'll see a screw that could use some tightening. I'm not talking about anything that should be checked by an FAA-certified mechanic—if the prop is loose, don't try to fix it yourself! I'm talking about the small stuff. You might also need it for your personal items, like your headsets, your handheld GPS or handheld radio mounts.

Every once in a while you just need a handy tool. Life is like that. Piloting is no different.

There's also a darker side to the usefulness of the Leatherman. If your airplane ever crashes and you're stuck inside mangled metal, you're going to wish you had a gadget to help you get out. The Leatherman can cut through airplane aluminum and can also help you remove screws to doors that might provide an escape route. It's a survival tool.

When you actually do make it to your picnic destination, because you flight-planned carefully, preflighted thoroughly and flew the airplane safely, you'll need a bottle opener for those sodas. You won't need it for the beers because you'll never forget the FAA regulation governing alcohol consumption that requires "8 hours from the bottle to the throttle." Right?

FLIGHT COMPUTERS

I reserved this space to talk about flight computers because, although the E6B is really all you need, the market is full of options that claim to be better, faster or easier to use.

I admit that I explored just about every electronic E6B alternative I could find. Not only did I want something more in line with my "digital" methodologies, but I just didn't trust myself to use a manual E6B properly. Some electronic options are quite impressive; others are simply cumbersome. If you think the manual E6B has a user-interface problem, you should try some of the electronic models.

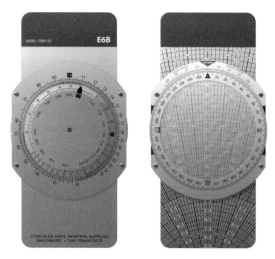

Figure 111: *E6-BIG* I keep a full-size metal E6B in my flight bag. Every now and then I need to tighten the screws that hold the rotating disc in place, but other than that, I can't imagine it ever wearing out.

Both options, manual and electronic, are good and both offer advantages.

MANUAL OPTIONS

An E6B is an E6B, but there are a few varieties on the market. There are large models, small models, metal models and even cardboard models.

Smaller units are tempting, but make sure that you can easily read the scales and markings.

I use a full-size metal unit, which is easy to read and durable. (Figure 111) The only problem I've ever had with it is that the screws that hold the circular unit together sometimes come loose. And do I love my Leatherman when that happens? You bet.

ELECTRONIC OPTIONS

While a manual E6B was once the only flight-calculating device available to pilots, electronic gadgets are commonplace now, and offer even more functionality. Whether or not you find them more useful is something to determine for yourself.

I won't try to steer you away from electronic devices by using the "dead batteries" mantra favored by CFIs and FAA examiners. Batteries are easy to find and many devices have battery indicators that can warn you when the level is low. If someone cautions you that the batteries in your device might fail when you need it most, remind that person that the battery indicator on your digital device is far and away more accurate than the fuel gauges the FAA has approved for your airplane.

Some electronic devices can be used during your FAA written exam. The basic rule is that if your device has a memory feature of any kind, it cannot be used. The rationale is that you might cheat by putting the answers to test questions into the unit's memory. Don't ask me how.

An E6B and a $2 drugstore calculator with no memory function is all you need for the written test, so don't tempt fate by taking a more sophisticated unit with you on the day of your test.

Personal digital assistants (PDAs) like the Palm Pilot or Windows PocketPC devices are not allowed during your written test, though they can very useful for other aspects of flight planning.

E6B

Electronic E6Bs offer the same functionality as their manual counterparts, but usually offer additional features such as functions for weight and balance, crosswind calculations and numeric and time conversions.

The advantage of electronic units is that it's easier to understand the results. Manual models are only as accurate as your interpretation of the result. An indication of "10" can mean 1, 10, 100 etc. If you read it wrong, the answer's wrong and it's not the unit's fault. This isn't a problem with the electronic units.

The problem with the electronic units—to me anyway—is that the user interface can be even more confusing than the wheel of fortune on the manual models. Interface design is an art that some software companies have simply not mastered. A poorly designed interface causes confusion and confusion causes distraction and we know where distraction leads. Small buttons with cryptic icons make things even worse.

Don't assume that because an electronic version is available that it's better.

FLIGHT PLANNERS

Flight-planning calculators and computer software are other siblings in the lair of the digital temptress. These cunning vixens lure number-weary pilots with the promise of easy, safe flight plans, only to suck from them any traditional flight-planning skills they ever acquired.

That said, they're wonderful.

Electronic flight planners know the locations of airports and navaids and quickly enable pilots to create connect-the-dots types of flight plans. Those with Internet connections can even download wind data into some programs automatically. Heading calculations are instantaneous and, of course, magnetic variation is considered automatically.

Electronic flight planners can be found for PDA devices, personal computers, and even as online services over the Internet.

I used an online service once to generate a flight plan from San Carlos, California to New York's JFK. I wanted to see how long it would take. The good news is that the flight would have taken far less time than I assumed it would. The bad news is that I would be dead right now if I had flown the flight that was planned for me.

Some of the aspects of flight planning are considered by the electronic options, but many are not. Distance, direction and wind calculations are the easy stuff. But what about VFR cruising altitudes? What about suitable emergency landing spots? What about weather avoidance?

What about the friggin' Rocky Mountains?

My online flight plan had me flying right over Denver, in a Cessna 172 no less. If I had been an idiot, I might have jumped into my airplane and flown it. But I knew I had dinner plans that evening in San Francisco and there was no way I could get back home in time. Besides, I don't own an airplane.

Some newer electronic planning systems do take terrain into account. But that still leaves emergency landing spots and other meaty issues unresolved.

Electronic flight planners tackle the science of flight planning, but they do not—and can not—solve the issues of art. Anyone who has used a GPS-based street navigation system has experienced this. The unit might say to take the highway for 18 miles and exit at Carlson Avenue, but the driver knows that it's 5:30 p.m. and the highway is backed up into yesterday. Surface streets would halve the commute, but the GPS will not concur because it cannot see the logic in a longer route being better for any reason.

Another limitation of electronic flight planners is that they don't know about local checkpoints, such as a water tower or a river's edge. Checkpoints like these are common to VFR flight planning. Some planners enable pilots to manually enter the lat/lon coordinates of checkpoints, but do we really want to go through all of that just to be able to push a button for a flight plan? Do you know the lat/lon coordinates for the water tower?

The biggest concern I have about electronic flight planners is that they enable pilots to quickly lose touch with their flight-planning skills. And they do little to encourage further development of those skills.

One might compare this theory to similar notions about calculators. Do we really need to remember how to do long division when a calculator is always available? Probably not. But when the fuel tanks are running dry or unforecast bad weather is dead ahead, that calculator isn't going to do you much good. Your skills as a flight planner and pilot are what will get your airplane down safely. If you rely on automated flight planning before the manual concept has become second nature, your first instinct when a diversion is necessary is going to be a menu choice rather than a heading choice.

MISCELLANEOUS ELECTRONIC TOOLS

Some aviation software falls neither into the E6B nor the flight-planning categories. Crosswind calculators, moving map GPS systems, traffic pattern heading calculators, and more, are common for PDA devices.

I sometimes use a crosswind calculator program in my PDA. It's quick and easy to use. I don't worry about it if the winds are calm or the direction is fairly well aligned with the runway. To be honest, this is just about the only practical use I've found for a PDA in the cockpit.

I also have another program that calculates wind correction headings and groundspeed. I use this to verify the information I determine manually. It's an easy way to get a second opinion on my "human" calculation efforts. That little program has caught many a mistake for me.

DIGITAL AVIATING

I can't pretend that the future of aviation won't include an increasingly significant digital fingerprint. After all, if a computer can accurately tackle the science, then one could reasonably argue that the pilot can better focus on the art. Other industries have benefitted from computer assistance: artists, accountants, architects. Why not aviators?

Musicians have some pretty sophisticated computer technology at their disposal too. An individual can orchestrate and perform an entire composition without the involvement of other musicians. But does this make composers of today better than those who lived centuries ago? Are the Back Street Boys better than Bach?

If aviation was music, I'd rather have Bach at the yoke if we lost an engine. I believe he'd have a better understanding of the art *and* science simply because he had no choice but to understand it all completely. He knew the core of his craft. Technology enables one to push the envelope further, but often at the expense of knowing the fundamentals of the process. You don't need to read music today in order to write a symphony. This wasn't true in Bach's day.

I'm not trying to diminish the value of technology in art or other arenas. Musicians use technology to propel music into new and interesting areas. Without the advent of synthesizers, for example, we wouldn't have seen the "new wave" of the 1980s, for which I have a personal affinity. Musicians and others have integrated technology into their work effectively and successfully.

Isn't it time for aviators to do the same?

In theory, this would be great. I'm just not so sure we're there yet as software designers, or users. Our technology is not foolproof, and we—the fools—have not mastered the use of technology as an *aid* rather than a *replacement*. We don't, for example, write software to assist the pilot in her duties, we write software to replace her duties. We don't have software that helps a pilot choose flight routes by showing options based on the pilot's preferences, we only have software that chooses routes, period. There's value in discussion, but thus far we haven't considered aviation software for "conversational" purposes, only for reference and decision making.

Even more important, however, is that few other professionals rely on consumer technology for life-dependant purposes. If a spreadsheet program crashes, the accountant survives. Industries that do rely on technology at mission-critical levels don't typically rely on consumer devices. Commercial jet liners like the 777, for example, have main computer systems and as many as two back-up systems. Further, this is software that has, in theory, undergone some pretty extensive testing. I can assure you that no such testing takes place in the offices of those writing software for consumers:

PILOT: *Mayday! Mayday! Mayday! Transcontinental Airways flight 2111; we've lost cabin pressure at 37,000 and our oxygen system has failed!*

ATC: *Roger that 2111, that's a known bug in your flight management system. Look for a fix in the 2.0 release, which is expected real soon now.*

PILOT: *Help us! Help us!*

ATC: *Wilco 2111, patching you through to technical support.*

"Welcome to MicroFlight technical support. Your expected hold time is 36 minutes."

Are you really willing to bet your life on the reliability of your home computer?

GPS navigation is a great example of technology than can be used to replace or just assist. It's hard to argue against the benefits of a little graphical airplane pointing in the direction you need to fly. GPS flying pretty much obsoletes any requirement for the pilot to understand traditional navigation.

But what does this do for a pilot's *situational awareness*? That little airplane might point you exactly where you need to go, but it's also more than willing to point you exactly where you tell it to, even if that's not where you really need or want to go.

This is exactly what brought down a 757 near Columbia, South America, back in 1995. The pilot told his flight computer to go to a certain navaid by entering its ID. Unfortunately, due to problems the pilot had using the computer's interface, the airplane did not head where he intended.

The 757's flight computer was more than happy to steer the airplane where it was told. It was programmed to perform navigation tasks, it was not programmed to "discuss" navigation options with the pilot. When the pilot entered the ID for the navaid he wanted—which turned out to be one he did *not* want—the flight computer obeyed and turned the airplane completely off course. Upon trying to correct the situation, the pilots flew the airplane into terrain.

But what if the computer had questioned the order: "The navaid you entered is not part of any approach to our destination airport. Confirm?" That simple question might have prompted the pilot to rethink what was happening *before* any heading change occurred.

The flight computers that are used in today's commercial jets are reliable. So reliable, in fact, that the pilots aboard that airplane were confused when the computer's display didn't match up to their printed charts. How could the computer be wrong? Those moments of confusion prevented the pilots from "flying the airplane," as we like to say. They lost their situational awareness because they had been depending on technology to fly their airplane.

And those pilots were right to assume that the flight computer was reliable. It performed exactly as programmed and did not fail. The failure was on the part of the computer's interface designer and the pilot.

Our manual E6B is a good example of technological perfection potentially limited by human error. The scales are accurate, but our misinterpretation of those scales could run our tanks dry.

Many handheld GPS units also have a feature that's a great example of technology *assistance* rather than technology *guidance*. These units can display a list of the nearest airports to your location, and even list the heading and distance to each one. Would I love this in an emergency? I would. So would Bach. Would I want the GPS unit to pick an airport and take over the flight controls? No way. Those wonderful GPS units were developed by error-prone humans. The closest airport might be only 3 miles away, but it might also be on the other side of a ridge that's 5,000 feet above my current altitude. Together, pilots and technology can make safer decisions than either can make alone.

Technology evangelists might say that I'm letting my human ego get in the way of reality. Technology is far less likely to screw up than I am. I admit that. Technology can also benefit from back-up systems, which I can't. Technology also has no mortgage, no income tax and no bad relationships. It's likely that it will always being "thinking" clearer than me.

If you think about it, the concept of pilots flying airplanes is really Old School in itself. Why not just fully automate aircraft? We already recognize that the vast majority of aviation disasters are due to pilot error. So, in theory, removing the pilot from the equation should reduce aviation accidents considerably.

We've had great luck fully automating processes over which we have complete control. Automated teller machines are a great example of this. Do you ever wonder, as they dole out those crisp $20 notes, if they ever hand out too many or too few? Apparently, if they do, they do so far less often than human tellers.

But this is, at least, in part because the process is controllable and constant. Twenty dollar bills are always the same. They are not larger one day, thicker the next. We control the "universe" of finance so we can intelligently automate it.

We do not control the universe of aviation. We don't control the weather nor do we control the forces of nature. If one day we do, then we can look into fully automating the process of moving metal through the air by manipulating those forces.

In the meantime, I believe that we're better off making technology an aviation partner and not an aviation authority.

CELLPHONES IN FLIGHT

Cellphones are forbidden for use on airborne aircraft, but this isn't an FAA regulation. The FCC forbids cellphone use in airborne airplanes because a cellphone at high altitudes can tie up many "cells" in the towers below.

That said, if you have one, take it with you when you fly. If you lose your radios in flight and need some help, call 1-800-WX-BRIEF. No one's going to throw you in jail for protecting the safety of your flight. We've also described some situations where the cellphone is handy and legal, such as when you're on the ground and need to file or close a flight plane with the FSS.

Figure 112: *YOU ARE HERE* For $500 or so a GPS can help you out of many navigation jams. You don't want to ever rely on GPS or any other electronics means of navigation, but then you don't ever want to wish you had one with you. The display on this unit shows the airplane's position with regard to the destination airport (LAL). The numeric displays indicate that the airplane's bearing and track are both heading 074° so there is no crosswind. The airport is 12.9 miles ahead. C'mon, who's your navigational daddy?

HANDHELDS – GPS AND RADIO

Here's where the big money can be spent. And aside from a good headset, this is where it *should* be spent. A handheld GPS and radio are great tools for pilots, especially students.

GPS

Some CFIs argue that using GPS thwarts a student's efforts to learn more traditional methods of navigation, like the VOR. This will certainly be the case if you fall victim to the accuracy, ease of use and reliability GPS offers. Who needs unsurpassed usefulness like that in the cockpit when we have an antiquated, confusing technology like the VOR?

This doesn't mean that as pilot-in-command of your aircraft you can't make the decision that having a handheld GPS along for the ride increases flight safety. (Figure 112)

It's difficult to belittle GPS technology. Simply put, it's decades better than VOR technology. But until such time the FAA decides to decommission VORs, student pilots will be required to learn how to use them. In fairness, the VOR is still a usable navigation technology. It's just not as straight forward as GPS.

I bought a handheld GPS before my first cross-country flight. My CFI was a bit nervous about it, but she trusted me when I assured her that I would never, ever actually turn the thing on.

GPS AS AN EDUCATOR

I couldn't wait to get into the airplane and turn my GPS on. I was totally amazed at the power of that little device. It was tempting to just follow the little airplane, but I soon discovered that the GPS offered some real educational advantages too.

I would continue to track VORs during my flights as I was taught, but by having the GPS follow along, I could see exactly how accurate the VOR was. I could see the difference in sensitivity between tracking a radial 5 miles from the facility and tracking one 20 miles out. When that VOR needle starts dancing around as you approach a facility, it's easy to think you're going off course. But the GPS convinced me I was doing well. I could experience the limitations of VOR technology while feeling perfectly safe that I was still on course. It's one thing for a groundschool instructor to warn students about VOR limitations, but it really sinks in when you can experience it first hand without concern that you're doing something wrong.

But the really cool thing about my GPS was that it could record my route. When I got home I could download that route into my computer and overlay it on a scanned chart. Hot damn! I could see exactly where I flew and how close I remained to my intended route line. Even my CFI was amazed by this. And then she yelled at me for using it.

The problem is that the process of overlaying a GPS route on the scanned chart isn't terribly easy to do. There's was no "make it happen" button in the software. I only did it once.

The process involved scanning the chart and bringing that scanned image into a program that would let me calibrate the image and download the GPS route data. Calibration involves defining the lat/lon coordinates of two or more points on the scanned image. This is easy on an aviation chart because the lat/lon coordinates are printed right on the chart.

There are a few programs on the market that can do this. I used a shareware Windows program called OziExplorer. There might be better options out there now to make it easier. The Macintosh platform has a program called GPSy that can do the same thing, but it didn't work with my GPS unit. If you plan to try this, make sure that your GPS has a way to record the route data and download it into your computer.

The GPS unit I used was a Lowrance Airmap 100. It's not the most deluxe unit on the market, but it sure works well. The screen is easy to read and it has some nice features. (The computer download option is one of the reasons I bought it.) Lowrance has a larger screen model, but I opted for the smaller size for portability reasons. The downside of the unit is that the user interface is clunky. Too make keystrokes are required to do anything. I would bet, however, that other handheld units suffer from this same shortcoming.

The price range of handheld GPS units starts at about $500 for monochrome ones like mine, and goes upwards of $2,000 for full-color models. Non-aviation units will technically work, but they will not have an aviation database of airports and navaids, which is essential.

PDA-based GPS antennae are also available. I would caution you to make sure that your PDA's screen is readable in bright daylight before you go this route. Also make sure that your petite PDA doesn't become a jumbo monster once the antenna is attached.

At first I figured that a single PDA would be the way to go. It could have the E6B and flight planning programs I wanted, and it could double as my airborne GPS unit. This seemed more efficient than having a PDA and a handheld GPS. But I couldn't find any PDA-based GPS systems that worked as well as the Airmap I bought. My main complaint was the readability of the screen. The Airmap was easier to read in sunlight. My PDA's screen was all but invisible in similar situations.

Check around before you buy. New stuff comes out all of the time. I would still prefer to have one unit that can do it all. I'll keep looking too.

I use my GPS less often now, but I still take it with me on every flight. If I'm flying to a small airport that might be hard to find, I turn it on as I approach the area. I mainly use traditional (anti-quated) navigation methods, but I'd rather find the airport safely then boast about how I found it without using GPS.

The other benefit of having GPS aboard is that I'll still have some means of electronic navigation if I ever lose my electrical system.

Someday GPS will be the standard means for navigation in aviation. Any experience you get with it now will only better prep you for the inevitable. I caution you, however, not to become reliant upon it. Not because it's GPS, but because it's an electronic means of navigation and as a VFR pilot you should only depend on your eyes and charts.

RADIO

I never bought a handheld radio during my training, but if I had to do over again, I would. (Figure 113)

Figure 113: *HANDY COM* Handheld radios offer emergency and training options that are invaluable to student pilots. Some radios have headset jacks that enable pilots to hear the signal through their headsets.

The obvious benefit of a handheld radio is that you've still got a communications option if your panel-mounted radios fail. Keep in mind, however, that handheld radios don't work as well as a panel-mounted ones. They don't have the reception range. Some have jacks for hooking them up to the airplane's external antenna, which helps, but most rental aircraft won't have the connection to the antenna that you'll need.

Handheld radios have non-emergency uses too. If you work near an airport you can grab a sandwich at lunch and sit and listen to the tower communications. The more you expose yourself to radio communications the sooner you'll become comfortable speaking on the radio. You can also listen to the ATIS broadcast and practice writing it down.

Smaller radios offer the obvious advantage of not being bulky in your flight bag. But make sure that you're not compromising power for size. Some slightly larger radios have greater range. The buttons on the smaller radios can also be a challenge for stubby fingers.

A LA CARTE VS. COMBO MODELS

Some handheld radios are combined with VOR receivers or even GPS units. There's ongoing debate about the usefulness of the VOR receiver in a handheld radio. Being underpowered, it's harder to get a reliable signal. And the VOR needle is a small vertical line in the radio's already tiny LCD display.

Most pilots I've talked to agree that they wouldn't rely on the VOR feature on the radio because they wouldn't trust it. But if the radio can receive VOR signals, then it can also be used to communicate with an FSS over a VOR, as we discussed earlier. But pilot/FSS communications options via VOR facilities are being phased out, so this benefit is limited.

If you ever lose your electrical system, you'll probably want to use you handheld radio for communication, not for navigation. Further, a handheld GPS unit will work much better for navigating during a difficult time like that.

So what about a radio/GPS combo unit?

This is another one of those ideas that looks great on paper. But the unit's aren't cheap and you lose that *moving map* feature that makes the GPS units so wonderful in the first place. Radio/GPS combo units also suffer from that small LCD display.

The urge to minimize your cockpit arsenal is prudent. But keep in mind that an emergency situation is not one for which you want to make compromises. Get the best communications option you can and get the best navigation option too. You won't likely find them in the same device.

Handheld radios are in the $400 to $600 range. They are a great safety backup and can also be a great learning tool. Combined with a (separate) handheld GPS unit, you greatly reduce the chance that an electrical system failure will become anything more than an inconvenience. Even at night.

These devices are worthy of the space they take in your flight bag and on your credit card statement.

FLIGHT SIMULATORS

A computer-based flight simulator cannot teach you how to fly an airplane. Learning to fly an airplane involves feeling the way the airplane responds to the way you manipulate the controls. Flight simulators cannot provide the user with the same experience.

It's hard to ignore the advancing quality of the flight simulators on the market today. The scenery is wonderful, the airplanes look great, and some programs even offer simulated ATC conversations and weather. All of this makes for great *entertainment* software, but don't assume it will help you learn to pilot an airplane any more than a game of Monopoly can help you develop a financial empire.

Flight simulators are popular for IFR training because the student is trying to learn to fly by instruments. Simulators emulate real flight instruments reasonably well, making them ideal in this situation. There are FAA-approved software simulators for IFR training. Most popular flight simulators are not approved by the FAA, meaning they might or might not be accurate. Sadly, most of the approved packages aren't as much fun because they focus on the flight instruments and not the reality experience.

I have heard a few CFIs claim that it was easier to teach VOR navigation to VFR students who had been flight simulator fans prior to starting their flight lessons. I've heard others claim it was hard to break students of bad habits they'd acquired behind the controls of a simulator.

I've never heard any CFI say that a flight simulator helped a student learn to fly the airplane.

9

Moving On

I hope this book has answered some of your aviation questions, I hope it has prompted new questions, and I hope your enthusiasm for aviation is stronger now than ever. And I hope you now see aviation as both art and science, and that you agree we're nowhere near understanding it completely or even adequately.

I haven't covered it all here, but I've covered a lot. I'm tackling the more advanced subjects of navigation, weather and flight planning in another book. Meet me there and we'll pick up where we left off.

In the meantime, remember that no one can teach you to be a good pilot. No one can teach you to be a safe pilot. "Good" and "safe" come not from memorizing what a CFI teaches you, but from learning to apply that knowledge effectively, each moment of every flight. That's a job you must do for yourself.

Even more importantly, remember that your flight training doesn't end after your checkride. In aviation, when you stop learning, your skills as an aviator become increasingly inadequate. Rules change. Techniques evolve. Stay on top of things.

The pilot you become will reflect the personal commitments you make.

Before you know it, aviation will become a part of you. You won't go more than an hour or so without the thought of an airplane entering your mind. It's like sex, only safer. Each time you hear that familiar sputter pass overhead you'll look up and wonder if it's one you've flown.

You'll see a greased landing in a strong crosswind and you'll smile at the sheer beauty of it. You'll sit on a commercial flight and listen to some flight attendant go on about FAA regulations and you'll think: "Let me tell *you* about FAA regulations, little boy!"

You'll meet other pilots and you'll be fast friends. You'll understand one another's core, no matter how different you appear on the outside.

You won't ever stop learning. You'll hear about aviation disasters and you'll contemplate what likely went wrong. They will affect you more deeply because you will imagine what the pilots were going through. It could have been you.

You'll watch news programs and chuckle at the absurd notions they offer for aviation incidents.

You'll become a pilot.

On the morning of September 11th, 2001, I watched my television as a news reporter theorized with her anchor desk about what prompted those pilots to crash their airplanes: Were they part of a terrorist network? Were background checks on U.S. pilots so lax that terrorists could be flying our nation's 767s without anyone being the wiser?

The world's thoughts and prayers focused on those lost that day, and on those trapped beneath the rubble in New York City.

But my thoughts were elsewhere.

I thought of the pilots flying in United States airspace that morning who heard ATC announce:

"By order of the FAA, and for reasons of national security, all pilots are to immediately land their aircraft at the nearest suitable airport."

No further explanation was given and those airborne pilots were left to wonder.

I thought of the air traffic controllers that sat before radar screens, powerless, as airplanes in their sectors turned toward targets, all the while wondering which "blip" would divert and disappear next.

I thought about the employees of United Airlines and American Airlines crippled with horror as they saw colleagues murdered.

I thought about the employees of Boeing who witnessed their miraculous machines turned into weapons.

I couldn't keep my eyes dry all day long and I knew I was not alone.

And that news reporter, sporting tailored Armani and that prefab look of angst that works so equally well for economy-crisis and guns-in-schools stories, stood there, artistically framed upon a backdrop of the smoke-consumed Manhattan skyline. She held an ear piece to her right ear, tossed her golden locks to the left, and shook her head in disbelief as she presumed, on national television, that *pilots* had caused this?

I knew better.

B

C

K

L

M

N